ENV ISIO NING EVIL

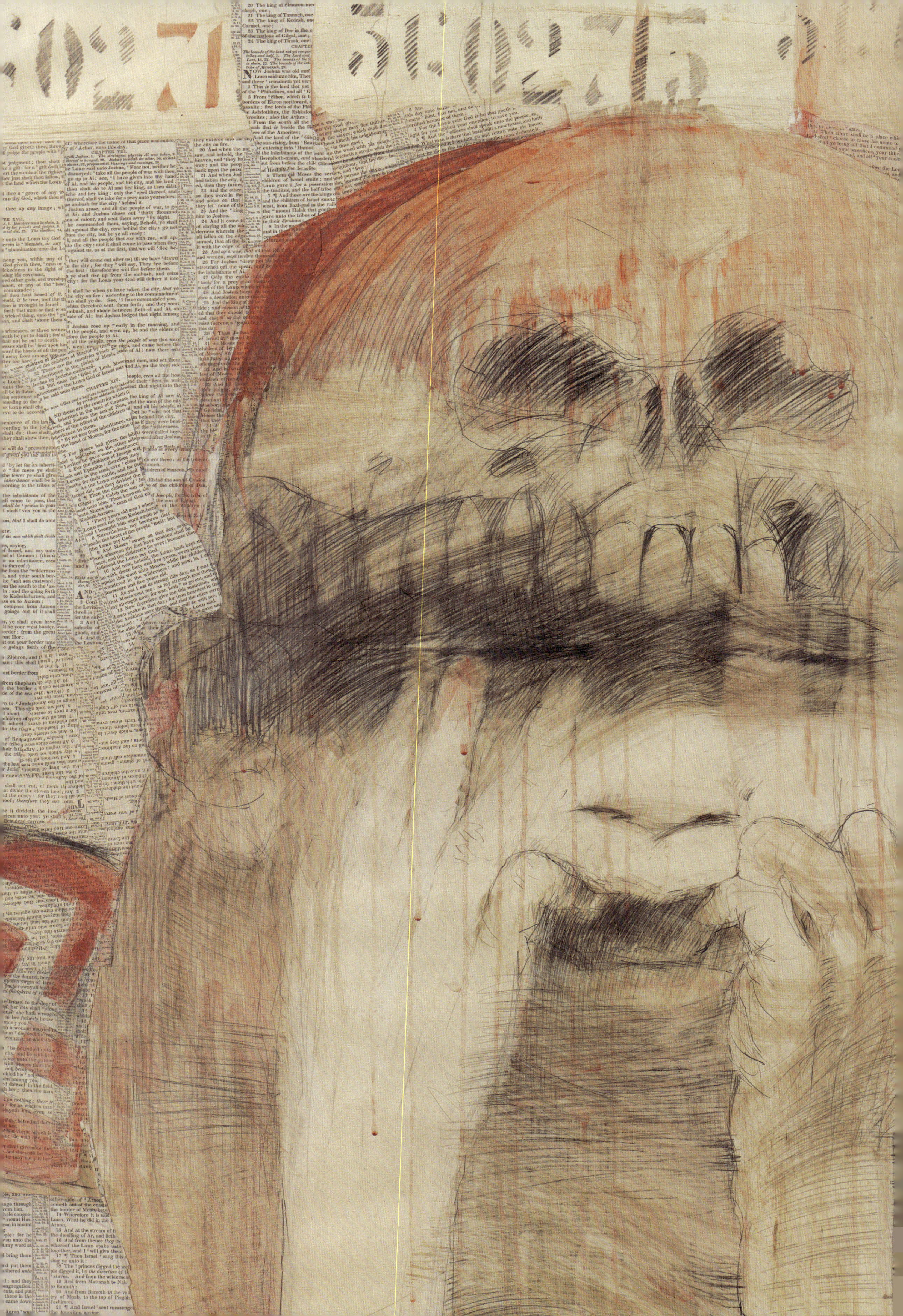

ENV ISIO NING EVIL

Rachel McGarry

With contributions by

Rabbi Barry D. Cytron

"The Nazi Drawings" by Mauricio Lasansky

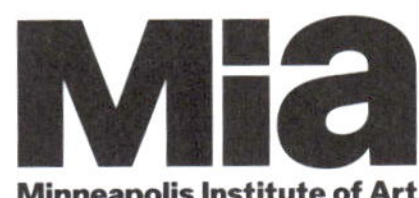

This catalogue was published in conjunction with the exhibition *Envisioning Evil: "The Nazi Drawings" by Mauricio Lasansky*, organized by the Minneapolis Institute of Art.

Exhibition curator: Rachel McGarry

Minneapolis Institute of Art, Minneapolis
October 16, 2021–June 26, 2022

The Baker Museum / Artis—Naples
September 2022–January 2023

Editor: Laura Silver
Designer: Jill Blumer
Photographer: Charles Walbridge
Digital image production: Joshua Lynn
Image acquisitions and permission: Kristin Lenaburg and Ian Karp
Indexer: David Luljak
Publishing and production management: Jim Bindas, Books & Projects LLC

Distributed by the University of Minnesota Press
111 Third Avenue South, Suite 290
Minneapolis, MN 55401-2520
www.upress.umn.edu

ISBN: 978-1-5179-1051-8 (pb)

Front and inside covers: Mauricio Lasansky, *No. 19* (details), 1961–66
Frontispiece: Mauricio Lasansky, *No. 27* (detail), 1961–66
"The Nazi Drawings," Levitt Foundation
© Lasansky Corporation

In artwork dimensions, height precedes width.

Printed in Canada

TABLE OF CONTENTS

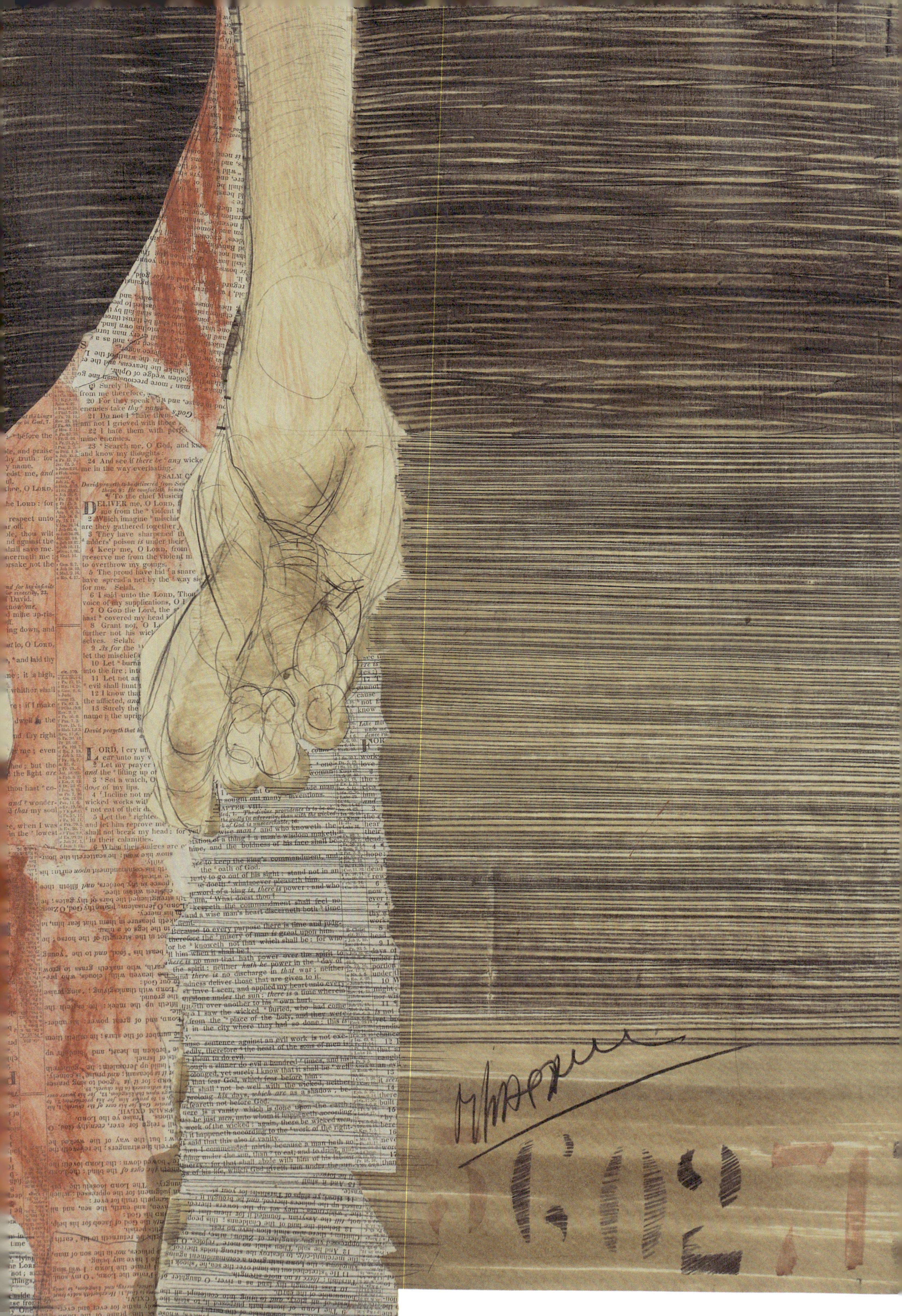

DIRECTOR'S FOREWORD

The Minneapolis Institute of Art is honored to present Mauricio Lasansky's "The Nazi Drawings," a commanding series that contributed to the growing awareness of the Holocaust in America. Created largely in the 1960s, the 33 outsize drawings are raw and expressive. Lasansky intended them to provoke an emotional and physical response in viewers, which is why it is so powerful to experience them in person. This catalogue is the first comprehensive examination of "The Nazi Drawings" to appear since the one that accompanied the original exhibition tour (1967–70), which drew enormous audiences and widespread critical acclaim.

The year 2020 marked 75 years since Allied troops liberated the Nazi camps. Scenes of the atrocities are unforgettable: starving prisoners, disease-ridden barracks, piled corpses. The Holocaust, the Nazis' attempt to exterminate all the Jews of Europe, resulted in the murder of 6 million Jews. In the wake of the overwhelming destruction of World War II, it took decades for the world to grasp the Jewish dimension of the Nazi horrors. As exhibition curator Rachel McGarry explores in one essay, many artists in the early 1950s focused on the theme of universal evil, rather than evil aimed at a specific group, and playwrights who adapted *The Diary of Anne Frank* for stage and film cut many of its Jewish references with the intention of drawing a wider audience.

A new awareness of the Holocaust emerged in the 1960s, with artists, writers, filmmakers, playwrights, and even television networks playing an important role. When Adolf Eichmann's trial unfolded on worldwide television in 1961, Nazi horrors came firmly to the fore. In her essay on "The Nazi Drawings," McGarry examines the influence of the Jerusalem trial, and how Lasansky incorporated the fiercely debated issues surrounding the Holocaust at the time into his series. Scholar Rabbi Barry D. Cytron's essay examines Christian teachings about Jews and Judaism prior to World War II and the subsequent impact of the Holocaust on those perspectives, and he discusses how Vatican II marked an official beginning for new understandings between the faiths.

From Mia, the exhibition will travel to the Baker Museum / Artis—Naples, in Florida. Mia is grateful to the Levitt Foundation for graciously lending "The Nazi Drawings" series in its entirety. Richard and Jeanne Levitt bought "The Nazi Drawings" from Lasansky, an artist they admired and knew as a friend, knowing it would fulfill his wishes to keep the series intact. The Levitts have deep ties to Minneapolis, dating from 1983 when Richard Levitt's banking career brought his family to our community. Their profound support of the arts was clear, with Mr. Levitt serving on Mia's board of trustees and Mrs. Levitt serving on the board of the Walker Art Center. The couple's impact has extended well beyond their 24 years in Minneapolis, and their philanthropy has enabled Mia to share these remarkable drawings with a new generation of visitors.

The financial support of our sponsors has been crucial. This catalogue and the exhibition were made possible through the generous support of Margaret and Angus Wurtele; Beverly Grossman; the John and Ruth Huss Fund; Erwin and Miriam Kelen; John and Nancy Lindahl; Sheila Morgan; Donna and James Pohlad, through the Eloise and Carl Pohlad Family Fund; the Lynne and Andrew Redleaf Foundation; Laurie and Ronald Eibensteiner; Stephen and Sheila Lieberman; Sheldon and Lili Chester; Andrew Grossman; Irving and Marjorie Weiser; and John and Marsha Soucheray.

Katherine Crawford Luber, PhD
Nivin and Duncan MacMillan Director and President
Minneapolis Institute of Art

Mauricio Lasansky, *No. 20* (detail), 1961–66, "The Nazi Drawings," Levitt Foundation

PREFACE AND ACKNOWLEDGMENTS

Many of us recall when we first began to grasp the facts of the Holocaust. Perhaps it was hearing survivors tell their stories, reading Anne Frank's diary, seeing *Schindler's List*, or visiting a memorial or museum. For me it was watching *Kitty: Return to Auschwitz* (Yorkshire Television, 1979), a documentary that aired in Minneapolis in 1981. A friend and I were doing cartwheels and flips in her basement and paying little attention to the television until a lively English-accented woman in her early fifties began to tell her story. It was Kitty Hart-Moxon, a Polish-English Holocaust survivor, who was returning to Auschwitz with an adult son to recount her experiences. They walk the abandoned camp as she details the horrors she witnessed and the suffering she survived. My friend and I watched the film frozen with shock and terror. Later, like many coming into consciousness in the 1980s, I assumed (wrongly) that America had entered World War II to put a stop to Hitler's attempted genocide of Europe's 10 million Jews. Of course, this was far from the truth.

Mauricio Lasansky began "The Nazi Drawings" in 1961, but the Nazi atrocities had been on his mind a long time. The artist had been haunted by "the millions and millions of people killed and screaming" since seeing the graphic newsreel footage of the camps in 1945. When I began to research the works, I was interested to learn why Lasansky deeply immersed himself in the subject of the Holocaust in the 1960s rather than in 1945. He completed the final work in the series, *Triptych*, in 1971, 26 years after the Nazi horrors had been laid bare. It had taken years for Lasansky to find the expressive language and fitting medium to convey his anger. When "The Nazi Drawings" toured North America from 1967 to 1970, they found a large, receptive audience at that moment too—something, it turns out, that was unlikely to have happened in the early postwar years.

While the Holocaust is considered one of the defining catastrophes of the 20th century, its significance was obscured amid the overwhelming calamity of World War II. Much of the press coverage was skeptical or nonexistent. Even when the Allies liberated the Nazi camps, the Jewish dimension of the tragedy was minimized or overlooked—victims were frequently described as political prisoners. While the footage and newsreels seared the Nazi atrocities into our collective memory, it took decades for public awareness of the Holocaust to take hold. The trial of Adolf Eichmann in Jerusalem in 1961 was a critical moment, as the essays here make clear. Art, literature, film, theater, and television also played a vital role in shining a light on the tragedy. Lasansky's "Nazi Drawings" were part of this effort. Now we have the honor of exhibiting this important series to a new generation of visitors. In the space of this volume, we attempt to reconstruct the context surrounding Lasansky's extraordinary undertaking: how the Holocaust happened, how it came to be forgotten, and how it was reexamined in the 1960s.

Many people deserve my heartfelt thanks for making this exhibition and publication possible. I want to begin by thanking Richard and Jeanne Levitt and the Levitt Foundation for entrusting us with "The Nazi Drawings." When I first proposed the show to the Levitts in 2017, they welcomed me into their California home (filled with stunning Lasansky prints). Before we had even finished lunch, they had become enthusiastic supporters of the exhibition and had generously agreed to loan the entire series. It was a great privilege to have met Mr. Levitt before his death, which occurred a few months after our meeting. He was truly a kind, magnanimous, thoughtful person, and the Levitts' exemplary philanthropy continues to enrich many communities and organizations. Mrs. Levitt and other members of the Levitt family, including Mark and Randall Levitt, have helped steward the exhibition. I'm particularly grateful to the Levitts' grandson, Elliot Levitt, who played an instrumental role from the very beginning.

This project would not have been possible without Erwin Kelen, whose passion for drawings has left a deep imprint on Twin Cities art museums. Erwin likes challenging, emotional, confrontational drawings and was immediately drawn to the power of Lasansky's series. As a child in Nazi-occupied Hungary, he witnessed firsthand the horrors committed by the Third Reich and its collaborators. He not only wished to support Mia's exhibition, but he arranged my introduction to the Levitts, spearheaded an ambitious fundraising campaign for the project, and assisted in securing a second venue. I am truly grateful to him and his wife, Miriam, and to the many generous donors who contributed to this show, all of whom are noted in the Director's Foreword.

We are greatly indebted to the Lasansky family. The Lasansky Corporation generously provided permission to reproduce Lasansky's artworks as well as family photos from the Lasansky archive.

Three of Mauricio Lasansky's children were especially valuable to my research: Phillip Lasansky, who sadly died in early 2020, the writer Nina Barragan, and the artist and professor Leonardo Lasansky, a longtime friend who introduced me to "The Nazi Drawings" a decade ago. These siblings shared their deep knowledge of the artist and many personal insights. I would also like to thank Mauricio's grandsons Diego Lasansky and Amadeo Lasansky, talented artists themselves.

The catalogue and exhibition are immeasurably richer for the contributions of Rabbi Barry D. Cytron. He has been a guiding light throughout this project, indispensable for his counsel and his prodigious knowledge of Holocaust literature and historiography. The essay he wrote examines the impact of the Holocaust on Christian and Jewish faiths and the interfaith dialogue of the postwar period. I am also indebted to Armin Kunz for his astute early reading of the catalogue text, which led to many improvements and fruitful discussions. Marla J. Kinney, whom I know as a brilliant editor, writer, and wordsmith, made invaluable contributions to this book. Her eternal patience and assurance at every stage deserve my boundless thanks.

Every exhibition is a collaboration, and at the Minneapolis Institute of Art I am grateful to have many talented colleagues who contributed in countless ways. I would like to thank Director Katherine Crawford Luber, Deputy Director and Chief Curator Matthew Welch, and Head of Exhibition Planning and Strategy Jennifer Komar Olivarez for their leadership and crucial support. My sincere thanks go to Mia's wonderful Prints and Drawings Department; Dennis Michael Jon, Marla J. Kinney, Kristin Lenaburg, and Tom Rassieur fully supported the project and covered for me when needed to meet the demands of our busy department. I'm grateful to the extraordinary staff of Mia's beloved Art Research and Reference Library: Janice Lurie, Head Librarian, and Meg Black, Mia's former Assistant Librarian, who heroically oversaw hundreds of interlibrary loan requests for me. Key technical support was provided by Steve Scidmore and Aaron Barger. I would like to thank Elisabeth Callihan and Karleen Gardner for their enthusiastic involvement in the show's programs and interpretation. Registrar Jennifer Starbright expertly arranged all exhibition loans. The dramatic gallery installation is the skillful work of exhibition designer Bill Skodje and lighting designer Jonathan Hamilton. Mike Dust, Head of Interactive Media and Senior Producer, helped shape significant aspects of the exhibition and film installation. I would also like to extend my thanks to Michaela Baltasar-Feyen, Dan Dennehy, Peggy Martin, Aubrey Mozer, and Kristin Prestegaard, who lent essential support at various stages of the project.

This catalogue would not exist without the expert guidance and dedication of many individuals. I would like to express my gratitude to editor Laura Silver and her remarkable attention to detail, thoughtful and sympathetic editing, and positive energy. I applaud Jill Blumer for her elegant design, sharp eye, and sensitivity to all aspects of printing books. Thanks go to Jim Bindas for overseeing book production. Kristin Lenaburg and Ian Karp worked tirelessly to obtain images and permissions, which greatly enhance the stories told on these pages. Splendid new photography of "The Nazi Drawings" is the work of Charles Walbridge. I extend special thanks as well to Josh Lynn, who devoted unstinting energy to digital image production.

The authors also wish to thank these friends and colleagues: Jill Ahlberg Yohe, Alejandro Baer, Carmen Bambach, Roberta Bartoli, Joey Bartolomeo, Melissa Bowling, Robert Cozzolino, Davida Cytron, Rebecca Diamondstein, Sascha Engel, Kaywin Feldman, Beverly Grossman, Toby Joyce, the Kordonowy family, Joe Larson, Doron Levene, Jan-Lodewijk Grootaers, Heidi Heller, Rena Hoisington, Lyle Humphrey, Nicole LaBouff, Michael Lapthorn, John Marciari, Mary McNamara, Constance McPhee, Lisa Michaux, Sam Molstad, Sheila Morgan, Teo Nguyen, Louise Rice, Casey Riley, Margot and Alex Rosenstein, Matthew Rutenberg, Molly Schlobohm, Vanessa Schmid, Eike Schmidt, Yehudit Shendar, Teddy Smetana, Nicole Soukup, Freyda Spira, Perrin Stein Kathleen Swenson, Thuan Micah Tran, Kathleen van Bergen, Betsy Vilett, Monroe Warshaw, and Gabe and Yvonne Weisberg. We remain deeply grateful for the love and encouragement of Phyllis Cytron, and Michael, James, and Louisa McGarry.

Rachel McGarry, PhD
Associate Curator, Minneapolis Institute of Art

INTRODUCTION TO "THE NAZI DRAWINGS"

Rachel McGarry

Fifty years ago, Mauricio Lasansky's landmark exhibition *The Nazi Drawings* opened in Iowa City, Iowa, the final venue of a nine-city tour that began in 1967. The Iowa City show marked the return of the drawings to the artist's adopted hometown, and the place where the series was conceived and partially created. The 33 monumental drawings, which confront the horrors of the Holocaust, continue to resonate today in their depiction of humanity's capacity for evil and the brutality and suffering that evil begets.

Lasansky, the son of Jewish immigrants, was born in 1914 in Buenos Aires, Argentina, and lived there until emigrating in 1943 to the United States, where he led a flourishing career as a printmaker. Throughout his life, his work often took on themes of war, human suffering, and social injustice. In 1961, after a few attempts that he considered failures, he felt ready to face the Nazi atrocities directly and began a project that became "The Nazi Drawings." The first 30 works were completed between 1961 and 1966. He added the three drawings of *Triptych*, completed in 1971, after the exhibition had finished its tour.

By the 1960s, Lasansky was an internationally known printmaker, but he decided that drawing—the most immediate, elemental medium—was best suited for this undertaking. "I tried to keep not only the vision of 'The Nazi Drawings' simple and direct but also the material I used in making them," he said. "I wanted them to be done with a tool used by everyone everywhere. From the cradle to the grave, meaning the pencil."[1]

The central theme of the series is the Holocaust, which Lasansky examined with a particular emphasis on the slaughter of women and children, especially children. Approximately 1.5 million Jewish children were murdered in the Holocaust. Throughout "The Nazi Drawings" Lasansky stenciled the number "5,602,715" on various sheets, sometimes many times, to signify the number of Jews the Nazis murdered, according to one estimate in circulation at the time. (In his "Kaddish" series of eight prints from 1976 to 1978, Lasansky put the number at 6,102,308.) Two of the newspaper articles collaged onto the drawings deal specifically with the Jewish dimension of the tragedy (see *No. 18* and *Triptych*). When Lasansky began the project, the Nazis' attempted genocide of the Jewish people was not yet universally called the Holocaust. The word, as discussed in the essay "The Holocaust in Press, Culture, and Art: Before and After Eichmann," was just beginning to be used in America to refer to this specific calamity. Even if "Holocaust" had carried the

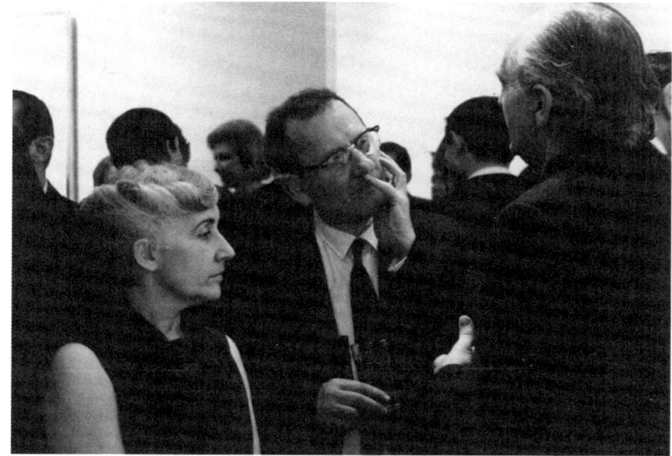

Fig. A.1 Mauricio and Emilia Lasansky at the opening of *The Nazi Drawings* exhibition, 1967, Whitney Museum of American Art, New York

association it has today, it seems unlikely that Lasansky would have put it in the series' title, since what he sought to convey was a more universal meaning. During the years the artist was working on them, Lasansky's wife, Emilia, had informally referred to them as "the Nazi drawings." Struggling to find a title, Lasansky realized that this phrase unified the group and captured the broader message he wanted to express: all the suffering inflicted by the Nazis, not only on the Jews but on the Roma and Sinti, Poles, Soviet POWs, and others. Lasansky firmly stated that he was concerned with all Nazi victims and the dangers of future exterminations and persecutions. Nazi Germany showed him, he said, "Everyone is in danger, any minority is in danger . . . everyone has the right to live."[2]

Lasansky was aware that the title could imply that the drawings were *by* Nazis rather than *about* Nazis. The misperception in fact led to some early, brief protests outside the Whitney Museum exhibition in 1967. The title inside the museum was corrected to include the word "The" (missing from the outside sign) to indicate that the phrase was a title rather than a description (fig. A.2). Once audiences saw the drawings, there was no confusion about what they were and how the artist felt about the Nazi massacres.

As it toured the country, the exhibition received widespread critical attention, with reviews in *Time* and *Look* magazines, the *New York Times*, the *Chicago Daily News*, and elsewhere.[3] At the Whitney, where the show was one of the inaugural exhibitions in the museum's new Marcel Breuer–designed quarters on Madison Avenue, visitors lined up around the block (fig. A.3). Also on display were shows dedicated to Louise Nevelson and Andrew Wyeth. The exhibition catalogue that accompanied the

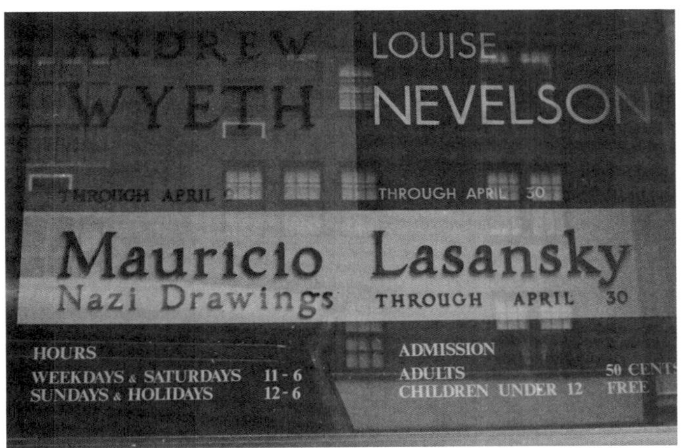

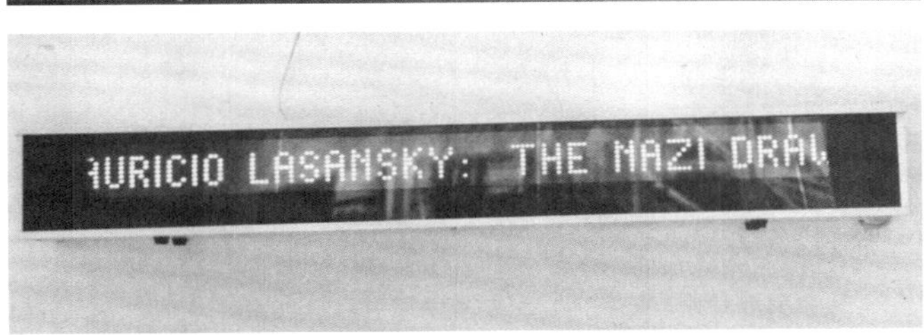

Fig. A.2 Whitney exhibition, 1967. The title in the museum lobby was corrected to include "The" because Lasansky wanted to clarify that the drawings were *about* Nazis, not by them.

show featured drawings 1 through 30 and an essay by the writer and professor Edwin Honig (Philadelphia, 1966). When the catalogue was reprinted 10 years later, *Triptych* was added (Iowa City, 1976).[4]

Given the popular response to "The Nazi Drawings," various institutions and dealers were keen to obtain individual works, but Lasansky wanted to keep the group together. He hoped that future audiences would see the series as a whole, and that they might take away lessons about compassion and the universal, precious value of each life. "You don't have to be a religious person to believe that life is sacred, that there are no inferior or superior races," he said.[5]

Richard and Jeanne Levitt of Des Moines, Iowa, stepped up to acquire the drawings for their family foundation in 1972, thus fulfilling Lasansky's wish to keep "The Nazi Drawings" series intact. At the time, the Levitts were prominent young art collectors, philanthropists, and Iowans, contributing in their community and later nationally to art, educational, civic, and Jewish organizations. During the more than two decades the couple lived in Minneapolis, Mr. Levitt served on Mia's board of trustees and Mrs. Levitt served on the Walker Art Center's board. The Levitts had met as students at the University of Iowa in the 1950s and were married for 65 years until Mr. Levitt's death in 2017 at age 87. The first works they bought together as budding art collectors were prints by Lasansky, acquired as newlyweds in Iowa City with their grocery money when Mr. Levitt was in law school. They got to know the artist and his family very well over the years.

The Levitt Foundation has taken great care to safeguard, preserve, and share "The Nazi Drawings," making the series accessible through loans and exhibitions. After acquiring the series in 1972, the family placed the works on extended loan at the University of Iowa Museum of Art, Iowa City, on the campus where the Levitts had met and where Lasansky had made his career in the United States as an artist and revered professor. The series was frequently on view in Iowa and lent periodically to shows at college art museums.[6] The works were evacuated from the University of Iowa along with the school's entire art collection just before the devastating flood of June 2008 hit Iowa City. In 2016–17, the Levitt family through its foundation funded a major preservation campaign of the drawings, conserving all 33 works. In addition, while Lasansky's original elegant brass frames were retained, new protective glazing and archival mounts were added, to better preserve the drawings and enhance their presentation. This is the first exhibition of the newly conserved works.

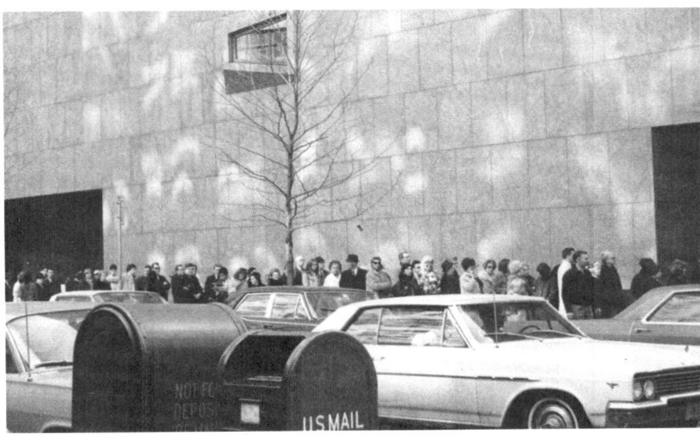

Fig. A.3 Visitors lining up to enter the Whitney when "The Nazi Drawings" were on view, 1967

The Nazi Drawings exhibition tour, 1967–70

Philadelphia Museum of Art, January 17–February 19, 1967
Whitney Museum of American Art, New York, March 22–April 30, 1967
Des Moines Art Center, Iowa, June 23–July 16, 1967
Tacoma Art Museum, Washington, September 22–October 22, 1967
Indianapolis Museum of Art, Indiana, January 7–February 4, 1968
Huntington Museum of Art, Huntington, West Virginia, March 1968
Museum of Contemporary Art, Chicago, June 1–July 7, 1968
Palace of Fine Arts, Mexico City, January–February, 1969
University of Iowa Museum of Art, Iowa City, January 11–March 1, 1970

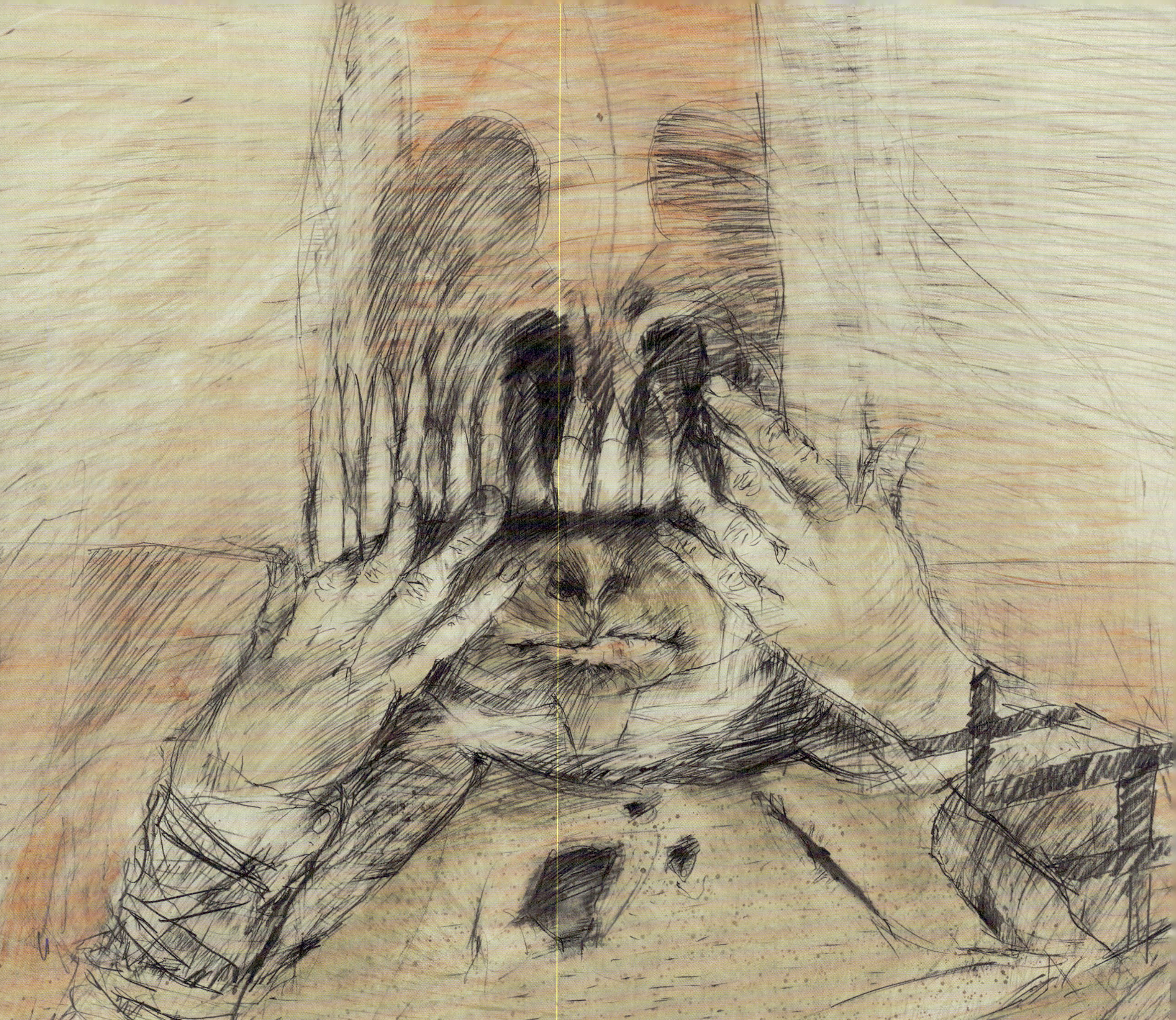

Mauricio Lasansky, *No. 21* (detail), "The Nazi Drawings"

NOTES

1. Mauricio Lasansky, *The Nazi Drawings* (exh. cat.), introduction by Edwin Honig, Philadelphia Museum of Art and eight other venues (Philadelphia, 1966).

2. Lane Wyrick and Mauricio Lasansky, "Interview with Lasansky," *The Nazi Drawings by Artist Mauricio Lasansky*, directed by Lane Wyrick (1999; Iowa City, Iowa: Xap Interactive Inc., 2004), DVD.

3. Charlotte Willard, "Drawings from Hell," *Look*, February 21, 1967, p. 79; Grace Glueck, "Non-Fairy Tale," *New York Times*, March 26, 1967; "Nameless evil," *Time*, March 31, 1967, p. 86; Hoke Norris, "A Cold Look at Horror," *Chicago Daily News*, April 29, 1970, pp. 3–4.

4. Mauricio Lasansky, *The Nazi Drawings* (exh. cat.), introduction by Edwin Honig, University of Iowa Museum of Art (Iowa City, 1976). A smaller-format exhibition catalogue was printed in Mexico City in Spanish, *Los Dibujos Nazis* (Mexico City, 1969).

5. Willard 1967, p. 79.

6. I would like to thank Elliot Levitt, Diego Lasansky, and Leonardo Lasansky for helping to fill in the exhibition history of "The Nazi Drawings." What follows is a partial record of that history. The drawings were shown at the University of Iowa Museum of Art, Iowa City, in 1970, 1972, and for extended periods while on long-term loan there from 1976 to 2008. Additionally, they were exhibited at Dickinson College, Carlisle, Pennsylvania, in 1974; Minnesota Museum of Art, St. Paul, October 14–29, 1977; Sarah Moody Gallery of Art, University of Alabama, Tuscaloosa, November 2–30, 1982 (organized by Cedar Rapids Art Museum, Iowa); Allen Priebe Gallery, University of Wisconsin, Oshkosh, October 10–November 3, 1985; and Cedar Rapids Art Museum, April 18–October 3, 2004, among other American museums.

NOTE TO THE READER

The authors, in considering the shifting understanding of the Holocaust in the period after World War II (1939–45), use the word Holocaust in this publication to mean the tragedy specific to the Jewish people as defined by the United States Holocaust Memorial Museum: "The systematic, state-sponsored persecution and murder of six million Jews by the Nazi regime and its allies and collaborators." It is interchangeable with the word Shoah, the ancient Hebrew word for *catastrophe* and the term favored in many countries.

The Nazis also persecuted, targeted, and killed other groups for their race, religion, political beliefs, sexual orientation, and disabilities—Roma and Sinti, ethnic Slavs (Belarusians, Poles, Russians, Ukrainians), Jehovah's Witnesses, Soviet prisoners of war, Communists, Catholics, homosexuals, people who were physically or mentally disabled, or physically or mentally ill, and others.

The Holocaust is at the very center of "The Nazi Drawings." However, Mauricio Lasansky's concern and empathy extended to all Nazi victims—and to what he described as future exterminations and persecutions of minorities.

THE HOLOCAUST IN PRESS, CULTURE, AND ART: BEFORE AND AFTER EICHMANN

Rachel McGarry

In retrospect, Auschwitz is the most important thing to know about World War II. But that is not how things seemed at the time. —Tony Judt, *Postwar: A History of Europe since 1945* (2005)[1]

The capture of notorious Nazi war criminal Adolf Eichmann in Buenos Aires in 1960 riveted the world and renewed focus on the Holocaust and the murder of 6 million Jews. Eichmann's trial in Jerusalem a year later, the first to be broadcast across the world, was seen in some form by an estimated 80 percent of television viewers.[2] As it unfolded, details emerged about the atrocities of Auschwitz, Treblinka, Sobibor, Ponary, Babi Yar, Buchenwald, Bergen-Belsen, and other Nazi killing sites across Europe during World War II. A worldwide audience heard about the Nazis' attempted genocide of Europe's 10 million Jews, an annihilation of a whole people that the Nazis obliquely called the "Final Solution of the Jewish Question." The Nazi program called for the extermination of other ethnic groups such as the Roma and Sinti, as well as groups deemed undesirable, such as mentally ill people, physically and mentally impaired people,[3] Jehovah's Witnesses, and homosexuals. Hitler was also intent on the mass killing of tens of millions of Slavs (Belarusians, Poles, Russians, Ukrainians) in his plans to colonize Eastern Europe—plans ultimately thwarted, but not before millions had died.[4] This essay, however, confines itself to the Holocaust, a tragedy specific to the Jewish people.

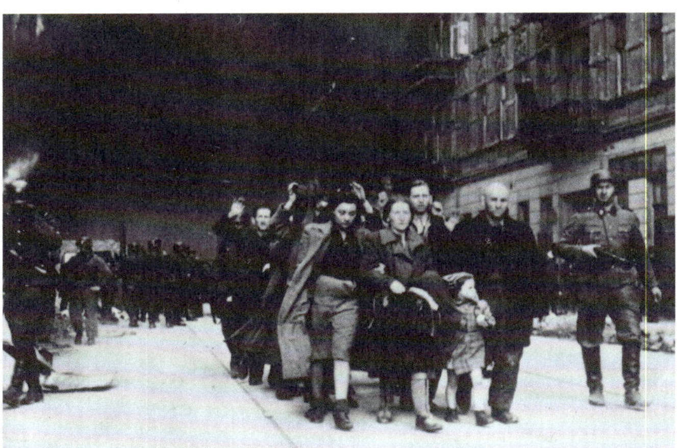

Fig. 1.1 Jews arrested during the Warsaw ghetto uprising (Poland), April 19–May 16, 1943. National Archives, Washington, D.C.
In 1942, the Nazis deported 265,000 Jews from the Warsaw ghetto to the Treblinka death camp. When deportations resumed in 1943, the Nazis met an armed revolt. Some 7,000 Jews died fighting; nearly 50,000 were deported to Auschwitz and Majdanek. The family at the head of this group of deportees has been identified as Madam Neyer between her son, Avraham Neyer, and his wife, Yehudit Tolb Neyer, with their daughter, whose name is unknown. Only Avraham survived.

Although the Nazis' systematic murder of Jews was repeatedly noted in reports during and immediately after the war, this reality was obscured amid the devastation of war, which had left 70 million to 85 million people dead. As will be explored, many other factors led to the catastrophe being downplayed or even concealed. In some cases, the Holocaust was simply too much to grasp. For many, it was only in the early 1960s, when survivors told their stories, most notably at the Eichmann trial, and when camp footage reappeared in film and on television, that Holocaust memories were awakened. It was at this moment that the world—including many artists, Mauricio Lasansky among them—began to grapple with the tragedy.

THE PLIGHT OF EUROPEAN JEWRY IN THE WARTIME PRESS: THE POLITICS OF OBSERVATION

I have learned that the Holocaust was a unique and uniquely Jewish event, albeit with universal implications. Not all victims were Jews, but all Jews were victims. I have learned the danger of indifference, the crime of indifference. For the opposite of love, I have learned, is not hate but indifference. Jews were killed by the enemy but betrayed by their so-called allies who found political reasons to justify their indifference or passivity. —Elie Wiesel, 1985[5]

Throughout the war, the plight and mass murder of the Jews was covered by the American press sporadically and unevenly. In the 1930s, U.S. newspapers often reported on Nazi persecution of the Jews, publishing stories about Kristallnacht, the Night of Broken Glass (1938), anti-Jewish legislation, harassment, pogroms, and theft of Jewish property. When Germany invaded Poland on September 1, 1939, and World War II ignited, attention shifted away from the issue just as it grew more urgent. The Nazis' systematic murder of the Jews began in the summer of 1941 in Eastern Europe, with mass shootings by *Einsatzgruppen* (mobile killing units within the SS—*Schutzstaffel*, or "protection squads") in Poland, Lithuania, and Ukraine. By early 1942, the gas chambers where millions would die were fully operational in a number of Nazi extermination camps. Throughout 1942, reports documenting mass murders and the dire conditions of the ghettos were smuggled out of Poland. (Ghettos were sealed-off areas in cities where Jews were interned.) These

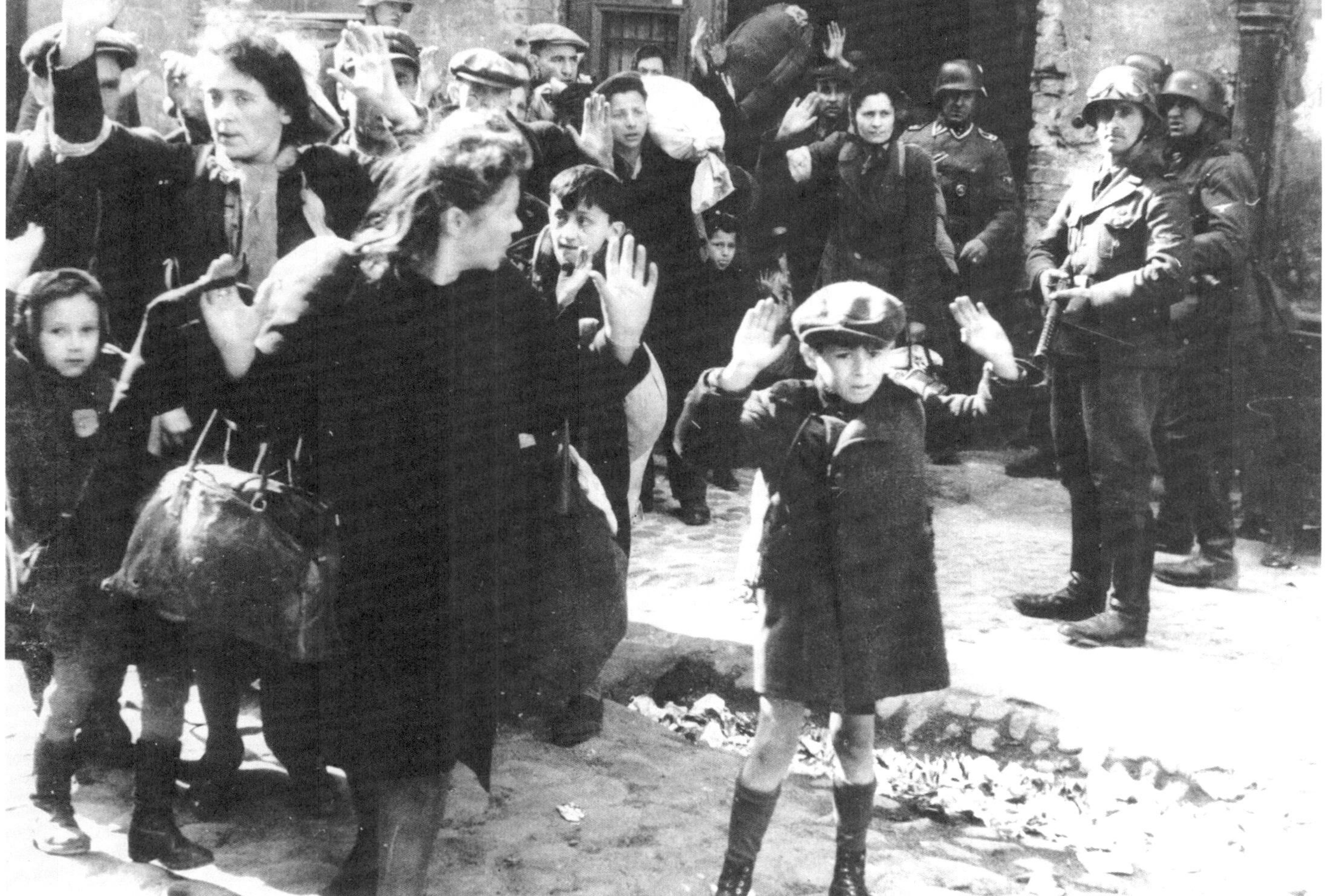

Fig. 1.2 Jews arrested during the Warsaw ghetto uprising (1943). United States Holocaust Memorial Museum, courtesy of the National Archives, Washington, D.C. Some of these victims have been identified, but the small boy at center, age six or seven, his hands raised in surrender, remains unknown. This iconic photo and fig. 1.1 come from the Stroop Report, an album SS Major General Juergen Stroop submitted to his superiors to document the destruction of the Warsaw ghetto by his forces. This photo was used as evidence in the first Nuremberg trial (1945–46), and in the 1969 trial in East Germany of a soldier in the photo.

included the Bund Report by Leon Feiner of the Jewish Resistance in Poland, which stated, among other things, that 700,000 Jewish victims had been slain in occupied Poland. There was also an eyewitness account of life in the Polish camps and ghettos by Jan Karski of the Polish Resistance,[6] among others. One document included a map of the Treblinka extermination camp.[7] A few Germans who witnessed the genocide or were privy to Nazi plans also leaked information. SS Officer Kurt Gerstein, for example, reported the gassings at Bełżec and Treblinka to a Swedish diplomat, a Catholic cleric, and a member of the Swiss press (and also the Dutch underground). The German industrialist Eduard Schulte secretly reported the Nazi plans to murder millions of Jews to the Jewish World Congress in Geneva.[8] Much of this crucial information was brushed off or not believed so was not circulated with any urgency.

The Bund Report made news when the British press followed up and featured the slayings prominently in June 1942. This prompted a public uproar and calls to provide a sanctuary for Hitler's victims.[9] The American press picked up the story but in shorter, diluted articles that often appeared deep inside the newspaper.[10] For instance, the *New York Times* opined that the 700,000 Jewish victims "probably includes many who died of maltreatment in concentration camps, of starvation in ghettos or of unbearable conditions of forced labor."[11] The reported use of gas chambers is mentioned at the end of the article. A *Times* article two days later put the mass murder aside, reporting that productive Jews "are placed in war industry, but the others are subjected to great hardships and sufferings. Among the latter the mortality due to starvation and ill-treatment is bound to be enormously high."[12] The story put the estimated number of Jewish victims in Nazi-occupied areas at between 100,000 and 1.5 million. The lack of consistent numbers in the American press throughout the war made reports seem less credible. Later in 1942, following efforts by Rabbi Stephen Wise, chairman of the World Jewish Congress, the U.S. State Department confirmed that the number of Jews murdered in an "extermination campaign" was 2 million.[13] In December the Polish government-in-exile, based in London, published *The Mass Extermination of Jews in German Occupied Poland*, a 16-page pamphlet detailing Nazi crimes against Jews in Poland. The United Nations and 11 Allied countries, including the United States, issued an immediate condemnation of "the cold-blooded extermination of the Jews." The condemnation was widely covered by the papers.[14]

When millions more Jews were reported to have been murdered at Treblinka in August 1943, *Times* readers saw the news on page 11.[15] One reason this was "buried" inside the paper may be that the story did not contain firsthand reporting. Throughout the war, many papers were unable to independently confirm the facts and figures of secret killing camps behind the front lines and so relied on reports from outside sources—sometimes a single source. News organizations, wary of propaganda, would frequently qualify these reports, which could lessen their impact.[16] This journalistic approach, reporting on reports rather than events, often made the atrocities feel less real and immediate. The *Times* continued in this vein, even in the face of powerful and persuasive reporting elsewhere.[17] In November 1943, *Times* reporter W. H. Lawrence, embedded with the Soviet Red Army, visited the site of the Babi Yar massacre near Kyiv, in Ukraine.[18] Two years earlier, 33,771 Jewish men, women, and children had been gunned down by Nazis and their collaborators in just two days. The slaughter continued over 1941, with an estimated 100,000 victims murdered—Jews, Sinti and Roma, Communists, and Soviet prisoners of war (POWs). The massacres were widely reported in the Soviet press, and several eyewitnesses had come forward.[19] Other American newspapers had described evidence of flesh, hair, and clothing at the scene.[20] Lawrence, however, wrote that he had no way to confirm "the truth or falsity" of "the alleged" massacre, and that there were no witnesses.

In the last year of the war, the press focused on day-to-day military advances and setbacks. By then, in historian Peter Novick's words, the Holocaust was "swallowed up in the larger carnage" of war.[21]

The failure of the American press to cover the Holocaust in spite of mounting evidence has been the subject of much scholarship, including: Deborah Lipstadt's *Beyond Belief: The American Press and the Coming of the Holocaust 1933–1945* (New York, 1986), Novick's *The Holocaust in American Life* (New York, 1999), and Laurel Leff's *Buried by the Times: The Holocaust and America's Most Important Newspaper* (Cambridge, 2005).[22] Lipstadt and Leff argue that the *New York Times*, long considered the U.S. "paper of record," misrepresented and downplayed the Holocaust with tragic consequences.[23] One might ask, for example, whether Eichmann would have been able to deport 425,000 Hungarian Jews to Auschwitz late in the war, between May and July 1944, if the world had been less ignorant of the Nazi war machine.[24]

There were many reasons, both unconscious and conscious, that the Holocaust was not broadcast more widely or diligently. Judt observes, "For the sad truth is that during World War II itself, many people did not know about the fate of the Jews and if they did know they did not much care. There were only two groups for whom World War II was above all a project to destroy the Jews: the Nazis and the Jews themselves. For practically everyone else the war had quite different meanings: they had troubles of their own."[25]

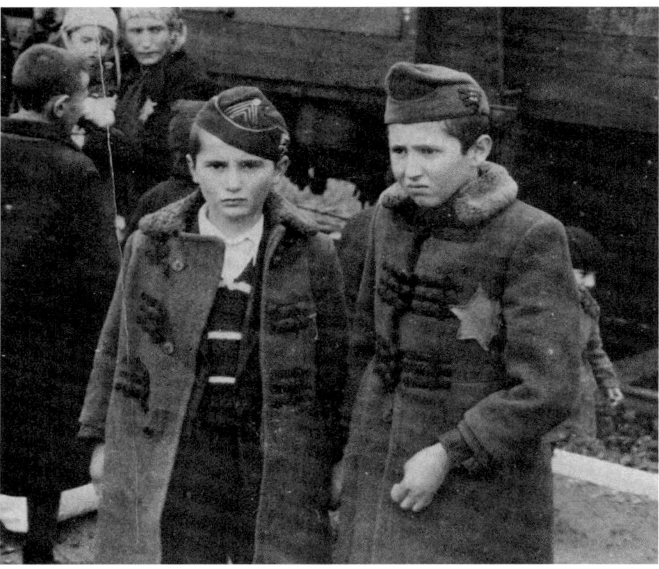

Fig. 1.3 Israel and Zelig Jacob, Jewish brothers from Hungary (Subcarpathian Rus, now Ukraine), awaiting selections at Auschwitz-Birkenau, May 1944. United States Holocaust Memorial Museum, courtesy of Yad Vashem, Jerusalem

The Jacob brothers, ages 8 and 10, were murdered in the gas chambers shortly after arriving at the camp. This is one of 193 photos taken by Nazi officials and compiled in the "Auschwitz Album." After the camp's liberation, the album was discovered by prisoner Lili Jacob, the boys' sister.

The U.S. government and its Allies minimized specific reports of atrocities against the Jews to universalize Nazi victims and secure broader support for the war.[26] Even though the British press pursued a number of stories about the Jewish genocide, Prime Minister Winston Churchill's government also suppressed information for fear of inflaming antisemitism in Britain.[27] The pressure of the Polish government-in-exile in London and contact with direct sources certainly influenced British reporting. In America, President Franklin D. Roosevelt had to contend with political groups like the America First Committee, which fervently promoted isolationism. The antisemitism of some of its membership (800,000 strong) is apparent in a speech given by the aviation hero and AFC spokesperson Charles Lindbergh, in Des Moines, Iowa, in September 1941. He argued, "If any one of these groups—the British, the Jewish, or the [Roosevelt] administration—stops agitating for war, I believe there will be little danger of our involvement."[28] By this date nearly 1 million Jews had been murdered by *Einsatzgruppen* in Eastern Europe.[29] Lindbergh continued, "Instead of agitating for war, the Jewish groups in this country should be opposing it in every possible way for they will be among the first to feel its consequences. . . . Their greatest danger to this country lies in their large ownership and influence in our motion pictures, our press, our radio and our government." Three months later, following Japan's attack on Pearl Harbor (December 7, 1941), the United States entered the war. The AFC disbanded, and Lindbergh tried to reenlist in the military but was rejected. Still, amid an enduring climate of isolationism and antisemitism, the government did not wish to give the impression that

American soldiers were fighting and risking their lives to save Jews. The press and Hollywood (a powerful force in shaping public opinion) likewise framed the war as saving humanity, not just specific ethnic groups. Movies focused on the battlefield, and those that alluded to Nazi camps gave a more prominent role to dissident prisoners than Jews.[30] Lipstadt and Leff see Jewish-owned papers like the *New York Times* as having assimilationist tendencies, which they believe also played a role. (Novick, Yehuda Bauer, and Dina Porat have shown that the Holocaust was underreported by Jewish papers in Palestine as well.[31])

Yet even if one acknowledges this entanglement of political considerations, one must ultimately not forget that the horror and scale of this tragedy were beyond imagination. The French philosopher and writer Raymond Aron, who was Jewish and a member of the Resistance, explained: "I knew, but I didn't believe it, and because I didn't believe it, I didn't know."[32]

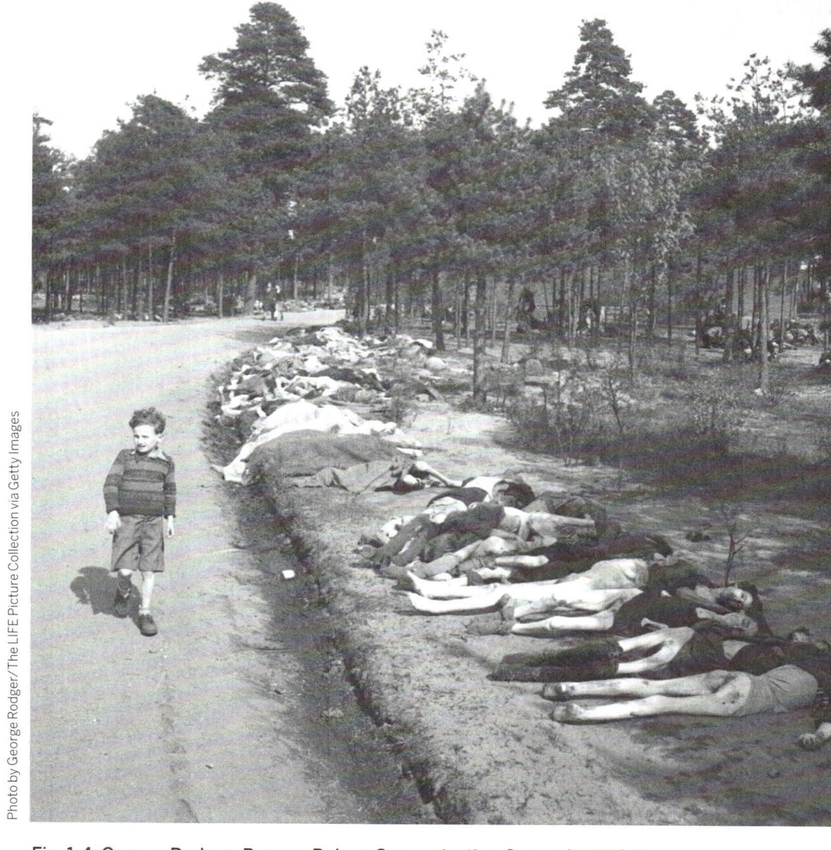

Photo by George Rodger/The LIFE Picture Collection via Getty Images

Fig. 1.4 George Rodger, *Bergen-Belsen Concentration Camp*, April 1945, silver gelatin print
Photojournalist Rodger accompanied the British 11th Armoured Division when it liberated the Nazis' massive Bergen-Belsen complex. This photo, in the *Life* story "The German Atrocities" (May 7, 1945), was captioned, "A Small Boy Strolls down a Road Lined with Dead Bodies near Camp at Belsen." The article made no mention of Jewish victims at the Nazi camps.

"HERE IS THE TRUTH!"[33] "THE WORLD MUST NOT FORGET"[34]

The things I saw beggar description. While I was touring the camp [Buchenwald] . . . the visual evidence and the verbal testimony of starvation, cruelty and bestiality were so overpowering as to leave me a bit sick. In one room, where they were piled up, twenty or thirty naked men, killed by starvation, [U.S. Army General] George Patton would not even enter. He said he would get sick if he did so. I made the visit deliberately, in order to be in position to give first-hand evidence of these things if ever, in the future, there develops a tendency to charge these allegations merely to "propaganda." —Gen. Dwight D. Eisenhower, supreme Allied commander, April 15, 1945[35]

With the liberation of the camps by Allied forces in 1944–45, the Nazi atrocities were laid bare.[36] The world began to see images of the death chambers and mass graves, the mounds of shoes, hair, and eyeglasses. The unprecedented horror, brutality, and scale of the tragedy started to become clear. As the Soviet Red Army advanced on the eastern front, the Nazis tried to destroy the gas chambers and crematoria. They evacuated weakened yet able-bodied prisoners in trains and on torturous marches west from Poland to Germany, resulting in some 30,000 to 45,000 more deaths. The Soviets liberated the extermination camps at Majdanek in Poland in late July 1944, arriving before it could be fully dismantled. But when they reached Treblinka, there was hardly a trace of the camp or the apparatus that murdered nearly 1 million Jews in its 396 days of operation. The Nazis had even removed the train tracks leading to the camp and planted lupines to hide their excavations.[37] The Red Army liberated Auschwitz on January 27, 1945. A few months later, U.S. and British forces saw firsthand the Nazi concentration and death camps too, beginning with the American liberation of Buchenwald (April 11), and the British of Bergen-Belsen (April 15).[38] (Bergen-Belsen is where Anne Frank, age 15, and her sister, Margot, age 19, spent their final months of the war. In the weeks before the British arrived, starvation and outbreaks of typhus fever, tuberculosis, and dysentery killed tens of thousands of prisoners, including the two sisters, who died of typhus.) The American and British armies filmed and photographed the camps, not just to document the Nazi crimes for later trials but to show the world—German citizens in particular—incontrovertible evidence of the atrocities. The supreme Allied commander, General Dwight D. Eisenhower, worried that stories of the Nazi camps would be dismissed as propaganda, invited U.S. statesmen and editors to fly to Europe immediately to see the camps in person.[39] Reading about mass killings was one thing; seeing the camps, or images of the camps, was quite another.[40] Footage and photographs circulated in newsreels, newspapers, magazines, books, and exhibitions.

Little of the boots-on-the-ground reporting from the liberated camps mentioned Jewish victims, which meant that the Jewish dimension of the Nazi crimes remained obscured. For example, Edward R. Murrow's famous radio broadcast from Buchenwald on April 15, 1945, did not mention Jews. Murrow vividly described what he saw, heard, and smelled: the heaps of clothes, the stacked corpses, the hundreds of orphaned children, "the living dead"—more than 20,000 "men from all Europe."[41] The first American newsreel on the camps, Universal's *Nazi*

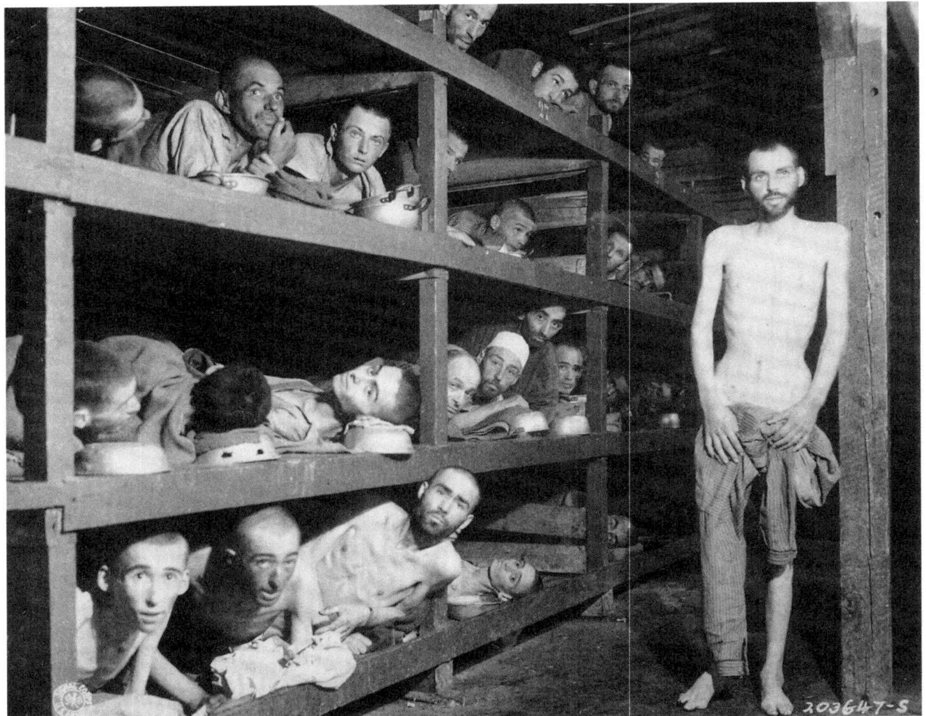

Fig. 1.5 Liberated prisoners in Barrack 56 of the "Little Camp" at Buchenwald concentration camp, April 16, 1945; photo by Private Harry Miller, U.S. Army 166th Signal Photo Company. National Archives, Washington, D.C.
"Little Camp" housed quarantined prisoners the Nazis had evacuated from camps in Poland on death marches as the Soviet army advanced. By 1945, dying inmates, mostly Jewish, were imprisoned in these barracks. Survivor and Nobel laureate Elie Wiesel is pictured on the second row of bunks, seventh from the left, next to the beam.

Murder Mills, made no mention of Jewish victims,[42] nor did *Life* magazine's six-page article on May 7, 1945, titled "The German Atrocities." The headline of the first story on Buchenwald in the *New York Times* is typical: "Prison Camp Is Overrun: 20,000 Political Captives Are Found at Buchenwald."[43] In subsequent *Times* coverage of the camps, when Jews were mentioned, it was late in the story, deep in the pages of the paper.[44] News organizations and military reports were more likely to describe prisoners by nationality than by ethnicity, as the *Times* did in another article on Buchenwald ("Twenty thousand prisoners were found, including 2,900 French, 3,800 Poles, 1,240 Hungarians, 570 Yugoslavs, 4,380 Russians, 324 Dutch, 622 Belgians, 550 Austrians, 242 Italians, 2,105 Czechs, 1,800 Germans . . .").[45] The first extended Soviet reports about Auschwitz took the same approach.[46] Even their ghastly reports of hundreds of thousands of children and infants murdered there failed to mention that they were Jewish.[47]

As Jews had been targeted for extermination rather than imprisonment, their survival was rarer.[48] Novick points out that an estimated one-fifth of the prisoners liberated at Buchenwald and Dachau were Jewish, greatly reduced by the harrowing death marches from Auschwitz in January.[49] Still, thousands of Jewish prisoners were among the liberated. Journalists reporting from the camps seem to have been so overwhelmed by the horror and the magnitude of death and suffering, few could see the historic calamity of the Holocaust before their eyes.[50] The critical Jewish thread was not grasped, was put aside, or was willfully ignored.[51] The same was true of the Roma and Sinti victims. Genocide was a newly defined concept.[52] The Nazi program to exterminate whole ethnic groups and to cleanse the population of groups they deemed undesirable remained hidden in the shadows. Despite early official reports that many millions of Jews were murdered,[53] the Jewish tragedy and its scale were lost. A survey in late 1944 showed that most Americans thought that Germans had killed about 100,000 or less in concentration camps. In May 1945, after extensive coverage of the liberated camps in newsreels and newspapers, people surveyed thought the Nazis had killed a *total* of about a million Jews and non-Jews in the camps.[54]

After America dropped atomic bombs on Hiroshima and Nagasaki, Japan, in August 1945, the world stood again in shock at the barbarity of modern warfare. The two blasts instantly killed between 100,000 and 165,000, and another 100,000 died from wounds, radiation, and burns in the days that followed or suffered illnesses from the nuclear fallout in subsequent years.[55] In Novick's view, "Hiroshima had a much greater impact on Americans than did the Holocaust, and a much more enduring impact."[56] Now it was the Americans who had perpetrated an unprecedented atrocity. The possibility of retaliation, should the bomb get into enemy hands, was terrifying, as was the threat atomic weaponry posed to the future of humankind. Around this time, President Harry S. Truman showed particular concern for the fate of Jewish survivors in Europe, and this made their plight front-page news.[57] Many survivors were living in the same camps as their Nazi captors, in unsanitary conditions, sometimes behind barbed wire. Shortly after the publicity, they had separate, improved facilities.[58] While Truman pledged justice for Jews in 1946, during the early Nuremberg trials of Nazi war criminals, only three Jewish survivors testified.[59] The French prosecutor never mentioned the deportations and mass murder of Jews at the proceedings.[60]

BEARING WITNESS TO A DEAFENING SILENCE

For many of us the hope of surviving merged with another, more precise hope. We hoped not to live *and* tell but to live *to* tell. —Primo Levi, 1966[61]

When I came to Israel, the slogan was "Forget." Until the late sixties—"Forget." And if you talk about the Holocaust, then, only the heroic part—partisans, not the camps. . . . In Israel, because it was a society of survivors and because they did not tell their children, there's a great dark hole in the lives of their children, and this hole can create curiosity. —Aharon Appelfeld, c. 1998[62]

Dear finder, search everywhere in every inch of soil. Tens of thousands of documents are buried under it, mine and those of other persons, which will throw light on everything that happened here. Great quantities of teeth are buried here. It was we, the Kommando workers, who expressly have strewn them over the terrain, as many as we could so that the world should find material traces of the millions of the murdered. —Zalman Gradowski, 1944, from notebook hidden near Crematorium II, Birkenau[63]

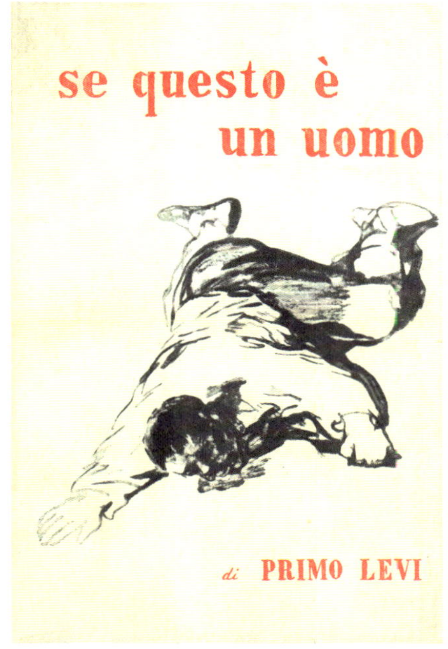

Fig. 1.6 Primo Levi, *Se questo è un uomo* (*If This Is a Man*), Turin, 1947
This cover illustration is an ink sketch by Francisco de Goya made in preparation for his famous 1814 painting *The Third of May 1808* (both works, Prado Museum, Madrid), which represents Napoleon's French troops executing Spaniards by firing squad. Levi's memoir of Auschwitz achieved belated acclaim in the 1960s.

If the press failed to convey the Nazis' genocidal intent toward the Jews, the memoirs, novels, poems, diaries, histories, and studies written by survivors brought the Holocaust graphically and emotionally into view, even if their initial readership was limited. The first wave of literature, written between 1945 and 1948 (see Timeline), came from Jewish and political prisoners alike. The breadth of languages—Czech, Dutch, French, German, Hungarian, Italian, Polish, Yiddish—reveals the terrifying reach of the Third Reich. The testimonials are uncannily consistent in their descriptions of the unnervingly routine and efficient Nazi death machine. Survivors wrote of the deportations (dark, crowded, suffocating cattle cars, days without food); the extermination camps (beatings, gas chambers, corpses, crematoria); the concentration camps (hard labor, selections, starvation, disease, unbearable cold). The stories of each narrator—which describe the loss of loved ones, personal sorrows and sufferings, bad luck and good—are both moving and wrenching.

Souvenirs de l'au-delà (*Memoirs from the Beyond*, Paris, 1946) by Olga Lengyel, a Hungarian nurse, recounts early in her story a fatal error she made upon arriving at Auschwitz-Birkenau.[64] (Birkenau was a death camp at the Auschwitz complex.) She persuaded her mother and 12-year-old son to leave her line, the one for able-bodied adults, and join her younger son in the line for the old and very young. She thought she was sparing them hard labor and giving comfort to her younger son, but she had unwittingly placed the two family members in the line destined for the gas chamber. After that, her existence at the camp seemed worse than death; she witnessed little children frozen to death, and mothers and their newborn babies murdered in the infirmary.

Primo Levi, an Italian chemist and Auschwitz survivor, published several books about the Holocaust (fig. 1.6). His first, *Se questo è un uomo* (*If This Is a Man*, Turin, 1947), describes a recurring dream in which he would be back in the warm comfort of his childhood home, telling his sister and friends about the brutalities of the Nazis.[65] No one believed him. It turns out that this was a dream that many prisoners shared, one that caused great anguish.[66]

These stories, drawn from fresh, raw memories, brought the nameless victims of Nazi atrocities to life and helped to humanize them. Levi described his need to share his story as "primordial and violent," as a means to free himself of its weight and bear witness.[67] He wrote the book furiously, in a matter of months, "obsessed by the fear that even one of my memories might be forgotten."[68] The Viennese psychotherapist Viktor Frankl, separated from his wife upon their arrival at Auschwitz, wrote his 1946 memoir in just nine days.[69] Lengyel said she wrote her book "to carry out the mandate given to me by the many fellow internees at Auschwitz who perished so horribly. . . . no Hitlers must ever be allowed to rise again."[70]

Worthy as these early memoirs were, their initial audiences were small. In the aftermath of war, the public wanted stories of resistance and rebellion, even if embellished to the point of mythology.[71] It was not until the 1960s, after the Eichmann trial, that stories from Holocaust survivors found critical and popular appeal. Frankl's book, issued in paperback in 1963 under the title *Man's Search for Meaning*, went on to sell more than 10 million copies. Translated into 24 languages and reprinted 73 times, it was named in a Library of Congress survey as one of the 10 most influential books in America.[72] After 1962, Lengyel's book received several new translations, including Japanese, Italian, Romanian, and Thai.[73] Levi's memoir achieved belated success and was even adapted for radio and theater.[74]

Given the significance the Holocaust now holds, the initial indifference to the subject may be surprising, but the world was not ready to listen. Survivors, in fact, reported in large numbers of having been discouraged from speaking about the subject.[75] Many kept silent or sought refuge in smaller, private survivor groups. Aharon Appelfeld, one of the most celebrated Hebrew writers of the 20th century, did not write about his experience of the Holocaust and as a postwar refugee until the 1960s, first publishing *Ashan* (*Smoke*, Jerusalem, 1962) and *Ba-gai ha-poreh* (*In the Fertile Valley*, Jerusalem, 1963).[76]

Elie Wiesel published his first book on the subject in 1956, a 900-page memoir of his experience at Auschwitz, *Un di velt hot geshvign* (*And the World Remained Silent*, Buenos Aires). His celebrated literary work *Night*, an abridged form of this book, was published in French in 1958 and English in 1960. It has since been translated into 30 languages, and more than 10 million copies have been sold in the United States alone.[77] Wiesel was awarded the Nobel Peace Prize in 1986.

Even Otto Frank had to wait to find interest in his daughter's diary. The original Dutch edition, *Het achterhuis, dagboekbrieven 14 Juni 1942–1 Augustus 1944* (*The House Behind, Diary Entries, June 14, 1942–August 1, 1944*, Amsterdam, 1947), was published in a small printing of 3,000 copies. It was rejected by 16 publishers in the United States and Great Britain before the first English edition was issued in 1952 as *Anne Frank: The Diary of a Young Girl*. It has been translated into 70 languages and has sold more than 30 million copies.

Zalman Gradowski was a Polish Jewish prisoner in the *Sonderkommando* (special command unit) at Auschwitz-Birkenau who worked as a slave laborer in the gas chambers and crematoria. He wrote an extensive, secret account of the Nazi extermination process, which he buried in a canteen. He was murdered on October 7, 1944, in a *Sonderkommando* revolt he helped organize (the revolt destroyed a crematorium). His notebook, discovered in March 1945 but not published until the 1970s,[78] describes the crimes he witnessed, where the victims were from, the screams he heard as people were sent to their deaths. Along with the notebook, Gradowski and other *Sonderkommandos* concealed vast evidence in a pit beneath the ashes of a crematorium, hoping it would be examined after the war. Manuscripts recovered from this pit have recently received broader attention.[79]

EARLY HOLOCAUST ART

If you live to leave this hell, make your drawings and tell the world about us. We want to be among the living, at least on paper. —Remark to Halina Olomucki from fellow prisoner at Auschwitz, 1943–45[80]

I felt obsessed, driven in fact by the overwhelming desire to put down every detail of this unfathomable place. I began to observe everything with an eye towards capturing it on paper . . . my commitment to drawing came out of a deep instinct of self-preservation and undoubtedly helped me to deny the unimaginable horrors of life at that time. —Alfred Kantor, 1971[81]

My drawings ought not to be subjected to scrutiny and aesthetic art criticism . . . I wish them to be considered a living and shocking document of a world of horror and torment. —Karol Konieczny, 1981[82]

A number of prisoners in the Nazi camps and Jewish ghettos recorded their experiences in art. Variously called witness art, camp art, inmate art, or Holocaust art (the latter as distinct from art confronting the Holocaust by artists who were not survivors or witnesses), it was initially appreciated mostly for its documentary value. Camp prisoners risked beatings, torture, and in some cases their lives to make art about what they were witnessing. Art materials were scarce, as were secret moments to make art, especially in the extermination camps.[83] Pen and pencil drawings were most common, but prisoners also used gouache, watercolor, and other media when they could find it. The artists went to great lengths to hide their works—in walls, pottery, jars, barracks. Art was buried underground or sewn into clothes. Some was smuggled to nonpersecuted friends outside confinement or given to escapees as evidence of crimes occurring inside the camps. Much was lost in the chaos of the closing days of the war, but some prisoners later returned and were able to retrieve bits and pieces of their work. Other art was found by liberating soldiers or other prisoners or years later, unexpectedly, by strangers.[84]

Since the 1960s there has been increased interest in the enormous trove of work that survives, judging from the proliferation of collections, publications, and exhibitions related to Holocaust-era art. Yad Vashem, Israel's official Holocaust memorial in Jerusalem, began receiving such art almost immediately after the center was founded in 1953. The collection became so large—more than 6,000 works—that a separate museum was founded in 1962, just as this category of art started being appreciated by the public, museums, and scholars.[85]

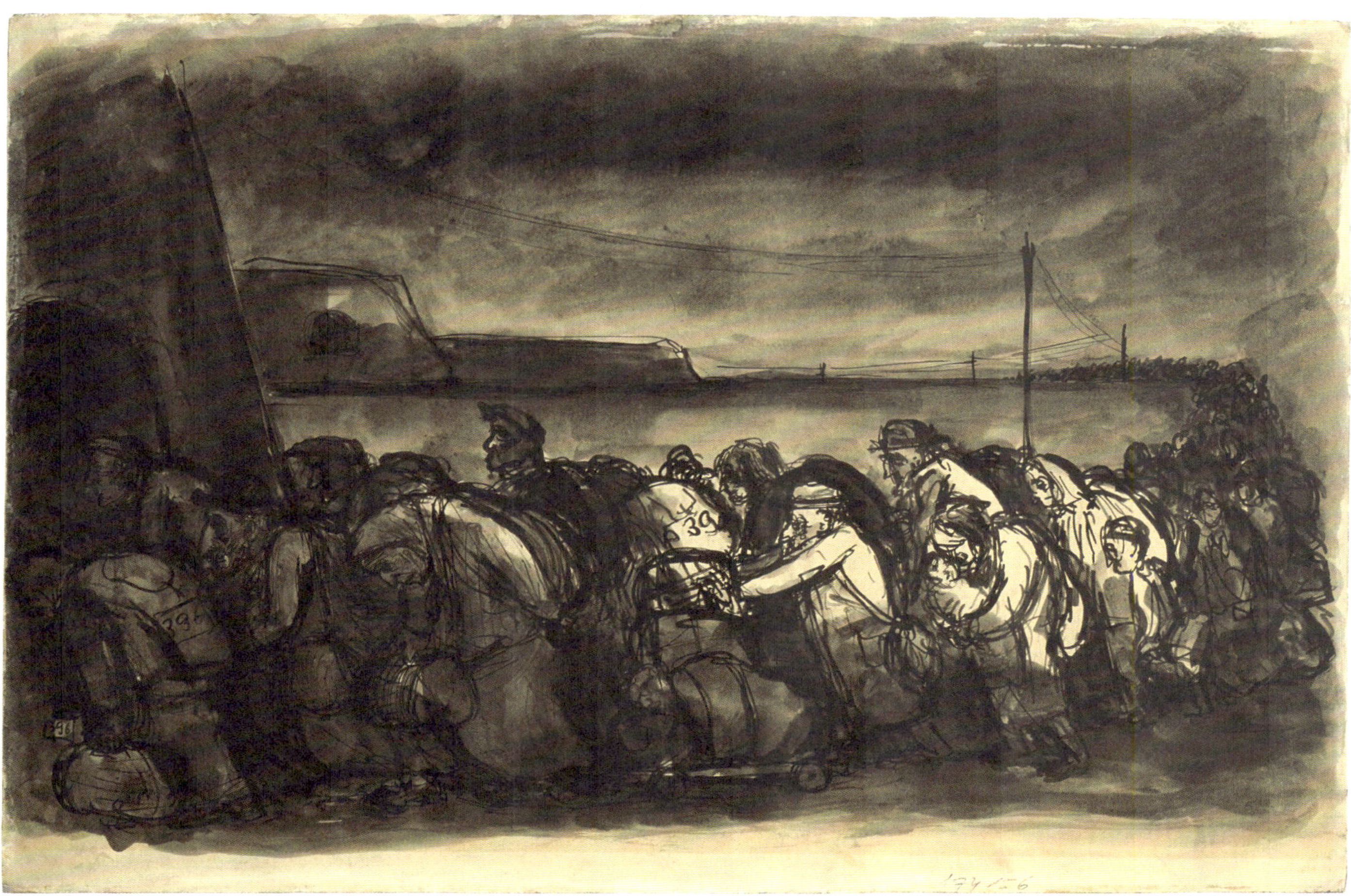

Fig. 1.7 Bedřich Fritta, *Incoming Transport II, Terezín*, 1943–44, pen and ink, brush and wash on paper, 20½ × 32½ in. (52.1 × 82.6 cm), Thomas Fritta-Haas on long-term loan to the Jewish Museum Berlin

The goals of these artists, who were both professional and amateur, were wide ranging, notes Ziva Amishai-Maisels in her monumental study *Depiction and Interpretation: The Influence of the Holocaust on the Visual Arts* (Oxford, 1993). First and foremost, they wanted to document the horrors and crimes they suffered or witnessed. They made art as a form of resistance and self-preservation, as an act of catharsis, and as an assertion of personal will and humanity in a cruel, totalitarian environment.[86] Some works commemorate those lost or record those present. Some express the anguish of the artist and the people being depicted. Other drawings convey the reality of camp life, meticulously recording buildings, people, crimes, and routines.

Much of the best-known Holocaust art was produced at the Czech ghetto–labor camp of Terezín (or Theresienstadt), near Prague, where 140,000 Jews were imprisoned from 1941 to 1945. A quarter of those died from the inhuman living conditions and another 84,000 were deported to extermination camps in Poland.[87] During the war, many detained at Terezín were put to work for the Reich as tailors, carpenters, doctors, musicians—and artists and architects. The latter two groups worked in the technical department, designing, drafting plans, and producing graphics and propaganda for the Nazis. This gave them access to art materials. The Jewish Museum in Prague houses more than 7,000 works of art produced at Terezín, including nearly 4,400 drawings by children.[88] Another impressive collection is at the Terezín Memorial and Ghetto Museum.

The work of Bedřich Fritta, one of the many talented artists imprisoned at Terezín, vividly captures the suffering, crowding, cruelty, and death he witnessed day in, day out.[89] His *Incoming Transport II, Terezín* (1943–44) (fig. 1.7) evokes the misery and exhaustion of new ghetto arrivals and the mental anguish of their long journey. Fritta, along with Felix Bloch, Leo Haas, and Otto Ungar, would pay dearly for making such work. Although these artists went to great lengths to hide it in building walls and in tin containers underground, the Gestapo saw a few drawings, probably because a collector had managed to smuggle some out of Terezín. Fritta, Bloch, Haas, and Ungar were arrested and interrogated by Eichmann and other SS officers. Despite three months of torture, none of the four revealed the hiding place of the other drawings. They were ultimately charged with disseminating "horror propaganda" abroad. Ungar's drawing hand was crushed and dismembered and some of his fingers had to be amputated. Bloch died from injuries sustained during the beatings, as did Fritta and Ungar, although Fritta and Ungar were deported to Auschwitz first, along with Haas.[90] (Haas was among the artists forced to draw victims

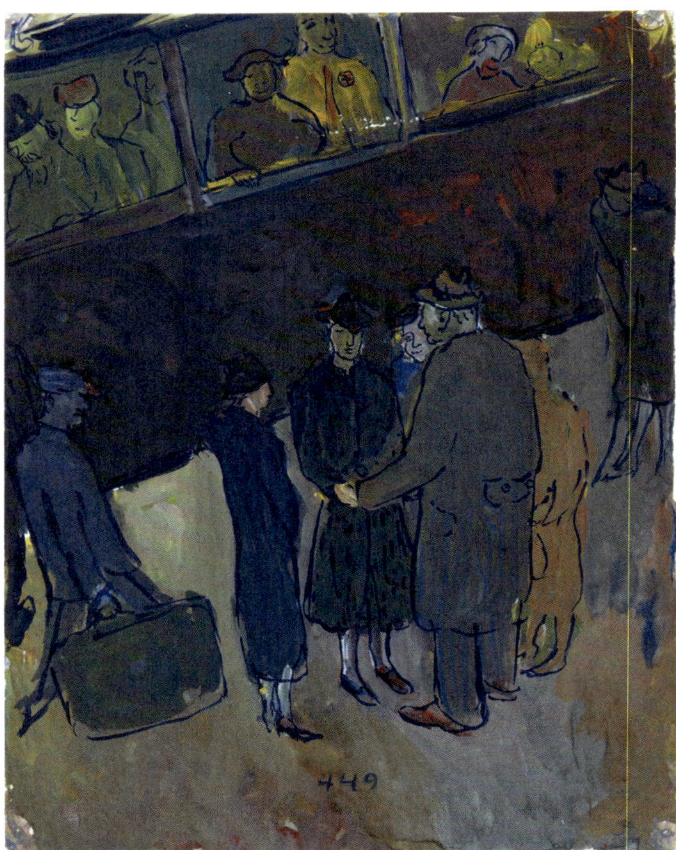

Fig. 1.8 Charlotte Salomon, *No. 449* [Charlotte Taking Leave of Her Family in Berlin, 1939], from the series "Life? or Theatre? A Musical Play," 1940–42, gouache on paper, $12\frac{13}{16} \times 9\frac{7}{8}$ in. (32.5 × 25 cm), Jewish Historical Museum, Amsterdam, inv. no. M004827

Salomon had fled Nazi Germany in 1939 for southern France, where she painted hundreds of autobiographical works. In this drawing, she bids goodbye to her father and stepmother at a Berlin train station.

of Dr. Josef Mengele's horrific experiments, including the pairs of twins whom Mengele tortured.[91]) Only Haas survived the war. He later returned to Terezín and retrieved hundreds of the hidden works.[92] Haas and his wife adopted Fritta's orphaned son; Fritta's wife, Hensi Fritta, had been imprisoned and starved to death after the initial discovery of the drawings. In 1947 Haas published 12 lithographs reproducing his drawings from the camps.[93] An exhibition of the Terezín painters' works was organized in London by the exiled Czech community in 1964.

One of the best-known Holocaust artists is Charlotte Salomon (1917–1943), a German Jewish woman who, at age 22, escaped persecution in Berlin in 1939 by fleeing to southern France with her grandparents. She took up painting in 1940 to cope with her grandmother's suicide (her mother had died of suicide in 1926, her aunt in 1917). Salomon was prolific, creating well over a thousand gouaches and sketches in the next two years. This burst of creativity produced poignant meditations on existence despite her isolation and abusive grandfather (whom she apparently secretly poisoned in 1943).[94]

Her autobiographical "Life? or Theatre? A Musical Play" ("Leben? oder Theater? Ein Singspiel") imaginatively and lyrically weaves together 781 gouaches and poetic texts about her life, family, lovers, dreams, anxieties, and surroundings. One shows her at a Berlin train station as she is leaving for France (fig. 1.8). Her father holds her hands as her stepmother brazenly places herself between their two sad faces; Salomon would never see them again. In late September 1943, she and her new husband were seized by the Gestapo. Two and a half weeks later, emerging from a cattle car in Auschwitz, the 26-year-old artist, five-months pregnant, was immediately gassed. Before being deported, she had left her art with her psychologist and friend, imploring him, "Keep these safe. They are my whole life." Her work represents a distinct category of Holocaust art, since the Holocaust and Nazi death camps, while looming large for the viewer given the artist's fate, are not represented. In 1947, Salomon's father and stepmother retrieved the cache—more than 1,700 paintings, sketches, transparencies with texts, and writings. Her work was first exhibited in Amsterdam in 1961, then in Tel Aviv in 1962, again reflecting the renewed interest in Holocaust material at this time. The following year, Emil Straus and the eminent German American theologian Paul Tillich published *Charlotte: A Diary in Pictures*.[95]

Immediately after the war, several political prisoners published books of their camp drawings. They include Henri Pieck from the Netherlands and Léon Delarbre and Boris Taslitzky from France. A successful painter and graphic artist (and former Soviet spy) before the war, Pieck published two books of his camp drawings in 1945.[96] His detailed studies of prisoners at Buchenwald give special attention to the prison badges and show political prisoners from many different countries (fig. 1.9).[97] Delarbre, a Resistance fighter, was in four separate camps. The spare drawings in his book of "clandestine sketches" isolate the suffering or deaths of single figures, or evoke the prisons' scale by depicting large masses of people.[98]

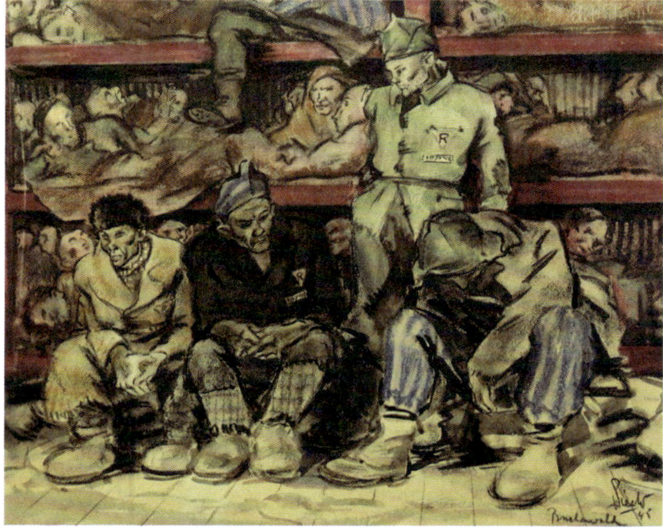

Fig. 1.9 Henri Pieck, *Interior of a Hut in the "Little Camp," Buchenwald*, 1945, graphite and crayon, $18\frac{5}{16} \times 15\frac{3}{16}$ in. (46.5 × 38.7 cm), Overloon War Museum, Netherlands

Pieck, an artist and a Communist, was imprisoned at Buchenwald for his resistance work in the Netherlands. The badges with an upside-down triangle and letter *R* identify these figures as Russian political prisoners. Pieck published this and other camp drawings in The Hague (1945) immediately after the war.

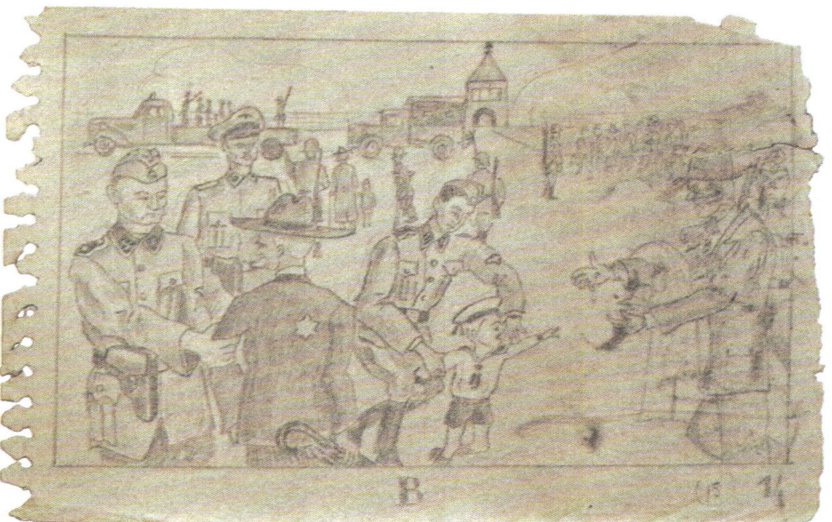

Fig. 1.10 Unknown author (signed MM), *The Separating of Families*, 1943, graphite and colored pencil on paper, 5⁵⁄₁₆ × 8³⁄₁₆ in. (13.5 × 20.8 cm), page 14 from the Auschwitz Sketchbook, collections of the Auschwitz-Birkenau State Museum, Oświęcim, Poland
An artist-prisoner at the Auschwitz-Birkenau camp secretly made 32 drawings documenting the extermination of Jews there. This one shows a young boy separated from his father during selections; he and an older Jewish man appear to be directed to the gas chamber. The drawing can be dated to the second half of 1943, when the main gate of the Birkenau camp, seen in the background, had only one wing.

Taslitzky's book of 111 Buchenwald drawings (1946) includes an essay by fellow prisoner Julien Cain, a former administrator general of the prestigious Bibliothèque Nationale, or national library, in Paris.[99]

Jewish prisoners generally are not conspicuously represented in these drawings by political prisoners. Even Taslitzky, who was Jewish, alluded to Jewish prisoners in only four of the 111 published drawings, identifying them with lightly sketched Stars of David on their prison jackets or listing Jews as part of a group in a title.[100] Cain, also Jewish, omitted any mention of Jews in his description of Buchenwald and instead focused on Taslitzky as the "artiste révolutionnaire," situating him in a long line of great French revolutionary painters.[101] The Jewish side of the story seems not to have concerned either artist or writer at the time. Both were arrested as political prisoners before the deportations of Jews had begun in France, which probably saved them from being gassed.[102]

One of the most significant works to survive from the Auschwitz-Birkenau camp is the Auschwitz Sketchbook (fig. 1.10), containing 32 small chalk and pencil studies by an artist-prisoner known only by the monogram MM. Found hidden in a bottle in the foundations of a cell block at Birkenau in 1947, the drawings were first published in 2011 and exhibited at the National Museum in Kraków, Poland, in 2017.[103] They portray the exterminations at Birkenau, focusing on Jewish victims in particular. Care is taken to identify guards and victims by their badges, and scenes can be located in precise areas of the camp.

Most of the drawings made by prisoners at Auschwitz were destroyed or lost. Only a handful of Halina Olomucki's Auschwitz drawings survive, in part because she destroyed some herself out of fear of being caught. But she managed to save hundreds from her time in the Warsaw ghetto in Poland by depositing them with a Polish friend before the ghetto's liquidation.[104] In the late 1940s and the 1950s, to fill this gap, the Auschwitz-Birkenau museum commissioned two former political prisoners of the camp, Władysław Siwek and Mieczysław Koscielniak, to create a series of works depicting life there. Their emphasis, understandably, was on the plight of ethnic Polish prisoners.[105]

The drawings Yehuda Bacon made in camp—he survived Terezín, Auschwitz, and Mauthausen—were mostly lost, but he said he drew "nonstop" after the war to document what had happened and to help him heal.[106] Just shy of 16 years old when the camps were liberated, Bacon was the only member of his family to survive. He testified at Eichmann's trial, and some of his sketches were introduced as evidence, as were works by Haas and Bloch.[107] Alfred Kantor acquired a blank sketchbook at an American displaced-persons camp after liberation and filled it from memory with drawings about his experiences at Auschwitz, Terezín, and the Schwarzheide concentration camp (near Dresden). He drew most of them in just two months.[108]

Many survivors produced their most important art about the Holocaust decades after the war, such as Samuel Bak, Zoran Music, Alice Lok Cahana, and Maryan S. Maryan.[109] Bak, like so many of his contemporaries, retreated into abstraction in the 1940s and 1950s before being drawn back to representational art in the 1960s and 1970s. He felt that the figure—distorted, attenuated, caricatured, and brutalized—was more effective at expressing his experience. As the scholar Yehudit Shendar writes, Bak "wrapped himself in silence" after the war and it was only years later, when "he could no longer keep the burden," that he "shed the cloak of silence" in his art.[110]

As with the literary accounts, art about the Holocaust and art made by Holocaust victims suddenly found a receptive audience in the 1960s. Levi's Auschwitz memoir only gained success in that decade, despite having been released in 1947. As Levi explained it, his words had fallen "into oblivion, partly because in that harsh period after the war, people had little desire to return in memory to the years of suffering they just endured."[111]

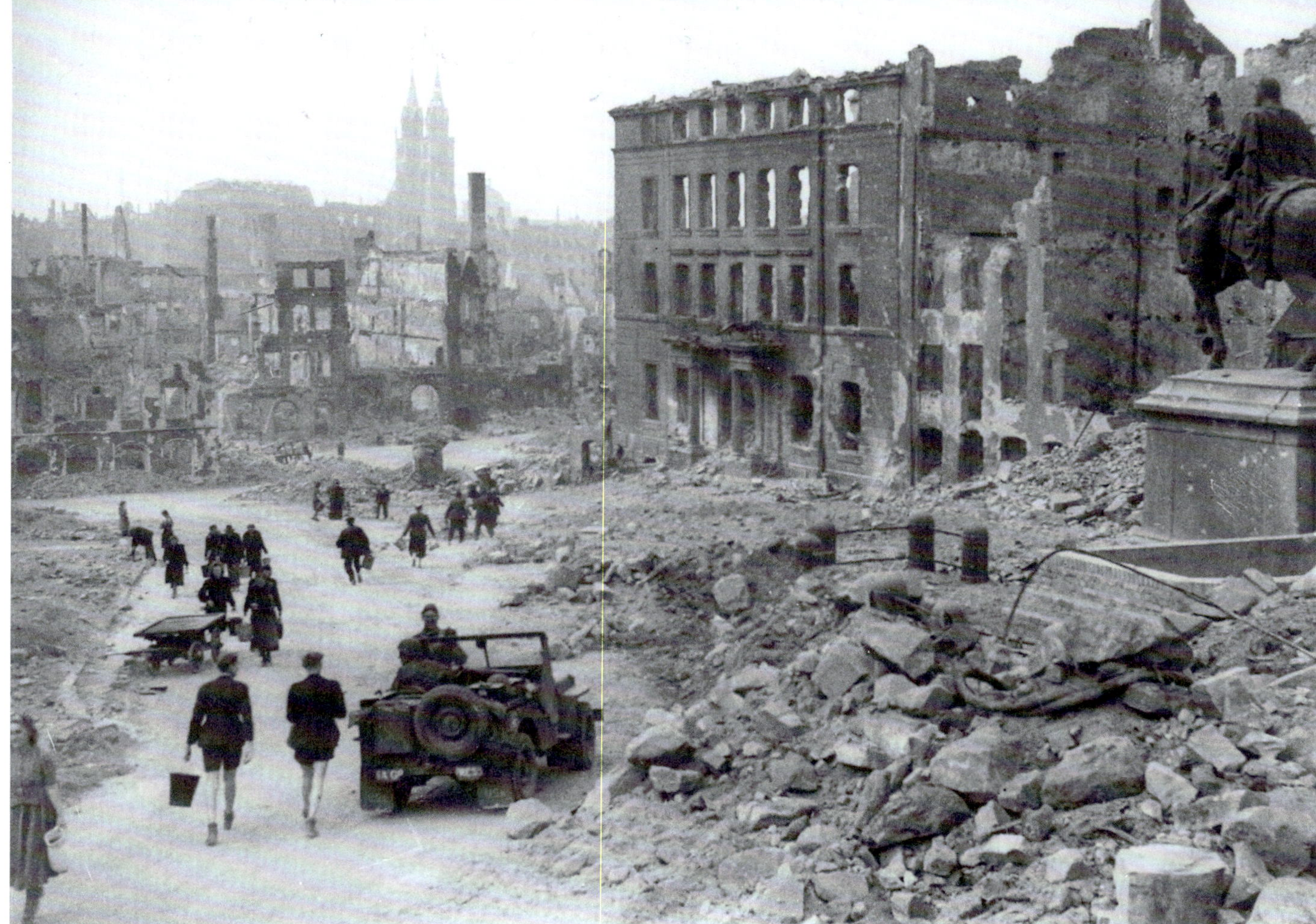

Fig. 1.11 Nuremberg, Germany, 1945. National Archives, Washington, D.C., American Commission for the Protection and Salvage of Artistic and Historic Monuments in War Areas
Nuremberg, home to the Nazi Party's massive propaganda rallies in the 1920s and '30s, lay in ruins after the war, nearly 90 percent destroyed. Here only the equestrian statue of Kaiser Wilhelm (1905) and the distant Gothic church of St. Lawrence appear to be intact.

STUNDE NULL, "HOUR ZERO"

In the circumstances of 1945, in a continent covered with rubble, there was much to be gained by behaving as though the past was indeed dead and buried and a new age about to begin. The price paid was a certain amount of selective, collective forgetting, notably in Germany. But then, in Germany above all, there was much to forget. —Tony Judt, *Postwar: A History of Europe since 1945* (2005)[112]

Germany surrendered to the Allies on May 7, 1945. The following day, "Hour Zero," as the Germans called it, marked the start of peace. The break with the past was cataclysmic. Much of Europe lay in ruins—the scale of destruction and misery was apocalyptic (figs. 1.11 and 1.12). In *Postwar: A History of Europe since 1945* (New York, 2005), Tony Judt catalogues the human loss and material devastation experienced by this "shattered continent."[113] He calculates that 36.5 million Europeans died between 1939 and 1945 from war-related causes, of which at least 19 million were civilians. Berlin, Dresden, Rotterdam, Kyiv, Minsk, Warsaw, and many other illustrious European cities were reduced to rubble. The total obliteration inspired a new cinematic genre, the "rubble films" of the late 1940s, set in these destroyed cities.[114] Warsaw lost 90 percent of its homes; Italy lost 1.2 million dwellings. In London, some 3.5 million homes were damaged, and the average wait for a new one was seven years. Twenty million Germans were homeless. The Soviet Union had 25 million people without homes, as well as 71,700 destroyed towns and villages and 32,000 destroyed factories. Hundreds of thousands of miles of railway tracks and roads across Europe were lost, and tens of thousands of bridges demolished. Wide swaths of arable land and forests were devastated, and hundreds of thousands of horses and livestock were dead—half of Yugoslavia's prewar population of such animals. There were massive food shortages, starvation, and increased infant deaths. Outbreaks of disease were widespread, stemming from malnutrition, sewage pollution, infections, and medicine shortages. Children suffered the most. In Berlin in December 1945, seven months after the war ended, one in four children died before their first birthday. Two years later, only half the city's rubble had been removed (mostly by hand).[115]

In September 1945, the United Nations and Western Allies had 6.8 million displaced persons (DPs)—concentration camp survivors, deportees, POWs, laborers, and orphans—in their care, mostly in DP camps across Europe. They were waiting to go home or, for the stateless or persecuted, to find a new home. The Soviet Union had 7 million refugees of its own to feed, house, and repatriate. This represented only part of the resettlement of tens of millions of people that took place. Between 1939 and 1943, Adolf Hitler, chancellor and führer of Germany (1933–45) and leader of the Nazi Party (1921–45), and Joseph Stalin, premier of the Soviet Union (1941–53) and secretary general of the Communist Party (1922–53), had deported, expelled, and/or transplanted some 30 million people. Those who survived the war had to be moved back, and, in some places, expulsions of ethnic minorities were ongoing.[116]

By late 1946, an estimated 250,000 Jewish refugees were in DP camps in Western Europe, mostly in Germany, of which some 50,000 were camp survivors.[117] Their numbers swelled following a wave of Polish pogroms in which hundreds of returning Jews were murdered.[118] Many were stateless or fearful of returning to their homes. The United States pressured Britain to open migration to Palestine and opened its own borders to refugees, welcoming by 1952 approximately 100,000 European Jews.[119] By 1951, some 332,000 European Jews had settled in Israel from DP camps in Germany and Soviet camps in Romania and Poland.[120]

European recovery took years, which is one reason, scholars say, that the Nazi barbarism toward the Jews was not acknowledged, comprehended, or memorialized. The process of forgetting began immediately with the removal of Nazi symbols and the destruction of incriminating uniforms and documents. At the same time, the trials of Nazi war criminals in Nuremberg in 1945–46 singled out specific high-ranking Nazis for blame, which had the unanticipated effect of making other Germans (and Germany's collaborators) feel like passive innocents. American denazification efforts sought to remove Nazis from civil service, but many who were fired were hired back a year or two later as judges or police officers or government officials.[121] Similarly, Nazi war criminals, including businessmen and camp doctors, had their sentences shortened or commuted within years of conviction. Whether guilty, compromised, or traumatized, Germans had little interest in examining the past.

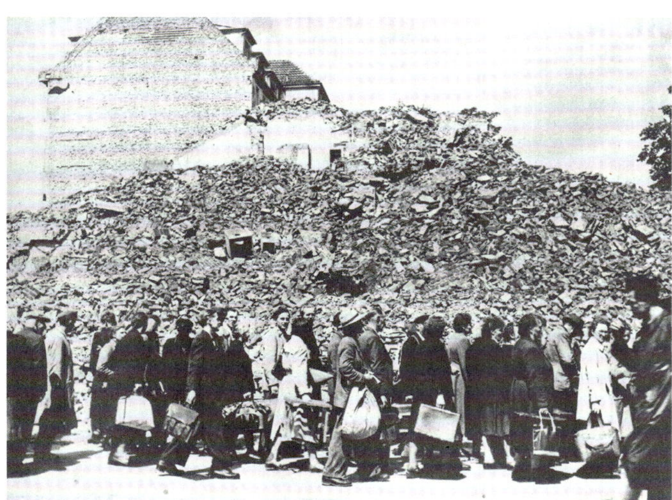

Fig. 1.12 People lining up with baggage in front of rubble in an unidentified German city, c. 1948–51. National Archives, Washington, D.C., photographs of Marshall Plan activities in Europe
Europe's efforts to rebuild after World War II were aided in no small part by George Marshall's European Recovery Program. The United States spent some $13 billion in Western Europe between 1948 and 1952.

THE TRAGEDY OF WAR HIDES THE TRAGEDY OF THE HOLOCAUST

If Germany seemed to ignore the Holocaust in the 1940s and 1950s, it was not alone. Judt observed that the "forgetting" was almost universal, extending from Italy to Britain, Poland to France.[122] Judt had cousins who were murdered in the death camps. Yet he said that for him, growing up in postwar England, "the silence seemed quite normal," and the Holocaust was seldom discussed in school or by the media at the time.[123] In the Soviet Union, where human losses were among the most devastating, with an estimated 16 million civilian deaths and 8.6 million military deaths, including 3.3 million Soviet POWs dying in German concentration camps, Stalin wished to make the Soviets both the greatest martyrs and the most important victors of the "Great Patriotic War."[124] This had the effect of marginalizing Jewish losses. Stalin's forced famines, starvations, and mass executions in Ukraine, Poland, Belarus, and within Russia's borders had left millions dead.[125] His gulag before, during, and after the war had a steady population of some 5 million political prisoners in forced labor. He wished to conceal his secret killing fields and prison camps.[126] Ukrainians and Latvians who had collaborated with the Nazis, or as POWs had been forced to work at the death camps, wished to bury the past (as seen with John Demjanjuk, whose decades-long odyssey disputing war crimes charges ended with his death in 2012).

Poland notably suffered huge wartime losses. Before the war, its Jewish population was 3 million. Afterward, it was approximately 75,000.[127] The surviving Jews, facing postwar pogroms and antisemitism, fled the country. Thus Poles largely forgot about their Jewish neighbors despite, as the filmmaker Claude Lanzmann shows in his documentary *Shoah* (1985), having taken over the houses of deported Jews and witnessing Nazi atrocities firsthand.[128] Ethnic Poles had experienced devastating casualties as well. Between 1.8 and 1.9 million were estimated to have been killed in the camps and through mass executions, uprisings, and forced labor. Some 1.5 million Poles were enslaved as laborers by the Reich, and hundreds of thousands were expelled to make room for German resettlement.[129] During the Communist era, genocide and antisemitism were not discussed at the Auschwitz-Birkenau Memorial and Museum in Poland, founded in 1947. Victims were listed by nationality, with no mention of their Jewish backgrounds, even though more than 90 percent of the 1.1 million murdered at the camp were Jews.[130]

Immediately after the war, France focused on the Nazi persecution of French citizens in general, not on the annihilation of the Jews in particular.[131] The Nazis had detained 1.8 million French soldiers as POWs since 1940, and, with the critical assistance of the Vichy collaborationist government, deported from France 140,000 French citizens and refugees, both political prisoners (largely Resistance fighters and Communists) and Jews. The survival rate for political deportees sent to concentration camps was much higher than for Jewish deportees, who were sent to extermination camps. (Fifty-nine percent of the 63,085 non-Jewish prisoners survived their imprisonment, whereas fewer than 3 percent of the 75,721 Jewish citizens and refugees lived.[132]) French law in 1948 restricted the term *déportés* to French citizens or political resisters; thus Jewish refugees sent from France to their deaths—the majority of the Jews who perished from the country, including Charlotte Salomon—were not counted. Jewish children murdered at Auschwitz who were citizens of France were described in French documents as "political deportees."[133] In this calculation, the Jewish tragedy was concealed.

In the early months of the liberations, the former German-occupied countries were focused on retribution, not Germany's ethnic cleansing. Waves of violence broke out across Europe. In France, this included an estimated 10,000 "extrajudicial" killings of collaborators (fig. 1.13).[134] There also was public shaming of women who consorted with the Germans—called "horizontal collaboration"—in occupied countries, including France, Belgium, the Netherlands, Italy, and Norway. Organized mobs rounded up the women, shaved their heads in city squares, and paraded them through the streets, sometimes stripped or covered with pitch or Nazi swastika symbols. As many as 200,000 babies were born to German fathers in France during the occupation (1940–44), 40,000 in Belgium, 20,000 in the Netherlands, 12,000 in Norway, and 4,000 in Finland.[135] Among the *collaboratrices* or *tondues* (shorn women) were Nazi sympathizers, women in love, teenagers, rape victims, and single mothers forced into prostitution for money and food. At least 20,000 women in France had their heads forcibly shaved following liberation.[136] Simone Touseau (fig. 1.14) was one of 11 women rounded up in Chartres, France, on August 16, 1944, along with 30 alleged male collaborators; three of the men were shot.[137] Touseau, a fascist sympathizer, had fallen in love with a German soldier while working as a translator. Accusations that she was an informant were never proved, but she was tried for "national degradation" and sentenced to 10 years in prison. In 1946 she learned that her German fiancé had died in the war. Released after two years, she lived as a recluse.[138] The large crowd in Robert Capa's photograph, walking briskly to keep pace with the humiliated Touseau and gawking with pleasure at her disgrace, captures the moral outrage and fury, pent up during the Nazi occupation and now unleashed in a spasm of schadenfreude.

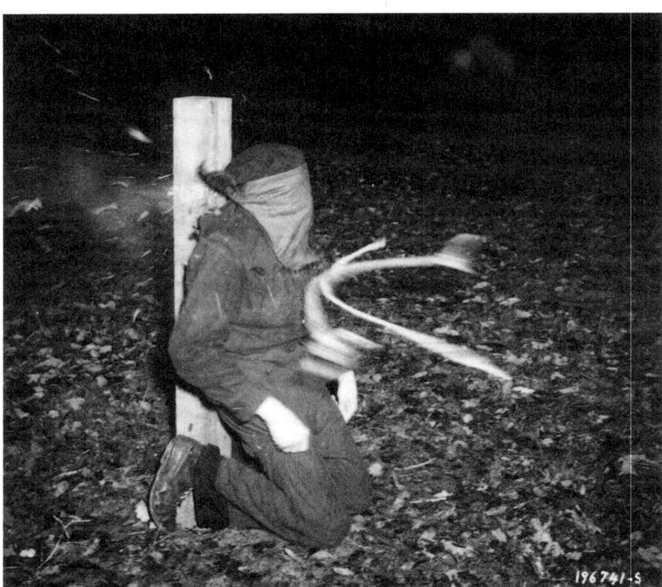

Fig. 1.13 A French collaborator murdered by a French firing squad in Rennes, France, November 21, 1944. National Archives, Washington, D.C. Waves of violent retribution broke out across Europe following the liberations of German-occupied countries. In France, an estimated 10,000 alleged collaborators were punished in extrajudicial killings.

Governments attempted to bring to trial citizens accused of collaborating with the Nazis and other crimes and to purge collaborators from the civil service with limited success.[139] (Only Germans were charged with crimes against humanity and war crimes in these early years.) Norway tried 3 percent of its population for Nazi collaboration, nearly 100,000 people; the Netherlands tried twice as many. In France a very small percentage of wartime collaborators were tried or lost their civil service jobs, and amnesties were granted and jobs reinstated a few years later.[140] By 1947, the mood had switched to national recovery and the future, signaling a nearly universal compulsion to forget the widespread collaboration and the moral compromises of the war.[141]

This climate was exemplified by a preference for heroic resistance stories and serviceable myths in literature, film, and popular culture. The French Resistance, which continues to hold an outsize reputation, had at its height at the end of the war an estimated 160,000 to 170,000 fully active members in a country of 35 million.[142] Their heroic efforts, undertaken at extraordinary risk, could have resulted in imprisonment, torture, and death. An estimated 70,000 French resisters died in concentration camps, in action, or by firing squad.[143] During the war, 70,000 French POWs escaped German captivity. Stories of resistance became the celebrated narrative of France after the war.

The writings of French political deportees imprisoned in German concentration camps received

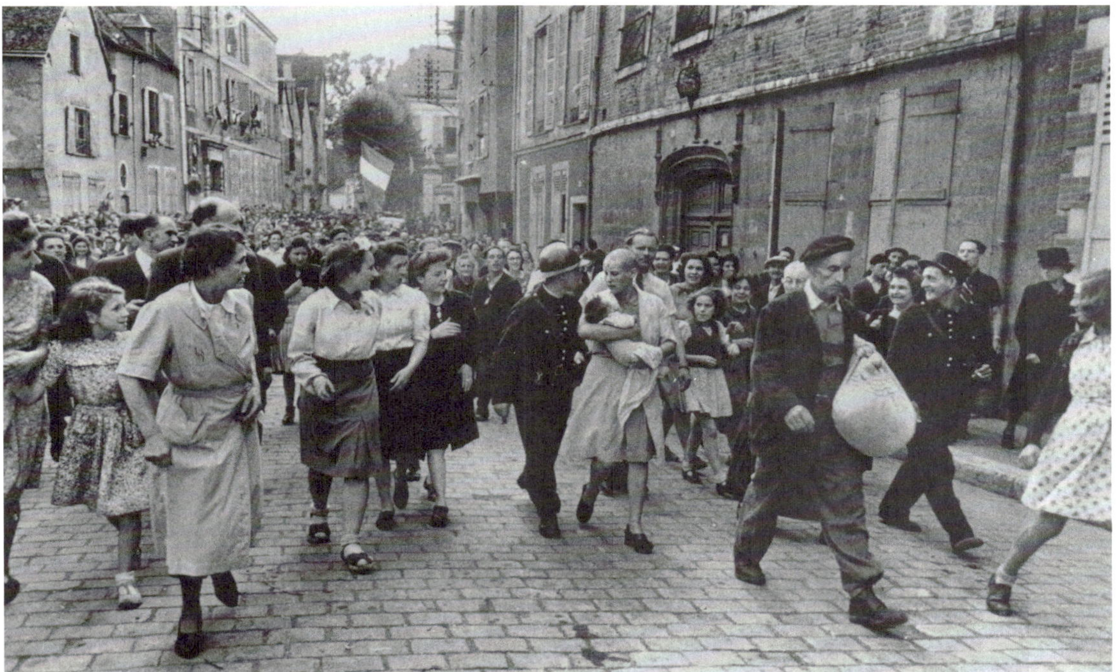

Fig. 1.14 Robert Capa, *Chartres, France, 1944*, August 18, 1944, gelatin silver print
Simone Touseau, whose baby was fathered by a German soldier, is publicly shamed in Chartres following the city's liberation. Her head forcibly shaved, she appeared in *Life* magazine, September 4, 1944, with the caption, "Woman collaborationist."

critical acclaim. (Few of France's political deportees were sent to extermination camps.) David Rousset, a French Resistance Communist arrested by the Gestapo in 1943, wrote about his time in the German salt mines and at Buchenwald in his 1946 book *L'Univers concentrationnaire* (*The Concentrationary Universe*, Paris). It received the prestigious Prix Renaudot literary award.[144] Jean Cayrol, a survivor of the Mauthausen-Gusen concentration camp complex, published *Poèmes de la nuit et du brouillard* (*Poems of the Night and Fog*, Paris, 1946), which was also awarded the Renaudot prize (1947), and later contributed to Alain Resnais's 1955 documentary *Nuit et brouillard* (*Night and Fog*). Robert Antelme, a political prisoner at Dachau and later the Gandersheim labor camp, wrote *L'Espèce humaine* (*The Human Species*, Paris, 1947), a philosophical consideration of concentration camps and humanity. Griselda Pollock and Max Silverman observe, "The public memory of war in France was largely written as a memory of Resistance to the German forces. The experiences of the deported political prisoners substantiated this comforting narrative."[145]

The first French postwar films also regaled audiences with resistance stories, among them René Chanas's *Le Jugement dernier* (*The Last Judgment*), in 1945, and René Clément's *Bataille du rail* (*Battle of the Rails*) and *Le Père tranquille* (*The Quiet Father*), both 1946.[146] That same year the newly opened Musée des Arts Modernes (Museum of Modern Arts) in Paris unveiled the sprawling exhibition *Art et résistance* (*Art and Resistance*), organized by friends of a French Communist Resistance group.[147] Visitors saw art by Resistance members hanging alongside works by Matisse, Bonnard, and Picasso. The subjects were wide ranging—barricades, patriots, partisans, martyrs, victors, allegories of France, the Resistance, liberation, victory—but only a handful dealt with the Nazi camps. Buchenwald survivor Boris Taslitzky showed a poster inspired by Louis Aragon's 1943 patriotic resistance poem, "I salute you, my France."[148] One work that alluded specifically to Jewish victims was the painting *Four Crematories under the Snow* by Irène Reno, the pseudonym of Rena Hassenberg. An accomplished Jewish artist born in Warsaw, she had emigrated to France in 1905.

The theme of resistance was not confined to the arts. Early Jewish memorials and Holocaust remembrance days honored the Warsaw ghetto revolt of 1943, a brave month-long armed resistance against the Germans. One of the first Holocaust memorials, Nathan Rapoport's Warsaw ghetto monument in Poland, was erected on the site of the former ghetto and unveiled on April 19, 1948, the revolt's fifth anniversary. The site has since become a more universal symbol of commemoration in Poland, with war veterans and political dissidents frequently gathering there, adopting the memorial as a symbol for the Poles' own uprising against the Nazis in 1944.[149] The first Holocaust museum, the Ghetto Fighters' House, now called the Yitzhak Katzenelson Holocaust and Jewish Resistance Heritage Museum, was founded by Holocaust survivors, including survivors of the Warsaw uprising, on an Israeli kibbutz in 1949. The founding date was also April 19. For Jewish organizations in the United States, Holocaust commemoration in the 1950s also centered on the Warsaw uprising, adopted as a symbol and marking the annual day of remembrance, Yom Hashoah, "Day of the Holocaust and Heroism."[150]

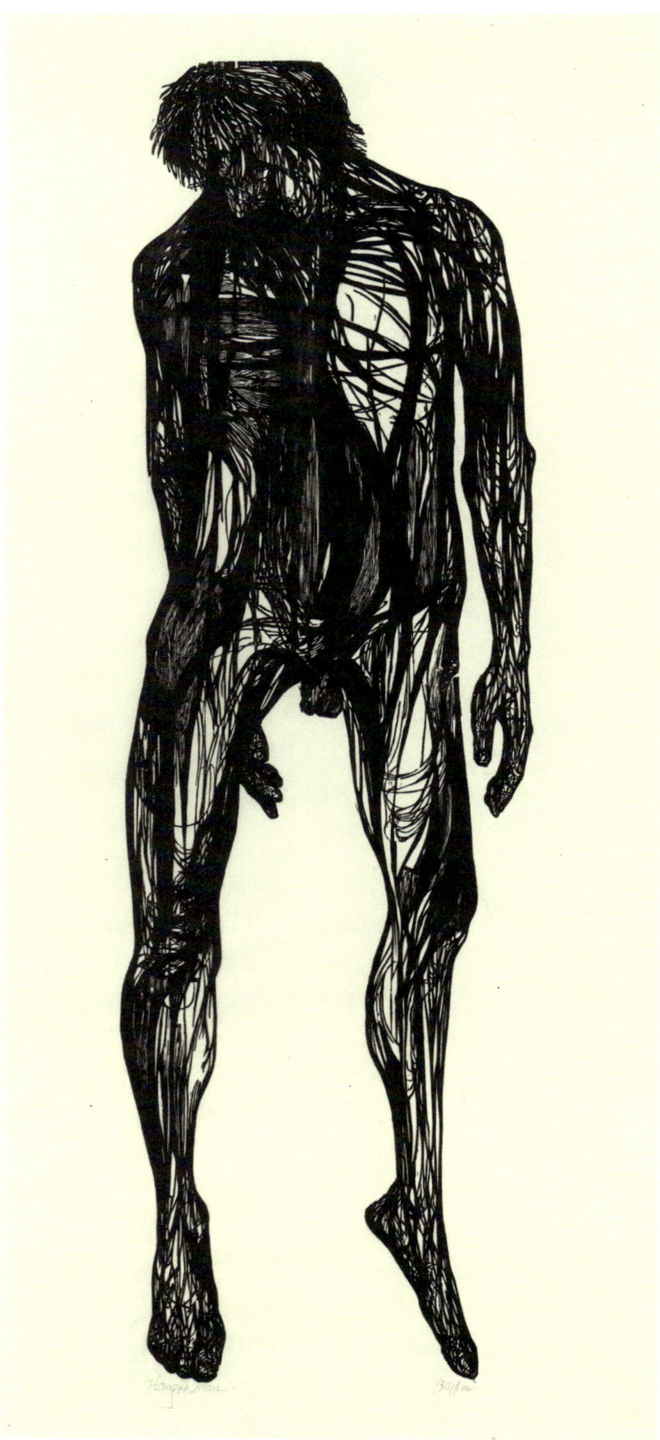

Fig. 1.15 Leonard Baskin, *Hanged Man*, 1955, woodcut, 78 × 36 in. (198.1 × 91.4 cm), Smithsonian American Art Museum, Washington, D.C., 1999.47

PORTRAYING EVIL: THE UNIVERSAL VERSUS THE SPECIFIC

There is a common presumption, although often erroneous, that early-postwar art, literature, and film about the war are about the Holocaust. However, as we have seen, the significance of the Jewish tragedy was not yet understood or given the attention we might expect in retrospect. In the postwar period, artists were generally drawn to symbolic language and purposeful ambiguities when depicting atrocities. The influential political thinker and journalist Hannah Arendt, herself a German Jew who fled Nazi Germany, wrote in 1945: "The reality is that the Nazis are men like ourselves; the nightmare is that they have shown, have proven beyond doubt what man is capable of. In other words, the problem of evil will be the fundamental question of postwar intellectual life in Europe."[151] The worldwide destruction and suffering of World War II, from Auschwitz to Hiroshima, Hamburg to Nanjing—in mass extermination camps, in cities destroyed by nuclear weapons or carpet bombing, and on the battlefield—starkly exposed humanity's shocking capability of violence and evil, in every corner of the globe, and on a new scale with the aid of modern technology. The killings and barbarisms seemed to dictate an approach by writers, scholars, and artists at this time to explore the problem of evil, and to universalize victims, perpetrators, and suffering, if a larger moral were to be learned and shared with a broader public.

In America, the war was experienced by most people at a distance. Abstract Expressionism was the predominant style of the 1940s and '50s. The monumental drip paintings, color-field paintings, and gestural abstractions, with numbered or music-inspired titles or no title at all, often retreated from such worldly, dark themes. There were certainly artists who wished to examine evil and war in their art, such as Leonard Baskin, Philip Guston, Jacques Lipchitz, Leon Golub, Nancy Spero, Rico Lebrun, and Mauricio Lasansky, but they needed a more concrete language. They adapted a widely varied, expressive figurative vocabulary, raw and tortured at times, to depict the brutality, mutilation, degradation, and evil of war.[152] Parallels in Europe might be found in the haunting, distorted figuration of Francis Bacon, Jean Dubuffet, and Pablo Picasso. What mattered first and foremost to many artists in this era was to convey the modern human condition and universal suffering.

Given this, it is curious how often art of this early period has been interpreted as having specific connections to the Holocaust.[153] The frightful, colossal figures in Baskin's "Dead Man" series (1951–55), and monumental woodcuts such as *Hydrogen Man* (1954) and *Hanged Man* (1955) (fig. 1.15), for instance, cannot be considered works

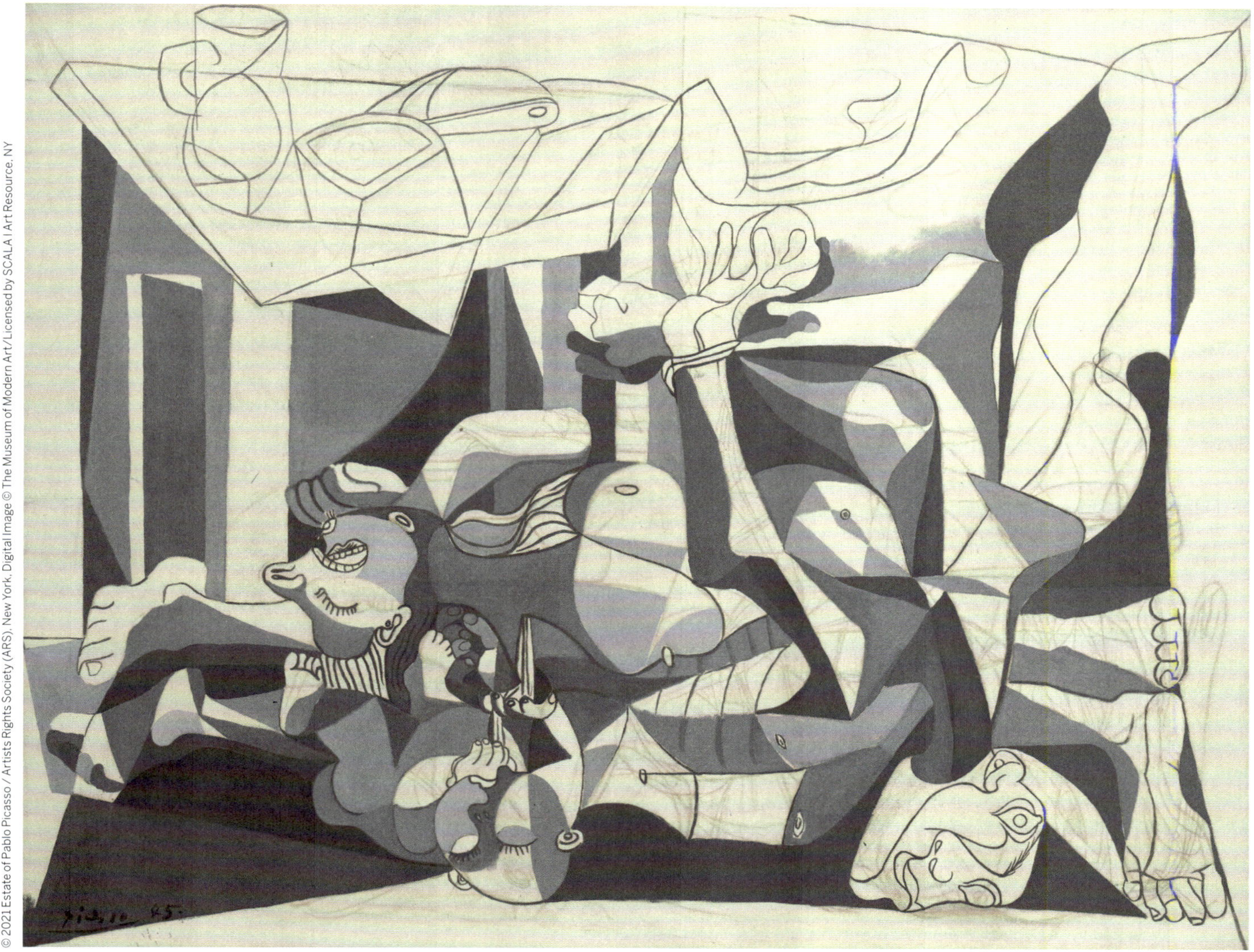

Fig. 1.16 Pablo Picasso, *The Charnel House*, 1944–45, oil and charcoal on canvas, 78⅝ × 98½ in. (199.8 × 250.1 cm), Museum of Modern Art, New York, 93.1971

about the Holocaust. Baskin, in fact, flatly refuted the suggestion.[154] Nor can Golub's *Damaged Man* (1955) and "Burnt Man" series (begun 1959) be put in that category. Golub's flayed and scorched figures serve as metaphors of violence, misery, mass annihilation. Specific details identifying the victims, perpetrators, places, and weapons are omitted (or merely alluded to, as in Baskin's *Hydrogen Man*, a kind of atomic war figure).

Another example is Picasso's *Charnel House* (1944–45) (fig. 1.16). Exhibited in the *Art et résistance* exhibition, it depicts a dead mother, father, and child crumpled beneath a dining table. It is often described as Picasso's response to the Nazi camps and photographs of the corpses,[155] but the table with napkins, pitcher, and food clearly locates the carnage in a home rather than a prison camp.[156] A more convincing suggestion, given the interrupted meal and Picasso's Spanish sympathies, is that the painting relates to an incident in the Spanish Civil War, the murder of a Republican family in their kitchen.[157] The common assumption that Picasso was particularly concerned with Jewish victims in this work or elsewhere cannot be substantiated.[158] The artist's symbolic language and purposeful ambiguities in the details universalize the tragedy, a strategy used by many artists in the era.

The Italian American artist Rico Lebrun was distinctive for specifically representing Nazi concentration camps in the 1950s, in his Buchenwald and Dachau series of paintings and drawings (1955–58). These brutal works, depicting dismembered corpses piled in pits, carts, and on floors, suggest a vast number of victims, their bodies degraded, their individual identities erased. While locating the slaughters in German concentration camps, the works do not highlight the Jewish genocide. They generalize the camp victims; these could be the bodies of political prisoners, Jews, Roma and Sinti, and Russian POWs.[159]

Ben-Zion, a Ukrainian-born Jewish artist living in the United States, was exceptional in the attention he gave to Jewish subject matter before, during, and immediately after the war and in his examination of the Holocaust. The 14 gouaches and oils in his series "De Profundis" (1943–46) depict small crowds of bearded older men praying.[160] The chaotic compositions are tightly cropped around the figures' heads, suggesting that the men are in danger or that death might be near. The allusion to the Holocaust is symbolic, but the artist's statement for a 1946 gallery exhibition in New York makes his intent clear:

> As people and countries are counting their losses after the defeat of the destroyers of Europe, the tribute of six million Jewish people, extinguished in the most fiendish way, has scarcely penetrated our conscience and we are still far from being able to create adequate symbols for this plight.

Ben-Zion said he chose "patriarchal types of Jews" for this series because "their humiliation was the deepest" and they were martyred despite their "strength of character and rare courage."[161] His early and explicit reference to the 6 million murdered Jews and timely artistic tribute to them are unusual. As Matthew Baigell observes in *Jewish-American Artists and the Holocaust* (New Brunswick, N.J., 1997), Ben-Zion has few parallels in the United States in this era. Marc Chagall can be considered one of them; he continued to explore Jewish subjects, persecution, and martyrdom while in exile from Nazi-occupied France in the 1940s and living in New York.

Perhaps more surprising, as Baigell explores, is how rarely Jewish artists (and writers and intellectuals) in America treated the Holocaust directly in the early postwar period.[162] Of his work in the 1950s, Golub, for instance, explained that he saw humanity as facing annihilation or mutation; thus his expressive figures showed "the stress of their vulnerability versus their capacities for endurance."[163] Ben Shahn said, "I wanted to reach further, to tap some sort of universal experience, to create symbols that would have some such universal quality."[164] His wife, Bernarda Bryson, said that Shahn did not depict the Holocaust because he wanted to avoid "ethnic self-pity."[165] (This changed for Shahn in 1965, when he began to make overt references to the Holocaust in his work.[166]) In Baigell's view, beyond the inclination to express universal themes, many factors inhibited Jewish artists from exploring the Holocaust in the 1940s and '50s: antisemitism, fear of being marginalized as a Jewish artist (even if proudly Jewish), persistent incomprehension of the tragedy, trauma, and an inability to express such a tragedy adequately.[167] As discussed in the essay "Mauricio Lasansky: A Life and Art of Compassion," Lasansky struggled with his first forays into Holocaust subject matter. He was not satisfied with *Dachau* (1946) and other early attempts, which he felt were "too aesthetic" to express the enormity of the destruction, and he abandoned the theme for more than a decade. Baskin and Hyman Bloom both reported being too overwhelmed by Holocaust photographs to make art about the tragedy. Baskin, the son of a rabbi, would dedicate himself to the subject of the Holocaust in the 1990s but said that in the early postwar years the topic felt too immense for art—an opinion shared by many.[168]

"To write poetry after Auschwitz is barbaric,"[169] German philosopher Theodor Adorno wrote in 1949. Seventeen years later he expanded on his famous remark:

> Perennial suffering has as much right to expression as a tortured man has to scream; hence it may have been wrong to say that after Auschwitz you could no longer write poems. But it is not wrong to raise the less cultural question whether after Auschwitz you can go on living—especially whether one who escaped by accident, one who by rights should have been killed, may go on living. His mere survival calls for the coldness, the basic principle of bourgeois subjectivity, without which there could have been no Auschwitz.[170]

These oft-cited words have multiple meanings. In one sense they proclaim the end of civilization; civilization perished at Auschwitz and it also created Auschwitz. The narrower, more common interpretation is that literature and art are barbarously inadequate to express the tragedy of the Holocaust, and thus meaningless, even offensive. Thankfully, Adorno's pronouncement has not been fulfilled. Life continues. Artists and writers continue to create. It took decades, but gradually the Holocaust was better understood.

TWO CASE STUDIES: A FILM AND A DIARY

Two milestones of film and literature played major roles in shaping how the tragedy was understood in the 1950s: Alain Resnais's documentary *Night and Fog* and Anne Frank's diary, published in English in 1952 and subsequently adapted for television, the stage, and the screen. They represent two approaches to the Holocaust in the decade before the Eichmann trial. An examination of these influential works will help to illuminate how the tragedy was understood just before Lasansky began "The Nazi Drawings."

Night and Fog

The 1955 French documentary *Nuit et brouillard* (*Night and Fog*) (fig. 1.17), directed by Alain Resnais and written by camp survivor Jean Cayrol, has been described as the first Holocaust film.[171] Just after its release, the French New Wave film director François Truffaut proclaimed it "the greatest film ever made."[172] It played an important role in shaping worldwide knowledge of the Nazi camps, yet not once does the 32-minute film mention the targeting of Jews for annihilation.[173] Actual Jewish prisoners appear only marginally, in just four shots, where they are identifiable by a Star of David on their clothes. The film's title comes from Hitler's Nacht und Nebel (Night and Fog) decree of December 1941, under which Resistance fighters were arrested and taken away in the middle of the night, with no word of their fate.[174] The narration describes the Night

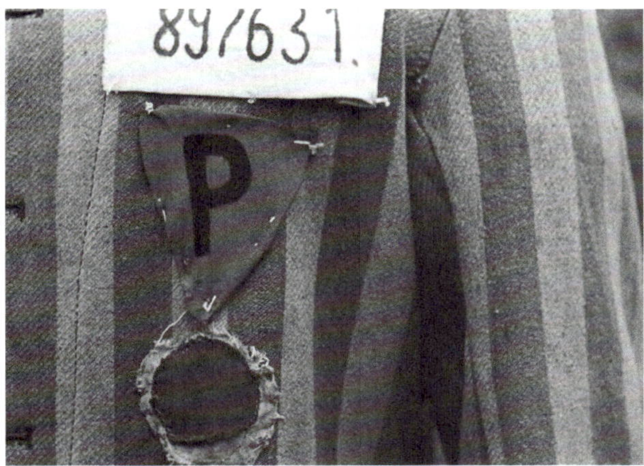

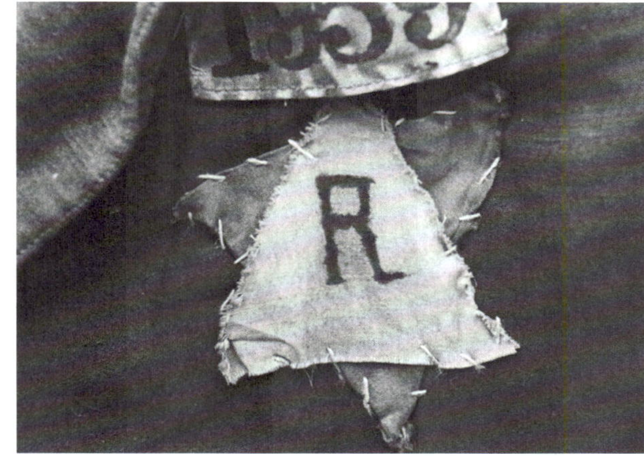

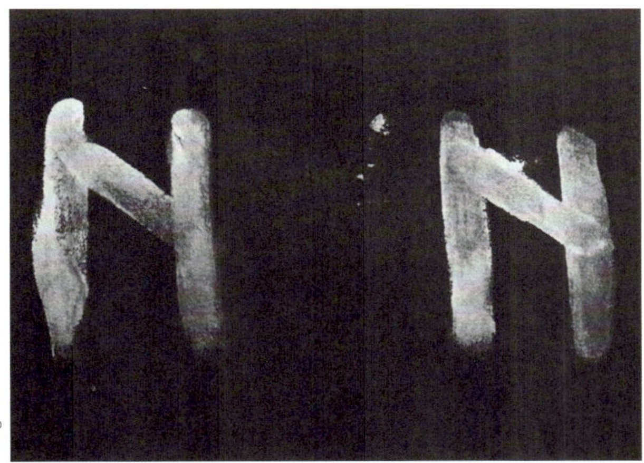

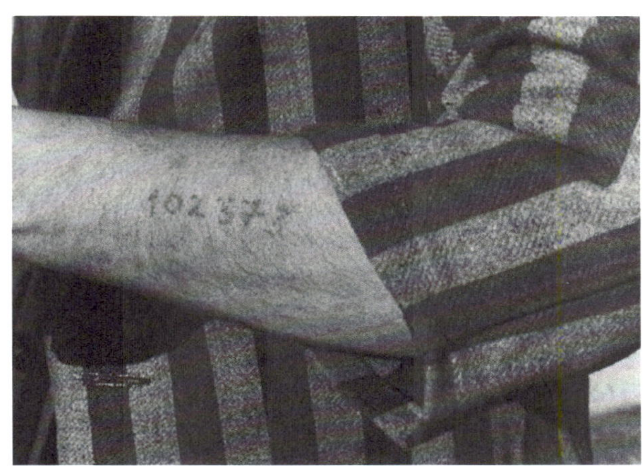

Fig. 1.17 Stills from the Alain Resnais documentary *Night and Fog*, 1955
The film describes the concentration camp hierarchy, with criminals and *Kapos* holding power over political prisoners. Jewish prisoners are briefly seen but not specifically mentioned.

and Fog prisoners as low in the camp ranks, beneath common criminals, *Kapos* (supervising prisoners, often drawn from criminal-prisoner ranks), and SS guards (who were considered "untouchable, addressed at a distance of three meters"). Jewish prisoners are not mentioned, and there is only one reference to Jews in the entire narration:

> Architects calmly design the gates meant to be passed through only once. Meanwhile, Burger, a German worker, Stern, a Jewish student in Amsterdam, Schmulski, a merchant in Krakow, and Annette, a schoolgirl in Bordeaux, go about their daily lives, not knowing a place is being prepared for them hundreds of miles away. One day their quarters are ready. All that is missing is them.

The film opens by surveying the "peaceful landscape" that surrounds Auschwitz 10 years after the war, including shots of the abandoned camp now overgrown with grass. Contemporary footage of this and other Nazi camps is then woven together with liberation footage, wartime photos of roundups and victims, and Nazi propaganda footage. We are presented with the macro and micro universes of the vast camp networks—the design and industry whose purpose was the death of millions—and the unremitting suffering of prisoners who are starved, scared, degraded, and tortured by *Kapos*, doctors, and disease.

The documentary grew out of the 1954 museum exhibition *Résistance, liberation, deportation* in Paris, which celebrated the 10-year anniversary of France's liberation from Germany.[175] Those behind the exhibition and film project (both government and private) were interested in France's resistance and the deportation experiences of French citizens. (One backer, the private group Réseau du Souvenir [Network of Remembrance], was established in memory of the deported "who died for freedom" and was structured "after the wartime resistance networks."[176]) Exhibition organizers Olga Wormser and Henri Michel were experts on deportation, having written *Tragédie de la déportation 1940–1945: Témoignages de survivants des camps de concentration allemands* (*Tragedy of the Deportation 1940–1945: Testimonies of Survivors of the German Concentration Camps*, Paris, 1954).[177] The authors can be credited with the idea of producing the film, and their book and exhibition served as the basis for it.[178]

The film's narration also reflected the personal experience of writer Cayrol, a political prisoner at Mauthausen-Gusen, who published his *Poèmes de la nuit et du brouillard* in 1946. The fact that he was at a concentration camp, as were most political deportees and resistance fighters, may explain the conflation of concentration camps and extermination camps in the film. (French Resistance members were rarely deported to extermination camps like Auschwitz, where much of the contemporary footage was shot.)

Resnais's overarching goal was to universalize the camps.[179] Both victims and perpetrators are intentionally generalized. Danger, the narrator tells us, lurks in ourselves now ("Are their [the executioners'] faces really different from our own?") and in the future ("We pretend it all happened only once, at a given time and place. We turn a blind eye to what surrounds us and a deaf ear to humanity's never-ending cry.") Resnais wanted these warnings of evil to serve as protests against France's actions in the current Algerian War of Independence (1954–62).[180] By emphasizing the repression of political prisoners and universalizing the Nazi subjugators, he was hoping contemporary audiences would make a connection to France's imperialism and abuse of power. (Resnais would go on to make the feature-length antiwar film *Hiroshima mon amour* in 1959.)

Resnais's abstraction of the camp experience and humanity, typical of the era, was also influenced by the Cold War. Now the free, civilized world had identified a new enemy: totalitarianism. Concentration camps came to be viewed as the most extreme totalitarian system, unprecedented in the power they exercised over individuals—their lives, deaths, identities (reduced to numbers), thoughts—for no utilitarian purpose. This model became the threat and ultimate terror for all citizens. Survivor David Rousset, in *L'Univers concentrationnaire* (Paris, 1946; *The Other Kingdom*, New York, 1947) and his provocative writings of the 1950s on Soviet gulags, and Arendt, in a number of works beginning with "The Concentration Camps" (1948), focused on this aspect of the camps.[181] Pollock and Silverman note that for Arendt and Rousset, the very concept of humanity seemed under threat for the first time in history and could be systematically eradicated by the totalitarian system.[182] In the late 1940s and early 1950s, it seemed as important to examine the system that created concentration camps and gulags (because this system endangered the future of civilization) as it did to expose the suffering and atrocity of the camps. Novick and Judt both have shown how the Cold War, which abruptly realigned political enemies and allies, marginalized the Holocaust.[183] To focus on the Nazi atrocities as a singular evil was inconvenient to the realpolitik; West Germany by the 1950s had become one of America's most important allies in continental Europe.[184] There was an explosion of literature on the topic, notably George Orwell's dystopian novel *Nineteen Eighty-four* (London, 1949), which introduced "Big Brother," "newspeak," "thought police," and "doublethink." Arendt's *Origins of Totalitarianism* (New York, 1951) examined and equated Nazi Germany and Stalin's Soviet Union and sought to expose the dangers of these tyrannical government structures where individuals are erased, facts and fictions collide, morals collapse, and bureaucracies disguise wrongdoing and eradicate perpetrators' guilty consciences. Whether in Nazi camps or Soviet gulags, camp prisoners, seen through this lens, become victims of a political system rather than an ethnic genocide.[185]

Although the producers of *Night and Fog* initially worried that it was too graphic, the documentary quickly achieved critical acclaim. It was widely distributed across Europe, Asia, and Australia in 1956 (the United States saw a limited release in 1962, but this grew in the 1970s).[186] Only journalists in Israel condemned the absence of the genocide. (Even so, the film was presented as evidence in the Eichmann trial, with Israeli prosecutors dedicating a quarter of their allotted screening time to it.[187]) Some footage of a French gendarme standing guard over deportations at a French transit camp was altered before the film's release at the insistence of French authorities to conceal France's collaboration in the deportations.[188] Over a decade after the war, France was not ready to face its collaboration with the Nazis; the original footage was not restored until 1997. Another controversy erupted at the Cannes Film Festival in 1956. The film had to be withdrawn from competition after objections by the German foreign ministry that it "would disturb the international harmony of the festival."[189]

While Jewish suffering under Hitler was tacitly understood in the 1950s, particulars of the Holocaust were not yet widely examined or valued. By focusing on the Nazi camps but leaving out or marginalizing the Jewish victims, *Night and Fog* grossly distorted the historical facts. Regardless of the reasons, the inclination of artists, writers, and filmmakers to universalize the victims and perpetrators of the Nazi camps and their suffering continued to mask the Jewish tragedy. Decades after *Night and Fog* was released, critics decried this aspect of the film. The Holocaust scholar Robert Michael writes:

> An otherwise historically and morally valid work, *Night and Fog* omits the particularity of the Jewish Holocaust and, in doing so, it emphasizes the universal at the expense of the particular . . . it silently buries six million Jews in universal genocide. It sinks the specific case of the central victims in a sea of generalities, and the Jews vanish with hardly a trace.[190]

In the 1950s, *Night and Fog* exerted great influence internationally in shaping perceptions of the Nazi camps. Today it is a staple of film classes, the subject of countless scholarly books and articles, and in 2003 was a selection of the Criterion Collection, a film company dedicated to the distribution and release of "important classic and contemporary films." Yet as Ewout van der Knaap notes, *Night and Fog* is "not a film about the Holocaust in its intention," but rather "a cultural artefact" and "a product of its time and situation."[191] Novick observes, "Every generation frames the Holocaust, represents the Holocaust, in ways that suit the mood." Collective memory forms and changes, and how something is remembered can reflect more about the circumstances and context of the present moment than the circumstances of the actual historical event.[192] Sensitivity to the Jewish dimension of the Holocaust developed only gradually, when individual stories of the 6 million victims came to light. The most important story to emerge in 1950s popular culture was that of Anne Frank, but even this had its complications.

Anne Frank's Diary

The story of Anne Frank in the fifty years since "The Diary of a Young Girl" was first published has been bowdlerized, distorted, transmuted, traduced, reduced; it has been infantilized, Americanized, homogenized, sentimentalized; falsified, kitschified, and, in fact, blatantly and arrogantly denied. . . . A deeply truth-telling work has been turned into an instrument of partial truth, surrogate truth, or anti-truth. The pure has been made impure—sometimes in the name of the reverse. —Cynthia Ozick, "Who Owns Anne Frank?" 1997[193]

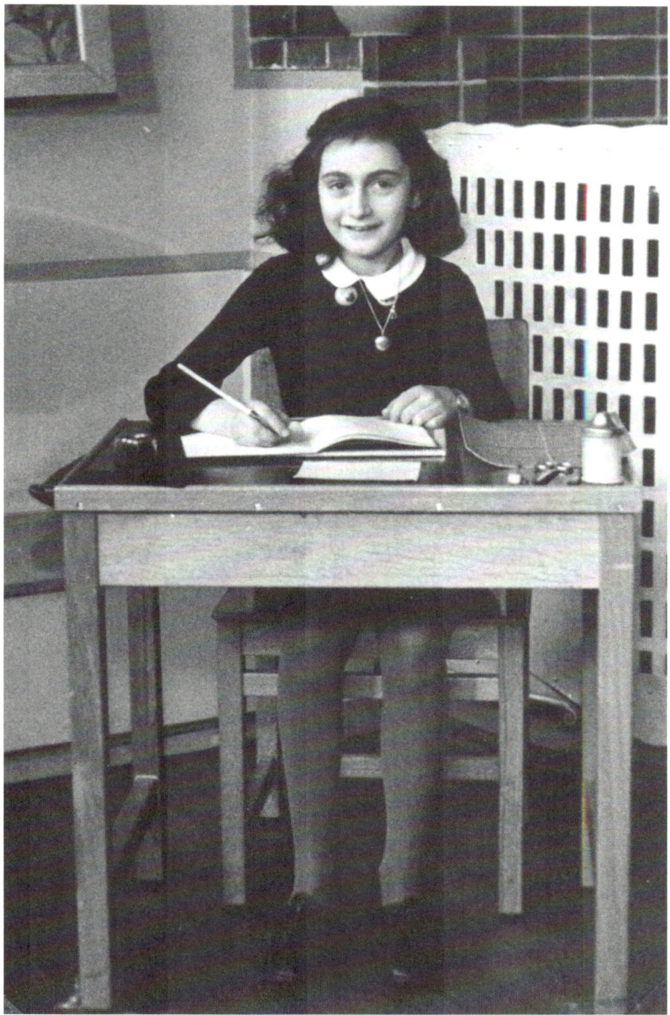

Fig. 1.18 Anne Frank, Montessori school photo, Amsterdam, December 1940. Photo collection Anne Frank House, Amsterdam
The Frank family went into hiding in Amsterdam on July 6, 1942, to escape deportation by the Nazis. They were found and arrested the following summer. Anne Frank died at Bergen-Belsen concentration camp in February 1945 at the age of 15.

The first inkling of Anne Frank's diary appeared in Amsterdam in 1947 when a Dutch publisher issued a few thousand copies under the title *Het achterhuis* (*The House Behind* or *The Secret Annex*).[194] It had been shepherded by Anne's father, Otto, the only member of the Frank family to survive the Holocaust. German and French editions appeared in 1950. After 16 rejections,[195] Otto Frank found two English publishers in 1952, in New York (Doubleday), where the book included an introduction by Eleanor Roosevelt, and London (Constellation Books). Now called *Anne Frank: The Diary of a Young Girl*, it opened the floodgates. A 30-minute television play aired on CBS in late 1952.[196] The play that debuted on Broadway in 1955 won a Pulitzer Prize and a Tony Award for best play. Over the next three years, it was performed in 30 countries in 21 languages. This was followed in 1959 by a Hollywood film directed by George Stevens, which was nominated for eight Academy Awards (it won three). By 1960, more than 700,000 copies of the book had sold in Germany alone, making it the best-selling paperback in German history at that time. Today it has been translated into some 70 languages, with more than 30 million copies sold.

The story of the young, Jewish Anne Frank (1929–1945), who hid from the Gestapo with her family in a building in the heart of Amsterdam, helped draw popular attention to the persecution and murder of innocent Jews. On July 5, 1942, when Anne's older sister, Margot, age 16, received a notice from the SS to report for forced-labor duty, the family sprang into action. They disappeared at 5:30 a.m. the following day. Anne, who had just received a diary for her 13th birthday, wrote a lively account of her family's next two years and one month in a small apartment hidden behind a wooden bookcase in the upper floors of a townhouse. They shared the tight quarters with another Jewish family, the van Pelses (called the van Daans in the diary), and a family friend, a dentist, Fritz Pfeffer (Mr. Dussel), Anne's roommate. As an author, Anne was charming, likable, and exceptionally talented. Readers could relate to her teenage musings, annoyance with adults and their constant lectures, irritation with her mother, Edith, and boy crushes. Her book went a long way in humanizing the Holocaust and individualizing one of the 6 million.

From the beginning, the book, play, and film were marketed as stories of hope. Cynthia Ozick, who has traced the alterations to Anne's texts through the years, believes that this misrepresented Anne and her dire situation and downplayed the gravity of the Holocaust. Ozick writes that "to believe the diary was 'a song to life' is to stew in an ugly innocence."[197] Anne lived in fear of being turned in by Dutch informers, arrested by the Gestapo, deported to a concentration camp, and murdered by the Nazis. All of these things did happen to the bright, innocent child we meet on the pages of her diary. Her terror and dread are palpable in this passage of her diary from April 11, 1944, reporting an incident when the Dutch police came late at night to search the townhouse after a burglary in the downstairs warehouse:

> At eleven-fifteen, a noise below. Up above you could hear the whole family breathing. For the rest, no one moved a muscle. Footsteps in the house, the private office, the kitchen, then . . . on the stairs. All sounds of breathing stopped, eight hearts pounded. Footsteps on the stairs, then a rattling at the bookcase. The moment was indescribable. "Now we're done for," I said, and I had visions of all fifteen of us [those in the annex and their Dutch helpers] being dragged away by the Gestapo that very night.
>
> . . . We've been strongly reminded of the fact that we're Jews in chains, chained to one spot, without any rights, but with a thousand obligations. . . . Who has inflicted this on us? Who has set us apart from all the rest? Who has put us through such suffering?[198]

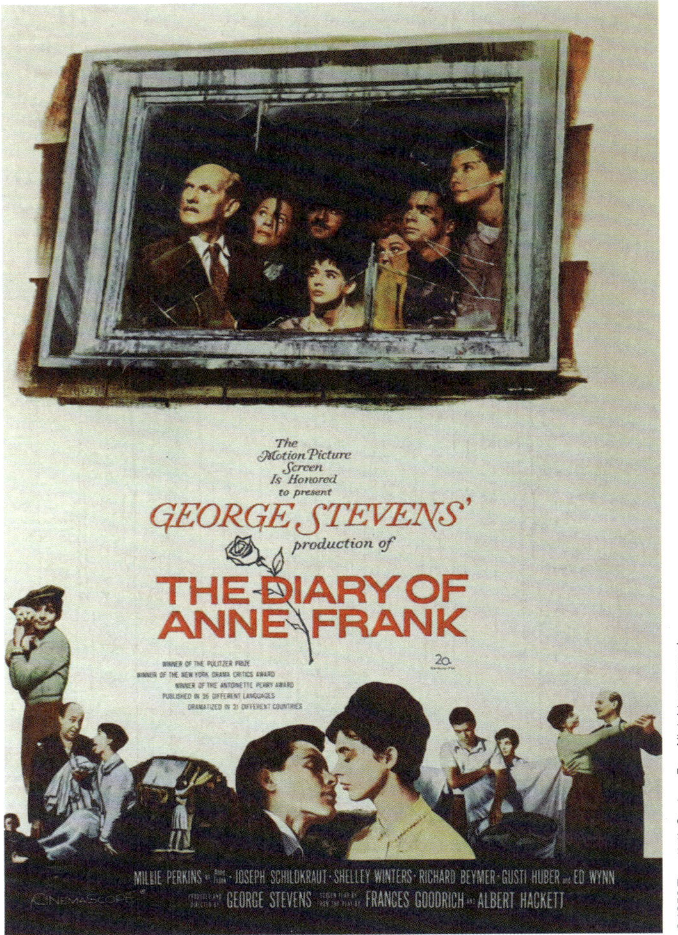

Fig. 1.19 Movie poster for *The Diary of Anne Frank*, 1959, directed by George Stevens

Less than four months later, the Dutch police, under the command of an SS officer, would return to arrest the eight in hiding, along with two of their Dutch helpers.

The success of Anne's story in the 1950s was due in part to the various attempts to universalize it. Along with Anne's thoughts about her body and other details, Otto had expunged passages about the Jewish faith and antisemitism in the Netherlands.[199] (These were restored after Otto Frank's death, in the definitive edition published in 1991.) The CBS television broadcast condensed the diary to an adolescent coming-of-age story, affirming the importance of faith and being true to oneself.[200] The play went much further. With Otto Frank's blessing, Anne's words and thoughts were altered to create an upbeat story that would attract audiences in the cheerfully optimistic era of postwar America.[201] Garson Kanin, who directed the 1955 play, called Anne's writings on the historic suffering of the Jewish people "an embarrassing piece of special pleading." In spite of his own Jewish heritage, he felt that "the fact that in this play the symbols of persecution and oppression are Jews is incidental, and Anne, in stating the argument so, reduces her magnificent stature."[202] When writers Albert Hackett and Frances Goodrich completed the script, many of the references to Jewish practices, Margot's Zionist beliefs, and Anne's worries about Jewish victims of Nazism were gone. Instead the staging (and the movie that followed) played up the comic elements and Anne's innocent romance with Peter van Pels.[203] The 1959 movie poster (fig. 1.19) suggests a romantic comedy with fun-filled high jinks rather than a heartrending tragedy of unimaginable scale. The carefree, Americanized Anne of the play and movie subsumed the real Anne; my paperback copy from the mid-1980s includes two photos of Anne—and eight photo stills from the film.

Even before the edits for Broadway and Hollywood, this most popular of Holocaust stories leaves most of the Holocaust out. Anne's last entry is dated August 1, 1944. Three days later everyone in the secret annex was arrested, held at Westerbork transit camp in the Netherlands, then deported to Nazi camps. The Franks were sent to Auschwitz, where Anne's mother died of starvation and fever. Anne and Margot were transferred to Bergen-Belsen, where they died of typhus in late February or early March of 1945. The diary has no details of the family's final months—the misery of the transit in cattle cars (without food, bathroom facilities, or a place to sit or rest), the separations from loved ones, the starvation, the cold, the lice-infested, diseased camp quarters, the agonizing illnesses and deaths. These very real facts are thus absent from the book, play, and movie.

The lack of grim details may also explain the enduring appeal of the story of Charlotte Salomon, the gifted young painter whose life and art have achieved cult status since the first posthumous exhibition of her art in 1961. Hundreds of publications—exhibition catalogues, monographs, biographies, coffee-table books, articles—have appeared since 2010 in languages ranging from Norwegian to Chinese.[204] Like Anne Frank, Salomon completed her work before her deportation, which means the Holocaust is not represented. The fate of these two brilliant young women at the hands of the Nazis, though known to their audiences, remains an abstract backdrop to their extraordinary works.

Scattered new signs of interest in the Holocaust arose in the late 1950s (see Timeline for highlights).[205] The televised *Judgment at Nuremberg* (CBS, 1959), written by Abby Mann, was particularly influential in the United States, presenting a fictional trial that incorporated actual camp-liberation footage and statistics of Jewish deaths.[206] The show gave new emphasis to the Jewish dimension of the Nazi crimes. Mann's 1961 movie adaptation, directed by Stanley Kramer, was nominated for 11 Academy Awards and featured an exceptional Hollywood cast—Spencer Tracy, Burt Lancaster, Judy Garland, Marlene Dietrich, and Montgomery Clift. Some of the actors reduced their salaries because of the social merits of the project. *The Final Ingredient* (ABC, 1959) focused on the Jewish experience of the camps, in this case Bergen-Belsen, but at the same time universalized the story to explore themes of faith and freedom.[207] Leon Uris's popular novel *Exodus* (New York, 1958), on the other hand, which became an Otto Preminger film starring Paul Newman (1960), focused on Holocaust survivors after the war, not only their plight as stateless, homeless refugees, but also the persistent trauma experienced from being at the camps. Such works helped set the stage for a new examination of the Holocaust and its victims. The world, now at some distance from the suffering, losses, and postwar rebuilding, was more prepared to grapple with the catastrophe. The arrest in 1960 of the Nazi war criminal Adolf Eichmann catapulted the Holocaust into the public sphere. Eichmann's 1961 trial in Jerusalem would forever change the way the Holocaust was understood and spoken about, from Tel Aviv to Iowa City, from Bonn to Buenos Aires.

EICHMANN EMERGES IN ARGENTINA

He [Eichmann] was quick to learn the ropes and was greatly valued by his manager. —Daimler-Benz employee, Argentina, 1960[208]

On May 11, 1960, at around 8 p.m. on the outskirts of Buenos Aires, Argentina, Adolf Eichmann was riding his usual bus home from work. As he walked from the bus stop in the dark toward the modest house he had recently built for his family, Israeli Mossad agents were waiting in two parked cars, one with the hood up to suggest car trouble. They seized Eichmann and forced him onto the floor of one of the cars. He was taken to a safe house to be physically examined and interrogated. After a few denials, SS *Obersturmbannführer* (Lt. Col.) Adolf Eichmann confessed his true identity, including his SS number. Israeli agents interviewed him over the next 10 days, then smuggled their fugitive on a plane to Israel, after first drugging him and giving him a false Israeli passport.

Eichmann had fled to Argentina 10 years earlier, in 1950. After the war, he had been interned in three American prisoner of war camps under various assumed names. As the Nuremberg trials of Nazi war criminals got under way in late 1945, he worried that his identity would be discovered. In January 1946, he fled a POW camp for northern Germany, where he worked as a lumberjack until he could get help leaving the country. Argentina had become a safe haven for Nazis under dictator Juan Perón (1946–55), who welcomed nearly 300 war criminals, including Dr. Josef Mengele, known as the "Angel of Death," and Klaus Barbie, the "Butcher of Lyon."[209] They used the so-called ratlines, or Nazi escape routes from Europe, which were supported by a network of Nazis, Catholic clergy in Europe and Argentina, and some well-placed Vatican officials. With their assistance, Eichmann made his way first to Rome, then Genoa, where some Church officials helped him secure a Red Cross passport with a new name, Ricardo Klement. He was 44 when he set sail for Argentina. His wife and three sons joined him two years later, guided by a deep network of National Socialists in Buenos Aires and Germany.[210]

When captured by the Mossad, Eichmann was working at a Mercedes-Benz factory and now had four sons.[211] In his free time, he gathered with former Nazis to reminisce. Apparently concerned with how history would remember his role in the genocide of the Jews, he wrote two manuscripts, one titled *The Others Spoke, Now I Want to Speak*. He also participated in extensive recorded interviews in 1957 with the Dutch Nazi collaborator and former SS journalist Willem Sassen in Argentina, which yielded more than a thousand transcript pages. Sassen sold abridged "memoirs" by Eichmann drawn from the interviews to *Der Stern* and *Life* magazines after the arrest.[212]

On May 23, 1960, Prime Minister David Ben-Gurion of Israel announced Eichmann's capture to the Knesset to astonishment and cheers. The event quickly made international news. On June 10, *Time* magazine broke the details of Eichmann's dramatic capture. (Mauricio Lasansky was no doubt interested to learn that Eichmann had spent 10 years in Buenos Aires, where he was born and raised.)

Eichmann, former head of Jewish affairs for the Gestapo, was accused of implementing the Nazi plan to annihilate the Jews and organizing the forced emigration and mass deportation of millions to Nazi extermination camps. He had not simply followed orders, but had undertaken his murderous assignment with apparent zeal, resourcefulness, and ambition. Controversies erupted at every stage of the case, beginning with his kidnapping. Argentina protested to the United Nations that its sovereignty had been violated, even though Eichmann, a fugitive, was not an Argentine citizen. But soon editorials in Argentina questioned the country's long history of harboring Nazi fugitives.[213] As many as 5,000 Nazis were said to have fled to Argentina after the war. Mengele lived and worked in Argentina under his own name. West Germany's belated efforts to extradite him in 1959 and 1960 had been stuck in bureaucratic limbo in Argentina, which gave the notorious doctor time to escape across the border to Paraguay and evade capture until his death in 1979.[214]

Another issue was the legality and jurisdiction of the Israeli court, as the State of Israel had not even existed when the crimes were committed. The American Telford Taylor, a prosecutor at the 1945–49 Nuremberg trials, argued that the Eichmann case would undermine international law and that describing Eichmann's actions as crimes against Jews specifically rather than crimes against humanity was dangerous.[215] Taylor also questioned whether Eichmann would receive a fair trial in Israel, echoing critics who, with a tinge of antisemitism, questioned whether a Jewish court and judges would be biased or vengeful. There were concerns that the trial would stir up anti-German feeling and antisemitism, and whether Israel would now assert itself as the representative for Jews worldwide. Some commentators worried that the Eichmann case would set a precedent that would upset the world order; might Allied soldiers who killed civilians, for instance, be subject to future arrests and trials? Hannah Arendt put it this way: "What are we going to say if tomorrow it occurs to some African state to send its agents into Mississippi and to kidnap one of the leaders of the segregationist movement there?"[216] As the proceedings got under way and the evidence was presented for the world to see, the court of opinion overwhelmingly sided with Israel's decision to prosecute Eichmann.[217]

ADOLF EICHMANN'S TRIAL IN JERUSALEM

We want to establish before the nations of the world how millions of people, because they happened to be Jews, and one million babies, because they happened to be Jewish babies, were murdered by the Nazis. We ask the nations not to forget it. —David Ben-Gurion, Israel's prime minister, 1960[218]

When I stand before you here, judges of Israel, to lead the prosecution of Adolf Eichmann, I am not standing alone. With me are six million accusers. But they cannot rise to their feet and point an accusing finger towards him who sits in the dock and cry: "J'accuse" [I accuse]. For their ashes are piled up on the hills of Auschwitz and the fields of Treblinka, and are strewn in the forests of Poland. Their graves are scattered throughout the length and breadth of Europe. Their blood cries out, but their voice is not heard. Therefore I will be their spokesman and in their name, I will unfold the awesome indictment. —Gideon Hausner, attorney general of Israel, opening statement of Eichmann trial, 1961

At Nuremberg the perpetrators and their documents had been the center; the victims had barely been a sidebar. [Attorney General Gideon] Hausner's determination that this trial would be founded on the human story of the Jewish victims' suffering stands, from a perspective of five decades, as the trial's most significant legacy. . . . the story of the Holocaust, though it had been previously told, discussed, and commemorated, was heard *anew*, in a profoundly different way, and not just in Israel, but in many parts of the Jewish and non-Jewish world. The *telling* may not have been entirely new, but the *hearing* was. —Deborah Lipstadt, *The Eichmann Trial* (2011)[219]

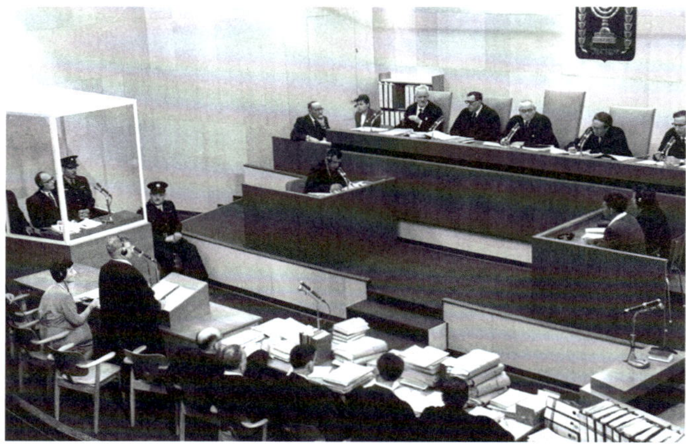

Fig. 1.20 Jerusalem's newly built public theater, Beit Ha'am (House of the Nation), a 756-seat auditorium, was turned into a courtroom for the Eichmann trial. Government Press Office of Israel, National Photo Collection
Courtroom translators provided immediate translations of the Hebrew proceedings and witness testimonies into German, French, and English. Using headphones, Eichmann, his counsel, and the international press could hear the translations. Television cameras and sound equipment were hidden in the walls to avoid intruding on the trial.

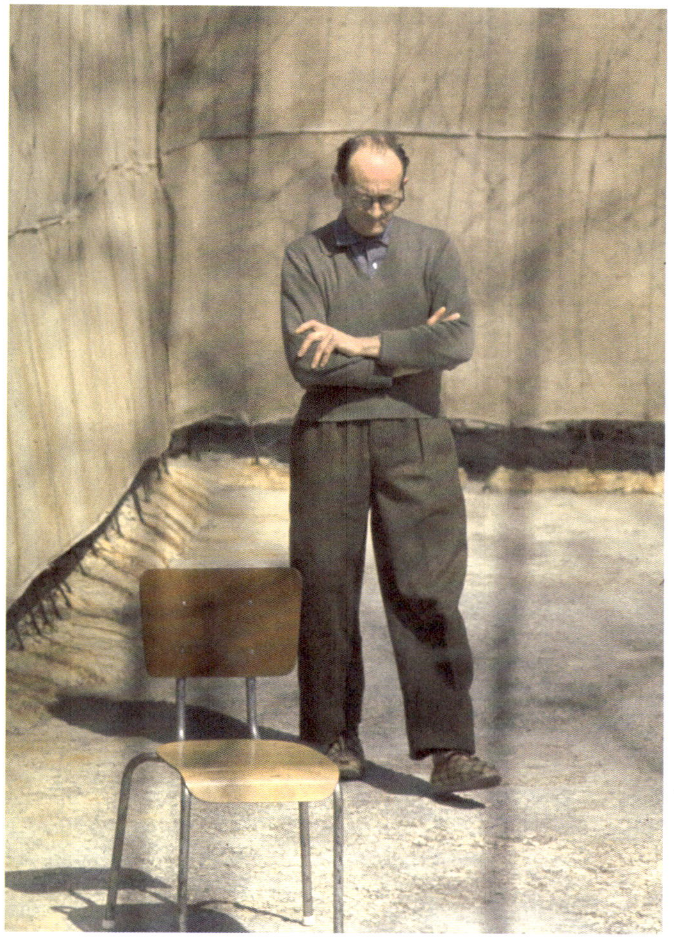

Fig. 1.21 Adolf Eichmann in the courtyard of his jail in Ramle, Israel, 1961; photo by John Milli. Government Press Office of Israel, National Photo Collection
Photos of Eichmann walking the prison yard appeared widely in the press in the early months of his trial. Commentators found the war criminal's look and demeanor disconcertingly "normal."

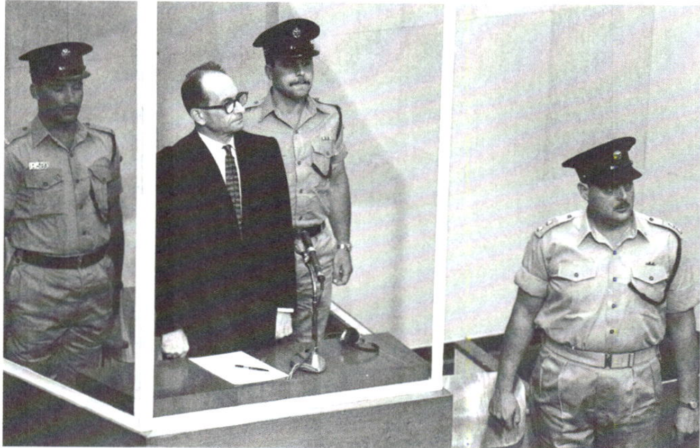

Fig. 1.22 Nazi SS *Obersturmbannführer* (Lt. Col.) Adolf Eichmann stands trial in Jerusalem, 1961. Government Press Office of Israel, National Photo Collection
Eichmann was indicted on 12 counts, including crimes against the Jewish people, crimes against humanity, and war crimes. He sat in a bulletproof glass booth and was protected by three Israeli guards during the proceedings.

Eichmann's trial began on April 11, 1961. It was staged in Jerusalem's newly built public theater, Beit Ha'am (House of the Nation), which had been turned into a courtroom for the event, with Eichmann seated (and displayed) in a bulletproof glass box (figs. 1.20 and 1.22). The presiding judges were Moshe Landau, Benjamin Halevi, and Yitzchak Raveh. Attorney General Gideon Hausner led the prosecution; Robert Servatius, a German defense lawyer who had served at the Nuremberg trials, led the defense. The official proceedings were conducted in Hebrew; witness testimonies, related in numerous languages, were simultaneously translated into English, German, and French.

In addition to the 756 seats in the Beit Ha'am auditorium for the press and general public, there was a live closed-circuit video feed in a hall at the Ratisbonne Monastery a few blocks away. By the sixth week of the trial, it was estimated that 45,000 people in Israel had seen the proceedings in the courtroom or hall. Some 350 foreign correspondents were in Jerusalem at the start of the trial. One news source reported that by May 18, 5,500 cables had been filed, 2,000 telex messages sent, and 2.5 million words of copy written.[220]

The Eichmann trial was one of the earliest televised trials and the first to be broadcast across the world—shown in 38 countries.[221] The television medium propelled the Holocaust into mainstream culture. Israel, which did not have television until 1966, contracted with Capital Cities Broadcasting Corporation in New York to film the proceedings and provide footage to broadcasting companies for a fee. In the United States, the major networks and the Public Broadcasting System each paid $50,000, which bought them one hour of trial footage a day while the trial lasted. Videotapes were flown out to subscribers daily.[222] Americans watched television coverage on the nightly news, in hour-long broadcasts of highlights (often shown during the dinner hour), and in special programs about Eichmann, the trial, the war, and the Holocaust.[223] These included fictional dramas and an episode of *The Twilight Zone*. Israelis primarily followed the trial on the radio, which was broadcast live in public spaces, restaurants, and homes. Schools were frequently canceled so students could listen.[224]

The literature that exists about the trial is extensive and begins with what was and in many ways remains its most controversial account, Hannah Arendt's *Eichmann in Jerusalem: A Report on the Banality of Evil* (New York, 1963), which grew out of her reporting for the *New Yorker*. It continues to draw scholarly attention.[225] Two more recent examinations of the trial are David Cesarini's *Eichmann: His Life and Crimes* (London, 2004) and Deborah Lipstadt's *The Eichmann Trial* (New York, 2011).

The survivors' testimonies during the trial are arguably its most enduring legacy, as Lipstadt observes, although their significance was fully appreciated only years later. Before these stories took center stage, the world was obsessed with Eichmann. Wearing glasses and ill-fitting dentures, his hair thinning, the 55-year-old former German officer disturbed many commentators

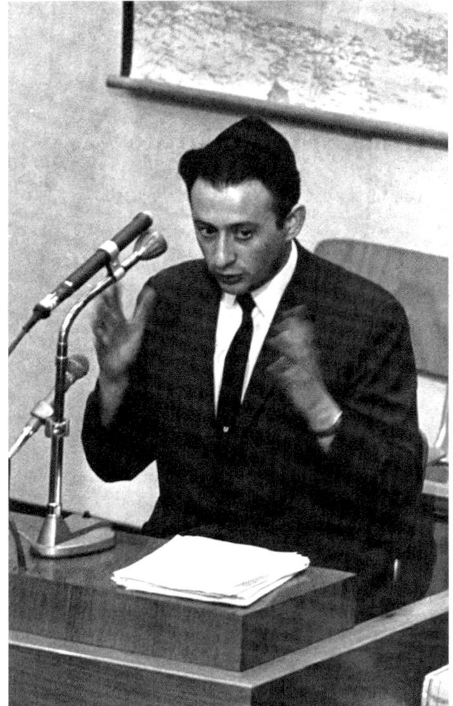

Fig. 1.23 Leon Wells, witness for the prosecution, Eichmann trial, Jerusalem, 1961. Government Press Office of Israel, National Photo Collection
As a forced laborer in a *Sonderkommando* unit, Wells witnessed the murder of thousands of men, women, and children. He was the only person in his extended 76-member Jewish family in Poland to survive the Holocaust.

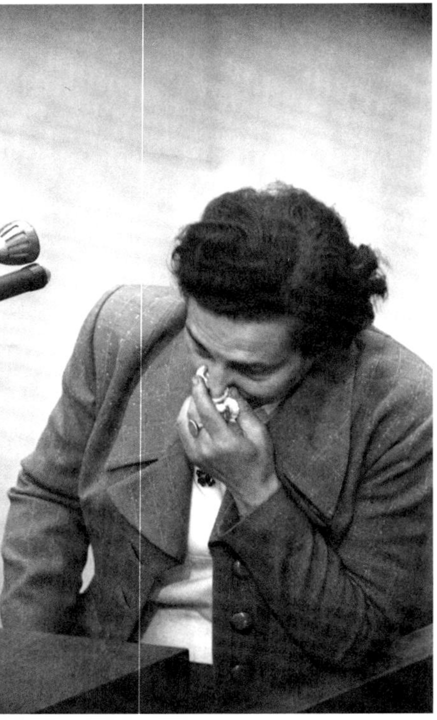

Fig. 1.24 Rivka Yosselevska, witness for the prosecution, Eichmann trial, Jerusalem, 1961. Government Press Office of Israel, National Photo Collection
Yosselevska testified about the massacre of her family in Belarus by SS *Einsatzgruppen* (mobile killing units) on August 14, 1942.

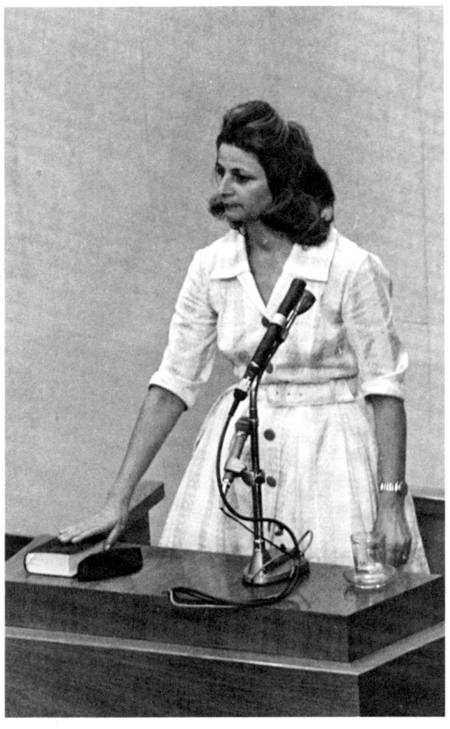

Fig. 1.25 Esther Goldstein, witness for the prosecution, Eichmann trial, Jerusalem, 1961. Government Press Office of Israel, National Photo Collection
Goldstein, a survivor of Auschwitz-Birkenau, testified about selections at the camp and the murder of family members and others from her Hungarian transport in 1944.

because he appeared so ordinary. Elie Wiesel, reporting for the *Jewish Daily Forward*, noted that journalists were surprised that he looked no "different from other humans."[226] Six psychiatrists certified Eichmann as "normal"—or as one psychiatrist declared, "More normal, at any rate, than I am after having examined him."[227] His ordinariness—or "banality," as Arendt controversially described Eichmann—demonstrated for her the particular danger posed to civilization by a kind of thoughtless, bureaucratic evil serving a totalitarian regime with no conscience.[228]

Life magazine featured three major stories on Eichmann between his capture and trial. The week the trial began, it ran an "intimate study" of his time in jail, with photos documenting his daily routine—eating, sleeping, brushing his teeth, walking the yard (fig. 1.21). This was preceded by its publication in back-to-back issues of his abridged memoirs, purchased from Eichmann's Nazi comrade in Argentina, Willem Sassen.[229] It was here that Eichmann famously declared, "To sum it all up, I must say that I regret nothing." His perplexing rationalization (and doublethink) is displayed in this statement:

> I was merely a little cog in the machinery that carried out the directives and orders of the German Reich. I was neither a murderer nor a mass-murderer. I was a man of average character, with good qualities and many faults. . . . Where I was implicated in the physical annihilation of the Jews, I admit my participation freely and without pressure. After all, I was the one who transported the Jews to the camps. If I had not transported them, they would not have been delivered to the butcher. Yet what is there to "admit"? I carried out my orders.[230]

Pleading not guilty to all charges "in the sense of the indictment," Eichmann said he felt legally clear of all responsibility by virtue of the chain of command. Yet simultaneously he admitted in his testimony in court to arranging the transport of millions of Jews to their deaths. Eichmann came across as a bewildering, cold-blooded, immoral, rule-abiding, inscrutable bureaucrat poisoned by virulent antisemitism.

Witness testimony began on April 24. The prosecution called 121 "background witnesses," including 90 survivors, to describe their experiences. Their stories were told in Hebrew, Yiddish, German, French, Polish, Hungarian, and English and simultaneously translated for spectators and the foreign press into Hebrew, German, French, and English. Television footage frequently cut to Eichmann's unmoved face as witnesses spoke. Over the course of the proceedings, the unfathomable statistic of 6 million murdered Jews came sharply into focus. The victims began to materialize as individuals, with names and families and stories.

Leon Wells (fig. 1.23), who eventually became a successful engineer living in the United States, testified about his three years in Nazi-occupied Poland. His father, mother, two brothers, and four young sisters were murdered; he was the only survivor of his extended 76-member family. It is estimated that in his hometown of Lwów (Lviv), fewer than 200 of the prewar population of 150,000 Jews survived. He wanted to die, he said (he attempted suicide once), but was resolved to try to live to bear witness. He was beaten and tortured in 1941, stood before shooting squads in 1942, and revolted with his *Sonderkommando* unit in 1943. Wells described working with his unit to excavate bodies of victims murdered by the Nazis, removing every trace of their flesh, hair, and bones, removing gold teeth and wedding rings, burning the bodies in massive pyres, and crushing bones and teeth in steel drums. He estimated that the unit burned remains of a few hundred thousand victims. He also witnessed the mass shootings of some 30,000 Jews by *Einsatzgruppen* in a ravine outside Lviv. Pressed by the Israeli prosecutor to account for why no one fought back, Wells explained that by 1943, having lost all of their loved ones, people had lost their will to live. Early on, he said, when Jews were still in the ghettos, any attempt to revolt was severely punished. The resister would be tortured before death and the resister's surviving family members—or random camp prisoners—would be murdered. Wells described one incident:

> Once a mother came with her child, and when she undressed she spat in the face of the SS guard. They took the child by the legs, knocked its head against a tree and put it in the fire, and hanged her by the feet. . . . The other women, seeing this, thought—"What's the use . . ." This happened quite a few times—especially for mothers not [willing] to undress [their] children.[231]

Wells, recalling this particular image, became agitated on the witness stand; his eyes showed a rush of adrenaline and terror. His *Sonderkommando* unit revolted after liquidation of the Janowska concentration camp, and he was one of the few to survive. After liberation, he returned to his family's home in Lviv and found it taken over by a Ukrainian family. A Red Army soldier accused him of collaboration because no Jews were supposed to be alive. He was forced into hiding. Months later he found refuge among the small number of Jewish survivors who had returned to the city.[232] He submitted testimony of his experience to Soviet officials and wrote a memoir that was published by the Polish Historical Commission in 1946. After the Eichmann trial, it was released as *The Janowska Road* (New York, 1963).[233]

Rivka Yosselevska (fig. 1.24) testified about the massacre of her family in Belarus by Nazi *Einsatzgruppen* on August 14, 1942. Her family was forced to stand in the execution line, undress, and assemble before a pit of corpses. Her father had kept his underclothes on, even

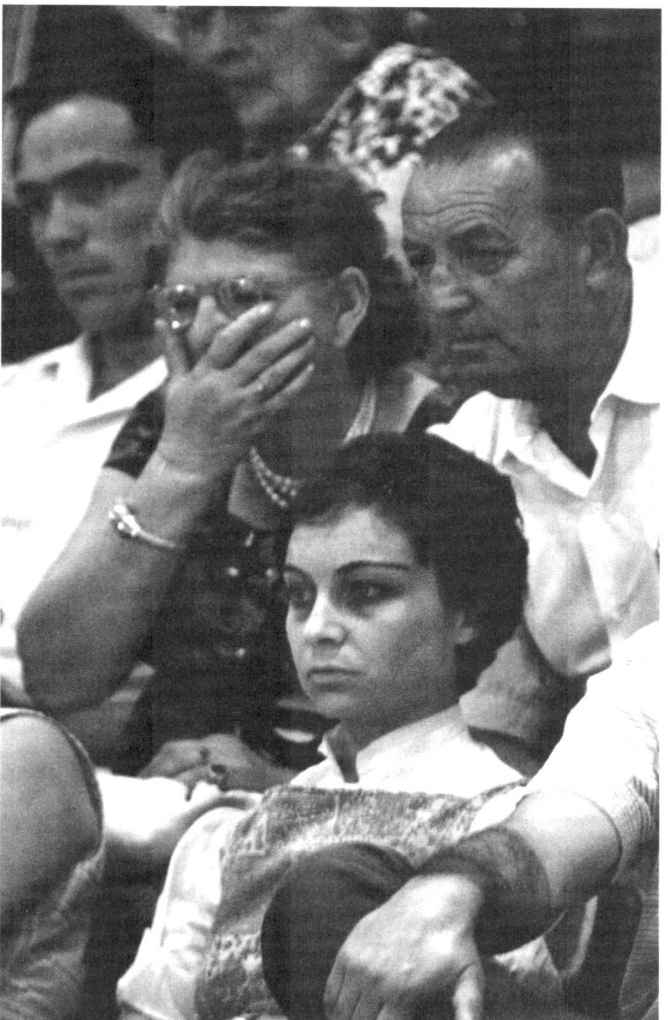

Fig. 1.26 Spectators at the Eichmann trial, Jerusalem, 1961. Government Press Office of Israel, National Photo Collection

though she begged him to comply. The guards tore off his clothes, beat him, then shot him. ("I saw it with my own eyes," she exclaimed in court.) Her mother was shot next, followed by her grandmother and her aunt, both holding nieces and nephews in their arms, then her two sisters. Then it was her turn. She held her young daughter in her arms. "We stood there facing the ditch. I turned my head. He [the guard] asked, 'Whom do I shoot first?' I didn't answer. He tore the child away from me. I heard her last cry and he shot her. Then he got ready to kill me, grabbed my hair, and turned my head about." His first shot missed her, so he loaded his pistol and shot again. The bullet grazed her and she fell into the pit, soon buried by more bodies, nearly suffocating but alive. After the Germans left, she tried to crawl out of the pile. As she did so, the dying grabbed her and bit her. Using all of her strength, she emerged covered with other people's blood and excrement. Yosselevska frantically called for her daughter and parents. There were children crying for their parents, people screaming in pain. The Germans returned to shoot the children. Days later a farmer helped her and got her into hiding.

As Yosselevska recounted these events, she appeared ashen and nauseated. She was shaking slightly and holding back tears. Her televised testimony switched back and forth from her to Eichmann, who appeared expressionless and calm, blinking intermittently. The *New York Times* featured a photo of Yosselevska on the stand, reporting that she was "buried alive" and provided "a ghoulish account of the mass execution of women and children."[234]

Martin Földi testified about his family being separated at Auschwitz-Birkenau, his wife and younger daughter sent to the left (to the gas chambers), he and his son to the right. The guard questioned him:

> "How old is the boy?" At that moment I could not lie, and I told him: 12 years old. And then he said: "And where is your mother?" I answered: She went to the left. Then he said to my son: "Run after your mother." After that I went on walking to the right and I saw how the boy was running. I wondered to myself how would he be able to find his mother there? After all, there were so many women and men, but I caught sight of my wife. How did I recognize her? My little girl was wearing some kind of a red coat. The red spot was a sign that my wife was near there. The red spot was getting smaller and smaller. I walked to the right and never saw them again.[235]

Nearly a hundred stories like this were recounted during the first two months of the trial. Survivor and writer Yehiel Dinur, known as "Ka-Tzetnik 135633" (Concentration Camp Inmate 135633), had just begun to describe the "planet" of Auschwitz when he collapsed and had to be hospitalized. His first words were stilted and distressed:

> They did not live, nor did they die, in accordance with the laws of the world. Their names were numbers . . . for close to two years, they left me and always left me behind . . . I see them, they are watching me [Dinur abruptly stands, walks a step, then returns to the witness chair], I see them. I see them standing in the queue.[236]

The Israeli historian and journalist Tom Segev wrote of Dinur's collapse, "All Israel held its breath. It was the most dramatic moment of the trial, one of the most dramatic moments in the country's history." Dinur did not return to the stand, and even decades later he refused to speak to anyone about his testimony, saying he lacked the strength to relive it.[237]

Esther Goldstein (fig. 1.25), like Földi, was part of the 1944 transports of Hungarian Jews to Auschwitz.[238] She described watching her sister being separated from her baby and young child; the children and her mother were sent to the gas chambers. While on the stand, she looked at photographs to identify those, including her family, who had been murdered.

Throughout the testimonies, there were outbursts and weeping among the spectators (fig. 1.26). Some fainted. Golda Meir, Israel's minister of foreign affairs and future prime minister, reportedly "wept bitterly" while attending the trial.[239] Arendt was not so moved, writing, "On trial are his [Eichmann's] deeds, not the sufferings of the Jews, not the German people or mankind, not even anti-Semitism and racism."[240] She was critical of nearly every aspect of the trial, although she believed that Eichmann was guilty and that death was the only appropriate sentence for his crimes.[241] (Such a sentence was not possible in West Germany, and a trial at an international court had hardly been forthcoming.) The trial, however, proved bigger than Eichmann's "deeds." This was true even for Arendt, a German Jew who had fled Nazi Germany in 1933 after being arrested by the Gestapo. As Tony Judt observes, Arendt remained fixated on the problems of evil and totalitarianism.[242] Her concern with Eichmann was focused on how he informed those philosophical inquiries. For most, however, worldwide awareness of the suffering of the Jews was the trial's principal contribution.

Eichmann received a guilty verdict on December 11, 1961. Following an unsuccessful appeal, he was hanged on June 1, 1962. Commentators, as well as Americans polled on the matter, generally believed that the proceedings were fair and transparent, and the judges were praised for their integrity. With all the Nazis hiding in plain sight, it was unclear that the international courts, the United Nations, or West Germany could be trusted to try the case, as they seemed unmotivated to arrest and prosecute war criminals before this landmark trial. A cascade of overdue arrests followed, with Nazi criminals tracked down in South America and Germany. A series of trials took place in West Germany beginning in 1963.[243] Also that year, West Germany extended its statute of limitations for murder so that Nazi crimes could be prosecuted (the statute was abolished altogether in 1979).[244] France enacted a "crimes against humanity" law of its own in 1964 to prosecute Nazi war crimes. And despite fears that the Eichmann trial would stir up new antisemitism, polls conducted in West Germany right afterward showed that antisemitism had dropped.[245]

AFTER THE TRIAL: THE HOLOCAUST EXAMINED

The sum total of the suffering of the millions—about a third of the Jewish people, tortured and slaughtered—is certainly beyond human understanding, and who are we to try to give it adequate expression? This is a task for the great writers and poets. —Judges Moshe Landau, Benjamin Halevi, Yitzchak Raveh, Judgment of Adolf Eichmann, District Court of Jerusalem, December 15, 1961[246]

Auschwitz lies on the other side of life and on the other side of death. There, one lives differently, one walks differently, one dreams differently. Auschwitz represents the negation and failure of human progress; it negates the human design and casts doubts on its validity. Then, it defeated culture; later, it defeated art, because just as no one could imagine Auschwitz before Auschwitz, no one can now retell Auschwitz after Auschwitz. —Elie Wiesel, 1989[247]

The most important thing about the Eichmann trial was that it was the first time that what we now call the Holocaust was presented to the American public as an entity in its own right, distinct from Nazi barbarism in general. In the United States, the word "Holocaust" first became firmly attached to the murder of European Jewry as a result of the trial. —Peter Novick, *The Holocaust in American Life* (1999)[248]

After months of wrenching testimony in a Jerusalem auditorium, the Jewish genocide could no longer be hidden in the shadows or engulfed by the mass casualties of World War II. The Holocaust was suddenly comprehended as something different, unprecedented, and catastrophic in its execution, reach, and speed. After Eichmann, "Holocaust" with a capital *H*, referring exclusively and universally to the Nazis' mass murder of the Jewish people, gradually took hold in the United States (fig. 1.27).[249]

The Eichmann trial marked a new focus on survivors (fig. 1.28) and their individual stories instead of the perpetrators. There had been efforts to collect testimonies earlier, notably, as historian Annette Timm highlights, by the Central Jewish Historical Commission in Warsaw, which gathered 7,300 written survivor testimonies beginning in 1944.[250] But this holding was not well known or easily accessible outside Poland. The trial brought survivors' voices to the international stage.

French filmmaker Claude Lanzmann's nine-hour documentary, *Shoah*, begun in 1974 (and released in 1985), took up where the trial left off.[251] Funded by the Israeli government, it set out to record the "living words" of those who could bear witness and to remember those who could not—the victims murdered by the Nazis at killing sites and death camps, which were then behind the iron curtain and largely unknown or forgotten in the West. He interviewed the trial witnesses and tracked down every participant he could find—death camp escapees, members of the *Sonderkommandos*, even perpetrators. The accumulated testimony paints the harrowing, gruesome details of the Nazi extermination process. Each survivor's story recounted in the film is unique, each escape from death a chance occurrence. Films like *Shoah* helped steer the Holocaust discourse away from universal suffering to emphasize instead the specific tragedies of 6 million murdered individuals.

The trial ushered in a new period of Holocaust research as well. William Shirer's best-selling *The Rise and Fall of the Third Reich* (New York), published in October 1960, quickly sold more than a million copies.[252] However, according to Novick's estimate, only about 2 to 3 percent of the book was devoted to the subject of the Holocaust.[253] Raul Hilberg's *Destruction of the European Jews* helped to rectify this gap. The manuscript had been

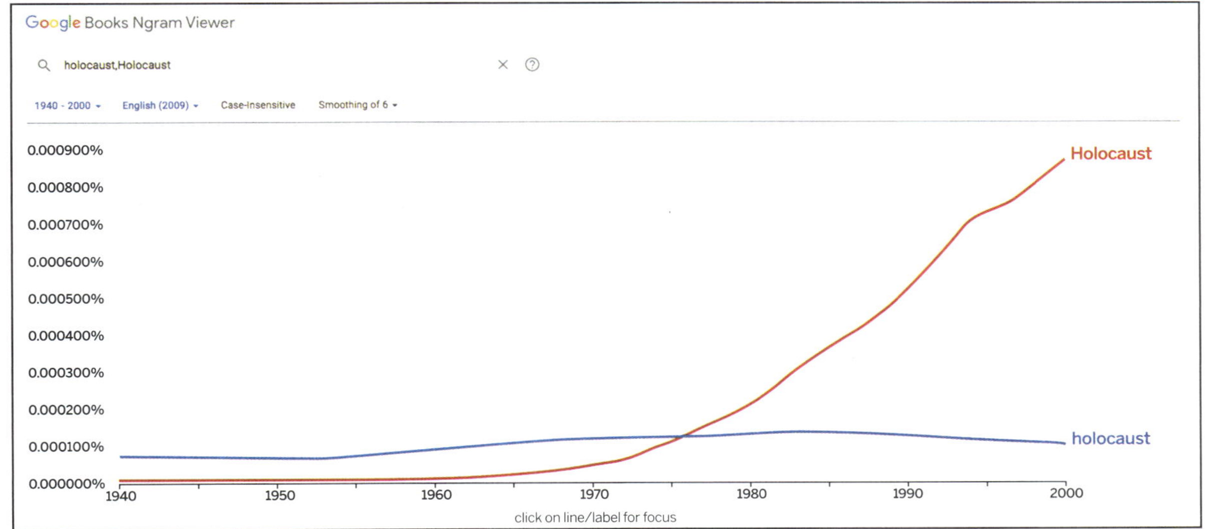

Fig. 1.27 The Google Books Ngram Viewer charts the use of "Holocaust" and "holocaust" in American English books between 1940 and 2000
The graph reflects an increased use of the capitalized version beginning in the 1960s, when the word, referring specifically to the Nazis' mass murder of the Jewish people, began to take hold. A similar trend occurred in British English books. This was likely a result of the Eichmann trial. (This Google graph has been visually enhanced for greater legibility.)

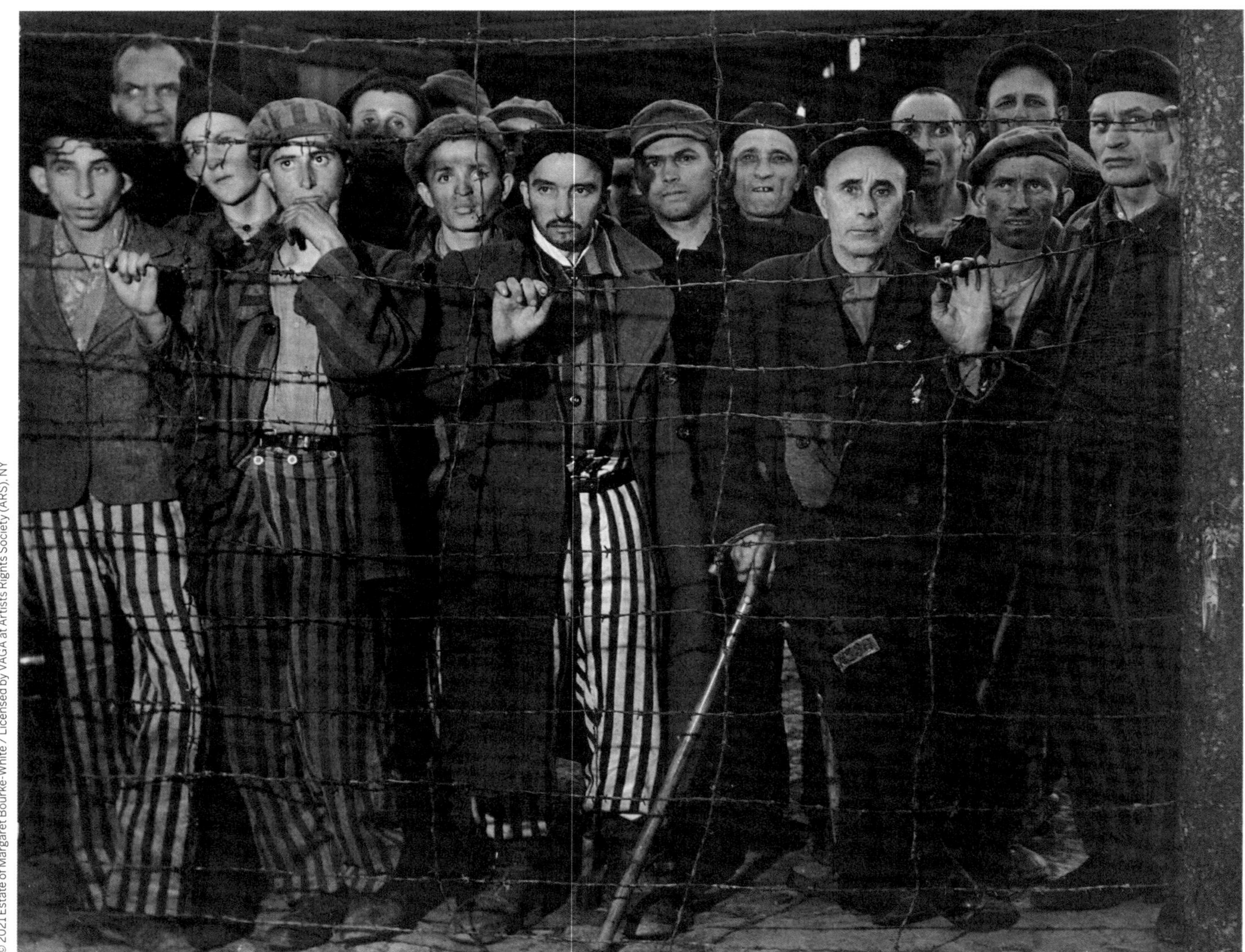

Fig. 1.28 Margaret Bourke-White, *The Living Dead at Buchenwald*, April 1945, ferrotype, Minneapolis Institute of Art, the Alfred and Ingrid Lenz Harrison Purchase Fund, 2012.47.1

Life published this photo in a special December 26, 1960, issue marking the magazine's 25th anniversary. The caption: "Grim Greeting at Buchenwald." Bourke-White joined journalists who accompanied General George Patton through Germany in the last month of the war. This portrait of camp survivors, showing their strength and dignity in the cruelest of circumstances, contrasts with the photos of piled corpses and barracks full of starving victims that the magazine published in 1945. It reflects the later era's new interest in survivors and their individual stories.

rejected by publishers since its completion in 1955. In 1961, in the wake of the Eichmann trial, the influential (and much critiqued) book was picked up by a small Chicago publishing house.[254] It is among the first of many major scholarly works in English to focus on the Holocaust.[255]

This intense accumulation of facts contributed to a new appreciation of the Holocaust, but many insights into the tragedy were to be plumbed in art, literature, film, theater, and television (see Timeline). Here stories and powerful visual and emotional experiences could be deployed to bring audiences to a deeper, more empathetic understanding of events. The early 1960s saw an explosion of material, from new (and rediscovered) survivor memoirs, published, reprinted, and translated, to best-selling novels like *Treblinka* (Paris, 1966) by Jean-François Steiner. Survivor Yehiel Dinur, whose memorable testimony at the Eichmann trial was discussed earlier, became known for his "Holocaust pulp fiction," which he published under his pen name and prison number, Ka-Tzetnik 135633. Movies and plays went a long way in shaping the world's collective memory of the Holocaust. These include Sidney Lumet's *The Pawnbroker* (1964), the artful documentary *Le Chagrin et la pitié* (*The Sorrow and the Pity*, 1969) by Marcel Ophuls, and the plays *Incident at Vichy* (1964) by Arthur Miller and *Der Stellvertreter: Ein christliches Trauerspiel* (*The Deputy: A Christian Tragedy*, 1963–64) by Rolf Hochhuth. The worldwide success of such works, as well as the controversies they often caused, demonstrates a new and broad interest in the Holocaust. As discussed earlier, it also became a central theme for many visual artists in the 1960s, including survivors Samuel Bak, Maryan S. Maryan, and Zoran Music. Many other artists began to explore the subject too, such as Gerhardt Frankl, Igael Tumarkin, Edward Kienholz, Jacob Landau, Sigmund Laufer, and Lasansky, to name just a few. Across Europe and the United States, memorials were erected (fig. 1.29) and textbooks were rewritten to acknowledge the Holocaust.[256] In 1962, West Germany passed a law requiring all schools to teach Germany's history between 1933 and 1945, including the attempted genocide of the Jews, a previously neglected subject. German schoolchildren and international tourists visited concentration camp museums in droves.[257]

The Holocaust came to influence many aspects of life—politics, international relations, law, religion (including, as Rabbi Barry D. Cytron explores in his essay in this catalogue, Roman Catholic doctrine), popular culture, and even tourism. Growing in significance with each subsequent decade, the Holocaust went from a vaguely understood aspect of World War II to one of the most momentous tragedies the world has ever known. Judt observes that in the 21st century, "Holocaust recognition is our contemporary European entry ticket," dictating, for instance, that Poland and Romania revise their discourse on the subject when they wished to join the European Union.[258] In Novick's view, by the 1970s the Holocaust was central to both Jewish identity in America and American culture at large.[259]

As Holocaust awareness grew, Jewish identity and culture became more appreciated around the world.[260] A burst of creative work about Jewish subject matter found large audiences, including the Broadway musical *Fiddler on the Roof* (1964), winner of nine Tony Awards, and Chaim Potok's novel *The Chosen* (New York, 1967). Russian artist Anatoli Kaplan, whose prints captured the lost world of the Jewish shtetl in Eastern Europe, gained an international following. Jewish culture, nearly destroyed in Europe, became something to be treasured across cultures. Hannah Arendt stated as much in her critique of the Israeli court's indictment of Eichmann, which charged him separately for crimes against the Jewish people (counts 1–4) and crimes against humanity (counts 5–7, 9–12). She argued for "the possibility that extermination of whole ethnic groups—the Jews, or the Poles, or the Gypsies—might be more than a crime against the Jewish or the Polish or the Gypsy people, that the international order, and mankind in its entirety, might have been grievously hurt and endangered."[261]

Popular culture proved particularly influential in shaping Holocaust awareness and memory in the 1970s, '80s, and '90s. In 1978, a reported 100 million Americans tuned in to watch the television miniseries *Holocaust: The Story of the Family Weiss*, a nine-and-a-half-hour (including commercials) television drama broadcast over four nights on NBC.[262] Critics, who included Elie Wiesel and Lanzmann, saw the production as commercialized,

Fig. 1.29 Treblinka Memorial by sculptor Franciszek Duszenko and architect Adam Haupt, 1964, Poland
This memorial, comprising 17,000 inscribed stones set like tombstones around an obelisk, is one of several monuments erected at former Nazi camps and extermination sites in the 1960s. Besides Treblinka, they include Sachsenhausen, Dachau, Auschwitz, Babi Yar, and Majdanek.

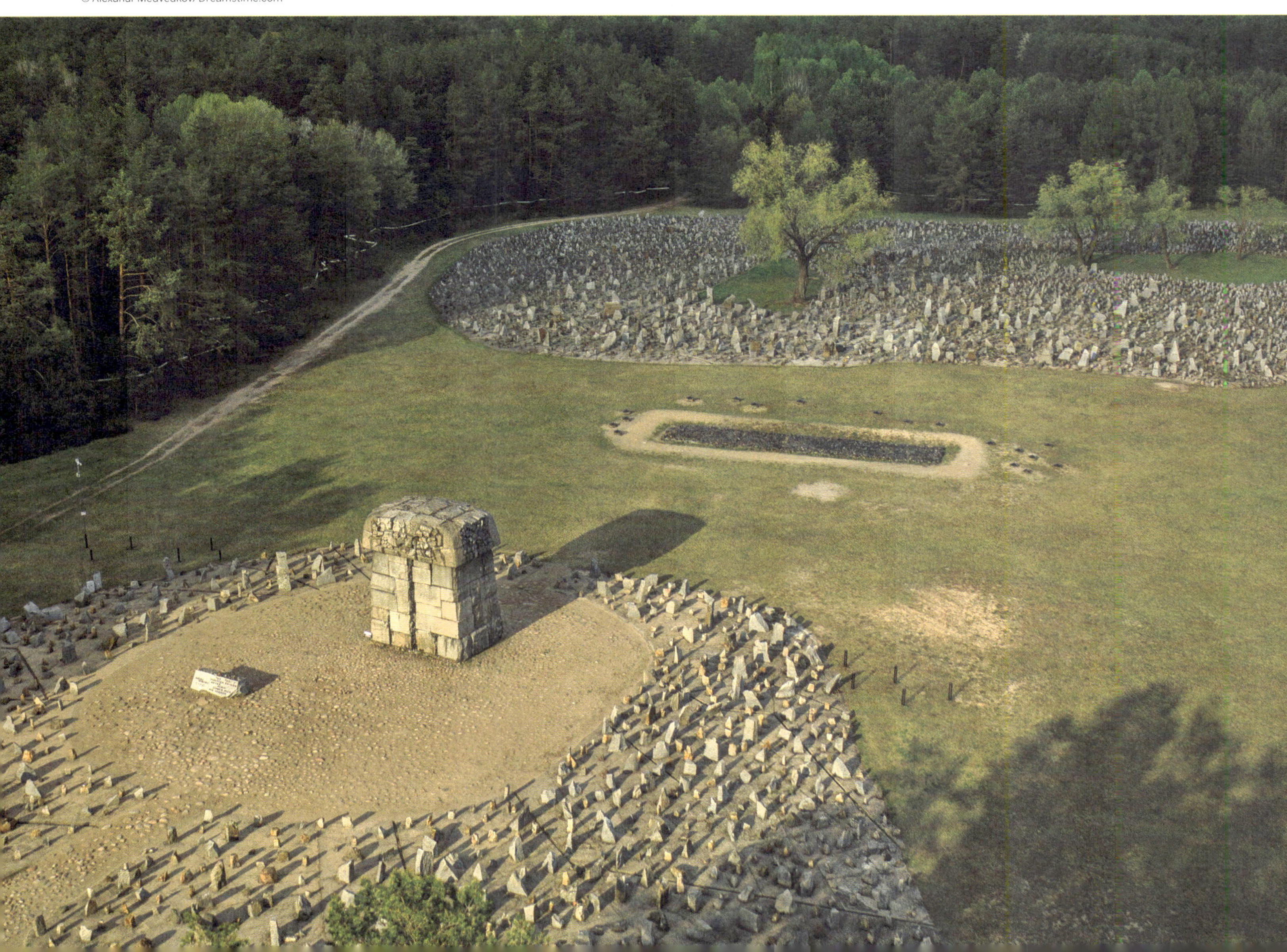

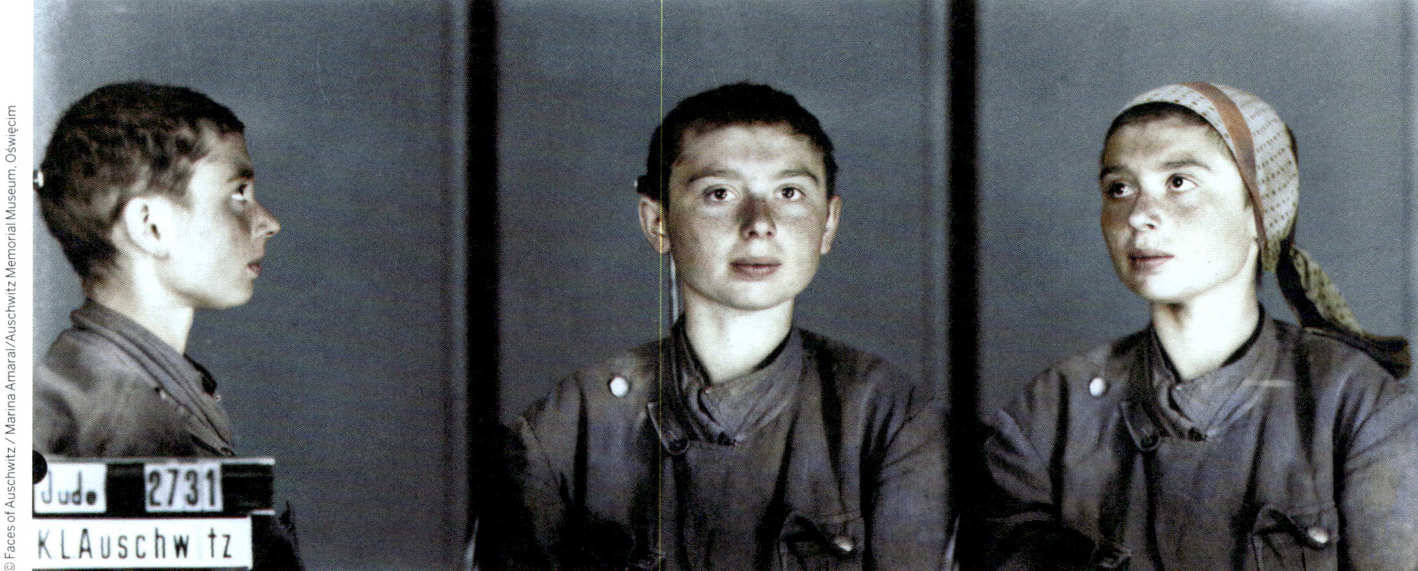

Fig. 1.30 Marina Amaral, *Prisoner 2731*, from the series "Faces of Auschwitz," 2018, digitally colored photograph, Auschwitz Memorial Museum, Oświęcim, Poland

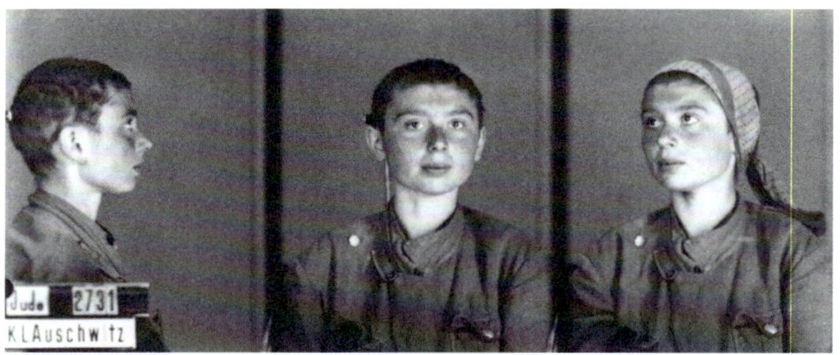

Fig. 1.31 Prisoner 2731, camp registration photo of a Jewish teenager, name unknown, deported from Slovakia, 1942, Auschwitz Memorial Museum, Oświęcim, Poland

offensive, and an insulting simplification of history. Lanzmann took aim with the quip, "There is no business like Shoah business."[263] Yet the show was extraordinarily successful in its reach. It was rebroadcast in West Germany in 1979, where it was seen by an estimated 20 million viewers, over half the adult population. The country, which had extended the statute of limitations for murder following the Eichmann trial, abolished it completely five months after the show aired.[264]

In 1989, Wiesel complained of the Holocaust becoming a fashionable subject in theater, film, and television, "exploited in the most vulgar sense of the word." In addition to the *Holocaust* miniseries, he cited *Il portiere di notte* (*The Night Porter*, 1974) and *Sophie's Choice* (1982) as trivializing and "insulting the dead." Still, an endless stream of fictional films, novels, and television shows followed. In 1993, Steven Spielberg delivered a story of hope with *Schindler's List*, based on the true story of Oskar Schindler, a German industrialist who saved more than 1,200 Jews during the war. It was black and white save for a red coat visible in certain scenes, inspired by Martin Földi's testimony at the Eichmann trial describing how he spotted his young daughter walking toward the gas chambers by her red coat. The film won seven Academy Awards and grossed $322 million worldwide. Critiques of Hollywood's misrepresentation, appropriation, and exploitation of the Holocaust are at times valid, but it is also true that these entertainments, in their best forms, draw attention to the subject in a way scholarship and high art cannot. By entering the world of popular culture, the tragedy becomes household knowledge.

Since the Eichmann trial, the survivor's story has remained the most powerful means of illuminating the Holocaust. Seventy-five years after camp liberations, as fewer and fewer survivors are left to share their stories, their voices are being preserved and heard through the efforts of Holocaust centers, archives, and documentarians. These include the witness testimonies from the Eichmann trial (available on YouTube thanks to Yad Vashem and the Israel State Archives, and the Steven Spielberg Jewish Film Archive at Hebrew University of Jerusalem) and the Fortunoff Video Archive at Yale University, with 4,400 Holocaust testimonies.

As we see with Lasansky's "Nazi Drawings" series, and with Rico Lebrun, Leonard Baskin (late in his career), and others, artists without firsthand experience of the Holocaust can create moving interpretations. George Segal and Rachel Whiteread each designed major Holocaust memorials in San Francisco and Vienna, respectively, and many major monuments have since followed, from Berlin to Ottawa, with an ambitious memorial now planned in the heart of London (next to the Houses of Parliament and Westminster Abbey), designed by David Adjaye and Ron Arad. Art plays a critical role in drawing attention to tragedies and uncovering injustices and abuses, and artists, architects, filmmakers, and writers, regardless of their identity, religion, or age, can sharpen our understanding of the past.

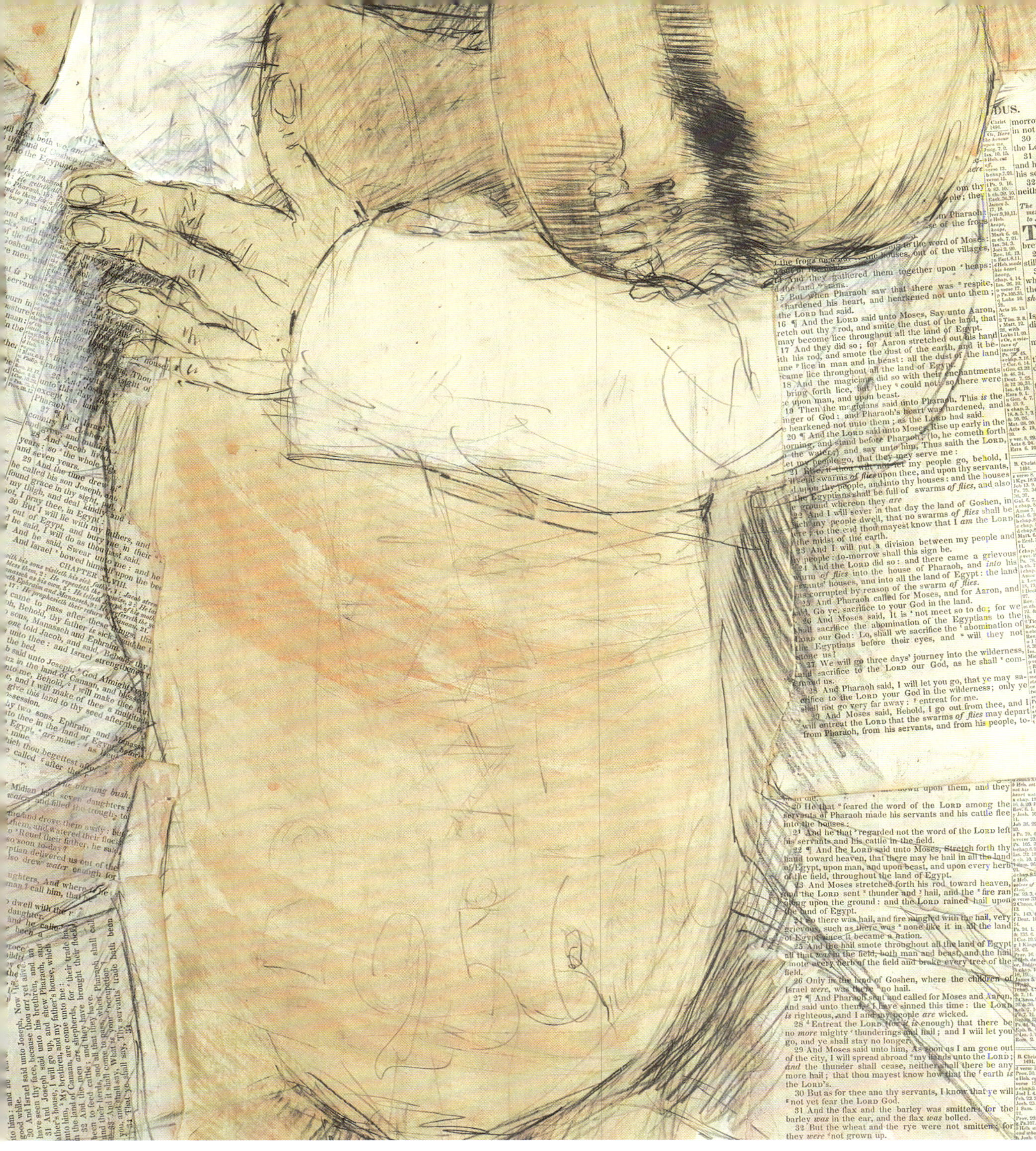

Mauricio Lasansky, *No. 23* (detail), "The Nazi Drawings"

The young Brazilian artist Marina Amaral (born 1994) brings Nazi victims hauntingly to life in her "Faces of Auschwitz" project, a collaboration begun in 2016 with the Auschwitz-Birkenau Memorial, in which she digitally colors prisoner registration photos. Only about 39,000 such photos survive, as the Nazis destroyed most of the camp's documentation during their hasty evacuations. Auschwitz-Birkenau is estimated to have imprisoned 1.1 million Jews, 140,000 Poles, 23,000 Sinti and Roma, 15,000 Soviet POWs, and 25,000 others, but that proportion is not reflected in Amaral's project. Jewish prisoners who were sent straight to the gas chambers upon arrival were not photographed and often not even registered, and after February 25, 1943, they were rarely registered at all.[265]

Among the few Jewish prisoners captured on film at the camp is this Slovak teen (figs. 1.30 and 1.31). Her name and birth date are not recorded, but her prison number, 2731, indicates that she was part of a deportation of Jews from Bratislava to Auschwitz on March 28, 1942, comprising 798 unmarried young women, age 16 and up.[266] With Amaral's sensitive coloring, the girl is transported from a distant, black-and-white past to the vivid present. We clearly see her unwashed face, chapped lips, roughly shorn brown hair, and dark eyes full of dread and despair. She seems to appear to us in the flesh, frightened and vulnerable. She is a startlingly immediate reminder of the very real individuals concealed in the staggering statistics of this tragedy: the 216,000 Jewish children murdered at Auschwitz, and the 11,000 Roma and Sinti children, 3,000 Polish children, the 2,000 Belarusian, Ukrainian, and Russian children also murdered there; and the millions and millions of others systematically exterminated because of their race and religion.

NOTES

1. Tony Judt, *Postwar: A History of Europe since 1945* (New York, 2005), p. 821.

2. Jeffrey Shandler, *While America Watches: Televising the Holocaust* (New York, 1999), p. 91. The estimate of 80 percent of television viewers' watching the Eichmann trial comes from the trial's television executive producer, Milton Fruchtman.

3. The Nazis' forced sterilizations of mentally ill people began in 1934 and were partly inspired by American eugenics programs, first legalized in some states in the 1890s, and rising significantly in 1927 following a U.S. Supreme Court case. In 1938 the Nazis expanded their program to carry out euthanasia, killing infants and children who were mentally ill and mentally and physically disabled. This "granting of mercy deaths," the euphemism employed by the Nazis, was ultimately expanded to the adult population, with an estimated 300,000 people murdered.

4. Timothy Snyder, *Bloodlands: Europe between Hitler and Stalin* (New York, 2010), pp. ix, 163, 244, 246, 411–13. Snyder estimates that the Germans murdered some 5 million non-Jewish civilians and prisoners of war in Eastern Europe through starvation and murder. He distinguished the term *genocide*, which includes the intention of the perpetrator to destroy a whole ethnic or religious group or race, from the term *mass killing*, which refers more broadly to purposeful policies of mass killing. While ethnic Belarusians, Poles, Russians, and Ukrainians were victims of mass killings, the Nazis had not intended to eradicate the entire Slavic population from Europe as they had with the Jews. Hitler, instead, planned to colonize Eastern Europe, destroy the existing nation states, expel, kill, and enslave the local "subhuman" populations, and exploit the land's natural and agricultural resources. Snyder writes, "If the German war against the USSR had gone as planned, thirty million civilians would have been starved in its first winter, and tens of millions more expelled, killed, assimilated, or enslaved thereafter."

5. Elie Wiesel, April 19, 1985, speech given at White House when accepting the Congressional Gold Medal from President Ronald Reagan.

6. Jan Karski met with Prime Minister Winston Churchill and Foreign Minister Anthony Eden in London in November 1942 about the "Jewish problem" in Poland, then traveled to the U.S. in July 1943 to meet with President Roosevelt and Justice Felix Frankfurter. He was frustrated with the failure to believe the horrors he reported and the indifference and inaction of the Allies. In 1944 Karski published a book detailing the Nazi extermination of Polish Jews, *Story of a Secret State* (New York, 1944). Claude Lanzmann's 2010 documentary *The Karski Report* features interviews with Karski from the 1970s.

7. There were many other scattered early sources detailing the Holocaust. See Comité d'information interallié Londres, *La Persecution des juifs, les conditions de vie dans les territoires occupés* (1942); World Jewish Congress, *Lest We Forget: The Massacre of the Warsaw Ghetto* (New York, 1943), which included a map of Treblinka death camp; and Jacob Apenszlak's *The Black Book of Polish Jewry* (New York, 1944), among others.

8. German industrialist Eduard Schulte secretly reported to Gerhard Riegner at the World Jewish Congress in Geneva German plans to deport and exterminate 3.5 to 4 million Jews in occupied countries, possibly with gas, beginning in the autumn. Riegner sent a telegram to New York and London offices of the World Jewish Congress. Rabbi Stephen Wise did not receive the telegram until August 28. Over a year later, the U.S. State Department confirmed information in the report, but also stated that some information was confused and fabricated. For further discussion, see Peter Novick, *The Holocaust in American Life* (New York, 1999), pp. 22–23.

9. The BBC reported on the Bund Report on June 2, 1942. For earlier coverage in Britain, following the outbreak of war, see, e.g., Raymond Daniell, "Nazi Tortures Detailed by Britain; Concentration Camp Horrors Told," *New York Times*, October 31, 1939.

10. See e.g., "1,000,000 Jews Slain by Nazis, Report Says," *New York Times*, June 30, 1942, p. 7. This article also includes other reports with significantly fewer victims ("several hundred thousand Jews").

11. "Allies Are Urged to Execute Nazis," *New York Times*, July 2, 1942, p. 6.

12. "Work Ability Sways Nazi Stand on Jews," *New York Times*, July 4, 1942, p. 4. The coverage also seemed to carry a note of skepticism.

13. "Wise Gets Confirmation," *New York Times*, November 25, 1942, p. 10; other papers across the country, *Miami Herald*, *Los Angeles Times*, *New York Herald*, etc., reported this on their front pages; see also more detailed story of Wise's findings the next day, "Slain Polish Jews Put at a Million," *New York Times*, November 26, 1942, p. 16, deep in the pages of the paper.

14. *New York Times*, December 18, 1942, front page, p. 10. One noteworthy early artistic condemnation is Leopold Méndez's 1942 linocut *Deportation to Death (Death Train)*, depicting the deportations of Jews in cattle cars. The print was included in Taller de Gráfica Popular's *The Black Book of Nazi Terror in Europe* (Mexico City, 1943), which included over 200 photographs and prints representing Nazi atrocities.

15. "2,000,000 Murders by Nazis Charged: Polish Paper in London Says Jews Are Exterminated in Treblinska [sic] Death House, Groups Slain in Cells, Steam Is Reported Used to Kill Men, Women and Children at Place in Woods," *New York Times*, August 8, 1943, p. 11. This story is mostly quotations from its source, *Polish Labor Fights*, a publication issued in London. It is difficult to determine the precise number of Jews and people in general murdered at Treblinka. The United States Holocaust Memorial Museum estimates 925,000 Jews were murdered; Snyder 2010 estimates 780,863 people; Yad Vashem estimates 870,000 people, of whom approximately 738,000 were Jewish.

16. *New York Times*, August 8, 1943, p. 11; Daniel Brigham, "Two Death Camps / Places of Horror . . . Mass Killing of Jews Described by Swiss," *New York Times*, July 6, 1944, p. 6. Novick notes (1999, p. 23) that editors had little hard news and often reported about the Holocaust from second- and third-hand reports. They frequently voiced skepticism for fear of publishing propaganda, as happened during World War I.

17. Vasily Grossman, "The Hell of Treblinka," *Znamya*, a Soviet literary journal, November 1944, https://www.facinghistory.org/holocaust-human-behavior/hell-of-treblinka-vasily-grossman, accessed January 14, 2020. Grossman, a Jewish Ukrainian writer who served as a war correspondent for the Red Army, wrote a powerful account of the mass murder of Jews at Treblinka II, where he reported that bones and teeth were visible in the ground and spare clues, like sacks of hair and remnants of photos of children, remained; for more on contemporaneous first-hand news reports, see Snyder 2010, pp. 278, 280. The carnage at Treblinka would not appear in the *Times* again until 1961, following testimonies of survivors at the Eichmann trial, despite Soviet reporters' confirming the mass killing of Jews when the Red Army overran the dismantled camp in 1944.

18. W. H. Lawrence, "50,000 Kiev Jews Reported Killed," *New York Times*, November 29, 1943, p. 3.

19. Arkadi Zeltser, "The Subject of 'Jews in Babi Yar' in the Soviet Union in the Years 1941–1945," in *Babyn Yar: Masove ubyvstvo i pam'iat' pro n'ogo*, eds. Vitaliy Nakhmanovych, Anatoliy Podol's'kyi, and Mykhaylo Tyaglyy (Kyiv, Ukraine, 2012), pp. 83–100; English translation available at International Institute for Holocaust Research at Yad Vashem; https://www.yadvashem.org/research/about/mirilashvili-center/articles/babi-yar.html, accessed December 20, 2020. The massacre had been reported in *Pravda* in 1941, among other places. There were further eyewitness reports in September 1943, Nazi prisoners who had been forced to exhume the mass burials to destroy evidence of the massacre. Eighteen managed to escape the gruesome operation.

20. For further discussion of the *Times* and Lawrence's uneven reporting of the Holocaust, see Deborah Lipstadt, *Beyond Belief: The American Press and the Coming of the Holocaust 1933–1945* (New York, 1986), pp. 245–50; Laurel Leff, *Buried by the Times: The Holocaust and America's Most Important Newspaper* (Cambridge, 2005), pp. 172–73; Novick 1999, p. 22.

21. Novick 1999, p. 20. "It was the overall course of the war that dominated the minds of Americans in the early forties. Unless we keep that in mind, we will never understand how the Holocaust came to be swallowed up in the larger carnage surrounding it."

22. See also Robert Ross, *So It Was True: The American Protestant Press and the Nazi Persecution of the Jews* (Minneapolis, 1980).

23. My own research on coverage of the Holocaust in the American press focused on the *New York Times*, examining the paper's reporting from 1933 to 1945. Thus the articles cited in this essay focus on the *Times*. Leff's

study also focused on the *New York Times*. She illuminates the role various personalities and relationships at the paper had on the coverage, as well as the influence of politics and culture of the era (Leff 2005). For a broader examination of the American press and other newspapers' coverage, see Lipstadt 1986.

24. Two prisoners, Rudolf Vrba and Alfréd Wetzler, escaped from Auschwitz in April 1944 and survived the dangerous two-week trek to Slovakia to report the mass murder of Jews at the camp. The anticipated arrival of hundreds of thousands of Hungarian deportees lent urgency to their escape plans, but their testimony, the Vrba-Wetzler Report, took months to reach Allied officials. Stories finally began appearing in the American and British press in June 1944, and Allied government officials began to make halted deportations only in July, after more than 400,000 Jews had been murdered, mainly at Auschwitz.

25. Tony Judt, "The 'Problem of Evil' in Postwar Europe," *New York Review of Books*, February 14, 2008, pp. 32–36.

26. Lipstadt 1986, pp. 250–55; Leff 2005, pp. 236–64.

27. Judt 2005, p. 808; Tony Judt and Timothy Snyder, *Thinking in the Twentieth Century* (London, 2012); *Times Literary Supplement*, October 4, 1996.

28. "Des Moines Speech," Charles Lindbergh: An American Aviator, accessed February 29, 2020, http://www.charleslindbergh.com/american first/speech.asp. In 1938, Lindbergh accepted a medal of honor from Germany, awarded by Nazi Hermann Göring; Lindbergh's racist views were articulated more blatantly in an article he wrote in *Reader's Digest*. He warns of the future of the white race "in a pressing sea of Yellow, Black, and Brown," and sees a war with Germany, "our own family of nations," achieved through foreign alliances, as committing "racial suicide." Charles A. Lindbergh, "Aviation, Geography and Race," *Reader's Digest*, November 1939, pp. 64–67.

29. Judt and Snyder 2012, p. 275.

30. Daniel Anker, dir., *Imaginary Witness* (U.S.; Anker Productions Inc., 2004). With the rise of Nazism, Hollywood executives, many of whom were Jewish, were wary of offending the German market (10 percent of film profits), and also of American antisemitism. Nonetheless, Senator Gerald Nye, in 1942, formed a committee to investigate a Jewish anti-German warmongering conspiracy in Hollywood. Following Pearl Harbor, Hollywood focused its war films on the battlefield and needed government approval for release. Numerous American filmmakers joined the war effort to film the war in Europe for the government, and filmed the liberation of the camps; see also Novick 1999, pp. 27–28. Novick cites a 1943 poll in which Hollywood executives voiced preference to show all victims of Nazism rather than focus on Jews. Both Anker and Novick cite *None Shall Escape* (Columbia Pictures, 1944) as a singular case in which Jewish victims are depicted. This film was not distributed internationally.

31. Novick 1999, pp. 35–36; Yehuda Bauer, *Jewish Reactions to the Holocaust* (Tel Aviv, 1989), p. 199; and Dina Porat, *The Blue and the Yellow Stars of David: The Zionist Leadership in Palestine and the Holocaust, 1939–1945* (Cambridge, Mass., 1990), pp. 41–42, 54–55, 62–63.

32. Lanzmann, *The Karski Report*, 2010.

33. Universal Studios, "Nazi Murder Mills," newsreel, April 26, 1945, narrated by Ed Herlihy.

34. Harold Denny, "'The World Must Not Forget,'" *New York Times Magazine*, May 6, 1945, pp. 8, 42–43.

35. Eisenhower, letter to George C. Marshall, U.S. Army chief of staff, April 15, 1945, "The Papers of Dwight David Eisenhower, The War Years IV," NAID no. 12005711, Eisenhower Presidential Library, Museum, and Boyhood Home, accessed December 16, 2019, https://www.eisenhowerlibrary.gov/sites/default/files/research/online-documents/holocaust/1945-04-15-dde-to-marshall.pdf.

36. The Soviets invited war correspondents to Majdanek extermination camp, the first camp to be liberated, on July 23, 1944. It was widely reported in the American press, with descriptions of mass graves and gas chambers; see, e.g., W. H. Lawrence, *New York Times*, August 30, 1944, front page, p. 9. Lawrence, one of the most outspoken skeptics of Nazi crimes against the Jews, including the slaughters at Babi Yar, finally believed in the Nazis' mass murder after visiting Majdanek. Interestingly, he begins six of the seven paragraphs of his front-page (unillustrated) story in the first person, stating, "I have just seen the most terrible place on the face of the earth," "I have been . . .," "I have seen," and so on. Still, *Times* editors felt compelled to back up Lawrence's reporting of the atrocities in their editorial page of same issue with this statement: "Mr. Lawrence, who is employed by this newspaper because he is known to be a thorough and accurate correspondent, quotes estimates of Soviet and Polish authorities that 1,500,000 'persons from nearly every country in Europe' were butchered here by the Nazis during the past three years"; "The Maidanek Horror," *New York Times*, August 31, 1944, p. 16. For further discussion on Lawrence, see Lipstadt 1986, pp. 245–50. Photos were published of Majdanek, but not as extensively as photos of the camps liberated by American and British forces. Western war correspondents did not see the other extermination camps built to annihilate the Jews—Chełmno, Sobibor, Bełżec, and Treblinka—which had been destroyed by the Nazis to hide their deeds, nor Auschwitz, which had been liberated by the Soviets.

37. Grossman 1944.

38. The camps liberated by American forces, such as Buchenwald and Dachau, and British forces, such as Bergen-Belsen, received far more attention in North America and Western Europe, in large part because the U.S. and U.K. forces extensively filmed and photographed the camps and invited the press and statesmen to the scene to bear witness. The footage and photographs were widely circulated. Thus American, British, and French newspapers and newsreels gave less attention to the extermination camps the Nazis destroyed, or Auschwitz, which the Soviets liberated and delayed releasing information about until after Germany's surrender to focus attention on the Soviet successes on the battlefield. Ignorance in the West of the Nazi extermination camps in Poland was compounded later by the iron curtain.

39. In a cable to Marshall, Eisenhower wrote, "We continue to uncover German concentration camps for political prisoners in which conditions of indescribable horror prevail. I have visited one of these myself and I assure you that whatever has been printed on them to date has been understatement. If you would see any advantage in asking about a dozen leaders of Congress and a dozen prominent editors to make a short visit to this theater in a couple of C-54s, I will arrange to have them conducted to one of these places where the evidence of bestiality and cruelty is so overpowering as to leave no doubt in their minds about the normal practices of the Germans in these camps." Eisenhower, cable to George C. Marshall, April 19, 1945, "The Papers of Dwight David Eisenhower, The War Years IV," NAID no. 12007738, Eisenhower Presidential Library, Museum, and Boyhood Home, accessed December 16, 2019, https://www.eisenhowerlibrary.gov/sites/default/files/research/online-documents/holocaust/1945-04-19-dde-to-marshall.pdf.

40. Barbie Zelizer, *Remembering to Forget: Holocaust Memory through the Camera's Eye* (Chicago, 1998), see especially pp. 141–69.

41. Edward J. Bliss, *In Search of Light: The Broadcasts of Edward R. Murrow, 1938–1961* (New York, 1967), p. 57. Murrow's Buchenwald visit on April 11 was broadcast on CBS radio on April 15, 1945. Murrow had reported about the Nazi extermination camps and murder of "millions of human beings, most of them Jews," on December 13, 1942, following the Polish government-in-exile report to the U.N. As discussed above, this was the brief time when the Jewish plight was the focus of the American press in its wartime reporting.

42. Narrator Ed Herlihy begins with the poor treatment of American POWs at the camps, and then describes the victims at the insane asylum and euthanasia center of Hadamar as "Poles, Greeks, Russians, any non-Germans." The newsreel first screened in American cinemas on April 26, 1945.

43. This Associated Press story was run by the *New York Times*, April 13, 1945, p. 11; see also "Dachau Captured by Americans," *New York Times*, May 1, 1945, front page, p. 5, where there is no mention of Jewish victims, only a "seething, swaying crowd of Russians, Poles, Frenchmen, Czechs, and Austrians, cheering the Americans in their native tongues." General Eisenhower's April 19 cable to Marshall quoted above also calls the camp victims "political prisoners."

44. See, e.g., Gene Currivan, "Nazi Death Factories Shock Germans on a Forced Tour," *New York Times*, April 18, 1945, p. 8; Harold Denny,

"Despair Blankets Buchenwald Camp," *New York Times*, April 20, 1945, p. 3. Jewish victims are noted more frequently in the *Times* when reports are being quoted, such as, April 29, 1945.

45. "Atrocity Report Issued by Army," *New York Times*, April 29, 1945.

46. Anita Kondoyanidi, "The Liberating Experience: War Correspondents, Red Army Soldiers, and the Nazi Extermination Camps," *The Russian Review*, vol. 69 (July 2010), pp. 428–62. The Red Army liberated Auschwitz on January 27, 1945, and the Soviets filmed footage of the camp shortly after liberation day (some of it staged). Only one war correspondent, however, was invited to Auschwitz, and he filed just a brief report. The Soviets delayed the more extensive report until after Germany's surrender on May 7, as Stalin wished to focus the world's attention on the Soviet victory in Berlin (May 2).

47. C. L. Sulzberger, "Oswiecim Killings Placed at 4,000,000," *New York Times*, May 8, 1945, p. 12. Sulzberger was reporting from Moscow on the Soviet State Commission investigation on Auschwitz, released on May 7.

48. Judt 2005, pp. 24–25. Jews suffered the worst. Those not murdered immediately upon their arrival at the camps were at the bottom of the hierarchy of the labor camps. Given the severity of their mistreatment and malnourishment, survival in the final days of the camp was rare. At Belsen, for instance, there had been no food for six days before the liberation. Of the Jewish prisoners still alive at liberation, four in 10 died in the first few weeks of their freedom. For discussion of prisoner hierarchies at the camps, with the Jews at the lowest rung, and the higher survival rates of "the privileged," see Primo Levi, *Se questo è un uomo* (*If This Is a Man*, Turin, 1947) and *I sommersi e i salvati* (*The Drowned and the Saved*, Turin, 1986) in *The Complete Works of Primo Levi*, ed. Ann Goldstein (New York, 2015), vol. 1, pp. 83–88, and vol. 3, pp. 2430–49. It is in this context that Levi discussed the complex "Gray Zone" and blurring of lines between persecutors and victims by the Nazis to achieve their ends. He absolved all low-functionary prisoners coerced into the totalitarian system for survival.

49. Novick 1999, p. 65.

50. The exception in the *Times* might be Anne O'Hare McCormick. See "Abroad: Victims of the Last Fury of the Nazis," *New York Times*, July 15, 1944, p. 12, in which she wrote, "Millions of human beings have perished at their will, not in battle alone, but before firing squads, in prison camps, in hundreds of murdered villages like Lidice, Distono and Oradour-sur-Glane, in the ghettos, box cars, and slaughterhouses where the Jews were hunted to death." See also O'Hare McCormick, "Abroad: Palestine Refugees Upset Appeal of Reason," *New York Times*, January 15, 1945.

51. Novick 1999, pp. 27–28. Novick generally sees these failures as a matter of complex circumstances, writers overwhelmed by the larger conflict, and also the result of Jewish prisoners surviving in smaller numbers at the liberated camps. Lipstadt, on the other hand, critiques the insensitivity and biases of the journalists; cf. Lipstadt 1989, pp. 254–56.

52. The term genocide combines *genos*, for tribe or race, with *-cide*, for killing. It was coined by the Polish Jewish lawyer Raphael Lemkin, who had fled Nazi Germany, in his book *Axis Rule in Occupied Europe* (Washington, 1944). The 1915 annihilation of Armenians by Ottoman Turks was the focus of his earlier work in Poland, which he cited as the first modern example of genocide. As Novick points out, Lemkin defined the Nazi genocide program "ecumenically," noting its "intent to wipe out the Poles, the Russians . . . and almost achieved their goal in exterminating the Jews and gypsies in Europe." Novick 1999, p. 100.

53. See, e.g., Sulzberger 1945. The most cited figure of 6 million for the Jewish death toll during the war likely came out of the Nuremberg trials; see testimony of Nazi SS Officer Wilhelm Hoettl, who credited Adolf Eichmann as source for the figure, stating that approximately 4 million were killed in camps, and 2 million in other ways, such as shooting squads. Nuremberg Trial Proceedings, vol. 3, Friday, December 14, 1945, Morning Session, Avalon Project, Yale Law School, https://avalon.law.yale.edu/imt/12-14-45.asp; see also Novick 1999, p. 334n23, and S. Rosenweig, "Letter to the Times," *New York Times*, August 24, 1946. In early 1946, President Truman cited 5.7 million murdered Jews ("Truman Pledges Justice for Jews," *New York Times*, February 26, 1946, p. 8), whereas Raul Hilberg calculated 5.1 million Jewish victims. See Hilberg, *The Destruction of the European Jews* (Chicago and London, 1961); more recently Snyder estimated the total to be 5.4 million Jews (Snyder 2010, p. 411).

54. Novick 1999, pp. 24, 288n9, citing Charles Herbert Stember et al., *Jews in the Mind of America* (New York, 1966), p. 141.

55. Rudolph J. Rummel, *Statistics of Democide: Genocide and Mass Murder since 1900* (Münster, 1998); see also James Yamazaki, "Children of the Atomic Bomb, A UCLA Physician's Eyewitness Report," accessed May 26, 2020, http://www.aasc.ucla.edu/cab/index.html. Yamazaki states that the estimate of 225,000 killed and wounded is overly conservative.

56. Novick 1999, p. 110. Interestingly, the word "holocaust" in the American press in the 1950s was used more frequently to describe the destruction caused by atomic bombs than the Nazi genocide of the Jewish people. (See, e.g., Harry Truman's 1953 State of the Union address or, in the *New York Times*, the phrases "hydrogen holocaust" (April 5, 1954) and "nuclear Holocaust" (July 14, 1957, p. 13).

57. Bertram Hulen, "President Orders Eisenhower to End New Abuse of Jews," *New York Times*, September 30, 1945, front page.

58. Judt 2005, p. 32.

59. "Truman Pledges Justice for Jews," *New York Times*, February 26, 1946, p. 8; Laura Jockusch, "Justice at Nuremberg? Jewish Responses to Nazi War-Crime Trials in Allied-Occupied Germany," *Jewish Social Studies*, vol. 19 (Fall 2012), pp. 107–47. It is true that a number of non-Jewish witnesses testified about the persecution of Jews, and Jewish lawyers and officials played important roles for the prosecution at Nuremberg, including Raphael Lemkin, who coined the term "genocide" in 1944, as well as Benjamin Ferencz, who was a chief prosecutor of the American military tribunal trials at Nuremberg in 1947–48.

60. Telford Taylor, *The Anatomy of the Nuremberg Trials* (New York, 1992), p. 296; Judt 2005, p. 805.

61. Foreword to the 1966 dramatized version of *If This Is a Man* (1947), in Levi 2015, vol. 2, p. 1173.

62. Philip Gourevitch, "Aharon Appelfeld and the Truth of Fiction in Remembering the Holocaust," *New Yorker*, January 5, 2018.

63. Mary Costanza, *The Living Witness* (New York, 1982), p. 135; Kazimierz Adamczyk, "Report and lament – Zalman Gradowski's notes from Auschwitz," *Acta Universitatis Lodziensis. Folia Litteraria Polonica*, vol. 8 (2017), pp. 187–203.

64. Lengyel wrote the book in Hungarian. It was translated into French as *Souvenirs de l'au-delà* for publication in France. The English translation was published in 1947 as *Five Chimneys: The Story of Auschwitz* (Chicago, 1947), and in paperback as *I Survived Hitler's Ovens* (New York, 1947). Doubts about Lengyel's Jewish origins have been put to rest by Marius Turda's recent documentary research, Marius Turda, "Redemptive Family Narratives: Olga Lengyel and the Textuality of the Holocaust," *Archiva Moldaviae*, vol. 8 (2016), pp. 69–82.

65. Levi 1947, in Levi 2015, vol. 1, pp. 56–58.

66. See also Elie Wiesel, "Art and the Holocaust: Trivializing Memory," *New York Times*, June 11, 1989, Arts and Leisure section, p. 1, and Haim Gouri's documentary film *The 81st Blow* (Israel, 1974). The title refers to the Israelis' doubting a survivor's account of being whipped 80 times.

67. Levi said, "I brought with me this primordial and violent impulse to narrate when I returned, and I wrote right away . . . because what I had experienced weighed inside me and I felt an urgency to free myself. Second, to satisfy a moral, civic, political duty to bear witness." Primo Levi, "Lo scrittore non scrittore" ("The Writer Who Is Not a Writer," lecture, Teatro Carignano, Turin, November 19, 1976), in Levi 2015, vol. 2, p. 1215. In 1947, Levi wrote: "Its origins go back, if not in practice, as an idea, an intention, to the days in the Lager [camp]. The need to tell our story to 'others' to make 'others' share it, took on for us, before the liberation and after, the character of an immediate and violent impulse, to the point of competing with other elementary needs. The book was written to satisfy that need: in the first place, therefore, as an interior liberation." Levi 1947, in Levi 2015, vol. 1, pp. 5–6.

68. "I needed to tell these stories: it seemed important that they not remain lying inside me, like a nightmare; they should be known, not just to my friends, but to everyone, the broadest possible audience." Primo Levi, *La tregua: letture per la scuola media* (*The Truce: Readings for Middle School Preface*, Turin, 1965), in Levi 2015, vol. 2, p. 1158.

69. Viktor Frankl's book was originally published as *. . . trotzdem Ja zum Leben sagen: Ein Psychologe erlebt das Konzentrationslager* (Vienna, 1946). The English translation (*. . . Nevertheless Say "Yes" to Life: A Psychologist Experiences the Concentration Camp*) was

published in the U.S. in 1959 and given the new title *From Death-Camp to Existentialism: A Psychiatrist's Path to a New Therapy* (Boston, 1959), then subsequently in paperback as *Man's Search for Meaning* (New York, 1963).

70. Lengyel 1947 (New York, 1995 ed.), pp. 225, 227.

71. Griselda Pollock and Max Silverman, *Concentrationary Cinema: Aesthetics as Political Resistance in Alain Resnais's "Night and Fog"* (1955) (New York, 2011), pp. 18–32; Sylvie Lindeperg *"Night and Fog": A Film History*, trans. Tom Mes (Minneapolis, 2014), p. 11; Judt 2005, pp. 61–62, 813–25.

72. Holcomb B. Noble, "Dr. Viktor E. Frankl of Vienna, Psychiatrist of the Search for Meaning, Dies at 92," *New York Times*, September 4, 1997. The LOC survey took place in 1991.

73. Lengyel's book had been immediately translated from French into English (1947) and received an early, albeit brief, review in the *New York Times* (August 3, 1947, "Records of Horror," Book Review, p. 16). It received renewed attention with an English reprinting in 1957, and then in the 1960s when it was translated into many languages and became available across the world (Tokyo, 1962; Bologna, 1967; Cluj, Romania, 1986; Bangkok, 1987; Mexico City, 1994; Laren, Netherlands, 2005). It was also reprinted in English a number of times (1972, 1982, 1995). Still, Lengyel's account, despite its early date and unique female perspective, has received less scholarly attention than expected (see Turda 2016, p. 3). In 1962, she founded the Memorial Library in New York, now called the Olga Lengyel Institute for Holocaust Studies and Human Rights, to educate teachers about the Holocaust. When Lengyel died in New York in 2001, it was overlooked by the *New York Times* obituary writers and only noted in a paid death notice (April 18, 2001).

74. Radio Canada produced a radio adaptation in 1962, followed by one produced in Italy by RAI and a theatrical adaptation (Ernesto Ferrero, "Chronology," in Levi 2015, pp. xxxvii–xliii). The publisher Einaudi rejected Levi's manuscript, but De Silva, a smaller publisher in Turin, published it. Franco Antonicelli, De Silva's founder, and a writer and antifascist activist during the war, recognized the significance of Levi's book, but it took audiences decades to catch up with him. Of the 2,500 copies De Silva published in 1947, just 1,400 copies sold. Einaudi subsequently acquired rights to the book and published a new edition in 1958, with a first run of 2,000 copies and second run of another 2,000. It was published in English in 1959 (London and New York) to modest success, with French and German editions in 1961.

75. Novick 1999, pp. 83–84, 107–9; Judt 2005, pp. 804–8.

76. The two stories by Aharon Appelfeld were first published in English with his book *In the Wilderness* (Jerusalem, 1965).

77. Joseph Berger, "Elie Wiesel, Auschwitz Survivor and Nobel Peace Prize Winner, Dies at 87," *New York Times*, July 2, 2016.

78. Z. Gradowski, "List, Dziennik," in *Wśród koszmarnej zbrodni. Rękopisy członków Sonderkommando* (Oświęcim, Poland, 1971), translated from Yiddish by Bernard Mark; see also *Amidst a Nightmare of Crime: Manuscripts of Members of Sonderkommando*, eds. Jadwiga Bezwinska and Danuta Czech (Oświęcim, Poland, 1973), for an early English source on Gradowski and other notebooks excavated from the Birkenau crematoria.

79. Since 2000, there have been a number of studies of Gradowski's manuscripts and others; for bibliography, see Adamczyk 2017.

80. Glenn Sujo, *Legacies of Silence: The Visual Arts and the Holocaust Memory* (exh. cat.), Imperial War Museum (London, 2001), p. 76; Costanza 1982, p. 134.

81. Alfred Kantor was a survivor of Auschwitz, Theresienstadt, and Schwarzheide; see Alfred Kantor and John Wykert, *The Book of Kantor: An Artist's Journal of the Holocaust* (New York, 1971), unpaginated.

82. Janet Blatter and Sybil Milton, *Art of the Holocaust* (New York, 1981), vol. 1, p. 142. Konieczny, from Poland, was imprisoned at Buchenwald. He assembled a 280-page notebook at the camp with contributions (drawings, poems, songs, caricatures) from fellow political prisoners, mostly Communists, 1943–45 (now in the Auschwitz-Birkenau Memorial and Museum); for Konieczny's biography, see Sujo 2001, p. 80.

83. Costanza 1982, pp. 43, 128–33. Pen and pencil drawings on paper were the most common; gouache or watercolor on paper were also made (or, rather, survive). Less common are paintings and sculpture. Felix Nussbaum, for example, executed his paintings while in hiding or on the run, rather than as a camp prisoner. A number of sculptures from the Auschwitz carpenter's workshop reportedly survive.

84. Costanza 1982, pp. 135–63. Costanza records various efforts by survivors to recover works after the war. Many were hidden with instruction as to where they should be sent if found. Esther Lurie, for example, requested that hers be sent to the Tel Aviv Museum. A cache of her work was found by Avraham Tory and donated to Yad Vashem, but almost all of the other 200 drawings and paintings she made in the Kovno ghetto were lost.

85. The full name of Yad Vashem is Yad Vashem: The World Holocaust Remembrance Center. Discussed further below are early exhibitions of Holocaust art such as Charlotte Salomon's work in Amsterdam in 1961 and Tel Aviv in 1962, and the art from the Terezín camp-ghetto in London in 1964. The Terezín Memorial collection of art was made mostly through donation after the museum first opened in May 1949. In 1960, Terezín hired a professional staff, and an inventory of the collection was undertaken at that time. For a description of the museum and memorial's holdings of this material, see Costanza 1982, pp. 154–62.

86. Ziva Amishai-Maisels, *Depiction and Interpretation: The Influence of the Holocaust on the Visual Arts* (Oxford, 1993), pp. 3–6; see also Costanza 1982, particularly quoting artist Alexander Bogen, p. xviii.

87. Sujo 2001, pp. 55–57.

88. An estimated 13,500 children of the 15,000 imprisoned at Terezín were deported and murdered at death camps. The Prague museum includes some 4,387 works by children at the Terezín ghetto-camp, and 2,922 works by adults.

89. Gerald Green, *The Artists of Terezín* (New York, 1969); Sujo 2001, pp. 48–61; Costanza 1982. Karl Fleischmann, in the medical division of Terezín, was a trained artist and made a number of drawings and wrote a number of poems about the camp that survive. He was deported to Auschwitz in 1944 and murdered. For a more extensive list of artists active at Terezín, see Sujo 2001, pp. 57–58.

90. Green 1969, pp. 1–2, 112–25. Fritta contracted dysentery and died days after arriving at Auschwitz; Ungar died a few months after liberation, from complications from his injuries at Terezín and the diseases he contracted at Buchenwald.

91. Costanza 1981, pp. 26–28.

92. This included nearly 200 drawings by Fritta. Large holdings of the Terezín works are held by the Jewish Museum in Prague and the Terezín memorial collection (Pamatnik, Terezín), which Haas donated, and approximately 100 are in the collection of his son, Thomas Fritta-Haas, on long-term loan to the Jewish Museum Berlin.

93. Leo Haas, *12 puvodnich litografii z nemeckych koncentracnich taboru* (*12 Original Lithographs of German Concentration Camps*, Prague, 1947), 6 pages, 12 plates. While 5,000 copies of the series were issued, it was probably not widely circulated in the U.S. and Western Europe. Only five copies are listed in WorldCat, "the world's largest network" of libraries, which includes American and major Western European research libraries; of those five, some were likely acquired recently.

94. Darcy Buerkle and Mary Felstiner, notes and translation of Salomon's "Letter to Amadeus Daberlohn" [Alfred Wolfsohn], with confession, in Judith C. E. Belinfante and Evelyn Benesch, *Charlotte Salomon: Life? or Theatre?* (New York, 2017), pp. 799, 805, 809. Information about the poisoning was made public only in 2012.

95. *Charlotte Salomon* (exh. cat.), Museum Fodor (Amsterdam, 1961); *Charlotte Salomon* (exh. cat.), Muze'on Tel Aviv (Tel Aviv, 1962); Emil Straus and Paul Tillich, *Charlotte Salomon, ein Tagebuch in Bildern, 1917–1943* (Hamburg, 1963); *Charlotte: A Diary in Pictures* (New York and London, 1963). In addition, Carlo Levi published *Charlotte, diario in figure di Charlotte Salomon, 1917–1943* (Milan, 1963). Salomon's parents donated her art to the Jewish Historical Museum, Amsterdam, in 1971.

96. Henri Pieck, *Buchenwald: Reproducties naar zijn teekeningen uit het concentratiekamp* (*Buchenwald: Reproductions of His Drawings from the Concentration Camp*), with foreword by R. P. Cleveringa (The Hague, 1945), which includes 24 camp drawings; and *Zeven origineele kleuren-litho's van beelden uit het concentratiekamp Buchenwald* (*Seven Original Color Lithographs of Images from Buchenwald Concentration Camp*) (The Hague, 1945).

97. Jewish prisoners are depicted in just two of Pieck's published drawings, identified by the titles of the works and one Star of David.

98. Léon Delarbre, *Dora, Auschwitz, Buchenwald, Bergen-Belsen, croquis clandestins* [clandestine sketches] (Paris, 1945). The book reproduces 44 of Delarbre's camp drawings.

99. Boris Taslitzky, *111 dessins faits à Buchenwald 1944–1945* (*111 Drawings Made at Buchenwald, 1944–1945*), preface by Julien Cain (Paris, 1946). Many of these drawings are now in the Museum of National Resistance of Champigny-sur-Marne. Also in 1946, Taslitzky exhibited three paintings he made after liberation, inspired by the camps, at Galerie La Gentilhommiere, Paris, in a show called *Testimony*. Taslitzky, a secular, assimilated Jew living in Paris, was the son of Russian Jewish émigrés. His father died in World War I fighting for the French. His mother was murdered at Auschwitz. During his imprisonment at the concentration camp Saint Sulpice-La-Pointe in 1944, he painted large political frescoes of resistance, many of which survive (in situ).

100. Taslitzky 1946, nos. 6, 9, 75, 79. The artist gave more direct attention to Roma at the camp, in terms of detailed studies and number of drawings.

101. Cain (1887–1974) discussed Taslitzky in line with Delacroix, Millet, Manet, and David, and also compared him to Goya and his savage truth-telling prints. He described the crowd from which Taslitzky drew, noting that many nationalities were present at the camp, as well as politicals and non-politicals and "some worrisome gypsy children." Cain 1946, p. 7.

102. The Vichy government removed Cain from his position as administrator general of the Bibliothèque Nationale because he was Jewish, a high-ranking Freemason, and also because he supported the former prime minister, Paul Reynaud, who wished to fight collaboration, rather than Pétain; Barbara Will, *Unlikely Collaboration: Gertrude Stein, Bernard Faÿ, and the Vichy Dilemma* (New York, 2011), pp. 243–44n10. Taslitzky's mother, however, was deported as a Jew, following the Vel d'Hiv mass roundup in Paris in the summer of 1942. She was murdered at Auschwitz.

103. Agnieszka Sieradzka, *The Sketchbook from Auschwitz; Szkicownik Z Auschwitz* (Oświęcim, Poland, 2011). The publication and exhibition were part of the Polish museum's efforts to make its archive more accessible.

104. See holdings of the United States Holocaust Memorial Museum, Washington, D.C., with 329 of Olomucki's works.

105. Sujo 2001, pp. 80–81 on this commission in particular, and pp. 72–81 on Auschwitz art. One of the earliest art exhibitions of the Auschwitz material was *In Memory of Human Tragedy* (exh. cat.), Jewish Museum in Prague (Oświęcim, Poland, 1978); see also, David Mickenberg et al., *The Last Expression: Art and Auschwitz* (exh. cat.), Block Museum of Art, David Museum, Brooklyn Museum of Art (Evanston, Ill., 2003). Many of Siwek's and Koscielniak's works are on display at the museum today. Some of the images serve more as propaganda than expressions of their personal experiences.

106. Yehuda Bacon, interview by Yad Vashem, accessed January 1, 2020, https://www.yadvashem.org/articles/interviews/yehuda-bacon.html. Everything Bacon brought to Auschwitz from Terezín was destroyed. David Olère is another noted artist of witness art; he produced drawings after the war about his experiences of Auschwitz and Mauthausen.

107. Batya Brutin, "The Pictorial Testimony during the Eichmann Trial in Jerusalem in 1961–1962," in *Post-Holocaust Studies in a Modern Context* (2019), pp. 44–69. Bacon's drawings were also presented as evidence at the Frankfurt Auschwitz trials in 1964, and, in 1996, in the failed lawsuit brought by Holocaust denier David Irving against Penguin Books and Deborah Lipstadt. The only member of his family to survive, Bacon emigrated to Israel and reported being greeted with silence when speaking too directly about his experiences after the war until the Eichmann trial; see also Yehuda Bacon, interview by Yad Vashem. His camp drawings were primarily private and remain mostly in his own collection, although he has donated some, including to the Ghetto Fighters' House museum. Alexander Bogen, Samuel Bak, and Alfred Kantor, among others, also kept their drawings to themselves in the early years. Before he died in 2010, Bogen gave 37 drawings depicting his activities as a Jewish partisan during the war to Yad Vashem.

108. Olivia Maccioni, Clare Manias, and Treva Walsh, "A Testament to the Artist: Restoring Alfred Kantor's Sketchbook and Portfolio," Museum of Jewish Heritage, June 5, 2019, https://mjhnyc.org/blog/restoring-alfred-kantors-sketchbook-and-portfolio/; see also Kantor and Wykert 1971. Some of Kantor's drawings from Terezín survive, but he had to destroy all of his early work from Auschwitz and most from Schwarzheide. His 1945 sketchbook was given by the artist to the Museum of Jewish Heritage, New York.

109. See also Stephen Feinstein, ed., *Witness and Legacy: Contemporary Art about the Holocaust* (exh. cat.), Minnesota Museum of American Art (Minneapolis, 1995), which features a number of later works by Holocaust survivors, such as Judith Goldstein, Netty Schwartz Vanderpol, and Edith Altman.

110. Yehudit Shendar, *An Arduous Road: Samuel Bak* (exh. cat.), Yad Vashem (Jerusalem, 2007).

111. Levi 1976, in Levi 2015, vol. 1, pp. 167–78.

112. Judt 2005, p. 62.

113. For these statistics, see Judt 2005, pp. 13–32, 18, 166, 235.

114. The first of the "rubble film" genre was the 1946 German film *Die Mörder sind unter uns* (*Murderers among Us*), directed by Wolfgang Staudte. With the ruins of World War II as its backdrop, it examined Nazi crimes and postwar trauma. Its production was licensed by the Soviet sector. Roberto Rossellini's quintessential Neorealismo film, *Germania anno zero* (*Germany Year Zero*), was partly filmed in the ruins of Berlin in the summer of 1947 and released in 1948.

115. Roberto Rossellini, dir., *Germany Year Zero* (Italy, Germany, 1948; Criterion Collection, 2009), DVD. Recovery in Germany, while almost miraculous, was slow. In 1950, 17 million people in West Germany were still needy or homeless, and the last DP camp closed only in 1957 (Judt 2005, pp. 32, 235).

116. Judt 2005, pp. 26–32. Poland, which had lost one in five of its prewar population, wanted all German nationals expelled—some 7 million people. Eventually some 13 million Germans from various European countries would have to be resettled in West Germany. Some 5.5 million Soviet nationals were repatriated by 1953, many against their will.

117. Novick 1999, p. 68.

118. Judt 2005, p. 804.

119. United States Holocaust Memorial Museum, "The Aftermath of the Holocaust," accessed December 27, 2019, https://encyclopedia.ushmm.org/content/en/article/the-aftermath-of-the-holocaust. Some 440,000 DPs in total had immigrated to the U.S. by the early 1950s. President Truman's December 1945 directive to loosen immigration quotas permitted 41,000 DPs to immigrate to the U.S., which included approximately 28,000 Jews; the 1948 Displaced Persons Act passed by Congress provided for 400,000 American visas to DPs, with an estimated 68,000 Jewish immigrants coming to the U.S. by 1952; Truman ultimately pushed for the Partition Plan in Palestine in 1947, despite the State Department and Pentagon's opposition, and supported the foundation of the Jewish State of Israel in 1948 (Novick 1999, pp. 72, 81–82).

120. Judt 2005, p. 32.

121. Judt 2005, pp. 52–61. In 1951 in Bavaria, 94 percent of judges and prosecutors were ex-Nazis; see also Novick 1999, pp. 86–101. Novick examines how the rapid escalation of the Cold War realigned U.S. interests in Europe and marginalized the Holocaust. Efforts to assist DPs shifted to those fleeing communism.

122. Judt 2005, p. 808.

123. Judt 2008, p. 33.

124. Judt 2005, pp. 18–19, 165–66, 652, 824–25. One in 11 of prewar population was dead in the Soviet Union; 78,000 Red Army soldiers died in the three-week Battle of Berlin.

125. Snyder 2010, pp. vii–viii. Snyder estimates that the Nazis and Soviets murdered 14 million civilians and prisoners of war through policies of deliberate mass murder between 1933 and 1945 in Eastern Europe in a zone he designates "the bloodlands," which stretches from central Poland to eastern Russia, through Ukraine, Belarus, and the Baltic States.

126. It was only in 1989, for instance, that the Soviet government officially acknowledged the Katyn massacre of 1940, where more than 20,000 Poles were executed following the Soviet invasion of Poland. During the war, the Soviets blamed the Nazis for the slaughter.

127. Only 2.5 percent of Poland's prewar population of Jews survived the Holocaust.

128. Claude Lanzmann, dir., *Shoah* (France, 1985; Criterion Collection, 2013), DVD.

129. Poland's 1947 figure of 3 million ethnic Poles killed during WWII has been rejected by more thorough documentation. It largely depends on where the borders of the country are drawn, since Stalin seized Polish land for the Soviet Union after the war (now Ukraine), and whether one counts deaths of Ukrainians and Belarusians

in Poland during the war, or deaths under Soviet rule (following the Molotov-Ribbentrop Pact of August 1939). Snyder puts the figure of ethnic Poles killed closer to 1 million (Judt and Snyder 2012, p. 42). Many scholars suggest a figure closer to 1.8 or 1.9 million. Polish intelligentsia, Catholic clergy, and military officers were also targeted, arrested as political prisoners or executed. An estimated 50,000 Polish children were kidnapped to be "Germanized," and those failing to meet Aryan criteria were sent to orphanages or extermination camps or forced into labor ("Non-Jewish Victims, Poles," United States Holocaust Memorial Museum, accessed February 15, 2020, https://www.ushmm.org/m/pdfs/2000926-Poles.pdf). Some 8 million foreign forced laborers were brought to Germany from Eastern Europe, mostly Slavs, from Poland, Ukraine, and Belarus; Snyder 2010, p. 244.

130. This same tactic was seen in the Soviet Union; the government acknowledged only Soviet victims at killing sites and camps, rather than Jewish victims in particular. In 1961, the publication of Vasily Grossman's novel *Life and Fate* was prohibited by the KGB for 250 years because it placed too much emphasis on the Nazi persecution of Jews (Sam Sacks, "Vasily Grossman: Loser, Saint," *New Yorker*, June 25, 2013). At the Babi Yar killing site, commemoration has evolved over the decades (see "About Project," Babyn Yar Holocaust Memorial Center, accessed April 8, 2020, http://babynyar.org/en/byhmc/about; and Linda Kinstler, "No Monument Stands over Babi Yar," *Atlantic*, September 30, 2016). The 1966 and 1974 erected memorials commemorated the "citizens of Kyiv." In 1991, on the 50-year anniversary of the massacre, a separate memorial honoring the Jewish victims was approved by the newly independent Ukrainian government. This would be the first of a number of markers erected at the site to memorialize the different victims murdered by the Nazis at the site. In 2016, on the 75th anniversary of the massacre, a government commission was formed to create a new memorial, museum, education, and research center at the site, and "to pay tribute to the victims, to tell the story of their lives and to explain the relationship between Jews and non-Jews in Kyiv and Ukraine" and "to show the danger of totalitarian, extremist nationalist and racist ideologies, and especially to show how it all began. And in contrast, to celebrate cultural, ethnic, religious and social differences," among other things. Construction will be completed in 2025–26.

131. Pollock and Silverman 2011, pp. 20–21; Lindeperg 2014, p. 11.

132. Annette Wieviorka, *Deportation et genocide: Entre la memoire et l'oubli* (Paris, 1992), p. 21. Pollock and Silverman 2011, p. 20, report a higher number of political deportees from occupied France, 115,000, with only 35 percent returning, that is, 40,250 people. Most of France's Jewish population was foreign-born at the start of WWII, thus refugees.

133. Judt 2005, p. 805.

134. Judt 2005, p. 41.

135. Maurin Picard, "200,000 enfants de soldats allemands seraient nés en France," *Le Figaro*, November 30, 2009; Josiane Kruger, *Née d'amours interdites: ma mère était française, mon père, soldat allemand* (Paris, 2008).

136. Philippe Frétigné and Gérard Leray, *La tondue, 1944–1947* (Paris, 2018); Judt 2005, pp. 42–43.

137. "The French Get Back Their Freedom," *Life*, September 4, 1944, p. 21.

138. Frétigné and Leray 2018.

139. Judt 2005, pp. 41–62.

140. Judt points out that during the occupation of France, a country of 35 million people, a mere 7,500 German administrators and civil and military police were deployed to run the country, as the French police and administrative staff could be relied on to administer Nazi policies (Judt 2005, p. 39). Similar local collaboration was found in Norway, the Netherlands, and Belgium.

141. Judt 2005, p. 808. Judt notes that what Henry Rousso called "Vichy Syndrome" to describe this forgetting happened across Europe.

142. Judt 2005, p. 33. Judt points out that the Nazis' move to send young Frenchmen to Germany as forced laborers at the end of the war led to an increase in the Resistance, which rose at that time to exceed the number of French collaborators.

143. Stéphane Simonnet, *Atlas de la libération de la France: 6 juin 1944–8 mai 1945: des débarquements aux villes libérées* (Paris, 2004), p. 68. Simonnet estimates that 43,000 members of French Resistance died in action, and 27,000 died in concentration camps as political deportees; Pollock and Silverman (2011, p. 20) estimate the deaths of French Resistance fighters in camps alone as 74,750. This number may include Jewish deportees who were French citizens, as the French government, as noted, counted casualties this way after the war.

144. It was subsequently published in English as *The Other Kingdom* (New York, 1947) and later in the U.K. titled *A World Apart* (London, 1951).

145. Pollock and Silverman 2011, p. 21.

146. *Le Père tranquille* (*The Quiet Father*) was released in the U.S. as *Mr. Orchid*. See also Philip Watts, "Of Heroes and Traitors: Two Early Films by René Clément," in *Rhine Crossings: France and Germany in Love and War*, eds. Aminia M. Brueggemann and Peter Schulman (Albany, N.Y., 2005), pp. 211–27, which examines *Bataille du rail* and *Les Maudits* (*The Damned*) of 1947.

147. Organized by the Francs-Tireurs et Partisans Français, the exhibition had over 450 works by Resistance members (including many amateur artists), as well as major and minor artists. Also on display were 100 children's drawings.

148. Martin Schieder, "Picasso libre," in *Les Arts à Paris après la libération. Temps et temporalités* (Heidelberg, 2019), p. 115; and Judt 2005, p. 822. The French title of Louis Aragon's poem is "Je vous salue ma France."

149. James E. Young, *The Art of Memory: Holocaust Memorials in History* (exh. cat.), Jewish Museum (New York, 1995), p. 25.

150. Novick 1999, pp. 104, 114, 138.

151. Hannah Arendt, *Essays in Understanding* (New York, 1945), p. 134.

152. For further discussion of this vein of artistic expression in 1940s and 1950s America and Europe, see Peter Selz, *New Images of Man* (exh. cat.), MoMA (New York, 1959), featuring 104 works by 23 artists.

153. Amishai-Maisels, in her monumental examination of the influence of the Holocaust on the visual arts, sees the Holocaust in many works of art where it seems unlikely to have been a consideration, particularly in the 1930s to 1950s, citing such work by Otto Dix, Paul Klee, Picasso, George Grosz, César Baldaccini, Jacques Lipchitz, and Leonard Baskin, among others. Some of these instances are discussed specifically below. In her deep focus on the Holocaust and synthesis of a vast number of artists and works—with 659 works illustrated—the writer overlooks other cultural and political influences in the postwar period, and fails to appreciate the belated understanding of the scale and tragedy of the Holocaust across the world. Her analysis of art executed during the war and after is informed retrospectively by attitudes about the Holocaust in the 1990s. This is seen throughout the book, but see especially, Amishai-Maisels 1993, pp. 28–29, 67–68, 83–86, 123–27. Ori Soltes makes this assumption throughout his book with regard to works from the 1940s and 1950s, including with Golub's *Charnel House*, 1946, and later *Burnt Man* (1960), which is more frequently associated with the Vietnam War, and with Lipchitz's *Prometheus Strangling the Vulture* (1943), among others. For this see Ori Soltes, *Fixing the World: Jewish American Painters in the Twentieth Century* (London, 2003), pp. 15–17, 78–81.

154. Leonard Baskin, *Leonard Baskin: Six New Woodcuts and Nine New Etchings* (Rockport, Maine, 1998); see also Amishai-Maisels 1993, pp. 28–31, 66, 83–86.

155. The speculative link of *Charnel House* to the Nazi camps dates beyond the last 30 years to just after its completion; see Christian Zervos, *Exhibition of Paintings by Picasso and Matisse* (exh. cat.), December 1945, Victoria and Albert Museum (London, 1945), unpaginated; Alfred H. Barr, *Fifty Years of Picasso* (exh. cat.), MoMA (New York, 1946), p. 250; Amishai-Maisels 1993, pp. 57–61, 391; Anne Baldassari, ed., *Picasso, Dora Maar: Il faisait tellement noir* (exh. cat.), Musée Picasso (Paris, 2006), p. 250; and Schieder 2019, pp. 115–16. Significantly, Zervos's and Barr's early connection of *Charnel House* to "German extermination camps" and "Buchenwald, Dachau, and Belsen" (respectively) makes no mentions of Jewish victims or the Holocaust. The date of the painting, begun in 1944 and completed between February and May 1945, further complicates the connection to the Holocaust, as most of the camp liberations were in April of 1945. The Soviets liberated Majdanek in July 1944 and Auschwitz in January 1945, but images of those camps were slow to come to Western Europe. Amishai-Maisels (1993, pp. 391–92n70) tries to work around the fact that Picasso began and completed the painting not only before the Western Allies liberated the Nazi camps, but also before there was any widespread understanding of the Nazis' attempted genocide of the Jewish people.

156. Amishai-Maisels 1993, pp. 59–60. Amishai-Maisels rather improbably interprets the still life in *Charnel House* as serving three functions for Picasso: imbuing the work with hope, serving as a personal symbol of the art he made in confinement during the war, and symbolizing the attempt of Germans and Jews to carry on life amid everyday slaughter.

157. Lynda Morris, *Picasso: Peace and Freedom* (exh. cat.), Tate Liverpool (London, 2010), p. 70. Morris notes that the murder of the Spanish Republican family had been the subject of a contemporary documentary film Picasso may have seen.

158. Amishai-Maisels (1993, pp. 57–58), among others, likely overstates Picasso's identification with Jewish people during the war and sympathies toward their plight, beyond connecting *Charnel House* to the Holocaust. She cites Picasso's statement, "All victims of the Nazis are my friends," which seems more likely to reflect his sympathies with the Spanish people and his alliance with the French Resistance. She also notes Picasso's mourning the loss of his Jewish friend Max Jacob, who died at the Drancy deportation camp near Paris. The artist had stood as *godfather* when Jacob was *baptized* in 1915 following his adult conversion to Catholicism (my italics); for other sources, see Amishai-Maisels 1993, pp. 391–92nn59, 60, 61, 71. Picasso, who remained in Paris during the Nazi occupation, had generally stayed clear of overt political statements in his art until Paris was liberated, although he had joined the Communist Party in 1944 to support his friends in the Resistance.

159. Leonard Baskin later considered Lebrun's works to be about the Holocaust (see discussion below), but they seem to represent all victims of Nazi crimes rather than Jewish victims in particular. The Israeli artist Naftali Bezem, who escaped Nazi Germany as a teen but whose parents were murdered at Auschwitz, also engaged early with the subject of the extermination camps and Nazi mass shootings, in the 1950s (Amishai-Maisels 1993, pp. 86–87, figs. 223–224). His 1953–54 painting *Mass Grave* depicts the murder of his family, and includes specific details of his father's Jewish identity. This work, however, was personal in nature and remained in the artist's collection in 1993. It was only after the Eichmann trial that Bezem felt compelled to work on the subject more, although in a less personal way, schematizing figures and employing symbolic subject matter, such as the Pietà.

160. Matthew Baigell, *Jewish-American Artists and the Holocaust* (New Brunswick, N.J., 1997), pp. 35–37.

161. Ben-Zion, *De Profundis Gouaches* (exh. cat.), Bertha Schaefer Gallery (New York, December 1946), Archives of American Art, roll N69-122, frame 265; see also Baigell 1997, p. 36.

162. Baigell 1997, pp. 18–19. Amishai-Maisels also makes note (1993, pp. 28–31, 66, 83–86) of the rarity of explicit Holocaust imagery in the 1950s and documents Baskin and others refuting its influence on their works in these years. But then, in her analysis of their work in the 1950s, she unconvincingly sees the Holocaust as ever present, in each image, whether inserted unconsciously, with substitute themes, or implicitly, from Baskin's *Dead Worker* (1949) to Lipchitz's works in the 1940s, such as his "Rescue" bronzes (1945, 1947) and later version of *Exile's Path*.

163. Selz 1959, p. 76. Golub's extended quote is, "Man is seen as having undergone a holocaust or facing annihilation or mutation. The ambiguities of these huge forms indicate the stress of their vulnerability versus their capacities for endurance." His use of "holocaust" with a small *h* at this time can refer both to nuclear holocaust or Nazi extermination; see discussion of postwar terminology in note 249 below. Golub's later work focused specifically on the Vietnam War.

164. Ben Shahn, "The Biography of Painting," in *The Shape of Content* (New York, 1957), p. 48.

165. Amishai-Maisels 1993, p. 78.

166. Baigell 1997, pp. 34–35. Baigell notes that Shahn's references tend to be "biblical rather than contemporary," and "Shahn, like other artists, reidentified with Judaism after the full extent of the Holocaust became known." Baigell also cites Amishai-Maisels 1993. As discussed further below, many Jewish artists and writers began to examine the Holocaust in their work in the 1960s, as well as their Jewish identity and heritage, when the world came to a deeper understanding of the tragedy.

167. Baigell 1997, pp. 18–19.

168. Baskin 1998. Leonard Baskin, despite assumptions otherwise, did not delve into the subject until the 1990s, with the Holocaust Memorial in Ann Arbor, Michigan (1994), and a series of Holocaust woodcuts (1996–98). In these works he represented the Holocaust symbolically as single figures, anguished, or ghoulish and terrifying, like *Specially Ordained Slaughter of Children* (1998). In his artist's statement about these prints, Baskin wrote, "Nearly forty years ago, the contemporary artist I admired above all others, Rico Lebrun, a friend and mentor, said to me, 'You must deal with the holocaust, it is the crucial theme of the century.' But I could not discover the plastic means or graphic modality that would allow my forging meaningful holocaust works." Incorporating Yiddish proverbs and Hebrew texts into the prints also helped empower him to take on the subject.

169. Theodor Adorno, "Kulturkritik und Gesellschaft" ("Cultural Criticism and Society"), 1949 essay published in *Soziologische Forschung in unserer Zeit. Leopold von Wiese zum 75. Geburtstag*, ed. Karl Gustav Specht (Cologne, 1951), pp. 228–40.

170. Adorno's quotation continues: "This is the drastic guilt of him who was spared. By way of atonement he will be plagued by dreams such as that he is no longer living at all, that he was sent to the ovens in 1944 and his whole existence since has been imaginary, an emanation of the insane wish of a man killed twenty years earlier." Theodor Adorno, *Negative Dialektik* (Frankfurt, 1966; *Negative Dialectics*, London, 1990), p. 358.

171. See, for instance, *Frankfurter Allgemeine*, July 5, 1956, as cited by Lindeperg 2014, p. 239.

172. François Truffaut, *Arts*, February 22, 1956.

173. There are numerous studies of *Night and Fog*, examining its reception, criticisms ("unjewishing the Holocaust"), and contextualizing its approach, including Ewout van der Knaap, ed., *Uncovering the Holocaust: The International Reception of Night and Fog* (London, 2006), especially van der Knaap, "The Construction of Memory in *Nuit et Brouillard*," pp. 7–34; and Warren Lubline, "The Trajectory of *Night and Fog* in the USA," pp. 149–64; and Pollock and Silverman 2011. For a comprehensive examination of the genesis, production, and legacy of the film, see Lindeperg 2014.

174. On December 7, 1941, Hitler issued the secret Nacht und Nebel (Night and Fog) decree ordering the arrest of members of the Resistance and political activists in Nazi-occupied Western Europe. Those arrested would vanish at night, with no report to their families, then be interrogated, tortured, and tried in secret courts. Possible outcomes were execution, imprisonment, or deportation to concentration camps.

175. The exhibition took place at the Musée Pédagogique (National Teaching Institute) in Paris.

176. The Réseau du Souvenir and Comité d'Histoire de la Deuxième Guerre Mondiale (Committee for the History of the Second World War) were the two most important and influential backers of many investors and international organizations involved in the project. They brought in film producer Anatole Dauman of Argos Films, who, in turn, commissioned Alain Resnais to direct the film and poet Jean Cayrol to write the narration; Lindeperg 2014, pp. 27–38.

177. Olga Wormser and Henri Michel, *Tragédie de la déportation 1940–1945: Témoignages de survivants des camps de concentration allemands* (Paris, 1954).

178. Lindeperg's book resuscitates the key contributions of Olga Wormser and Henri Michel to the production of *Night and Fog*, which went well beyond their film credit as historical advisers. They conceived of the film project, undertook all the research, found and selected the wartime and camp footage, developed the narrative structure (which mirrored their exhibition), scouted the film locations, and worked on the documentary from start to finish. Lindeperg takes a close look at Wormser, a pioneering historian who dedicated herself to researching the Nazi camps in the early postwar years, and examines how Wormser focused on French deportees rather than the plight of the Jews, despite being Jewish. (This fact Wormser never mentioned in her unfinished memoir or discussions of her career.) Wormser traveled to Bergen-Belsen in 1945 as part of an official French delegation seeking to document the fate of the French prisoners. When she went to Auschwitz-Birkenau in 1946, she continued to focus on tracking down the names of deported French citizens. The word "Jew" appears only once in her extensive account of her visit to this camp; Lindeperg 2014, pp. 2, 8–11, 28–35, passim.

179. See van der Knaap 2006, pp. 18–19, 33; Lubline 2006, pp. 152–57; Lindeperg 2014, pp. 11–12; and Pollock and Silverman 2011, pp. 8–37. For discussion of the emphasis in the U.S. on

universalism with regard to the Holocaust, see Novick 1999, pp. 85–88, 112–16. Novick discusses the role that the threat of the Cold War played in shaping conversation around the Holocaust and that of the ebullient mood of postwar America in muting it.

180. Alain Resnais interview in *L'Express*, January 31, 1956, in Lindeperg 2014, p. 125. Other conflicts, such as the Vietnam War, would also be addressed in this way, by artists and writers. Lubline (2006, pp. 153–54) notes that *Night and Fog* would be put to use in America by protesters of the Vietnam War, who organized screenings for large audiences in 1967.

181. Rousset, a Communist, was an anti-Stalinist Trotskyite and one of the first French Communists to critique the Soviet dictator and his abuse of power outspokenly. The Hungarian-born journalist and novelist Arthur Koestler, author of *Darkness at Noon* (London, 1940), who fled France following Germany's invasion, is another. Hannah Arendt, "The Concentration Camps," *Partisan Review*, vol. 15 (1948), pp. 743–63; see also Arendt's "Social Science Techniques and the Study of Concentration Camps," *Jewish Social Studies*, vol. 12 (January 1950), pp. 49–64.

182. Pollock and Silverman 2011, pp. 18–32, see especially p. 27.

183. Novick 1999, pp. 85–88; Judt 2005, pp. 56–62, 125.

184. Judt and Snyder 2012, pp. 132, 220–30.

185. Novick 1999, p. 87.

186. Lindeperg 2014, p. 206; for U.S. distribution and reception, see Lubline 2006, pp. 149–52.

187. Lindeperg 2014, pp. 222–30. The film was first screened in Israel in 1960, where it was both praised and critiqued. At the Eichmann trial in 1961, some 15 minutes of the one hour granted to the prosecution for screening Nazi atrocity footage was dedicated to *Night and Fog*. The prosecutor, Gideon Hausner, argued that the film helped make the facts presented in the trial documents and survivor testimonies "more alive and tangible."

188. Lindeperg 2014, pp. 141–55.

189. Lindeperg 2014, pp. 156–72. The film, in the end, was shown at Cannes but could not compete for the Palme d'Or prize. A few years after its release, there were also some early objections to the self-consciously aesthetic style of the film, in the wake of the scandal surrounding Gillo Pontecorvo's 1959 feature film *Kapò*. *Kapò* was heavily criticized by French director and critic Jacques Rivette for a tracking shot that captures the electrocution of a prisoner. Rivette describes the Italian Jewish filmmaker's approach as aestheticizing atrocity. This sparked a debate about the representation of the Holocaust in film that continues today. For further discussion, see Lindeperg 2014, pp. 247–49, and Lubline 2006, pp. 161–64.

190. Robert Michael, "The Holocaust in *Night and Fog*," *Cineaste* (December 1984), pp. 36–37.

191. Van der Knaap 2006, p. 33; see also Lubline 2006.

192. Novick 1999, pp. 120, and 3–6, with his reading of Maurice Halbwachs's collective memory.

193. Cynthia Ozick, "Who Owns Anne Frank?" *New Yorker*, October 7, 1997, p. 78.

194. The full Dutch title, *Het achterhuis, dagboekbrieven 14 Juni 1942–1 Augustus 1944*, is translated either as "The Secret Annex," or "The House Behind, Diary Entries, June 14, 1942–August 1, 1944." It was published by Uitgeverij Contact in Amsterdam, 1947.

195. Eric Colleary, "Anne Frank and the Archive," *Ransom Center Magazine*, October 6, 2015. Knopf's 1950 rejection letter described the book as "very dull reading. The style, occasionally effusive, never compelling, is not at all distinguished. The perceptions, naturally childish, are never sparked by originality. It is not in any way a literary achievement." It goes on to say that the subject is no longer timely, as it would have been five years earlier. The letter is now at the Harry Ransom Center at the University of Texas, Austin.

196. Shandler 1999, pp. 62–64. The telecast was written by Morton Wishengrad for the Jewish Theological Seminary. The show aired as part of a Sunday-night series seeking an ecumenical message.

197. Ozick 1997, p. 78.

198. Anne Frank, *Anne Frank, The Diary of a Young Girl, The Definitive Edition*, eds. Otto Frank and Mirjam Pressler (New York, 1995), pp. 252, 258.

199. Ozick 1997, p. 82.

200. Shandler 1999, pp. 62–64.

201. For America's postwar upbeat mood, see Novick 1999, pp. 112–14.

202. Ozick 1997, p. 85; Novick 1999, p. 118.

203. Ozick, 1997, pp. 84–87. Ozick also examines the role of Lillian Hellman in reshaping the narrative for the stage. Meyer Levin, who had worked with Otto Frank in securing an English-language publisher, wrote his own adaptation of the diary for the stage, with the understanding that he was Frank's chosen playwright. He sued Otto Frank when his script was rejected, and complained loudly in the press that Anne's story had been "de-Judaized" by the Kanin/Hackett play; for a discussion of scholarship in recent years arguing, instead, that Anne's Jewish identity was only peripheral (Robert Alter) or so limited as to be grounds to expel the diary from the canon of celebrated Holocaust texts (Lawrence Langer), see Novick 1999, pp. 117–20.

204. Of late, see, for example, Griselda Pollock, *Charlotte Salomon and the Theatre of Memory* (New Haven, Conn., 2018); Judith Belinfante et al., *Charlotte Salomon, Life? Or Theatre?: A Selection of 450 Gouaches* (Cologne, 2017); the international best-selling novel inspired by Salomon's life, David Foenkinos, *Charlotte* (Edinburgh, 2018); Astrid Schmetterling, *Charlotte Salomon: Bilder eines Lebens* (Berlin, 2001; 2017); Judith Herzberg et al., *Charlotte Salomon: leven? of theater?* (Amsterdam, 2015); Toni Bentley, "The Obsessive Art and Confession of Charlotte Salomon," *New Yorker*, July 15, 2017; Frédéric Martin and Anne Hélène Hoog, *Vie? ou Théâtre?* (Paris, 2015; English translation, New York, 2017), among many others.

205. See Shandler 1999, pp. 44–79, who traces the appearance of sporadic, important television programs in the 1950s that address the Holocaust or include Jewish characters.

206. Novick (1999, pp. 112–14) argues that this television program downplayed the Jewish story, but Germany's anti-Jewish racial laws were a central theme, shown in the flashbacks to the 1938 pogroms and at the heart of the testimony of one of the main witnesses. Additionally, Jewish death statistics in the camps were noted in the show's voiceover during the screening of the footage in the court but were absent from the original U.S. Army narration.

207. Shandler 1999, pp. 64–69.

208. Gaby Weber, *Daimler-Benz und die Argentinien-Connection* (Berlin, 2004), p. 91.

209. Uki Goñi, *The Real Odessa: Smuggling the Nazis to Perón's Argentina* (London, 2002).

210. Bettina Stangneth, *Eichmann before Jerusalem* (New York, 2014), pp. 108–9, 164. Eichmann's first job in Argentina was working as a government contractor developing a hydroelectric plant in Tucumán for a Perón-sponsored organization that employed numerous German immigrants. The famous photos of Eichmann wearing a poncho, or riding on horseback, date from this period, when he was surveying land in the hills and mountains of Tucumán province in 1952. Those photos are sometimes erroneously identified as relating to Eichmann's rumored work as a gaucho in Paraguay or Brazil in 1955.

211. Eichmann's oldest son, Klaus Eichmann, was a schoolmate of Silvia Hermann, the daughter of Lothar Hermann, a German Jewish émigré and Dachau camp survivor, who had immigrated to Buenos Aires in 1938. Lothar Hermann tipped off the German Jewish prosecutor Fritz Bauer in Frankfurt, a report Bauer confirmed with an unnamed second source. Bauer did not trust West German officials, as there were many former Nazis flourishing in public service, despite the Allies' denazification efforts. Bauer hoped ultimately to extradite Eichmann to West Germany but thought Israel would more likely act on the intelligence information and bring Eichmann to justice. Bauer contacted Mossad in 1957. It took some years for Israel to confirm Eichmann's identity and garner support for the operation to capture him. Eichmann's arrest led to subsequent Nazi trials in West Germany, prosecuted by Bauer in Frankfurt, albeit with more lenient sentences. For an in-depth account of the Eichmann hunt by multiple entities in the 1950s, including Israel, Bauer, the CIA, Tuviah Friedman, and Simon Wiesenthal, see Stangneth 2014. The Nazi hunter and Holocaust survivor Wiesenthal exaggerated his role in the capture of Eichmann, which he recounted in two books, *Ich jagte Eichmann* (*I Hunted Eichmann*, Gütersloh, Germany, 1961) and *The Murderers among Us* (New York, 1967). The books made Wiesenthal famous and drew attention to his efforts to track down and prosecute Nazi criminals. For differing accounts of Wiesenthal's role, see Lipstadt 2011, pp. 5–8, and Stangneth 2014, pp. 127–46.

212. Eichmann's extensive archive in Argentina has been recently studied by Stangneth (2014).

The publication of Eichmann's abridged memoir appeared in *Der Stern*, July 1960, and in *Life* as a two-part story, "Eichmann's Story Part I: I Transported Them . . . to the Butcher," and "Eichmann's Own Story Part II: To Sum It All Up, I Regret Nothing," *Life*, November 28, 1960, and December 5, 1960.

213. Juan de Onis, "Argentina Cools to Former Nazis," *New York Times*, June 19, 1960, p. 10, who cites specifically the Argentine papers *La Prensa* and *La Razon* as newly critical of the Nazi presence in the country. De Onis also discusses the Mengele case specifically, and the failure of Argentina to extradite him to West Germany.

214. Mengele, called the Angel of Death for his role in the Auschwitz selections for the gas chambers and his cruel, fatal "medical" experiments on prisoners, lived in Argentina under his own name in the 1950s. He worked openly for his family's international business selling farm machinery.

215. Telford Taylor, "Large Questions in the Eichmann Case," *New York Times Magazine*, January 22, 1961, p. 11.

216. Hannah Arendt, *Eichmann in Jerusalem: A Report on the Banality of Evil* (New York, 1963; all citations refer to the 2006 edition), p. 264.

217. George Salomon, "America's Response," *The American Jewish Year Book*, vol. 63 (1962), pp. 85–103; see especially p. 101, which reports Gallup poll results stating that 50 percent felt Israel was the appropriate place to try Eichmann, 36 percent favored an international court, 71 percent thought it was positive to be reminded of Nazi atrocities, and 71 percent thought Eichmann had a fair trial.

218. Ben-Gurion's response to the question, "What do you hope to achieve by bringing Eichmann to trial?" *New York Times*, December 18, 1960.

219. Deborah Lipstadt, *The Eichmann Trial* (New York, 2011), pp. 192–93. The italics are Lipstadt's.

220. *Jewish Telegraphic Agency Daily News Bulletin*, vol. 28, no. 97, May 19, 1961.

221. Shandler 1999, pp. 89–93, 278n28; Tom Segev, *The Seventh Million: The Israelis and the Holocaust*, trans. Haim Waltzman (New York, 1991), pp. 350–51; *Jewish Telegraphic Agency Daily News Bulletin*, vol. 28, no. 97, May 19, 1961.

222. Shandler 1999, pp. 89–93, 278n28.

223. Shandler 1999, pp. 114–27; E. Z. Dimitman, "How Television Is Watching the Eichmann Trial," *TV Guide*, May 6–12, 1961, pp. A2–A3; and also daily television guides in the *New York Times* and the *Des Moines Register*, for instance, listing half-hour, hour-long, and 90-minute programs daily, on many channels, and in prime time. Special programs, such as "Verdict for Tomorrow: Summary of the Adolf Eichmann Trial," aired on December 11, 1961, and "The Trial of Adolf Eichmann," in August 1961. The latter drew high ratings, 68 percent of the total television audience, according to one report (John Shanley, "TV: Two Documentaries. 'Berlin Acts of War?' and 'The Trial of Adolf Eichmann' Break Summer Lull," *New York Times*, August 16, 1961).

224. Segev 1991, pp. 350–51.

225. Hannah Arendt's five-part series on the Eichmann trial appeared in the *New Yorker* between February 8 and March 16, 1963, and within months as a book, *Eichmann in Jerusalem: A Report on the Banality of Evil* (New York). From the start, Arendt's controversial book and its characterization of Eichmann and criticism of the cooperation of the *Judenräten* (Jewish Councils), albeit forced, with the Nazis, among many other points, sparked an international furor that made her a pariah, or for a time "American Jewish Public Enemy Number One" (Novick 1999, p. 134). Much of the criticism has dissipated in the intervening decades, as in, e.g., Tony Judt, "At Home in This Century," *New York Review of Books*, vol. 42, April 6, 1995, pp. 9–14; and Amos Elon, "The Excommunication of Hannah Arendt," Introduction, Penguin Edition, in *Eichmann in Jerusalem* (New York, 2006). Nonetheless, criticisms of Arendt's book endure. Recently Bettina Stangneth (2014, pp. xvi–xxi passim) took aim at Arendt's characterization of Eichmann as a shallow, obeying, thoughtless bureaucrat, portraying quite a different view of the accused.

226. Lipstadt 2011, p. 56.

227. Arendt 1963, 2006 ed., pp. 25–27. These were prison evaluations. Arendt wrote that another of the psychiatrists "had found that Eichmann's whole psychological outlook, including his relationship with his wife and children, his mother and father, his brothers and sisters and friends, was 'not only normal but most desirable.'—and finally the minister who paid regular visits to him in prison after the Supreme Court had finished hearing his appeal reassured everybody by declaring that Eichmann was 'a man with very positive ideas.'"

228. Stangneth 2014. Stangneth, in examining Eichmann's life in Argentina, with a careful review of thousands of pages of Eichmann interviews, many unpublished, critiques Arendt's characterization of Eichmann and argues, instead, that he was a murderous, megalomaniac antisemite and that his persona of appearing normal and powerless was cultivated for the trial as a defense.

229. The two-part story, "Eichmann's Story Part I: I Transported Them . . . to the Butcher," and "Eichmann's Own Story Part II: To Sum It All Up, I Regret Nothing," *Life* magazine, November 28, 1960, pp. 19–25, and December 5, 1960, pp. 146–61.

230. Eichmann in *Life*, November 28, 1960, p. 21.

231. Testimony of Leon Weliczker Wells, Sessions 22–23, May 1–2, 1961, Adolf Eichmann Trial, District Court of Jerusalem; Yad Vashem Eichmann Trial Channel, accessed April 8, 2020, https://www.youtube.com/watch?v=CkupLm3G74E&t=1493s; for transcript of Wells's testimony, see Nizkor Project, session, 23/3, accessed April 8, 2020, http://www.nizkor.com/ftp.cgi/people/e/eichmann.adolf/transcripts/Sessions.

232. Waitman Wade Beorn, "Leon Wells Journey," Lviv Interactive, Center for Urban History of East Central Europe, accessed April 8, 2020, https://lia.lvivcenter.org/en/storymaps/wells/.

233. A later English edition of Wells's book was published as *The Death Brigade* (New York, 1978).

234. Homer Bigart, "Court Hears Story of a Woman Who Was Buried Alive in Common Grave," *New York Times*, May 9, 1961, p. 16. Testimony of Rivka Yosselevska, Session 30, May 8, 1961. For transcript see Nizkor Project, session 30/4, accessed April 8, 2020, http://www.nizkor.com/ftp.cgi/people/e/eichmann.adolf/transcripts/Sessions. Her televised testimony is partially preserved by British Pathé, "Woman's Evidence at Eichmann Trial," accessed April 8, 2020, https://www.britishpathe.com/video/womans-evidence-at-eichmann-trial.

235. Földi and his family were on one of the Hungarian transports to Auschwitz in late May 1944; Testimony of Martin Földi, Session 53, May 25, 1961. For transcript, see Nizkor Project, session 53/04, accessed April 8, 2020, http://www.nizkor.com/ftp.cgi/people/e/eichmann.adolf/transcripts/Sessions/.

236. Testimony of Yehiel Dinur, Session 68, June 7, 1961. For transcript, see Nizkor Project, session 68/01, accessed April 8, 2020, http://www.nizkor.com/ftp.cgi/people/e/eichmann.adolf/transcripts/Sessions/.

237. Segev 1991, pp. 3–11.

238. Testimony of Esther Goldstein, Session 70, June 8, 1961. For transcript see Nizkor Project, session 70/5, accessed April 8, 2020, http://www.nizkor.com/ftp.cgi/people/e/eichmann.adolf/transcripts/Sessions/.

239. See, for instance, *Jewish Telegraphic Agency Daily News Bulletin*, vol. 28, no. 84, May 2, 1961, which reports two spectators being ejected from the court after shouting at Eichmann, with one fainting twice, as well as Golda Meir, who "wept bitterly" despite efforts to act inconspicuously.

240. Arendt 1963, 2006 ed., p. 5.

241. Elon 2006, p. xviii. Arendt criticized the State of Israel (as a former Zionist), the jurisdiction of the court, the legality and precedent of the case, its function as a show trial, and quibbled about every detail of the proceedings—the translators, the charges, the prosecutor (whom she accused of vanity, press courting, outbursts, and pursuing Israel's nationalist agenda), and even some of the witnesses. Arendt, a German Jew, revealed biases against Eastern European Jews throughout her reporting on the trial, particularly berating the Galician-born prosecutor Hausner. On Arendt's German-ness, see Judt 1995, and on age-old tensions between German Jews ("yekkes") and Jews in Palestine and Eastern Europe in the 1930s, see Segev 1991, pp. 35–64.

242. Judt 1995, p. 9. Judt also notes that in 1953, Arendt had written that "totalitarian crimes are very inadequately described as murder and totalitarian criminals can hardly be punished as murderers." For her, totalitarian domination has "exploded our traditional categories of political thought." Hannah Arendt, "A Reply," *The Review of Politics*, vol. 15, no. 1 (January 1953), p. 80.

243. Clippings from the *Daily Iowan* covering the Frankfurt Auschwitz trial in 1964 were incorporated by Lasansky in *No. 18* of "The Nazi Drawings." The Frankfurt Auschwitz trials, December 20, 1963–August 19, 1965, charged 22 defendants (mostly low-ranking SS officers) under West German law for their roles in the

Holocaust at the Auschwitz-Birkenau death camp. Eighteen were sentenced to prison, eight served life sentences. The effort was led by German state prosecutor Fritz Bauer, who was Jewish and had been imprisoned in a Nazi concentration camp in 1933 before escaping into exile. Bauer was a key figure in the capture of Eichmann but was stymied by the German government in his efforts to extradite and try Nazi war criminals in Germany, in large part because many former Nazis held high-ranking positions in the German government. More than 360 witnesses were summoned to testify, including 210 survivors.

244. Judt 2005, pp. 810–11. The statute had formerly been limited to 20 years. It had been extended in 1969 before being abolished.

245. "German Anti-Semitism Drops," *New York Times*, May 31, 1962, p. 3.

246. "Documents were submitted describing the Holocaust in the East, but the bulk of the evidence consisted of statements by witnesses, 'brands plucked from the fire,' who followed each other in the witness box for days and weeks on end. They spoke simply, and the seal of truth was on their words. But there is no doubt that even they themselves could not find the words to describe their suffering in all its depth. . . . If these be the sufferings of the individual, then the sum total of the suffering of the millions—about a third of the Jewish people, tortured and slaughtered—is certainly beyond human understanding." Judges Moshe Landau, Benjamin Halevi, Yitzchak Raveh, Judgment of Adolf Eichmann, District Court of Jerusalem, December 15, 1961.

247. Wiesel's quote continues, "The truth of Auschwitz remains hidden in its ashes. Only those who lived it in their flesh and in their minds can possibly transform their experience into knowledge. Others, despite their best intentions, can never do so." Elie Wiesel, "Art and the Holocaust: Trivializing Memory," *New York Times*, June 11, 1989, Arts and Leisure section, pp. 1, 38.

248. Novick 1999, p. 133.

249. American press, writers, and the public gradually adopted the word "Holocaust" in the 1960s to refer to the Nazi genocide of the Jewish people, following the Israeli press, although initially it was rarely capitalized. The early Greek and Latin definition, "burnt whole" or "a burnt whole offering," appears in the Bible among other places. Before the Eichmann trial and for a few years after, the word was frequently used to describe destructive, deadly fires, and in the 1950s more often in discussions of the destruction of atomic bombs (See, e.g., Harry Truman's 1953 State of the Union, or *New York Times*' reference to "hydrogen holocaust" (April 5, 1954) or "nuclear holocaust" (July 14, 1957, p. 13). Alongside these usages in the 1940s and 1950s, "holocaust" was also sporadically used to refer to the Nazi genocide of the Jews. As late as 1957, however, the word was employed (surprisingly, to modern readers) in the title of a book about a torpedoed Nazi battleship which left nearly 2,000 German soldiers dead in 1943, *Holocaust at Sea: The Drama of the Scharnhorst* by Fritz-Otto Busch, from the original 1952 German title *Tragodie am Nordkap: Untergang des Schlachtschiffes "Scharnhorst"* (Tragedy at the North Cape: Sinking of the Battleship "Scharnhorst"). Novick notes that the 1948 Israeli Declaration of Independence's reference to "the Nazi *shoah*" ("catastrophe" in Hebrew) appeared as "the Nazi holocaust" in the official Israeli translation into English (Novick 1999, p. 133). Nonetheless some scholars have argued that the term holocaust is offensive in light of its associations with religious sacrifice and its Christian overtones, which might cast Nazis "into a quasi 'priestly' role to sacrifice Jews to God." Zev Garber and Bruce Zuckerman, "Why Do We Call the Holocaust 'The Holocaust?' An Inquiry into the Psychology of Labels," *Modern Judaism*, vol. 9 (1989), pp. 197–211. Given the sustained and wide usage of "Holocaust," such a reading seems to have gained little traction. For an informative account of the evolving meanings and uses of "Holocaust," "holocaust," and "Shoah," see Anna-Vera Sullam Calimani, "A Name for Extermination," *Modern Language Review*, vol. 94 (October 1999), pp. 978–99.

250. Annette F. Timm, "Testimony in Holocaust Historiography," in *Holocaust History and the Readings of Ka-Tzetnik*, ed. Annette F. Timm, pp. 37–66. The commission was founded in Lublin, Poland.

251. Today, Lanzmann's original 185 hours of filmed interviews are held jointly by Yad Vashem and the United States Holocaust Memorial Museum.

252. Shirer's book was selected by the Book-of-the-Month Club in November 1960, causing sales to skyrocket. After it won the National Book Award in 1961, a paperback edition was issued, which also quickly sold a million copies. In 1962 *Reader's Digest*, which had a circulation of 12 million readers per month, serialized an abbreviated version of the thousand-page book over three issues, March, April, May 1962; Gavriel D. Rosenfeld, "The Reception of William L. Shirer's *The Rise and Fall of the Third Reich* in the United States and West Germany, 1960–62," *Journal of Contemporary History*, vol. 29 (January 1994), pp. 95, 100–101.

253. Novick 1999, p. 128.

254. Raul Hilberg's *Destruction of the European Jews*, 788 pages, published by Quadrangle Books in 1961, began as Hilberg's PhD dissertation at Columbia University, New York. In addition to there being less interest in the subject in the 1950s, publishers also hesitated to accept the book because of its length, similar to Shirer's book.

255. Hilberg's book was preceded in the 1950s by Gerald Reitlinger's *The Final Solution: The Attempt to Exterminate the Jews of Europe, 1939–1945* (London, New York, and Berlin, 1953) and Léon Poliakov's *Harvest of Hate* (Philadelphia, 1954), translated from the French edition in 1951. As Novick pointed out, both books were printed and distributed in the U.S. by small publishers, and neither was reviewed in general-circulation press, Novick 1999, p. 103. Hilberg's book in contrast was widely read and reviewed. Hilberg was criticized, in particular, for his characterization of Jewish victims as passive and partly culpable for failing to fight. Arendt, who relied heavily on Hilberg, attracted furor for implicating the Jewish Councils "in the destruction of their own people," which she called "the darkest chapter of the whole dark story." Arendt 1963, 2006 ed., p. 117. As Novick and Judt have both argued (Novick 1999, pp. 139–42; Judt 1995, p. 11), Arendt may have stated the case insensitively, but considering or even condemning the role of the *Judenräten* in administering policies in the ghettos was not new and was worthy of examination. There had even been prosecutions in Israel, and one case in New York. Her complex, at times rambling analysis uncomfortably blurred the line between pure evil and pure good.

256. For changes in textbooks, see Gerd Korman, "Silence in the American Textbooks," *Yad Vashem Studies*, vol. 8 (1970), pp. 183–202; Novick 1999, pp. 103, 307n2; Judt 2005, p. 809.

257. Judt 2005, pp. 810–11. Judt notes that between the late 1960s and 1970s, school groups visiting Dachau increased more than tenfold.

258. Judt 2005, p. 803.

259. Novick 1999, pp. 2–7, 198–200, where he discusses efforts to sacralize the Holocaust as a central symbol of Judaism and to place it "at the core of American Jewish thought."

260. For further discussion of the strengthening of Jewish identity with the rise of Holocaust knowledge in 1960s and 1970s, see Novick 1999, chaps. 8–10, especially pp. 6–7, 201–3. Novick sees the Holocaust gradually becoming central to Jewish identity as well. For discussion of artists in particular, see Amishai-Maisels 1993, especially pp. 123, 318–20.

261. Arendt 1963, 2006 ed., pp. 275–76.

262. Novick 1999, pp. 209, 333n5. Some estimate as many as 120 million watched in 1978. It was rebroadcast in the U.S. in 1979.

263. "Pery Broad," United States Holocaust Memorial Museum, accessed March 1, 2020, https://collections.ushmm.org/search/catalog/irn1004810. Lanzmann used the expression in discussing the *Holocaust* miniseries in his secretly filmed interview with Pery Broad, a former Auschwitz guard, in 1979. The original quip is attributed to the Israeli statesman Abba Eban in the 1950s.

264. Judt 2005, p. 811.

265. Auschwitz-Birkenau was estimated to have been the murder site of 1.1 million people. As Jewish prisoners were at the bottom of the camp's hierarchy, the paradox of Auschwitz was that those marked as criminals or political prisoners might receive different (thus better) treatment in their transport or selection; Testimony of Raya Kagan, Trial of Adolf Eichmann, District Court of Jerusalem, Session 70, June 8, 1961. For transcript, see Nizkor Project, session 70/03, accessed April 8, 2020, http://www.nizkor.com/ftp.cgi/people/e/eichmann.adolf/transcripts/Sessions.

266. *Prisoner 2731*, Faces of Auschwitz, accessed May 29, 2020, https://facesofauschwitz.com/gallery/prisoner-2731/. She was on one of the first transports of women to Auschwitz, most of whom were dead by the end of 1942.

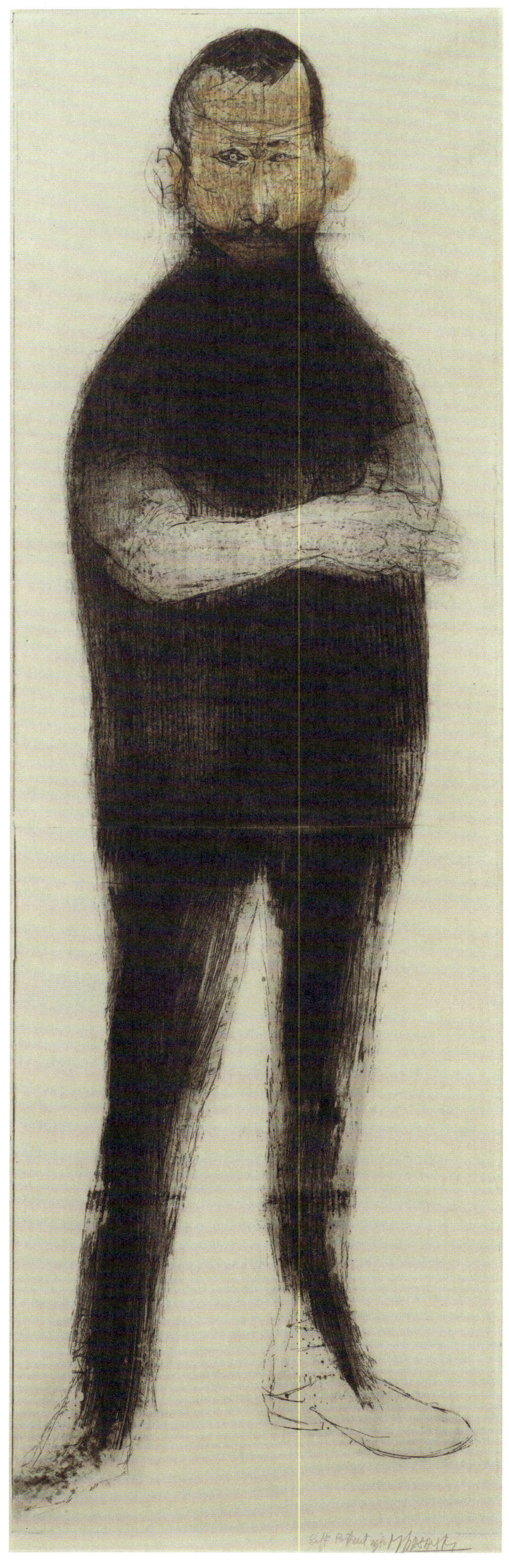

Fig. 2.1 Mauricio Lasansky, *Self-Portrait*, 1959, color engraving, soft-ground etching, aquatint, open-bite, water ground, and electric stippler, 68¼ × 21⅝ in. (173.4 × 54.9 cm), Minneapolis Institute of Art, the Edith and Norman Garmezy Prints and Drawings Acquisition Fund, 2003.213.5

MAURICIO LASANSKY: A LIFE AND ART OF COMPASSION

Rachel McGarry

Mauricio Lasansky (1914–2012) was a successful artist with an international reputation when he began his ambitious "Nazi Drawings" series in 1961. He had exhibited widely in solo and group shows across South America, the United States, and Europe. Before this drawing series, his reputation was based exclusively on his prints. *Time* magazine declared Lasansky "the nation's most influential printmaker" in 1961.[1] The previous year, the American author and art critic Selden Rodman went even further, saying, "Lasansky is considered by many to be the world's outstanding printmaker."[2] By 1960 some 50 public collections across four continents—South America, North America, Australia, and Europe—held his work.[3] Lasansky's broad recognition as a major artist was noteworthy given the historic bias against printmaking as a minor art compared to painting and sculpture.[4] Critics, curators, artists, and collectors celebrated his prints for their technical sophistication, vibrant colors, monumental size, and complex combinations of intaglio techniques that included engraving, soft-ground etching, aquatint, and drypoint; for some later works, as many as 50 plates were required to produce a single print.

BEGINNINGS IN ARGENTINA

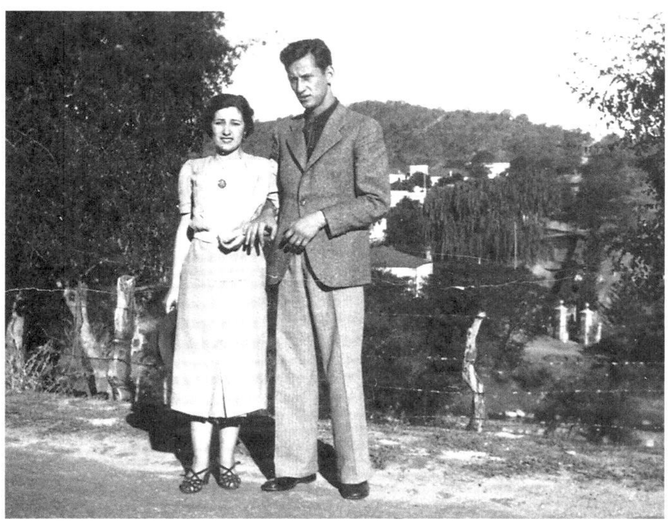

Fig. 2.2 Mauricio and Emilia Lasansky, 1938, Córdoba, Argentina, shortly after their marriage

Mauricio Leib Lasansky was born on October 12, 1914, in Buenos Aires, Argentina. His parents were Jewish immigrants from Lithuania. Lasansky's father, Abrahm Isaac Lasansky [Laschansky] (1883–1938), lived in Vilna (Vilnius), the capital of Lithuania, then part of the Russian Empire.[5] Vilna had a vibrant Jewish community, which, at the time of Abrahm's departure in 1904, made up more than half of the city's population. Initially, Abrahm and his brother, Cecilio, emigrated to the United States and worked as engravers at the Philadelphia Mint, thus pursuing the family trade of engraving and printing.[6] By 1908 or 1909, the brothers had moved to Buenos Aires. Here Abrahm married Ana Kahn [Kagan] (1888–1971), an immigrant from Kovno (now Kaunas), Lithuania. Cecilio worked as a printer; Abrahm went into the photo business, hand coloring family portraits, usually tintypes or ferrotypes, and traveling around the country to market his skills. Abrahm and Ana had seven children, six boys and one girl; Mauricio was the third child. Two of his younger brothers died in infancy of influenza, and his oldest brother, Guillermo, who assisted in Abrahm's photo business, died in his 20s.

From a young age Mauricio showed uncommon talent in music and art. His father played cornet and composed music, and Mauricio excelled at the violin. At age 13, he began taking art lessons, presumably in drawing. At age 15, he and a close neighborhood friend, Luis Barragán, Jr. (1914–2009), started an art academy called Arte por el Arte (Art for Art).[7] The boys and their art-minded friends gathered at the Barragán house, located in the Villa Devoto neighborhood on a street aptly named calle Juan Gutenberg, after the famous 15th-century German printer and inventor of movable type.[8] Like Lasansky, Barragán went on to become an accomplished artist, as did other friends in the group, among them Orlando Pierri and Bruno Venier.[9]

It was at the Barragán house that Mauricio encountered Luis's sister, Emilia Barragán (1917–2009). They first met in 1926, when he was 12 years old and she was 9. Emilia and Luis's parents, like Mauricio's, were immigrants who had met and married in Buenos Aires. Their mother, Pilar Fernández (1894–1952), had emigrated as a child from a small village near Toledo, Spain. Their father, Luis Barragán (1884/86–1954), had come from a town northwest of Madrid, where family members specialized in devotional art.[10] Both Pilar and Luis Barragán were Roman Catholics. It is no surprise that Mauricio was drawn to the Barragán household, which nurtured a passion for art. In addition to young Luis, sibling Julio Barragán (1928–2011) became a successful artist in Argentina.[11] Mauricio and Emilia married in a civil ceremony on December 16, 1937, and remained devoted to each other for nearly 72 years, until Emilia's death in 2009. Her interest in art was apparent throughout her life. Her energies were dedicated to supporting her husband's artistic career

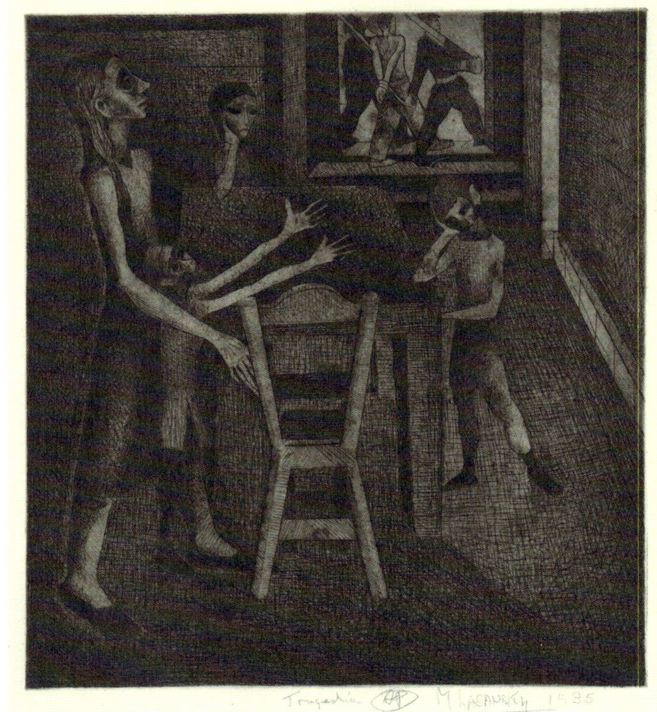

Fig. 2.3 Mauricio Lasansky, *Tragedy* (*Tragedia*), 1935 (1980 edition), drypoint, 15 × 13 7/16 in. (38.1 × 34.1 cm), Annex Galleries, Santa Rosa, Calif.

and helping to manage his art business, encouraging the creative talents of their six children, and running their busy, art-filled house.[12] She shared with her husband a deep interest in collecting art, particularly African and pre-Columbian art.[13] In Emilia, Mauricio had found a muse and a sympathetic life partner.

Before settling down, Lasansky formalized his artistic training. In 1933 he was accepted into the Escuela Superior de Bellas Artes in Buenos Aires. He entered as a sculpture student but quickly switched his focus to printmaking. As he explained, "One day I just wandered into the print department, and I smelled all that ink and my old ancestors came out. It just hit me. It gets into your veins."[14] With precocious facility, he experimented in an array of techniques—zincography, linocut, etching, drypoint, lithography. Despite his lifelong attention to craft (he became renowned for his mastery of printmaking processes), he was concerned less with beauty ("beauty for beauty's sake," as he put it) than with examining the human condition.[15] Outside of portraits and early forays into surrealism, he used art as a vehicle for shining a light on injustice. This made printmaking—the age-old medium for social criticism—a natural fit.

Lasansky's early prints, from the 1930s, depict hunger, death, and the plight of those living in urban and rural poverty. Lasansky later remarked, "My great teacher was the Depression. There were lots of ugly things then."[16] Empty dishes, thin children, deathbeds—his earliest work embodies the Nuevo Realismo movement of 1930s Argentina, highlighting the struggles and conditions of the poor in a realistic, if spare, figurative language.

Lasansky's prints could be overtly political. *Tragedy* (1935) (fig. 2.3) depicts a family grieving the arrest of their father, who is marched out of a barren interior by armed soldiers. The print is an explicit critique of the upheaval and oppression experienced in Argentina in the '30s. This was the so-called Infamous Decade, when fascist military leaders quelled their opposition through arrest, torture, and execution at the hands of a newly formed military police.[17] Leaders targeted socialists, anarchists, and workers and removed foreigners through deportation. In *Tragedy* we see a sensitivity to the suffering of women and children that would be a major theme for Lasansky throughout his career.

He exhibited his prints frequently in the 1930s and won numerous first prizes from the start.[18] He also contributed illustrations to left-leaning, antifascist magazines in this period. His zincograph *Prisoners* (1934) depicts the arrest (and suppression) of people on strike. Strikes by unionized workers and farmers occurred frequently and often turned violent. In 1935, the print appeared on the cover of *Izquierda: Critica y Accion Socialista* (*Left: Criticism and Social Action*) (fig. 2.4).[19] The image was reprinted in 1936 in *Revista Impulso! Critica, Letras, Polemica* (*Impulse Magazine: Criticism, Letters, Polemics*), this time with a statement by the artist. Proclaiming his solidarity with the labor movement, Lasansky wrote, "My humble but safe hand for the workers of 'fontamara' Argentina. I will fight for art for the proletariat."[20] Fontamara is a fictional Italian town in Ignazio Silone's acclaimed 1933 novel of the same name about peasant farmers suffering at the hands of exploitative fascists.

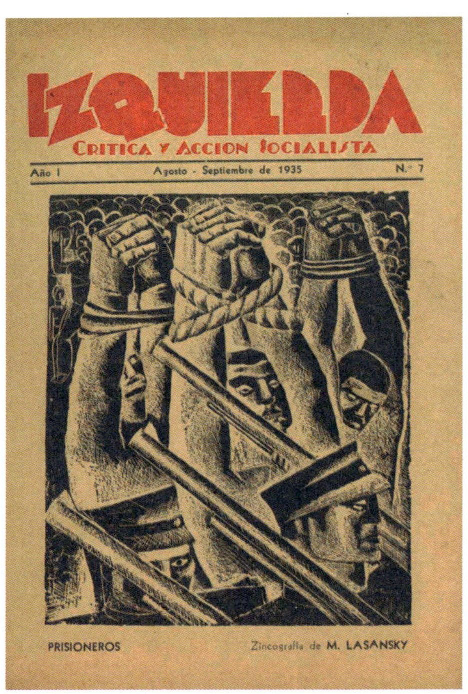

Fig. 2.4 Cover of *Izquierda: Critica y Accion Socialista*, August–September 1935, with Mauricio Lasansky's 1934 print *The Prisoners*

Lasansky's activities as a muralist in Argentina, recently brought to light by the art historian Carolina Romano, reveal that Lasansky used more than one artistic means to fight suffering and injustice.[21] He collaborated with Luis Barragán, Jr., on at least two large-scale murals, *América* (1935), painted in Buenos Aires, and *Labor Court* (1936), painted in the province of Córdoba.[22] Lasansky had moved to Villa María, in Córdoba, in 1936 to become director of the Escuela Libre de Bellas Artes at the Universidad Nacional. At the time, he was just 22 years old. Neither mural survives, but reproductions in contemporary magazines, along with a related Lasansky print, enable us to reconstruct them. *América*, measuring 42 square meters, depicted a wake for a group of dead men and women, lying prostrate, surrounded by mourners; Lasansky's 1935 drypoint *The Victims*, also called *Cadavers*, depicting corpses lined up on tables with only their bare feet visible, may give a sense of how it looked.[23] The Córdoba fresco can be partially reconstructed from a photograph of part of the destroyed mural and reproductions in magazines.[24] It showed a trial of a condemned worker and relates to the use of court cases to oppress the lower classes and preserve the country's power structure. Both murals were commissioned by people known to be politically active socialists, for their private homes. These images were published in antifascist, anti-imperialist magazines, indicating that the patrons and artists wanted to disseminate the politically charged message behind each work.

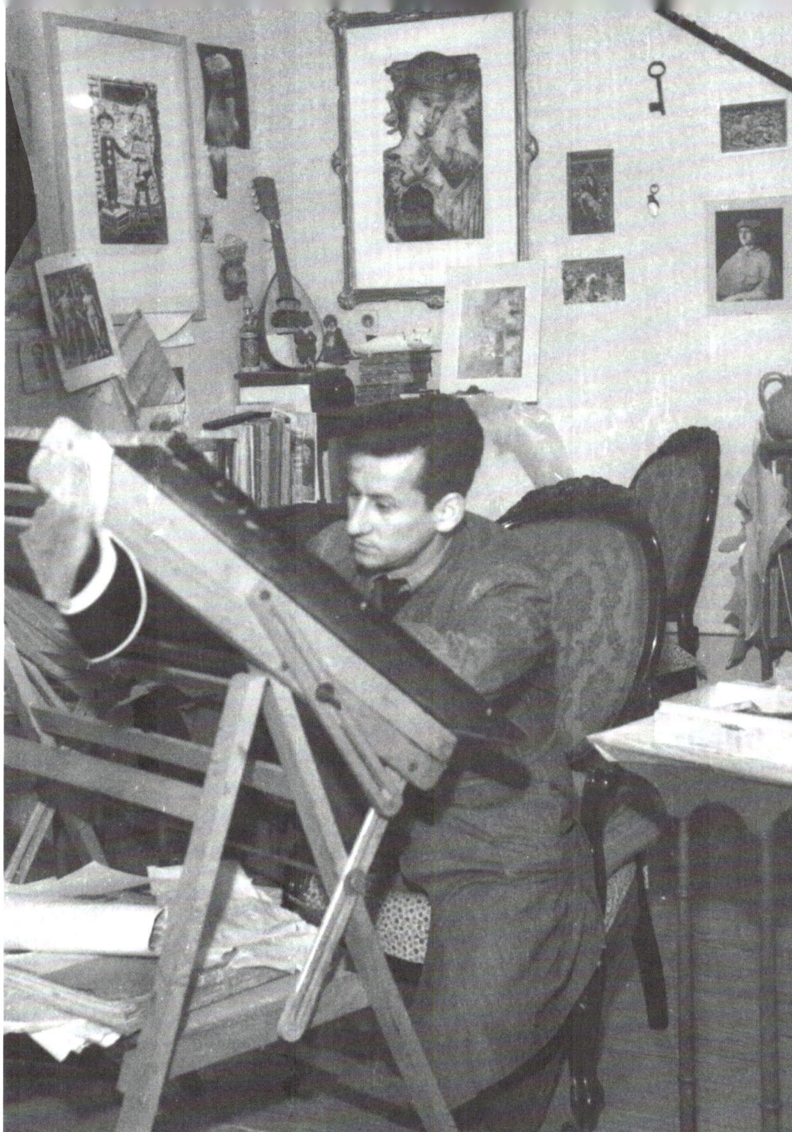

Fig. 2.6 Mauricio Lasansky at work in his studio, Córdoba, Argentina, c. 1942
Framed on the wall are Lasansky's prints *Carnival* (1936) and *A Sleepwalking Romance* (1940). Reproductions of famous works of art are also tacked up, including Dürer's *Adam and Eve* (1504), Venus de Milo (Hellenistic, Louvre, Paris), Trajan's relief from the Arch of Constantine (Roman, 2nd century CE, Rome), Raphael's *Portrait of a Cardinal* (c. 1510–11, Prado, Madrid), an unidentified Pietà panel painting (Spanish?, 15th century?), and a Renaissance battle painting, perhaps by Paolo Uccello (c. 1450).

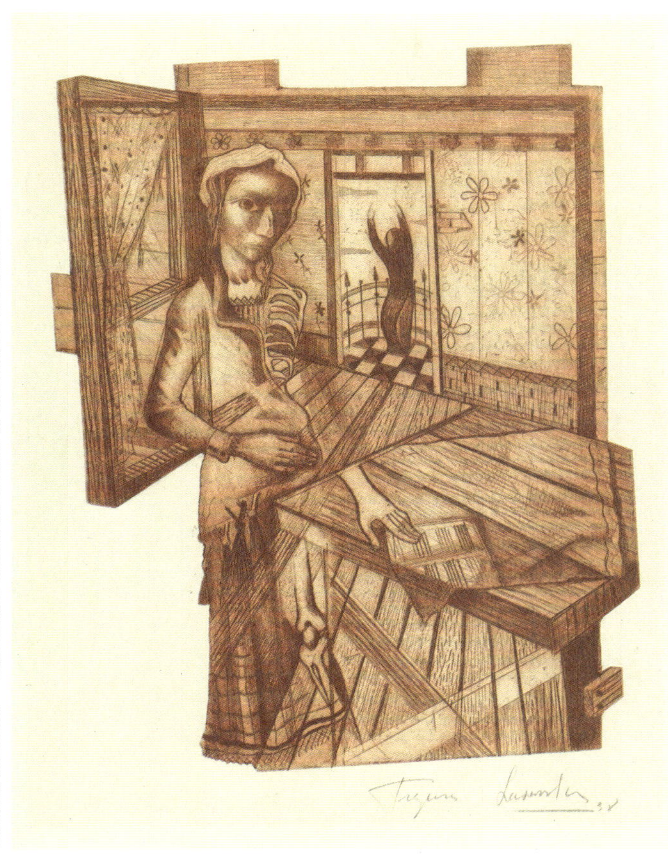

Fig. 2.5 Mauricio Lasansky, *Figure (Figura)*, 1938, drypoint, 22¹/₈ × 15³/₁₆ in. (56.2 × 38.5 cm), Museum of Modern Art, New York, Inter-American Fund, 711.1942

In 1939 Lasansky was appointed director of the Escuela de Manualidades Amadeo Auchter, in the city of Córdoba, a city with a strong history of liberal, antifascist politics and a center of progressive learning.[25] To support his young family—William (Guillermo) was born in 1938 and Nina (Rocio) in 1943—Lasansky spent his years in Córdoba province teaching, organizing exhibitions, and producing art, all while running two successive art schools. The style and subject matter of his prints alternated between regionalism and surrealism, the latter executed in a refined style and often featuring dreamlike settings with animals or beautiful figures inspired by Emilia, such as *Figure* (fig. 2.5) from 1938.[26] As the 1930s drew to a close, Lasansky focused more on psychological pathos than physical and emotional suffering. Portraiture became important now, too, and would remain so throughout his career.

NELSON ROCKEFELLER CREATES A MARKET FOR LATIN AMERICAN ART

While Lasansky's talents and hard work brought him early success within Argentina, luck played a role in propelling him onto the international stage. That luck was largely due to the machinations of Nelson Rockefeller, the American millionaire, businessman, and statesman with business interests in Latin America. One of Rockefeller's many strategies for protecting those interests in the first half of the 1940s was a well-funded diplomatic initiative involving the United States and South America. Two prominent New York museum officials visited Argentina in 1942 as part of this diplomatic effort. After they encountered Lasansky and his prints, the artist had his entrée into the U.S. art world.[27]

In 1940, President Franklin D. Roosevelt, at Rockefeller's urging, and against the backdrop of escalating war, founded what became known as the Office of Inter-American Affairs, or OIAA, with Rockefeller as its head (fig. 2.7). In addition to fighting the rise of Nazi and fascist influence in South America, the agency promoted "increased hemispheric solidarity and inter-American cooperation."[28] At stake for Rockefeller were investments in the region (particularly in Venezuela and Mexico) by his family's oil business, subsidiaries of Standard Oil Company. He set to work fostering economic, cultural, and political relations, promoting trade, securing natural resources (which would be needed in the war effort), developing health and sanitation programs, and more, even recruiting animation pioneer Walt Disney (fig. 2.8) and actor-filmmaker Orson Welles to travel to South America to make movies and radio programs.[29]

Rockefeller, who had a particular affinity for the visual arts, tapped his deep network at American museums to organize artistic exchanges.[30] He had served on the board of the Metropolitan Museum of Art fresh out of college, in 1930, and was a longtime trustee (and one-time president) of the Museum of Modern Art. He urged these New York museums to collaborate with two others, the Whitney Museum of American Art and the Brooklyn Museum, to assemble exhibitions of contemporary American art and send them on a "50,000-mile tour in South America," circulated by the OIAA.[31]

There was a lively exchange of art going in the other direction as well. Rockefeller called on these same four museums, in addition to the San Francisco Museum of Art, to organize touring exhibitions of Latin American art. Between 1941 and 1944, countless shows traversed the United States, with titles such as *Paintings from Ten Latin American Art Republics, Graphic Arts of Mexico and Argentina, Cuban Painting Today*, and *Faces and Places in Brazil*.[32] In Washington, D.C., the Pan American Union alone organized 27 circulating exhibitions of Latin American art, including a number presented at the Smithsonian National Museum.[33] The Library of Congress unveiled new murals by the Brazilian artist Candido Portinari in 1942, and the Brooklyn Museum opened new galleries dedicated to Latin American art in 1943.[34] Macy's staged a three-week Latin American Art Fair in 1942 that attracted an estimated 825,000 people to its New York store.[35] The OIAA produced an eight-minute documentary on the fair—a piece of triumphant propaganda celebrating Pan-American relations (as well as American consumerism).[36]

This massive initiative created an acute demand for Latin American art and artists in the United States. Lasansky benefited from Rockefeller's campaign when Lincoln Kirstein, the Museum of Modern Art's consultant on Latin American art,[37] purchased one of his prints for the museum during an art-buying trip in South America in 1942, Lasansky's *Figure*, from 1938 (see fig. 2.5).[38]

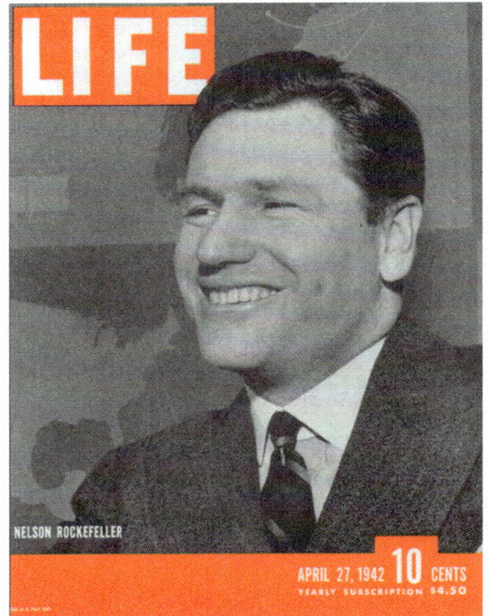

Fig. 2.7 Nelson Rockefeller, *Life*, April 27, 1942; photo by Myron Davis
Rockefeller headed the Office of Inter-American Affairs (1940–44), which President Franklin D. Roosevelt founded at Rockefeller's urging. Rockefeller's efforts to further U.S. and Latin American relations extended beyond policy and business to artistic collaboration, which benefited Lasansky.

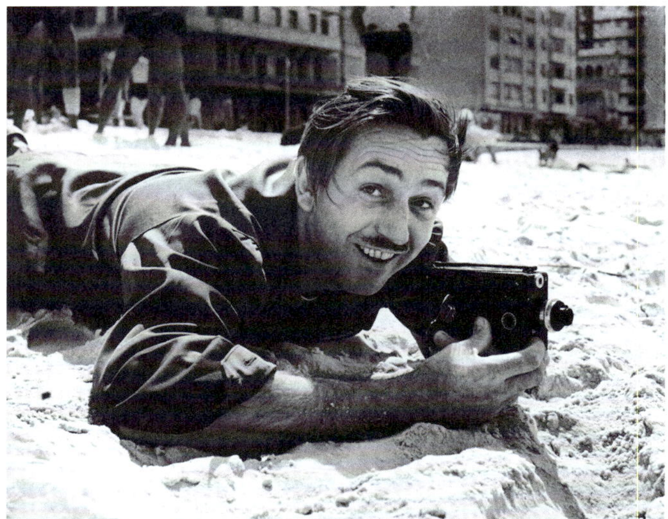

Fig. 2.8 Walt Disney filming in Rio de Janeiro, Brazil, 1941; photo by Hart Preston
Disney and his films were wildly popular in Latin America. The animated *Saludos amigos* (*Greetings, Friends*, 1942), set in Latin America, was inspired by Disney's goodwill tour for the Office of Inter-American Affairs and was produced with a federal loan guarantee. In 1943, the OIAA helped Disney produce *The Grain That Built a Hemisphere*, a short animated documentary about corn that was reportedly seen by more than a million people and won an Academy Award.

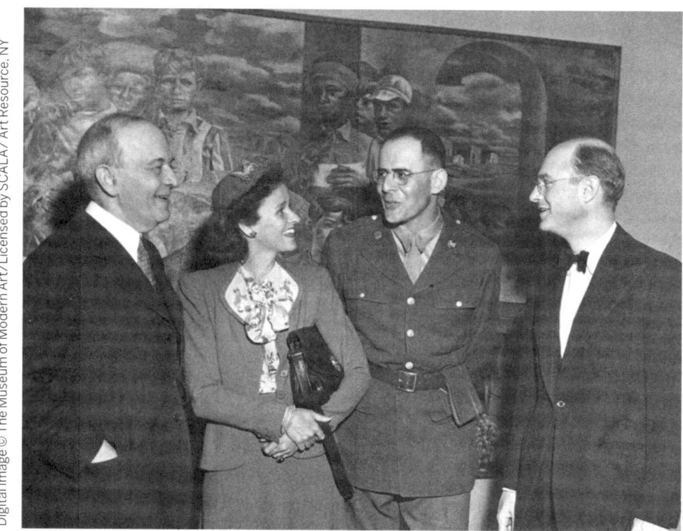

Fig. 2.9 Opening of *The Latin-American Collection of the Museum of Modern Art*, March 30, 1943, photographic archive, Museum of Modern Art, New York
This exhibition featured works purchased in South America for MoMA by its consultant Lincoln Kirstein, including Lasansky's *Figure* (1938). Kirstein, in uniform, had returned from military duty to attend the event. With him are Stephen Clark and Betsy Cushing Roosevelt Whitney (at left) and John Abbott (at right).

(Kirstein was also tasked with secretly reporting to his friend Rockefeller on the fascist activities he saw.) MoMA, then just 13 years old, wanted to build what it termed a "panoramic" collection of modern art; Rockefeller initiated and funded the formation of its Latin American department and art collection. His largess stemmed from his family's business interests in Latin America,[39] and also their passion for Latin American art, particularly on the part of his mother, Abby Aldrich Rockefeller, one of MoMA's founders. In the 1930s, the Rockefellers commissioned major murals from two Mexican artists: *Man at the Crossroads* by Diego Rivera, with its scandalous portrait of Lenin, at Rockefeller Center (destroyed in 1934), and *The Epic of American Civilization* (1932–34) by José Clemente Orozco at Dartmouth College. Rockefeller's mother gave MoMA its first Latin American work of art, an Orozco painting, in 1935.[40] While Kirstein was buying art in South America, MoMA director Alfred Barr was doing the same in Mexico and Cuba. The 195 works they acquired, along with other work in MoMA's collection, were exhibited in New York in 1943 (fig. 2.9). Included in the landmark show, *The Latin-American Collection of the Museum of Modern Art*, was Lasansky's print *Figure*.[41]

Lasansky's good fortune grew when he met Francis Henry Taylor, director of the Metropolitan Museum, who was also touring Argentina in 1942, lecturing, acquiring art, and organizing exhibition exchanges.[42] Taylor wanted to strengthen the U.S.–Argentina relationship on behalf of the OIAA and also increase Rockefeller's support of the Met.[43] He was reportedly in search of pre-Columbian art,[44] which Rockefeller himself collected. (Rockefeller gave his pre-Columbian collection to the Met in 1969.) Among the loans Taylor negotiated were works from Argentina's Society of Watercolorists and Engravers.[45] When these appeared in *Argentine Prints* at the Met in the fall of 1943,[46] Lasansky's 1941 drypoint *Portrait of Emilia* was among them.[47]

Taylor was impressed with Lasansky and recommended him for a Guggenheim Fellowship. The Guggenheim Foundation had established its Latin American Fellowship in 1929 to foster "better international understanding . . . among the American republics." Kirstein and Taylor sought the foundation's support for talented people they had met on their travels to South America.[48]

Lasansky won a Guggenheim Foundation Latin American Exchange Fellowship in 1943 to fund a year of work in New York. It was the first of five Guggenheims he would receive. The award could not have come at a better time. Argentina had just undergone the military coup that ultimately led to Juan Perón's rise to power. Antisemitism and anti-immigrant feelings had been on the rise in the country for a decade,[49] but the Jewish community was further alienated after the coup when religious education was reinstated in public schools. The government also flooded universities with right-wing appointments.[50] In 1943, art by artists deemed Communist (or even sympathetic to Communists) was purged from Argentina's museums, and books by writers similarly suspected were removed from libraries and publishing houses.[51] Lasansky, whose prints had appeared in socialist, antifascist periodicals, may have felt vulnerable during this crackdown.

LASANSKY IN NEW YORK

Lasansky arrived in New York to begin his fellowship on October 20, 1943, one week after his 29th birthday. The Met's *Argentine Prints* exhibition, which featured one of Lasansky's works, had closed just three days earlier. Before him lay 12 months to see and make prints. Away from his wife and two children, he dove in, beginning with a deep study of the Met's vast print collection. He took it all in—old masters (Mantegna, Schongauer, Rembrandt), modern artists (Goya, Daumier), and living artists (Nolde, Picasso). No such treasury of original prints existed in Argentina, and the experience subtly reverberated in Lasansky's imagery and technique for the next five decades.

Lasansky also worked in the celebrated print studio Atelier 17, recently relocated to New York from Nazi-occupied Paris by its founder, the British artist Stanley William Hayter. Hayter favored intaglio and applauded experimentation in all intaglio techniques. He did not believe in a division of labor: everyone got their hands dirty; artists worked their own plates and often printed their own prints. Housed at the New School for Social Research, Atelier 17 attracted a range of talent, from established European artists fleeing World War II to young Americans. In 1944, Lasansky worked alongside Marc Chagall, Joan Miró, Jacques Lipchitz, Jackson

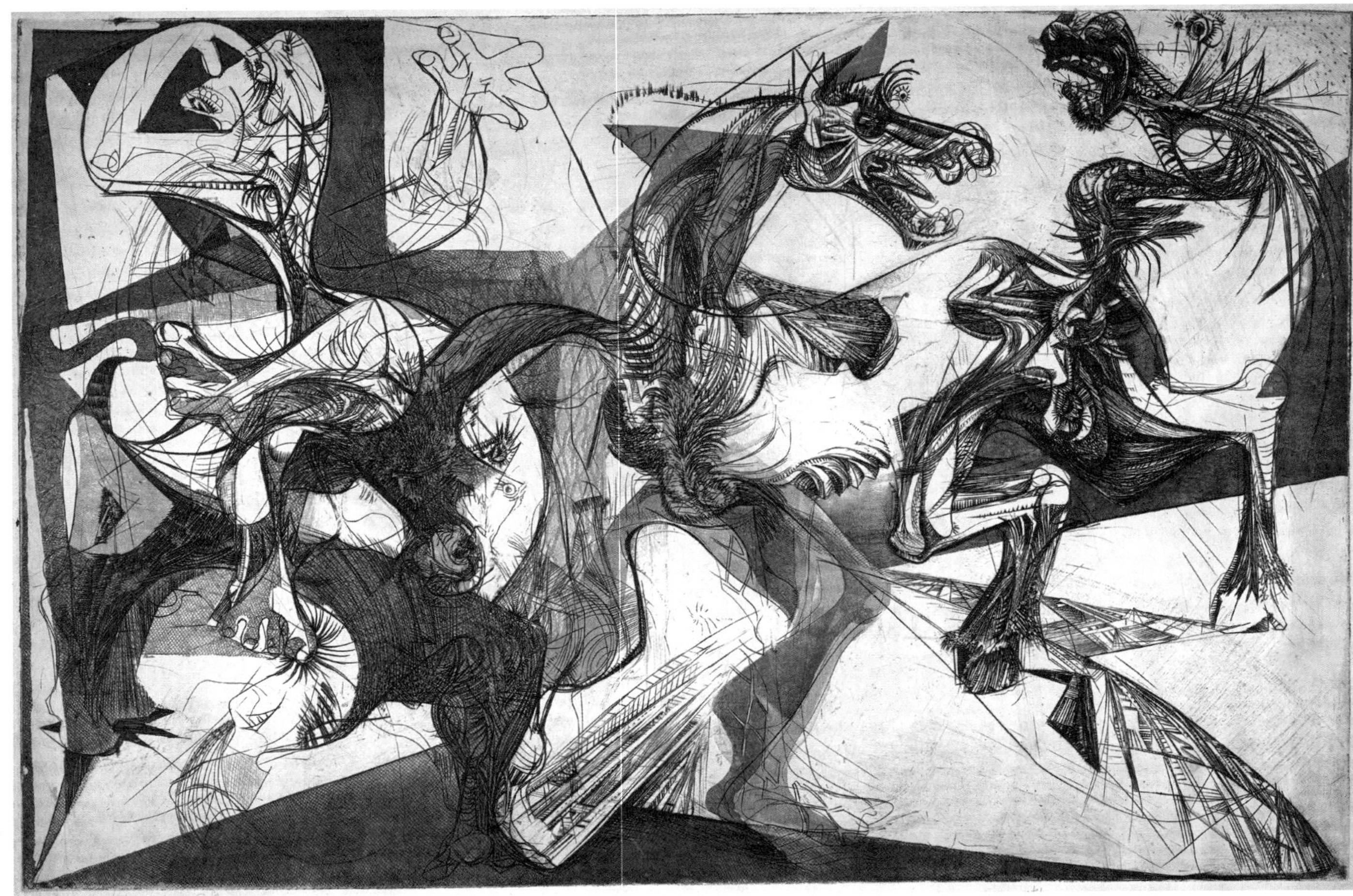

Fig. 2.10 Mauricio Lasansky, *Apocalyptical Space*, 1944–45, engraving, soft-ground etching, aquatint, drypoint, burnishing and scraping, 16 × 23⁹⁄₁₆ in. (40.6 × 59.9 cm) (plate), Minneapolis Institute of Art, gift of C. G. Boerner in honor of Dennis Michael Jon, 2009.19.5

Pollock, Sue Fuller, and Alexander Calder, among others. An exhibition organized by MoMA that summer, *Hayter and Studio 17: New Directions of Gravure*, included three prints by Lasansky.[52] The show traveled to 11 venues—from Baltimore to St. Paul, Minnesota, to San Francisco—promoting the reputations of the featured artists across the country.

Despite the star power inside Atelier 17, the biggest influences on Lasansky in the mid-1940s were Picasso and Hayter, notably Hayter's lyrical Abstract Expressionism. Lasansky's *Apocalyptical Space* (fig. 2.10) of 1944–45 is an homage to Picasso's antiwar painting *Guernica* (1937).[53] Picasso's symbolic language is evident in Lasansky's ferocious composition, presumably inspired by the horrors of World War II. The print depicts several dystopian horselike figures bucking, kicking, and savagely braying, while a lone rider, arms raised in agony, silently screams. The scene might additionally allude to the biblical Four Horsemen of the Apocalypse—War, Famine, Death, and Conquest (or Pestilence)—an image that would have resonated against the contemporary backdrop of wartime devastation. Albrecht Dürer's famous 1498 *Four Horsemen* woodcut was well known to Lasansky.[54]

While his mature Argentine prints had already achieved impressive technical complexity, his Atelier 17 prints represent yet another leap forward. *Apocalyptical Space* combines engraving, soft-ground etching, aquatint, and drypoint, along with burnishing and scraping, to create an array of rich texture and tone. Close inspection reveals elaborately worked surfaces and a mastery of challenging techniques. Since Lasansky liked to compose directly on the plate, without preparatory drawings, his line and composition retained a high degree of spontaneity. He proved a quick study under Hayter and believed ardently in his teacher's underlying approach to printmaking: imaginative, personal experimentation to the point of attacking, shredding, or even destroying the copper plate if necessary—indeed, as if in battle.[55]

Allowed to renew his Guggenheim Fellowship, Lasansky had Emilia and the children join him in New York. In November 1944, the San Francisco Museum of Art, which had taken the lead in OIAA efforts to stage Latin American art shows in the American West, organized an exhibition of Lasansky's prints.[56] In 1945, *Sun and Moon (Sol y luna)*, similar in subject, technique, and scale to *Apocalyptical Space*, won first prize in an exhibition sponsored by the Philadelphia Print Club.[57]

In 1945, bolstered by yet another Guggenheim, his third, the artist set about finding a teaching position outside New York.

IOWA: A "MIDWEST ARGENTINIAN" BECOMES AMERICA'S MOST INFLUENTIAL PRINTMAKER[58]

The recommendation to bring Lasansky to the University of Iowa in Iowa City, where he would remain for the rest of his career, came from the head of the Guggenheim Foundation, Henry Allen Moe. Iowa had built a prominent art and art history department, thanks in part to faculty members Grant Wood (1934–d. 1942), H. W. Janson (1938–41), and Philip Guston (1941–45).[59]

After a brief stint as a visiting lecturer, Lasansky was hired as an assistant professor in 1946 and promoted to full professor in 1948. During his 40-year tenure, he established Iowa as the preeminent printmaking program in America and the first to offer a master's of fine art in printmaking. Lasansky trained a generation of artists in sophisticated intaglio techniques. (He boasted, "We have a new breed: the completely trained printmaker.")[60] By 1958 some 25 print departments at American colleges and universities were run by Lasansky students.[61]

In 1947, Lasansky established the Iowa Print Group to organize touring exhibitions and juried competitions for his students. In the catalogue for the exhibition *A New Direction in Intaglio: The Work of Mauricio Lasansky and His Students*, organized by the Walker Art Center in Minneapolis in 1949, it was noted that "well over 50 percent of all prizes in important juried print exhibitions in the country have been awarded to Lasansky and his former and present students."[62]

During his early years in Iowa, as the news of the Nazi camp atrocities gnawed at him, Lasansky printed an edition of *Dachau* (1946), a plate he had begun in New York (fig. 2.11). It was his first work to examine the Nazi camps directly. The Dachau concentration camp, located in a suburb of Munich, was established in 1933 for political prisoners. It was liberated by American forces on April 29, 1945.[63] News articles described thousands of corpses stacked in piles like wood, and 39 railroad cars

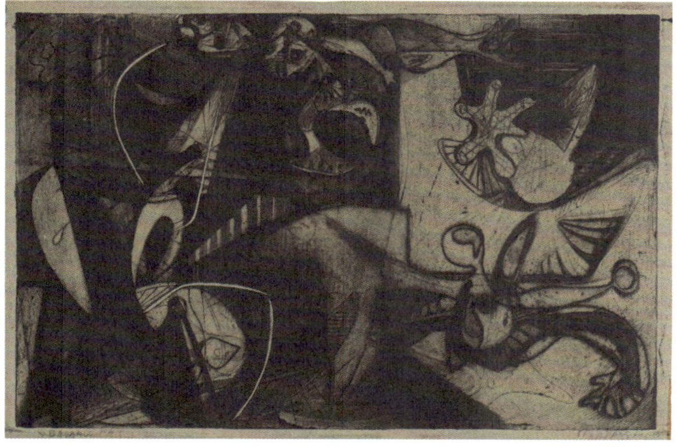

Fig. 2.11 Mauricio Lasansky, *Dachau*, 1945–46 (working proof), engraving, soft-ground etching, aquatint, drypoint, burnishing and scraping, 15⅝ × 23¹¹⁄₁₆ in. (39.8 × 60.1 cm) (plate), Lasansky Corporation

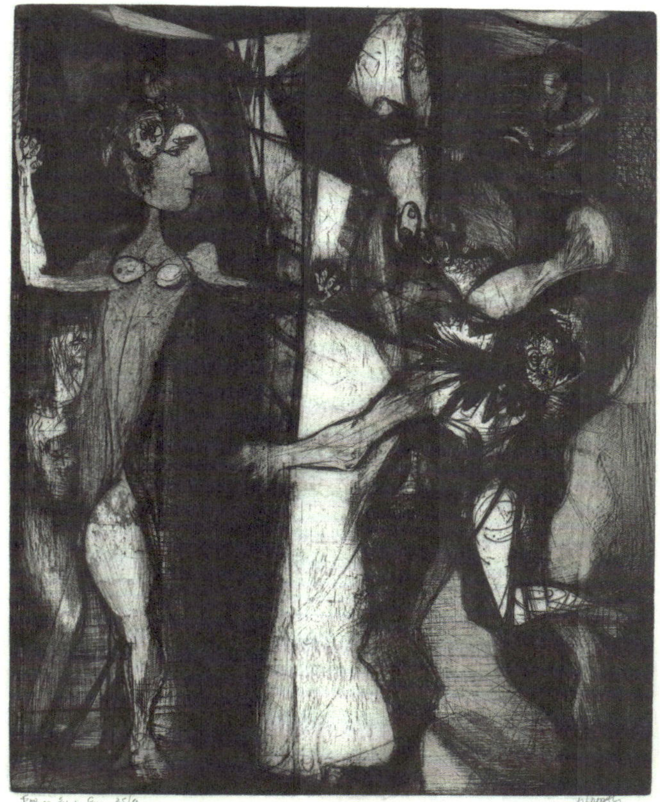

Fig. 2.12 Mauricio Lasansky, *For an Eye an Eye I*, 1946–48, etching, soft-ground etching, aquatint, open-bite, scraping and burnishing, 27 × 21¼ in. (68.6 × 54 cm) (plate), Minneapolis Institute of Art, given in memory of Mauricio and Emilia Barragan Lasansky, from their son Leonardo and grandson Amadeo Galgo Lasansky, 2012.100.1

full of victims who had starved or suffocated. Lasansky again turned for inspiration to Picasso, this time his painting *Charnel House* of 1944–45 (MoMA, New York, p. 29, fig. 1.16),[64] which depicts a Republican family murdered in their kitchen, an incident from the Spanish Civil War.[65] Lasansky's work presents the victims less tangibly as human beings than Picasso's. He employed a rough technique—scratching and gouging the surface of the printing plate with dissonant, jarring lines—as if to evoke hostility. However dark this image of massacred innocents may be, the abstract forms and lack of detail distance them from specific atrocities. The title *Dachau* is all that helps us connect this print to the Nazi horrors.

Lasansky's four-print series "For an Eye an Eye" (1946–48) again takes up the themes of war and violence. Adapting a strongly figurative mode still indebted to Picasso, Lasansky represented vengeful, murderous figures attacking, torturing, and killing one another. In Plate I (fig. 2.12), a woman stands protectively before a smaller, childlike figure while reaching through prison bars toward a bleeding figure restrained by a shadowy, monumental man. As the series progresses, the woman, now ensnared in the contagion of violence, becomes more monstrous, less human. In the final plate, faces and bodies are scarred and mutilated. The surfaces of the printing plates seem to have been gashed and defaced with similar fury. There are no details to locate the nightmarish scenes

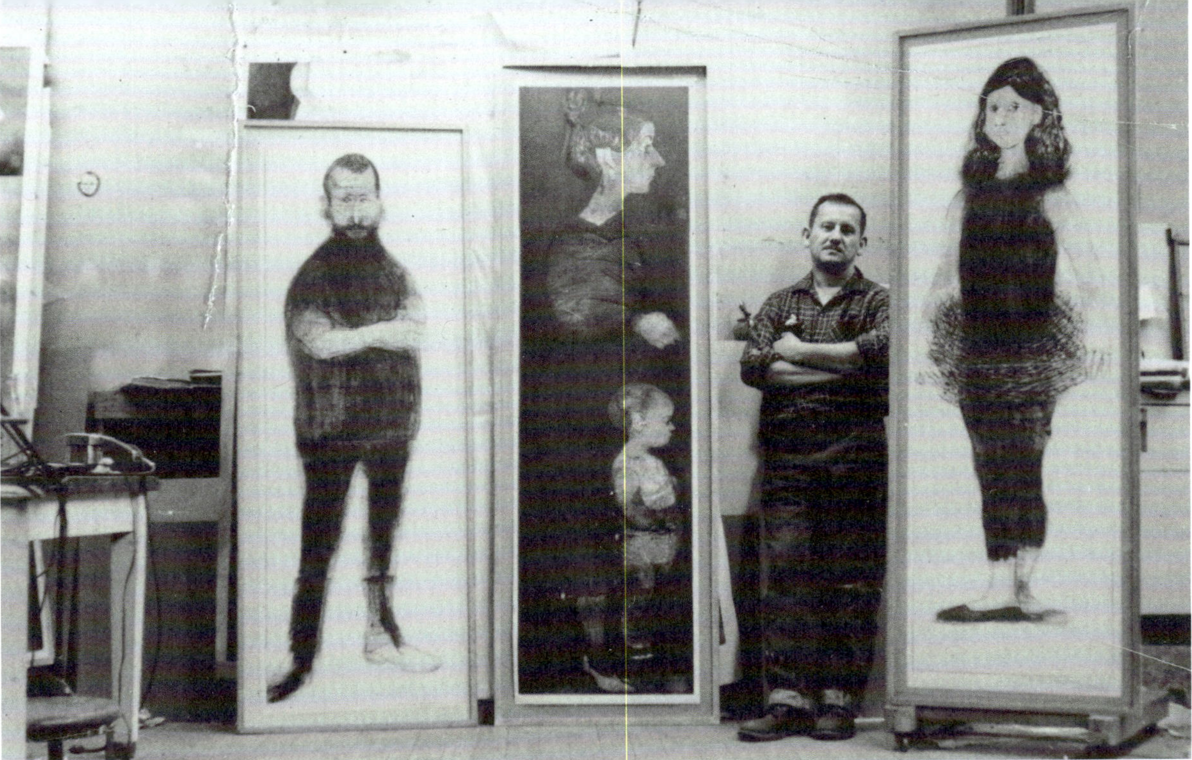

Fig. 2.13 Lasansky in his Iowa studio, 1959
Lasansky made these three large-scale prints in 1959: *Self-Portrait*, *My Wife and Tomás*, and *My Daughter Maria Jimena*.

in a concentration camp or identify the figures as Nazis or prisoners.[66] Instead these are meditations on the human condition. The nude, abstract figures are allegories of revenge and the degradation of war. Among his largest prints up to that time, the series is a virtuoso display of intaglio printmaking and emotionally wrenching content. This exceptional print series may be among the works Lasansky expressed dissatisfaction with in terms of his early attempts at representing the Nazi atrocities. In interviews about *The Nazi Drawings* exhibition in 1967–70, he discussed how his various attempts over the previous 25 years to treat the subject had been problematic:

> The Hitler years were in my belly . . . But I was too worldly about them, too esthetic. The trouble was I thought of them as art. But then I decided the hell with it. Why don't I just put down what I feel? The fact is that people were killed—how cool can you play that?[67]

He seemed to conclude that abstraction was inadequate for communicating the meaning and significance of the subject[68] and ultimately that the printmaking medium may not have suited his ends either. Thus Lasansky abandoned the Holocaust for some time. From his earliest days as a printmaker, he had been concerned with themes of social justice and making "ethical" activist art.[69] On the subject of the Holocaust, however, he had yet to discover the right language to express himself.

SOJOURN TO SPAIN

I think the universe is concentrated in a human being. The figure is a vehicle for my expression, the universal.
—Mauricio Lasansky, 1976[70]

In 1953, having earned his fourth Guggenheim Fellowship, Lasansky and his wife packed up their family of six and moved to Spain for a year. Before establishing themselves in Madrid, they traveled around Spain in a car Lasansky had bought in Paris.[71] Emilia's parents were born in Spain, and this sojourn was a chance for a Barragán reunion. Emilia's parents traveled from Argentina for a visit, as did her brother Luis Barragán, Jr., and his wife. The Lasanskys saw where Emilia's parents grew up; they toured museums and medieval churches and watched elaborate Catholic processions, complete with bleeding polychrome sculptures and members of fraternal organizations masked in *capirotes*, or pointed hoods.[72] They also witnessed the deprivations of life under Spanish dictator Francisco Franco.

Lasansky immersed himself in Madrid's Prado Museum. His daughter Nina called it his second home. His prolonged study of the Prado's Spanish art, particularly the paintings of El Greco (a Greek artist Spain had adopted as its own), Goya, and Velázquez, pointed Lasansky in a new artistic direction. In a 1976 interview, he called Velázquez "the greatest of all"—special praise that he bestowed on just two other artists, Goya and Picasso. Of Velázquez, he explained, "He had such respect for human dignity that all his skills as an artist were on the surface. He glorified man. He made the little dwarf [*The Boy from Vallecas (Francisco Lezcano)*, 1635–45, Prado] the most moving thing, it tears your heart out. It is not sentimental at all, it is warm and moving." Lasansky also admired the painter's rejection of props. "That's one of the things I learned from Velázquez," he said.[73]

Lasansky's prints immediately began to reflect these influences. Portraits of family members and self-portraits had been constants in his career (fig. 2.13). Thus he was never far from the figure, even during his most abstract periods. In Spain, released from the grip of Abstract Expressionism, which dominated the American art scene in the 1940s and '50s, he embraced figurative art. His increasingly naturalistic style is on display in *Spain* (*España*), from 1956, and *Birth in Cardiel* (*Nacimiento en Cardiel*), from 1958, two enigmatic narratives full of foreboding. By drawing figures in motion or foreshortened, embellished or with a degree of unfinish, not unlike the brushwork of Velázquez or the pen and etched lines of Rembrandt, the artist demonstrated his masterful draftsmanship in depicting the human form. And here, too, the underlying presence of Picasso can still be felt—now no longer the expressive exaggerations of the *Guernica* years but instead the haunting stillness of the early Blue Period. For Lasansky the printmaker, Picasso's first foray into printmaking, his seminal *The Frugal Repast* (*Le Repas frugal*) of 1904 and the Spanish master's "Saltimbanques" etching series of 1905–6, would surely have left an impact.[74]

There was also a new psychological presence in these works. His sitters now appeared solemn and dignified if a little aloof, qualities he admired in Velázquez. Lasansky's portraits could have the captivating aura of a Spanish infanta, as in *My Daughter Maria Jimena* (1959) and *Tomás* (1962) (figs. 2.13 and 2.14). We can further see the artist looking at Goya's royal portraits for inspiration. The portraits also grew larger, often to life size, enhancing their physical and emotional presence. His prints became more pictorial, utilizing color as a key design element. *Tomás* shows the more restrained, earthy palette he adopted in the late 1950s and would later employ in "The Nazi Drawings."

Back at the University of Iowa, Lasansky flourished as he developed his personal figural style. His many successes in the 1950s have been thoroughly recounted in the literature and therefore do not need to be repeated here. They include numerous exhibitions, acquisition of his work by major museums, print prizes, and coverage in the national press. The attention culminated in a midcareer retrospective in 1960 sponsored by the Ford Foundation and circulated by the American Federation of Arts. The catalogue was written by the respected print curator and print dealer Carl Zigrosser.[75]

By 1960 Lasansky had formulated the figurative language and mode of expression that he would deploy to haunting effect in "The Nazi Drawings." The moment had come for him to return to the Holocaust theme. His earlier attempts on the subject had not satisfied him. "The drawings were in my belly for 25 years, I tried to do them two or three times, but they were fragmentary," he said.[76] The revelations surrounding Adolf Eichmann's capture in 1960 and trial in 1961 jolted the world from its collective amnesia. Across the globe and in Iowa City, the tragedy could be put aside no longer.

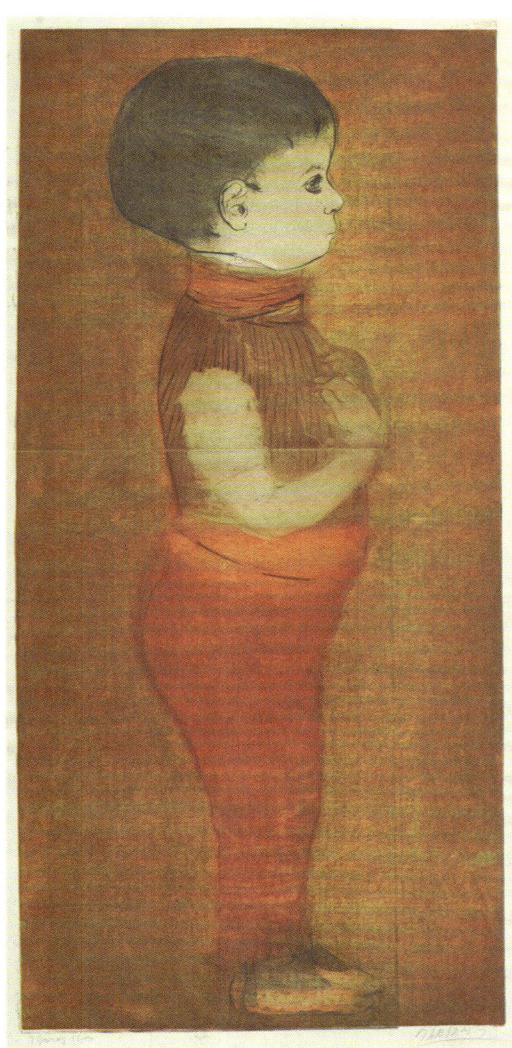

Fig. 2.14 Mauricio Lasansky, *Tomás*, 1962, color engraving, soft-ground etching, aquatint, electric stippler, drypoint, and scraping, 40¾ × 19 in. (103.5 × 48.3 cm) (plate), Minneapolis Institute of Art, gift of Kate Butler Peterson, 2010.107.4
Lasansky's youngest son, Tomás, was born in 1957.

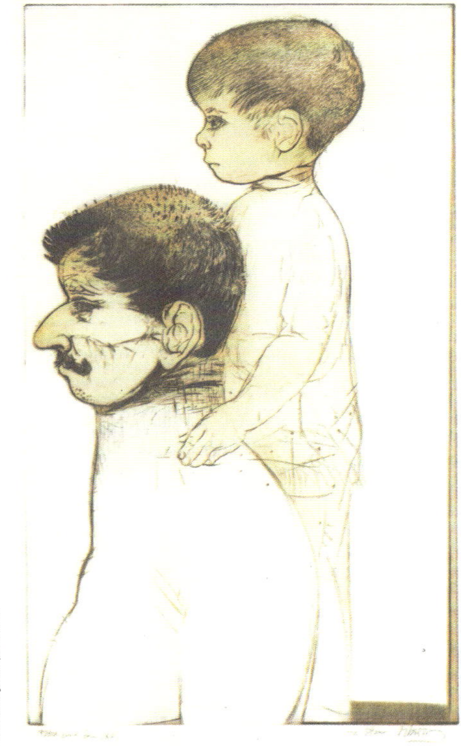

Fig. 2.15 Mauricio Lasansky, *Father and Son* (*Felipe*), 1958, engraving, scraping, and electric stippler printed in yellow ochre and black, 3513/16 × 20 15/16 in. (91 × 53.2 cm) (plate), Myron Kunin Collection of American Art, Minneapolis
For this work, Lasansky adapted a 1957 self-portrait to include his three-year-old son, Phillip, born Luis Felipe.

NOTES

1. "Iowa's Printmaker," *Time*, December 1, 1961, p. 68.

2. Selden Rodman, *The Insiders: Rejection and Rediscovery of Man in the Arts of Our Time* (Baton Rouge, La., 1960), p. 111, fig. 62.

3. Carl Zigrosser, *Mauricio Lasansky* (exh. cat.), American Federation of the Arts (New York, 1960), p. 15. Lasansky's career after moving to the U.S. is well documented in the literature. In addition to Zigrosser, see John Thein and Phillip Lasansky, *Lasansky, Printmaker* (Iowa City, University of Iowa, 1975), with a complete catalogue of his prints before 1973, a chronology, exhibition history, and bibliography, and a foreword by Carl Zigrosser and essays by Alan Fern ("The Prints of Mauricio Lasansky") and Stephen Rhodes ("Themes and Images in Mauricio Lasansky's Prints"); see also Joann Moser et al., *Mauricio Lasansky: A Retrospective Exhibition of His Prints and Drawings* (exh. cat.), University of Iowa Museum of Art and other venues (Iowa City, 1976), with essays by Joann Moser and I. Michael Danoff, and an interview by Jan K. Muhlert with the artist.

4. Rodman 1960, fig. 62. For Rodman, Lasansky's "prodigious" and "revolutionary" technique gave printmaking "for the first time in history the potentialities of a major art." Lasansky, however, would have taken issue with this statement; many of the towering geniuses in the history of art that Lasansky most admired, such as Rembrandt and Goya, had executed some of their most important work as prints.

5. I am grateful to Nina Barragan, pen name of Rocio Lasansky Weinstein, Mauricio Lasansky's eldest daughter, for sharing her research into her family's heritage with me.

6. Abrahm Laschansky arrived in New York on May 16, 1904, aboard the *Norge*, which had sailed from Copenhagen; see https://libertyellisfoundation.org/passenger-result. The ship manifest records the following details about Laschansky: age 21; single; male; "Calling or Occupation," laborer; yes, able to read and write; Nationality, Russian; "Race or People, Hebrew"; Last Residence, Russia; "Final Destination, Brooklyn"; yes, possessing a ticket to final destination, paid for by "self"; possessing $157; never visited the U.S. before; staying with a cousin (name illegible), at 136 Manhattan Avenue, Brooklyn; and passing important list of questions that would exclude him from staying: no prison history, not a polygamist, not an anarchist, not coming under contract to labor in U.S., in good health, not "Deformed or Crippled."

Some of the U.S. immigration questions, such as defining Jewishness as a "Race," as well as health and mental requirements, are of interest in light of Nazi policies developed a few decades later. In addition to the immigration survey, upon arrival to the U.S. a physical exam was required to prevent the entrance of infectious diseases as well as immigrants with birth defects, disabilities, and the "feeble minded"—a practice reminiscent of Nazi policies. The Nazis' forced sterilizations of the mentally ill beginning in 1934 was inspired, in part, by American eugenics programs, first legalized in some states in the 1890s, and rising significantly in 1927 following a U.S. Supreme Court case.

7. Julio Sánchez Gil, *Artistas Hispano-Argentinos vinculados a la Sierra de San Vicente: Buenos Aires/Toledo* (exh. cat.), Sociedad de Amigos de la Sierra de San Vicente (Toledo, Spain, 2010), pp. 22–25; Julio Sánchez Gil, *Barragán: Nexo artístico Cardiel-Buenos Aires* (exh. cat.), Cardiel de los Montes (Toledo, Spain, 2015).

8. Gil 2010, p. 23.

9. Throughout the 1930s, these artists, like Antonio Berni, would alternate styles and subjects between Nuevo Realismo and Surrealism. After Lasansky moved to Córdoba, Barragán, Pierri, and Venier exhibited surrealist works together as the Grupo Orión in 1939 and 1940; see Guillermo Fantoni, *La Luz en la tormenta: Arte moderno entre dos guerras* (exh. cat.), Museo Provincial de Bellas Artes Rosa Galisteo de Rodríguez (Santa Fe, Argentina, 2017), p. 17.

10. Gil 2010, p. 22.

11. The exhibition *Barragán: Nexo artístico*, cited in note 7, organized by Gil in 2015 in the Spanish hometown of Pilar Fernández Barragán, Cardiel de los Montes, pays homage to the Barragán family of artists in Argentina. Like the Lasansky family, many members of the next generation of the Barragáns became professional artists. For further information on the careers of the Barragán brothers, see Marta Bendersky, *Luis Barragán: En pintores Argentinos del siglo XX* (Buenos Aires, 1981); Mauricio Neuman, *Julio Barragán* (Buenos Aires, 1980); and Luciana Sudar Klappenbach, "Julio Barragán," in *El patrimonio artístico de El Fogón de los Arrieros*, pt. 1, pp. 37–38.

12. Emilia and Mauricio Lasansky's six children have been active in the arts: William (Guillermo), born 1938, a sculptor; Nina (Rocio), born 1943, a writer; Leonardo, born 1946, an artist and printmaker; Jimena, born 1947, a dancer and choreographer; Phillip (Luis Felipe) (1954–2020), manager of the Lasansky Corporation and estate; and Tomás, born 1957, a painter and printmaker. Many of their 10 grandchildren are artists as well.

13. For the Lasansky collection of African and pre-Columbian art, see sale catalogue, "African, Oceanic and Pre-Columbian Art Including Property from the Krugier and Lasansky Collections," Sotheby's, New York, May 16, 2014. For reminiscences of life in the Lasansky house and details about their art collection, including a Spanish Romanesque Corpus Christi sculpture in wood (now Cedar Rapids Art Museum, Iowa) and Goya prints, see Nina Barragan, "When Fiction Becomes Memory," *North American Review*, open-space, September 17, 2019.

14. Lasansky interview, Muhlert 1976, p. 17.

15. Hoke Norris, "A Cold Look at Horror," *Chicago Daily News*, April 29, 1970, p. 4. In Lasansky's words, "The artist should do what he needs to do. He should decide which way to go, esthetic or ethical. They are the two ways — the artist who works for beauty alone — Botticelli, Leonardo, beauty for beauty's sake — and then the very ethical artists — Michelangelo as in the Sistine Chapel, Goya in Spain. Nobody makes better art for me than Goya."

16. *Time*, 1961, p. 68.

17. For Lasansky's print, see Carolina Romano, "El arte nuevo de Mauricio Lasansky: Contextos de su producción artística inicia," *Separata*, vol. 20 (December 2017), p. 34, ill.; and Thein and Lasansky 1975, no. 16, where the lithograph is listed but not illustrated. For discussion of social unrest and political and military surveillance and policing in Argentina in the 1930s, see Laura Kalmanowiecki, "Origins and Applications of Political Policing in Argentina," *Latin American Perspectives*, vol. 27 (March 2000), pp. 36–56.

18. For specific prizes Lasansky was awarded in Argentina, see Carolina Romano, "Mauricio Leib Lasansky," in *Diccionario biografico: Un archivo de la cultura de Córdoba*, Proyecto Culturas Interiores, accessed November 15, 2019, http://culturasinteriores.ffyh.unc.edu.ar/ifi002.jsp?pidf=RV2U2WA1D&po=DB; and Zigrosser 1960, p. 13. Zigrosser noted that Lasansky won 18 first prizes in print exhibitions in Argentina.

19. For Lasansky's print, see Thein and Lasansky 1975, no. 8; for this issue of *Izquierda: Critica y Accion Socialista*, no. 7 (August–September, 1935), see http://americalee.cedinci.org/wp-content/uploads/2017/05/Izquierda_n7.pdf.

20. See Romano 2017, p. 32, for discussion of work in *Revista Impulso! Critica, Letras, Polemica* (April 1936).

21. The details of Lasansky's life in Argentina, his first 29 years, are recounted only sparingly in the literature, but thanks to the recent research of some Argentine art historians cited above, more details can be filled in. Carolina Romano provides a wealth of new information about Lasansky's Argentine period, including an in-depth discussion of his frescoes; see Romano 2017, pp. 25–41. Romano has an illustration of a fragment of Lasansky and Barragán's *Labor Court* fresco, which measured 20 square meters, as well as illustrations related to their *América* fresco, which measured 42 square meters. The latter is connected to Lasansky's 1935 drypoint *Las Víctimas* (Thein and Lasansky 1975, cat. no. 25, not illustrated); see Romano 2017, pp. 29 and 30, ill.; for further literature, see p. 39n13–15.

22. Romano suggests the cover illustration by Lasansky and Barragán published in *América Libre* (December 1935) depicting four soldiers might relate to a third mural; see Romano 2017, p. 30, ill.

23. Romano 2017, p. 29, ill. Romano is the first to illustrate this print by Lasansky in the modern literature. She identifies it as *Las Victimas*. Thein and Lasansky 1975, in the catalogue raisonné (with which Mauricio Lasansky assisted), list two prints with this title but illustrate only one (nos. 24–25). Lasansky Gallery, instead, identifies the images as being Lasansky's print *Cadaver* (Thein and Lasansky 1975, no. 18, where it is listed

but not illustrated, although it is described there as being a lithograph). Romano tracked down an early reproduction of the print illustrated (in reverse) in *Revista Impulso! Critica, Letras, Polemica*, May 1937, where it is titled *The Victims (Las Victimas)*. It is also possible that Thein and Lasansky 1975, no. 25 and no. 18, are one and the same. Romano reports that an early exhibition catalogue includes a reproduction of a fragment of the *América* fresco; *M. Lasansky. Presenta grabados y fotos de frescos* (exh. cat.), Galiera Depiel Goré (Tucumán, Argentina, 1936).

24. Romano illustrates a thumbnail photograph of the destroyed fresco fragment and notes that reproductions of the fresco were published in *Revista Unidad* and *Frente Unico*; Romano 2017, pp. 30 (ill.), 39n14. She cites an earlier article she published on the murals in *Revista Avances*, vol. 23 (2013–14), pp. 371–83, which I was unable to locate in any U.S. library.

25. For Lasansky's Córdoba years, see Nina Barragan, "A Few Days in Córdoba: Mauricio Lasansky and Stefan Zweig," *Art Times Online Journal*, February 2014; and Romano 2017, pp. 27–30.

26. For Lasansky's print, see Thein and Lasansky 1975, no. 40.

27. The officials were Lincoln Kirstein, a consultant for MoMA, and Francis Henry Taylor, director of the Metropolitan Museum.

28. Before its name was shortened, the agency was called the Office for Coordination of Commercial and Cultural Relations between the American Republics. Nelson Rockefeller served as coordinator of inter-American affairs from 1940 until 1944, when he was appointed assistant secretary of state. The idea for the agency's founding can largely be credited to Rockefeller as well; see Noel F. Busch, "Close-Up: Nelson A. Rockefeller," *Life*, April 27, 1942 (cover story); see also William S. Lieberman, "The Nelson Aldrich Rockefeller Collection," in *Twentieth-century Art from the Nelson Aldrich Rockefeller Collection* (New York: Museum of Modern Art, 1969), p. 27.

29. Walt Disney made the animated films *Saludos Amigos (Greetings, Friends)*, 1942, and *The Grain That Built a Hemisphere*, 1943. The trip also inspired the subsequent Disney film *The Three Caballeros*, 1944. Orson Welles traveled to Brazil in 1942 to film Rio's Carnival, as well as to shoot part of his film *It's All True*, coproduced by the OIAA and RKO Pictures—where Nelson Rockefeller was a major stockholder and board member. Welles waived his pay to support the war effort. He lost support from the producers well into production, and the film was never finished. More successful was the radio program he made for OIAA, *Hello Americans*, 1942–43, about the varied history, culture, music, and governments of the countries of Latin America and the Caribbean. Rita Hayworth and Bing Crosby were among the other American talents Rockefeller tapped to travel to South America.

30. The enormous influence the OIAA wielded on numerous independent public art museums across the U.S. was highly unusual; a federal agency (shaped by high-stakes personal business interests) essentially dictated an entirely new exhibition program in these four years.

31. Elizabeth McCausland, "Art in Wartime," *The New Republic*, May 15, 1944, p. 679.

32. MoMA's efforts were especially energetic hosting and circulating Latin American shows around the U.S. For a list of shows organized from 1941 to 1945, see "Circulating Exhibitions, 1931–1954," *The Bulletin of the Museum of Modern Art*, vol. 21 (1954), p. 12. One of MoMA's exhibitions sponsored by the OIAA, *Brazil Builds*, was sent not only around the U.S., but also to Mexico City, Brazil, and London.

33. For a list of shows, see "Past Exhibitions: 1940s," Art Museum of the Americas of the Organization of American States, accessed March 10, 2020, http://museum.oas.org/exhibitions/exhibitions_past_1940s.html. First Lady Eleanor Roosevelt's visit to a Latin American photography show at the PAU was covered in the *New York Times*, January 11, 1943. The Corcoran Gallery in Washington, D.C., also organized shows.

34. Portinari executed the four murals in the Hispanic Reading Room of the Library of Congress in 1941–42, *The Discovery of the Land, Entry in the Forest, Teaching of the Indians*, and *Discovery of Gold*. While Nelson Rockefeller attended their unveiling, Portinari was not in attendance. He had traveled to New York to execute a portrait of Abby Aldrich Rockefeller, Nelson's mother and a founder of MoMA, before returning to Brazil. While in Washington the year prior, Portinari had executed portraits of Nelson's three-year-old twins, Mary and Michael.

Commercial galleries such as Wildenstein and Perls, both in New York, also capitalized on this new interest in art "by our Good Neighbors to the South," as one reviewer wrote in the *New York Times*, March 13, 1944.

35. For attendance figure, see *New York Times*, February 8, 1942: for a study of the Macy's fair, see Lisa Crossman, "Macy's Latin American Fair: A Temple Built on the Anxieties of Inter/Americanism," *Material Culture Review*, vol. 79 (Spring 2014), pp. 60–77. Nelson Rockefeller served on the fair's advisory committee.

36. The eight-minute film was coproduced by Macy's. James H. Smith, *Pan-American Bazaar* [Office of the Coordinator of Inter-American Affairs; R. H. Macy and Company, Inc., 1942], 16 mm film, from Indiana University Library Moving Image Archive, https://media.dlib.indiana.edu/media_objects/1v53jx16x.

37. Kirstein deferred his military duty (America had entered the war on December 7, 1941) until early 1943 and went to South America twice, in 1941 and 1942, promoting two different inter-American artistic programs. Accompanying him in 1941 were the choreographer George Balanchine and their newly formed American Ballet Caravan. They staged a number of performances in South America and collaborated with local artists, musicians, dancers, and writers. For his 1942 trip for MoMA, he traveled through South America, from May through October. The museum gave him a $5,000 salary, $3,500 for expenses, and $12,500 to spend on art; see Martin Duberman, *The Worlds of Lincoln Kirstein* (Evanston, Ill., 2008), p. 373. Kirstein later cofounded the New York City Ballet.

38. Lasansky, *Figure (Figura)*, 1938, etching and drypoint, MoMA, Inter-American Fund, 711.1942. Rockefeller's large donation to MoMA for Latin American art purchases was the "Inter-American Fund."

39. Nelson Rockefeller served as director of Creole Petroleum Corporation, a subsidiary of Standard Oil of New Jersey, from 1935 to 1940. In 1937 he traveled to Venezuela, where the company was deeply invested in oil fields and production; see Nelson A. Rockefeller Personal Papers, Rockefeller Archive Center, https://dimes.rockarch.org/xtf/media/pdf/ead/FA339/FA339.pdf, p. 2. He reportedly visited every country in Latin America that year (Busch 1942, p. 84). When Mexico nationalized its petroleum production in 1938, his family's Venezuelan oil investments appeared acutely at risk. Rockefeller took another extended trip to South America in 1939 and submitted a proposal to create the OIAA to President Roosevelt upon his return. For discussion of labor unrest at Creole oil fields in Venezuela and Nelson Rockefeller's ill-fated attempts to win over workers, see Gerald Colby and Charlotte Dennett, *Thy Will Be Done: The Conquest of the Amazon and Evangelism in the Age of Oil* (New York, 1995). This book also presents an in-depth look at the Rockefeller family's vast holdings in South America, including Brazilian ranches, commercial banks, factories, and mines, and Nelson's public works to secure their safety.

40. Orozco's *The Subway*, 1928, oil on canvas, MoMA.

41. Lincoln Kirstein, *The Latin-American Collection of the Museum of Modern Art* (exh. cat.), MoMA (New York, 1943), March 31–June 6, 1943; Lasansky *Figure* print is listed on p. 88.

42. While the Lasansky literature usually reports that Taylor met the artist in Argentina in 1940 or 1941 (see, e.g., Fern 1975, p. 13), Kirstein reported seeing Taylor frequently in Argentina in the summer of 1942, lecturing on Italian paintings and purchasing art for the Met. Kirstein found Taylor bumbling and "all piss and vinegar," among other things (Duberman 2008, p. 380). Taylor's reputed blundering is on display in his oft-repeated remark about Lasansky's thorough study of the Metropolitan Museum of Art's collection of 150,000 prints. Taylor reportedly quipped, "It took an 'Indian' from South America to have the perseverance and guts to look at every print in the Museum" (Zigrosser 1959, p. 6). This statement is not only bigoted but inaccurate given Lasansky's heritage.

Taylor's correspondence records his activity working on exhibition exchanges between the U.S. and Argentina and confirms the 1942 date of his trip. In a note to Laurance Roberts, director of the Brooklyn Museum, who was organizing a South American show (of watercolors) in 1943, Taylor suggested contacting Alfredo González Garaño, founder of the Sociedad de Acuarelistas y Grabadores, whom he called "a swell guy and very pro-U.S." Taylor also reported to Roberts that the Met's print loans from the society were secured in exchange for material the Met had sent for exhibition in Argentina; see Letter, Laurance P. Roberts, Brooklyn Museum, November 6, 1942, box 2, folder 11, Francis Henry Taylor records, the Metropolitan Museum of Art Archives, New York. An exhibition review also notes Taylor's arrangement of the loans during a trip to Latin America "last summer," thus 1942; Carlyle Burrows, "Argentine Prints," *New York Herald Tribune*, September 5, 1943.

43. A letter from the Met's director's office to the American embassy in Buenos Aires, written just before *Argentine Prints* opened, stated that the Met had secured an article on the show in *The American Magazine of Art*, to be written by Teresa Umlauff, "who is at present doing research work at the Museum under the auspices of the Committee for Inter-American Artistic and Intellectual Relations." Letter from Horace H. F. Jayne, vice director, Metropolitan Museum, to Hayward Keniston, American embassy, Buenos Aires, August 25, 1943, Exhibitions - 1943 - Argentine Prints, 1942–1946, Office of the Secretary Records, the Metropolitan Museum of Art Archives, New York.

44. Kirstein reported that Taylor's purchasing on the trip was focused on "Death and Tombs" (Duberman 2008, p. 380), suggesting pre-Columbian art.

45. Just 42 of the 104 prints sent by the watercolor society on loan were selected by A. Hyatt Mayor, the Met's print curator, to be displayed in the Met's exhibition. There was considerable overlap in Argentine artists between the Met's and MoMA's 1943 shows. For a complete list of works lent and displayed at the Met, see "Argentine Prints," Shipping Receipts 1943, Registrar's Office, the Metropolitan Museum of Art, New York. I wish to thank Mary McNamara from the Met's Registrar's Office for assisting in researching this exhibition.

46. The show comprised a selection of prints by "modern Argentine artists"; September 4–October 17, 1943; Metropolitan Museum of Art "News Release," September 4, 1943. Attempts to tour the exhibition around the U.S. failed, as a release from customs duty could not be secured from the State Department. The Grolier Club in New York, however, showed an additional dozen Argentine prints from the group; see Robert Sugden to Dudley T. Easby, interdepartmental memo, Re: Argentine Prints, September 12, 1946, Exhibitions - 1943 - Argentine Prints, 1942–1946, Office of the Secretary Records, Metropolitan Museum of Art Archives, New York. The author wishes to thank Melissa Bowling, archivist, Metropolitan Museum of Art, for her assistance in researching this exhibition.

47. Thein and Lasansky 1975, no. 47, drypoint printed in sienna ink. Lasansky lent only this print, which was given an insurance value of $200 where values of $100 or $150 were more common. Only Alfredo Guido, Lasansky's teacher at the Escuela Superior de Bellas Artes, Buenos Aires, had higher-value prints, with two works valued at $250 and three at $200. Guido lent seven prints; four were exhibited; see "Argentine Prints," Shipping Receipts 1943, Registrar's Office, the Metropolitan Museum of Art, New York.

48. Kirstein recommended writer Victoria Ocampo to Henry Allen Moe at the Guggenheim Foundation, who invited her to come to the U.S. in 1943 to give a series of lectures; see Duberman 2008, p. 383, and Doris Meyer, *Victoria Ocampo: Against the Wind and the Tide* (Austin, Tex., 1979). Kirstein also recommended the Colombian anthropologist Gregorio Hernández de Alba; see Kirstein to Henry Allen Moe, November 11, 1942, Lincoln Kirstein Correspondence and Notes, series I, Museum of Modern Art Archives.

49. Following an antisemitic incident at the Escuela Superior de Bellas Artes in 1934 during Lasansky's student days, Alfredo Guido, the school's director, cited Lasansky's exceptional success there as evidence that the school did not and would not tolerate antisemitism at any time. Guido noted that a special dedication had been made to a Jewish student [Lasansky] who was a sculptor and engraver ("la dedicación especial que se ha tenido para con un alumno escultor y grabador incorporado este año"); see Alfredo Benavídez Bedoya, "Castagnino fue expulsado de la escuela de la Carcova en 1934: Una sequela de persecuciones," *Pagina 12*, November 4, 2003.

50. Michael Burdick, *For God and Fatherland: Religion and Politics in Argentina* (Albany, N.Y., 1995), pp. 53–55.

51. "Argentine Art 'Purged,'" *New York Times*, September 27, 1943.

52. MoMA's press release noted 11 nationalities represented among the artists. It stated that the show comprised 50 prints, plus a number of copper plates and matrices, but the final exhibition checklist records 60 prints, in addition to copper matrices, plaster casts, book covers, and other illustrations. "Master Checklist" for *Hayter and Studio 17: New Directions in Gravure*, Exhibitions, Museum of Modern Art, accessed November 21, 2019, https://www.moma.org/calendar/exhibitions/2777?locale=en. Lasansky's three prints in the show were: *Horse* (*Caballo*), 1944, engraving; *The Tear* (*La Lágrima*), 1944, color intaglio; and *Horse Breaker* (*Doma*), 1944, engraving, all lent by the artist. Each print on the checklist was assigned a handwritten value; Lasansky's were $20, $30, and $40, respectively. The notations "sold" next to Abraham Rattner's print *Among those who stood*, lent by the dealer Paul Rosenberg, and "NFS" [not for sale] next to Chagall's, suggest that most of the prints were for sale. Incidentally, a number were being offered for less than Lasansky's, such as André Masson's *Le Génie de l'espèce*, for $18, or Sue Fuller's *A Sailor's Dream*, for $10.

The venues of the 1944–46 tour are recorded by Christina Weyl. It traveled to Cincinnati Modern Art Society, Ohio; Baltimore Museum of Art, Md.; St. Paul Gallery and School of Art, Minn.; Detroit Institute of Arts; San Francisco Museum of Art; Fort Worth Art Association, Tex.; Museum of the Cranbrook Academy of Art, Bloomfield Hills, Mich.; University of Washington, Seattle; School of the Museum of Fine Arts, Boston; Cornell University, Ithaca, N.Y.; Vassar College, Poughkeepsie, N.Y.; see "Atelier 17 Group Exhibitions: A Chronology," Christina Weyl, accessed December 6, 2019, https://christinaweyl.com/atelier-17-group-exhibition-chronology/.

53. Thein and Lasansky 1975, no. 64. Mia's impression, inscribed by the artist, "my litel [*sic*] 1944 Christmas card to Sue / M Lasansky" was given by Lasansky to Sue Fuller, a fellow Atelier 17 printmaker. While the edition of the print, comprising 10 impressions, is dated 1945, this inscription indicates that the artist completed work on the plate and printed this impression before late December 1944.

54. I am grateful to Mia curator Tom Rassieur for suggesting that Lasansky's composition may be an oblique reference to Dürer's print.

55. Christina Weyl, *The Women of Atelier 17: Modernist Printmaking in Midcentury New York* (New Haven, Conn., 2019), pp. 96–97. According to Sue Fuller, Lasansky adopted Hayter's preference for the engraver's burin, which was uncompromising and required brute force to carve lines into the copper plate, over the etching needle, which Hayter considered "lady-like," in its soft, malleable lines drawn on a prepared plate ; see Weyl 2019, p. 252n11.

56. Jessica Lemieux, *Finding Aid to the San Francisco Museum of Modern Art Exhibition Records, 1934–ongoing* (San Francisco, 2008), pp. 25, 51, 140.

57. "Mauricio Lasansky of Argentina, Best in Philadelphia Show," *New York Times*, April 14, 1945, p. 13.

58. Lasansky is quoted in 1970 as describing himself as a "Midwest Argentinian"; see Norris 1970, pp. 3–4.

59. H. W. Janson was an art historian. Lasansky had teaching offers from the Art Institute of Chicago and the University of New Mexico, Albuquerque (Norris 1970, p. 4). However, he wished to live and work far away from big cities and the art establishment and preferred the simplicity of Iowa, which he felt was also "the most American place" of the three; see Norris; Zigrosser 1975, p. 9; and Fern 1975, pp. 15–16. At the time Iowa hired Lasansky, it wanted to expand its arts programs, given the war's end and anticipated influx of student veterans entering school supported by the G.I. Bill.

60. *Time*, 1961, p. 68.

61. "Paperbacks of Painting," *Time*, June 2, 1958, p. 64.

62. William M. Friedman, *A New Direction in Intaglio: The Work of Mauricio Lasansky and His Students* (exh. cat.), Walker Art Center, Minneapolis, and Colorado Springs Fine Arts Center (Minneapolis, 1949). This show featured work by Carroll Cassill, Ernest Freed, Barbara Fumagalli, Ray French, Arthur Levine, Malcolm Myers, and James Steg. See also *Mauricio Lasansky and the First Generation: Lee Chesney, Barbara Fumagalli, Arthur Levine, Janet K. Ruttenberg, Donn Steward* (exh. cat.), University of Iowa (Iowa City, 2014). Lasansky also trained artist Miriam Schapiro and MoMA print curator Riva Castleman.

63. See, e.g., "Dachau Captured by Americans Who Kill Guards, Liberate 32,000," *New York Times*, May 1, 1945, front page and p. 5. This article erroneously described Dachau as an extermination camp. While tens of thousands of prisoners died here from disease, starvation, cold, and, less frequently, hangings and shootings, Dachau was a concentration camp, not an extermination camp. A gas chamber was built in a barrack but not used. Thus Jewish prisoners were not part of the regular population. But thousands of Jews were present at the time of the liberation, having arrived from death marches and evacuations from the extermination camps to the east (Griselda Pollock and Max Silverman, *Concentrationary Cinema: Aesthetics as Political Resistance in Alain Resnais's "Night and Fog"* [1955] [New York, 2011], p. 11).

64. Ziva Amishai-Maisels, *Depiction and Interpretation: The Influence of the Holocaust on the Visual Arts* (Oxford, 1993), pp. 245–46, 462.

65. Lynda Morris, *Picasso: Peace and Freedom* (exh. cat.), Tate Liverpool (London, 2010), p. 70. Given the date of the work, it is often wrongly assumed (by his contemporaries Zervos and Barr and by a number of later writers) that the painting represents Picasso's response to Nazi camps and photos. The work was begun in 1944, which largely precludes this theory. Furthermore, the scene is clearly set in a domestic interior, with a dining table with food, napkins, and a pitcher, not a camp; see Christian Zervos, *Exhibition of Paintings by Picasso and Matisse* (exh. cat.), December 1945, Victoria and Albert Museum (London, 1945), unpaginated; Alfred H. Barr, *Fifty Years of Picasso* (exh. cat.), MoMA (New York, 1946), p. 250; Amishai-Maisels 1993, pp. 57–58.

66. Even without specific allusions, the literature consistently ties the "For an Eye an Eye" series to the Nazi barbarism; see, e.g., Zigrosser 1975, p. 10; Danoff 1976, p. 13. Both authors knew the artist personally and wrote about the series for publications with which Lasansky was directly involved. Amishai-Maisels's assertion that Lasansky's *Pietà* and *Near East (Pietà)* of 1948 incorporate Holocaust-related imagery cannot be substantiated. She also sees the latter referring to the Israeli War of Independence; Amishai-Maisels 1993, p. 246. For other reading of the two prints, see William Friedman and Ann Wittchen, *Intaglios: The Work of Mauricio Lasansky and Other Printmakers Who Studied with Him at the State University of Iowa* (Iowa City, Iowa, 1959). The State University of Iowa changed its name to the University of Iowa in 1964.

67. Charlotte Willard, "Drawings from Hell," *Look*, February 21, 1967, p. 79; Grace Glueck, "Non-Fairy Tale," *New York Times*, March 26, 1967, Arts and Leisure section, p. 24; and Norris 1970, p. 4, with published quotes from Lasansky; see also Amishai-Maisels 1993, pp. 246, 462n18–19 (citing unpublished interview). Lasansky's statement is about his various failed attempts earlier in his career to treat the subject of the Nazi murders prior to "The Nazi Drawings," rather than about "For an Eye an Eye" in particular.

68. Amishai-Maisels 1993, p. 246; Danoff 1976, p. 13.

69. Norris 1970, p. 70. Lasansky said, "[The artist] should decide which way to go, esthetic or ethical."

70. Lasansky interview, Muhlert 1976, p. 17.

71. For details of the trip, Lasansky's daughter Nina has written two accounts of the family's year in Spain; see Nina Barragan, "Mauricio Lasansky: View from a Spanish Bridge," *Kansas Quarterly*, vol. 14 (Fall 1982), pp. 5–18, and Barragan 2019.

72. Leonardo Lasansky described for me the memorable Holy Week processions in Valencia the family saw.

73. Lasansky interview, Muhlert 1976, p. 18.

74. I am grateful to Armin Kunz for pointing out Picasso's enduring influence in these works, particularly the Spanish artist's first prints.

75. Lasansky's retrospective opened at the Art Institute of Chicago in March 1960 and traveled to the Brooklyn Museum of Art in November 1961, among other venues.

76. Lasansky interview, Willard 1967, p. 80. There is an undated photo of Lasansky in his studio with a large preliminary sketch tacked to the wall relating to *No. 30* in "The Nazi Drawings." The rough study shows a figure standing with his hands covering his eyes. The head (and arms?) of a barely sketched second figure is seen looming above the primary figure's shoulders. The photo, taken between 1958 and 1962, shows how the subject festered in the artist for years before he made the final series.

ART AND FAITH: CRAFTING A RENEWED RELATIONSHIP AFTER AUSCHWITZ

Rabbi Barry D. Cytron

On April 11, 1961, in a Jerusalem auditorium hastily converted into a courtroom, case no. 40/61, the Attorney General vs. Adolf, son of Adolf Karl Eichmann, was called to order. Two weeks into the trial, after preliminaries and opening arguments, the calling of witnesses commenced. Among the first was a 46-year-old woman, wearing an unadorned box jacket and darkened eyeglasses.

> **Attorney General**: With the Court's permission, I shall now call the first witness, Mrs. Ada Lichtman. The first testimonies are meant to prove the period of small-scale terror in the occupied areas in Poland.
>
> **Presiding Judge**: [*to witness*] Do you speak Hebrew?
>
> **Witness Lichtman**: Not too well, perhaps Yiddish would be better.[1]

In the subsequent decades, both the trial and that particular moment have attained a pivotal place in our understanding of mid-20th-century judicial and world history. Ada Lichtman (fig. 3.1), born in Poland, was one of 47 prisoners to survive the Sobibor death camp. Her testimony was unprecedented on many levels, beginning with her request to bear witness in Yiddish. Hearing her speak in her native tongue was apparently unnerving—and electrifying: "You shivered on hearing the words of the language of the slaughtered and the burned."[2] It was more than just the words themselves. This is how legal scholar Lawrence Douglas describes her presence:

> ... from the moment Lichtman took the oath, the Eichmann trial assumed a radically different tenor. ... during her entire time on the stand her eyes remained concealed behind dark sunglasses. She appeared, then, to be blind (though she was not), an impression made all the more striking as the dramatic force of her testimony found focus in the words, "I saw everything." Her physical appearance in the courtroom suggested ... a witness who has been blinded by what she has seen. No longer capable of sight, all that she can see is the vision of atrocity that has been permanently burnt upon an inner retina.[3]

Ada Lichtman's presence, alongside some one hundred other survivors, was certainly one of the defining features of the trial. It was also the most contested. The trial's other innovations—the first to be broadcast and telecast around the world, the first to

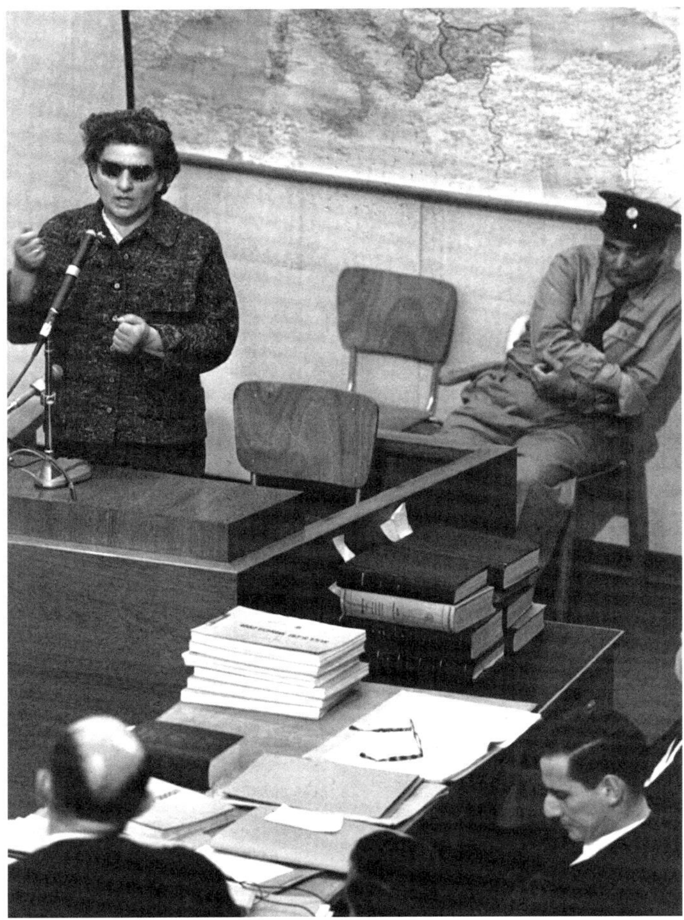

Fig. 3.1 Ada Lichtman, witness for the prosecution, Eichmann trial, Jerusalem, 1961. Government Press Office of Israel, National Photo Collection
Lichtman was one of the few survivors of the Sobibor extermination camp.

emphasize genocide as a discrete element of World War II, the first to underline the fate of European Jews at the center of a juridical deliberation—were met largely with ready acceptance. By contrast, survivor testimony occasioned persistent negative judgment, from the Israeli three-judge panel during the proceedings and by observers commenting in the years after: many of the men and women brought to the witness stand admittedly had no direct connection to the defendant.

Gideon Hausner, the attorney general who led the prosecution, would vigorously defend his decision to call those survivors. Their testimony, he argued, was absolutely crucial. How else to record the incremental process by which Europe was emptied of most of its Jewish inhabitants? Only through the presence and the words of those who experienced it—enactment by enactment, SS *Aktion* by SS *Aktion*,[4] trainload by trainload—could the calamity be fittingly, though never fully, comprehended. As Hausner wrote:

> The only way to concretize it was to call surviving witnesses, as many as the framework of the trial would allow, and to ask each of them to tell a tiny fragment of what he had seen and experienced. The story of a particular set of events, told by a single witness, is still tangible enough to be *visualized*.[5]

Today, how do we meet the prosecutor's challenge, to "visualize" as Hausner called it, "the fantastic, unbelievable apparition that emerges from the Nazi documents"?[6] To meet that responsibility, both in our generation and for future ones, we now require Mauricio Lasansky's "The Nazi Drawings."

The early 1960s, during which Lasansky was beginning the drawings, coincided with an increasing public awareness of the events that had prompted him to undertake his work. As is now understood by historians, the Eichmann trial shattered the widespread silence—either willful or merely uninformed—that had largely obscured the Nazi crimes for the prior 15 years. In the years following the trial, the pace of global recognition and study of the events significantly quickened.

The coverage of the trial, including some early, sensationalist reporting about Eichmann, gave way to more judicious, thoughtful analysis. Scholars across the academic disciplines sought to plumb the meanings and implications of what had befallen the targeted communities. Filmmakers and playwrights, novelists and memoirists found ready audiences. Even the idiom of 20th-century mass murder was being transformed. The Nuremberg trials (1945–49) had employed the subdued terminology of *war crimes* and *conspiracy against peace*. By the 1960s, the terms *Sonderbehandlung*[7] (special treatment), *Final Solution*, and *genocide*, along with the words *Holocaust* and *Shoah*, had entered the vocabulary of 20th-century evil.

Moreover, the Holocaust as a discrete field of specialization was just about to materialize, occasioned by the pioneering and hard-won publication in 1961 of Raul Hilberg's *Destruction of the European Jews*. His research and conclusions would indelibly stamp the discipline, and, to this day, his analysis and initial conclusions remain the touchstone, though no longer the final word, for our study of the entire epoch.

Hilberg opens his study with a compelling summary of the antecedents that prepared the way for the annihilation of Europe's Jews:

> The missionaries of Christianity had said in effect: *You have no right to live among us as Jews*. The secular rulers who followed had proclaimed: *You have no right to live among us*. The German Nazis at last proclaimed: *You have no right to live*. . . . the German Nazis did not discard the past; they built upon it. They did not begin a development; they completed it.[8]

These frequently cited words may provide some historical backdrop for the presence of so many religious symbols and personages appearing throughout "The Nazi Drawings." The cruciform seems ever present, sometimes faintly discernible, other times quite pronounced.

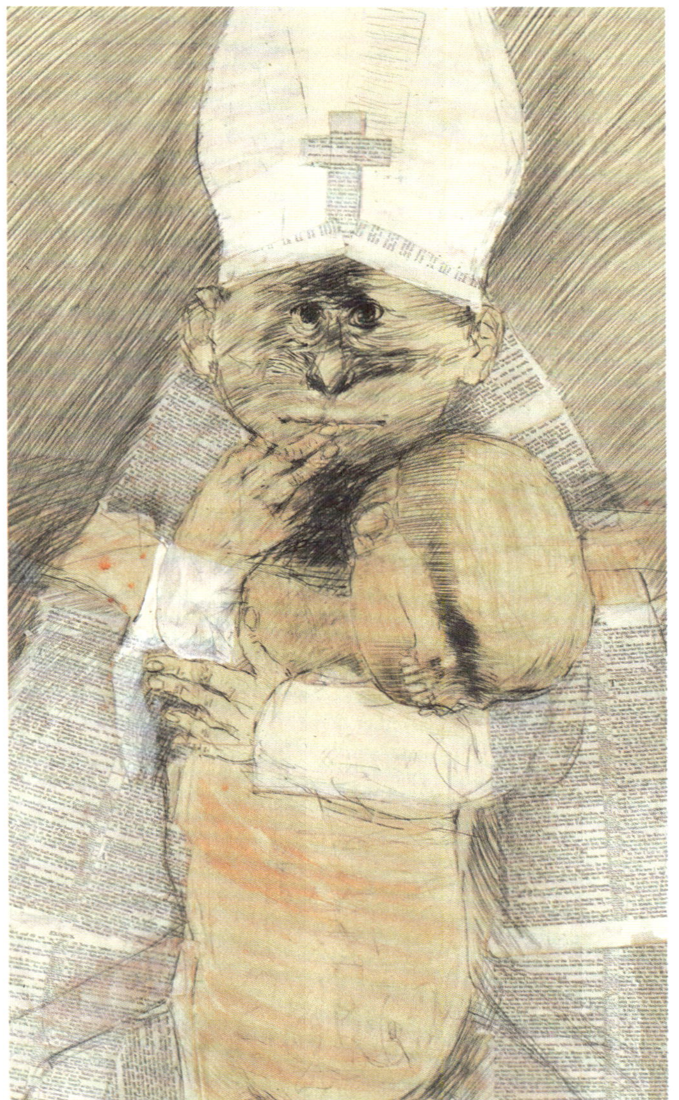

Fig. 3.2 Mauricio Lasansky, *No. 23* (detail), "The Nazi Drawings"

Outlines of clergy clothed in cassock and collar, chasuble and miter, populate the final set of portrayals. A church leader (fig. 3.2) cuddles an infant victim, his facial expression inscrutable, his cope enigmatically inscribed with the words of Genesis and Exodus, *the* founding biblical texts of the Jewish people.

Should we view these disturbing images as an instantiation of Hilberg's triadic argument, a material realization of his assertion of theology's relationship to the gas chambers? Or perhaps we should understand them as referencing the heated controversy surrounding German playwright Rolf Hochhuth's *The Deputy*. The play, which had premiered in Berlin in 1963 (and was mounted later that year in London and the following year in New York), depicted the wartime pope, Pius XII, as not only silent about but indifferent to the fate of the Jewish victims.[9] That argument about the pope's dealings seems to find an echo in literary critic Edwin Honig's essay for the 1966 exhibition catalogue *The Nazi Drawings*: "Lasansky focuses here [in drawings *No.* 22 and *No.* 29] on the irreconcilability between the slaughter of the innocents and the unaiding witness of the established church."[10]

That storm of controversy had erupted not only as Lasansky was at work on the drawings but during the same years the Catholic Church was absorbed in examining its stance vis-à-vis the Jewish people and their faith. In 1958, with the death of Pius XII, a new pontiff had been elected. Soon after taking the reins of the Church, John XXIII announced his intention to call for an ecumenical council to reappraise the Church's basic tenets, including a reformulation of its ritual practice and the shaping of its stance in response to the post–World War II world then unfolding. Spurred on by a fateful meeting with French Jewish scholar and Holocaust survivor Jules Isaac, the pope urged the synod, now known popularly as

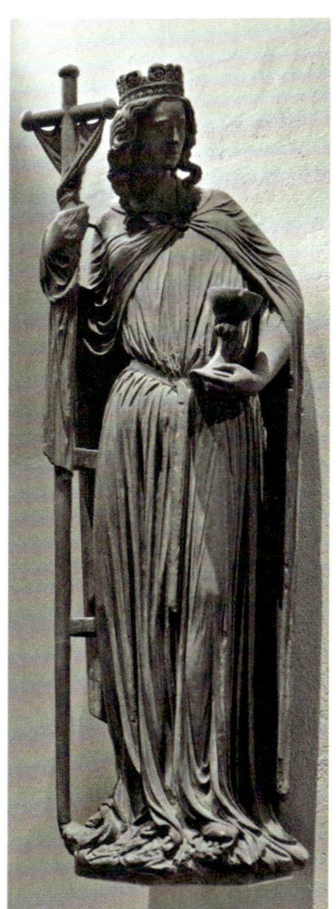

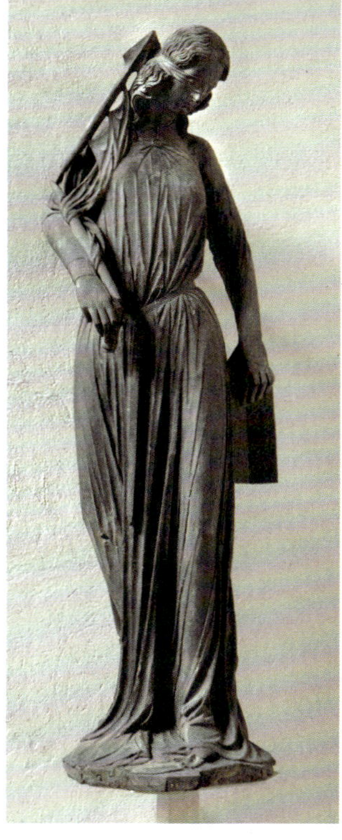

Fig. 3.3 ***The Church and the Synagogue*****, c. 1220–30, pink sandstone, formerly Strasbourg Cathedral, south portal, now in the Musée de l'Oeuvre Notre-Dame, Strasbourg, France**
The personification of Church (or Ecclesia) at left is upright and triumphant in contrast with Synagogue (or Synagoga) at right, portrayed as bowed, blinded, and broken.

Vatican II (1962–65), to also undertake an assessment of its historic teachings about Judaism.

In the more than half century that has elapsed, our understanding of the fraught relations between Jews and Christians, central to the council's work in this area and clearly salient to Lasansky's drawings, has been dramatically transformed. The interrogation by scholars and theologians of this troubled history has been nothing short of extraordinary.

Ancient texts, holy scripture, classical theological treatises, numerous papal bulls, and Catholic religious art (fig. 3.3), alongside the complicated history of interactions, interdictions, and persecutions, have been scrutinized and dissected. In response, multiple Church bodies have upended long-standing postures, committing themselves to inward reflection and then public pronouncement. In so doing, they have sought to scrutinize the role of their religious doctrines, and their faithful, in fostering an environment of enmity, hoping thereby to find a new beginning "after such knowledge."[11]

In addressing the alleged complicity of the Christian faith in the Holocaust, historians, popular essayists, even novelists have weighed in with a range of judgments. One helpful way of grappling with the many competing positions is through the studies of Marc Saperstein, a distinguished medievalist, ordained rabbi, and university leader. His review of the literature touching on this issue is not only the most comprehensive, but the most nuanced and balanced, too.[12]

Rabbi Saperstein employs a useful taxonomy to classify the multiple perspectives on Christian doctrine's connection to the Shoah. Many adopt what he labels a "model of continuity." Its advocates maintain that Nazi antisemitism advanced directly from "anti-Judaism," the term regularly applied to historical Christian denigration of Jewish faith. That disparagement, both theological and social, comprises several distinct strands.

New Testament texts and the early Church fathers had spoken of Jewish belief as "superseded," permanently displaced from divine favor. That was due to the "blindness" of the Jews during Jesus' time, both to his message and the meaning of his life. Moreover, the Jewish people were held to be ultimately responsible for his crucifixion, as well as willfully oblivious to the significance his death was said to confer. Finally, that double badge of shame was considered compounded by ongoing Jewish intransigence in refusing to embrace the Christian faith. Those adopting the "continuity model" detect an unerring trajectory from this complex of vilifications to the 19th- and 20th-century calumnies that culminated in mass extermination.

Those holding to the "continuity model" regularly rely on various metaphors to make their case. They may speak of Christian doctrine as providing the *roots*, the *indispensable seedbed*, or the *spawning ground* for the genocide. Others invoke "scientific" language, speaking of antisemitism as *evolving* from Christianity's negative tropes about Jews and their faith, or its being the *lethal metastasis* of such animus. While Saperstein recognizes the appeal of invoking such metaphors, he contends that scholarship requires firmer evidence than mere clever phrasing to demonstrate historical causality.[13]

In sharp contrast, other writers maintain that the hatreds of modernity were predicated on absolutely different rationales and emerged from far different circumstances. Here, for example, is how Salo Baron, the doyen of 20th-century Jewish historians, stated it when, as an "expert witness," he offered testimony in the opening

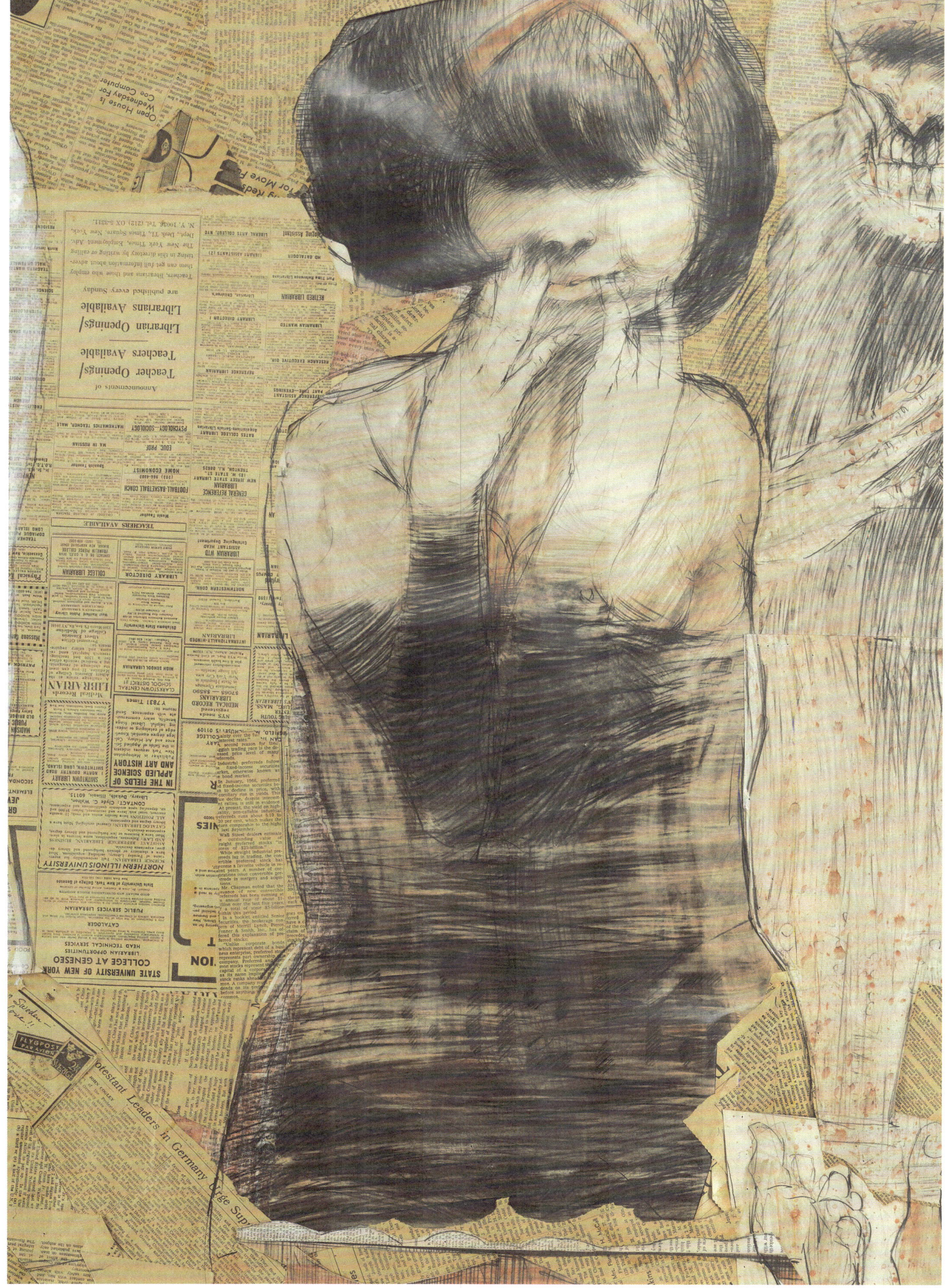

Fig. 3.4 Mauricio Lasansky, *Triptych*, left panel (detail), "The Nazi Drawings"

days of the Eichmann trial: "I want to say that the Nazi movement not only did not turn the clock back . . . but it brought to the world new elements which had no precedent, and which were distinct from the whole history of anti-Semitism of two thousand years and more."[14]

Saperstein groups assessments such as Baron's (whom he does not quote) as belonging to "models of discontinuity." Those adopting this position often stress the importance of Saint Augustine's having set the parameters that guided medieval Christendom's treatment of Jews. Scattered across his writings, Augustine had offered bifurcated counsel, commending that Jews be both shielded and shamed. They were to be protected as "living witnesses" to the Old Testament, the source of the new faith, but they were to live a degraded existence as punishment for rejecting Jesus and his teachings, and for their alleged culpability in his death.[15]

There is ample historical evidence that Augustine's teachings served to protect Jewish communities throughout the Middle Ages. Speaking in large measure for many advocates of the discontinuity model, one noted Jewish theologian puts it this way: "Before the twentieth century, the Christian religious tradition was both the source of much traditional anti-Jewish hostility and an effective barrier against the final murderous step. Something changed in the twentieth century."[16]

Though Saperstein judiciously evaluates writers on both sides of this question, there can be little doubt where his allegiance lies. That is best indicated, perhaps, by his pointed rebuttal to a scholar who had argued that Christianity was the "cause" for the Holocaust:

> Many things "helped make [the Holocaust] possible," including World War I and the Treaty of Versailles, a world-wide depression, the charismatic personality and rhetorical power of Hitler, the invention of the machine gun and the technology of gas chambers and crematoria, the steam engine for railroad transportation and IBM cards for keeping efficient records, American isolationism, sophisticated techniques of indoctrination and propaganda. How does one rank the importance of such factors, in comparison with the teachings of the church?[17]

The debate Saperstein so ably surveys focuses on matters of interpretation and analysis that may ultimately be impossible to resolve. Nevertheless, one can easily imagine that those on both sides of the question would applaud the monumental strides that have been taken by institutional Christianity to right the grave wrongs of the past. That process of religiously inspired contrition began publicly just as Lasansky must have been readying the final triptych that brought "The Nazi Drawings" to their culmination. We know this because of a *New York Times* story incorporated into the triptych itself.

The headline for that August 8, 1965, news piece, partially visible in the left panel on the lower left (fig. 3.4), reads, "Protestant Leaders in Germany Urge Support of Vatican Draft on Jews."[18] Not only the headline but its date is noteworthy. As noted earlier, Pope John XXIII had convened the Second Vatican Council in 1962. The participating bishops were nearing the conclusion of their work and had saved one of the most vexing questions, that of the relationship of the Catholic Church to the Jewish people, for the final months. Would the ancient charge of deicide be overturned? Would the language of the Vatican text make reference to antisemitism, to genocide, to the young State of Israel? And what impact would interfaith initiatives in Rome have for other Christian denominations across the globe?

In its own way, that *Times* headline and report Lasansky collaged into *Triptych* speak to the subsequent history of Jewish-Christian relationships. The article had highlighted leaders of the German Lutheran Church urging the council to move for adoption of statements that would not just heal, but herald a new beginning for Jews and Christians. The Vatican II declaration *Nostra aetate*, promulgated on October 28, 1965, accomplished both those aims. The sparse declaration condemned antisemitism, lifted the blanket charge of responsibility for the death of Jesus from off the Jewish people, and insisted that Jewish people and their faith must not be "presented as rejected or accursed by God."[19] It's no exaggeration to say, as one interfaith activist did on the 50th anniversary of its proclamation, that "there have been more positive Christian-Jewish encounters since 1965 than there were in the first 20 centuries of Christianity."[20]

Many mainline Protestant denominations followed in the footsteps of Rome. In some cases, such as those of the Presbyterian (PCUSA, 1987), Episcopal (1988), and Lutheran (ELCA, 1994) communities, they go beyond the Vatican declaration, associating their statements more directly with the Holocaust. In 1998, the Vatican would finally issue its own study of those years, entitled "We Remember: A Reflection on the Shoah."

Approaching "The Nazi Drawings" in our day promises, then, to be a noticeably different experience than when they were initially shown. In the 1960s, one can safely assume that many viewers were puzzled, perhaps taken aback, maybe even highly offended by the artist's allusions to Christianity's implication in the Nazi genocide. Over the last 50 years, as has been noted, scholars and clergy, both Christian and Jewish, have labored to forthrightly illumine the entangled relationship between religious teachings and the Nazi genocide. That has led to sustained efforts at bridge building between the two faith communities.

Those efforts are a testimony to the power of truth telling and open confrontation with the past, as well as resolute, intentional commitment to communal reconciliation. With the wisdom and courage demanded in sustaining those efforts, it may be possible to realize the world Lasansky looked forward to when he wrote: "Man's dignity is a force and the only modus vivendi by which man and his history survive."[21]

NOTES

1. Testimony of Ada Lichtman, Session 20, April 25, 1961. For transcript see Nizkor Project, B'Nai Brith Canada, accessed April 28, 2020, http://nizkor.com/hweb/people/e/eichmann-adolf/transcripts/Sessions/Session-020-07.html.

2. Tom Segev, *The Seventh Million: The Israelis and the Holocaust*, trans. Haim Watzman (New York, 1993), p. 350.

3. Lawrence Douglas, *The Memory of Judgment: Making Law and History in the Trials of the Holocaust* (New Haven, Conn., and London, 2001), pp. 102, 104.

4. *Aktion* was the German euphemism for an operation involving the mass assembly, deportation, and murder of Jews by the Nazis during the Holocaust.

5. Gideon Hausner, *Justice in Jerusalem* (New York, 1966), p. 292, emphasis added.

6. Hausner 1966, p. 292.

7. The Nazi euphemism first employed in the T4 death programs for "invalids" and those who were mentally disabled and later applied to the use of death chambers and Zyklon B gas.

8. Raul Hilberg, *The Destruction of the European Jews* (Chicago and London, 1961), pp. 3–4, emphasis added.

9. In early 2019, Pope Francis announced that the Vatican Secret Archives, which contain many thousands of documents about the wartime pope, were to be opened. "The Church is not afraid of history," he emphasized when heralding this decision. The pope was true to his word, and in March 2020, scholars began poring over the documents, only to have their efforts disrupted by the COVID-19 pandemic. It will take many months/years of sustained scrutiny by specialists to determine precisely what new evidence those records provide about what Pius XII knew and did. Alas one thing is likely to result. In an era of hyperpartisanship and routine claims of "fake news," few minds will be dissuaded from the positions they have already staked out. See Gillian Brockell, "Pope Pius XII was silent during the Holocaust. Now Vatican records may reveal whether he collaborated with the Nazis," *Washington Post*, March 3, 2020, https://www.washingtonpost.com/history/2020/03/03/pope-pius-holocaust-vatican-records/. See also David Kertzer's essay in the *Atlantic*, "The Pope, the Jews, and the Secrets in the Archives," August 27, 2020, https://www.theatlantic.com/ideas/archive/2020/08/the-popes-jews/615736/. Kertzer, a Pulitzer Prize recipient, has written extensively about the wartime pontiff. An earlier book, *The Kidnapping of Edgardo Mortara* (New York, 1996), was adapted by playwright Alfred Uhry as *Edgardo Mine* in 2002.

10. Edwin Honig, "The Nazi Drawings of Mauricio Lasansky," in Mauricio Lasansky, *The Nazi Drawings* (exh. cat.), Philadelphia Museum of Art and eight other venues (Philadelphia, 1966), p. 7 of a nine-page essay, unnumbered.

11. These words are from T. S. Eliot's poem "Gerontion" (1920). A middle stanza opens with the words, "After such knowledge, what forgiveness?" These lines are cited in several post-Holocaust writings, most notably in the chronicle of Eva Hoffman, *After Such Knowledge: Memory, History and the Legacy of the Holocaust* (New York, 2004).

12. See Marc Saperstein, *Moments of Crisis in Jewish-Christian Relations* (London and Philadelphia, 1989), pp. 38–50; his more extended treatments of this subject may be found in his "Christian Doctrine and the 'Final Solution': The State of the Question," in *Remembering for the Future: The Holocaust in an Age of Genocide*, vol. 2, eds. John K. Roth and Elisabeth Maxwell (Hampshire, U.K., and New York, 2001), pp. 814–41; and "Christian Doctrine and the Death Camps: The Ambiguities of Influence," in *Interpreting the "Spirit of Assisi": Challenges to Interfaith Dialogue in a Pluralistic World*, eds. Maria Diemling and Thomas J. Herbst (Canterbury, U.K., 2013), pp. 49–69.

13. Saperstein 2001, pp. 825–26.

14. "Eichmann Trial, Session 12 and 13, Testimonies of A. Less and S. Baron," April 24, 1961, from the United States Holocaust Memorial Museum, Steven Spielberg Film and Video Archive, video, 1:03:25, https://collections.ushmm.org/search/catalog/irn1001039.

15. See Jeremy Cohen, *Living Letters of the Law: Ideas of the Jew in Medieval Christianity* (Berkeley, Calif., and London, 1999), pp. 19–65.

16. Richard L. Rubenstein, *The Cunning of History: Mass Death and the American Future* (New York, 1975), p. 5.

17. Marc Saperstein, "An Indictment: Half Right," review of *The Popes Against the Jews: The Vatican's Role in the Rise of Modern Anti-Semitism*, by David Kertzer, *Commonweal*, September 28, 2001, pp. 19–21.

18. John Cogley, "Protestant Leaders in Germany Urge Support of Vatican Draft on Jews," *New York Times*, Sunday, August 8, 1965, p. 54.

19. "Declaration on the Relation of the Church to Non-Christian Religions, Nostra Aetate," Holy See, accessed April 15, 2020, http://www.vatican.va/archive/hist_councils/ii_vatican_council/documents/vat-ii_decl_19651028_nostra-aetate_en.html.

20. Rabbi A. James Rudin, "On 50th Anniversary of Nostra Aetate, a Glass Half Full," *National Catholic Reporter*, October 28, 2015, https://www.ncronline.org/blogs/ncr-today/50th-anniversary-nostra-aetate-glass-half-full.

21. Lasansky 1966, artist statement, p. 4 of unnumbered text; see p. 102 in this volume.

"THE NAZI DRAWINGS"

Mauricio Lasansky, *Nos. 1–30* and *Triptych*, 1961–71
Lent by the Levitt Foundation

No. 1

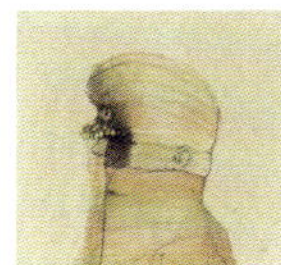

No. 2

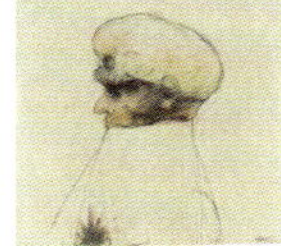

No. 3

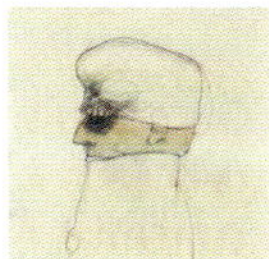

No. 4

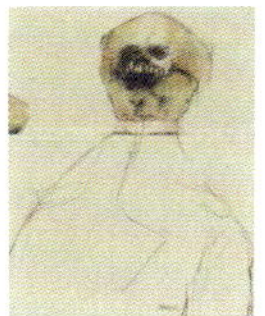

No. 5

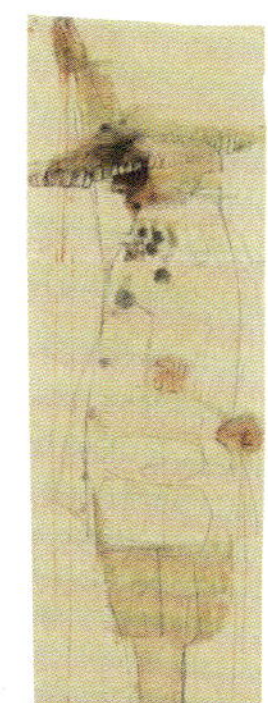

No. 6

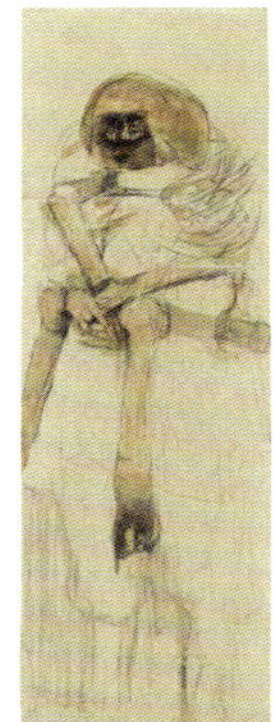

No. 7

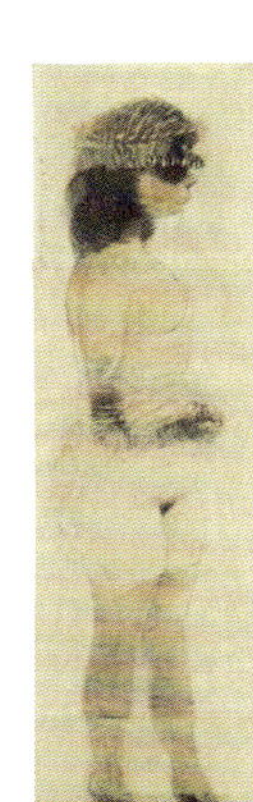

No. 8

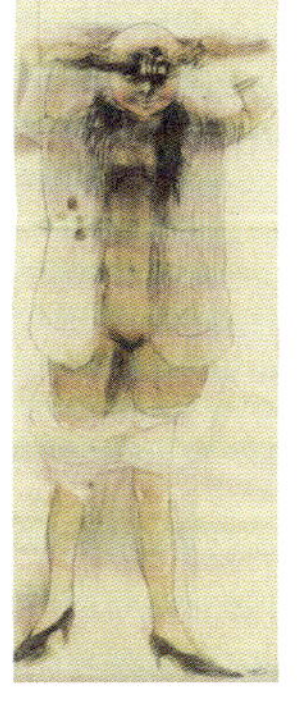

No. 9

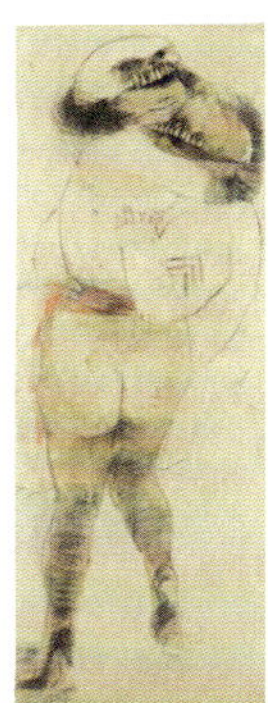

No. 10

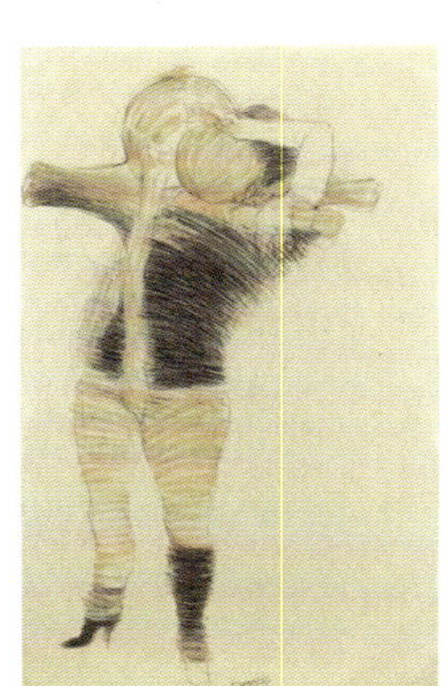

No. 11

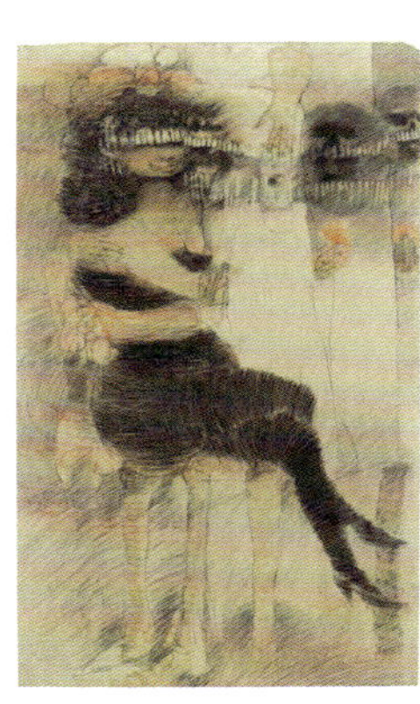

No. 12

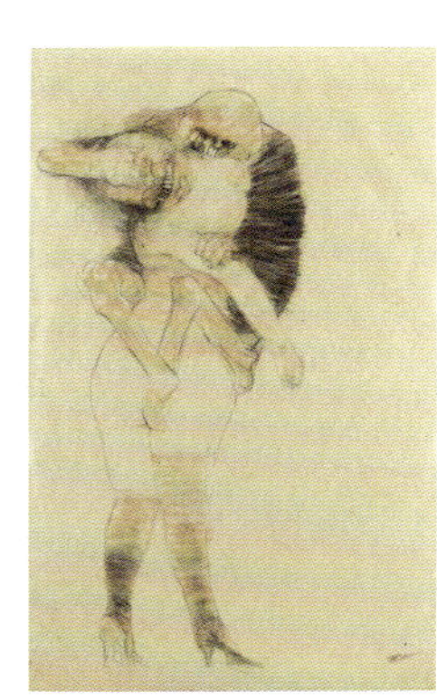

No. 13

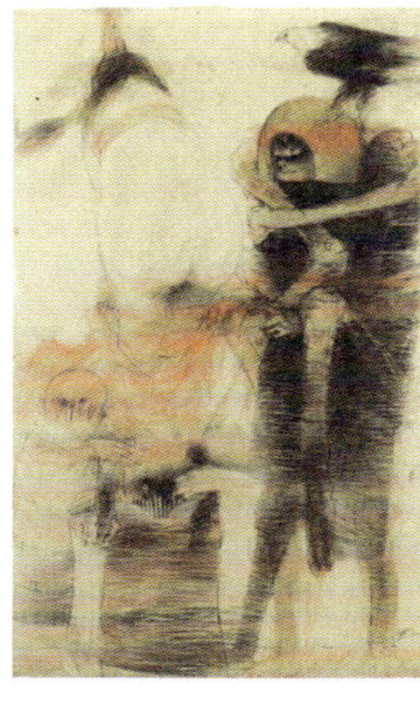

No. 14

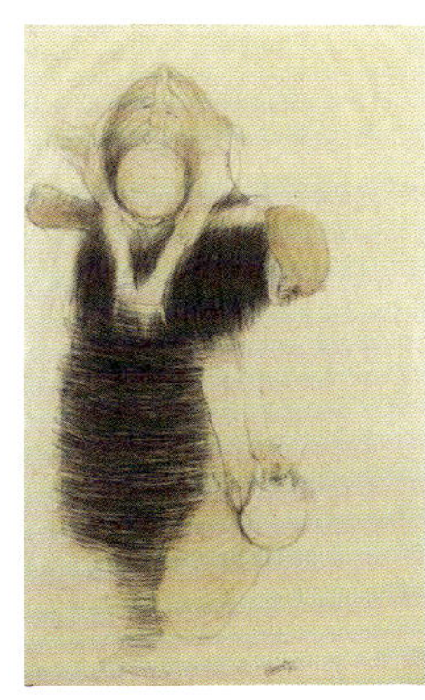

No. 15

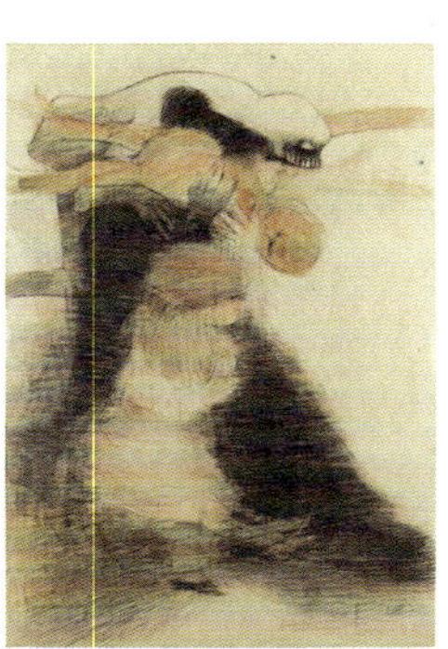

No. 16

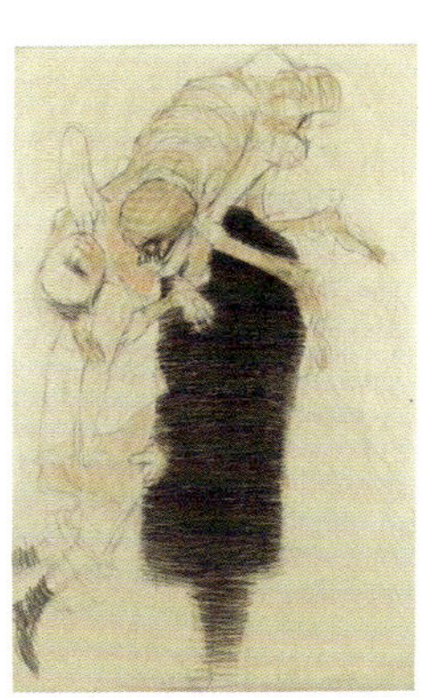

No. 17

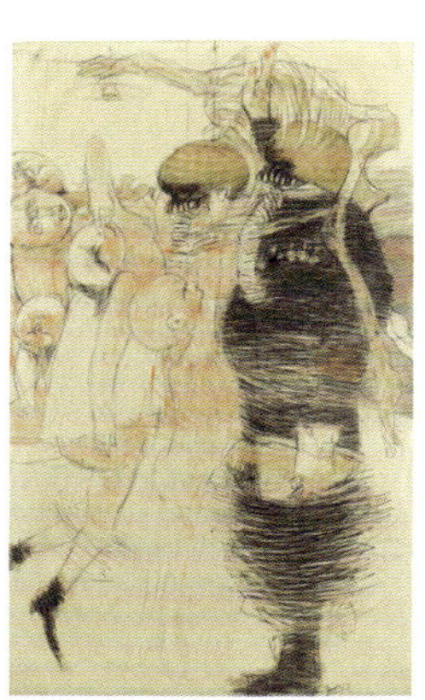

No. 18

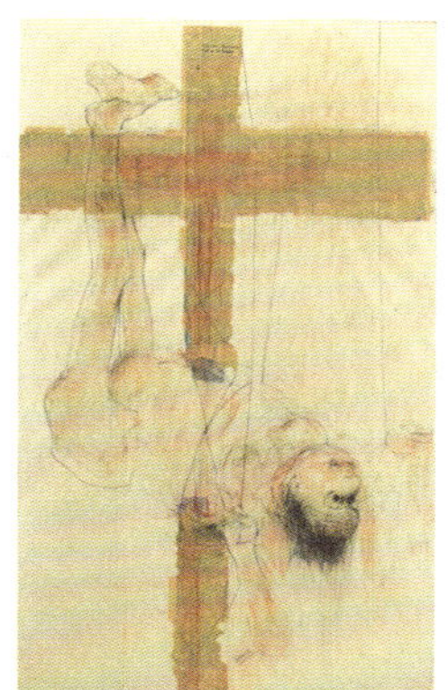

No. 19

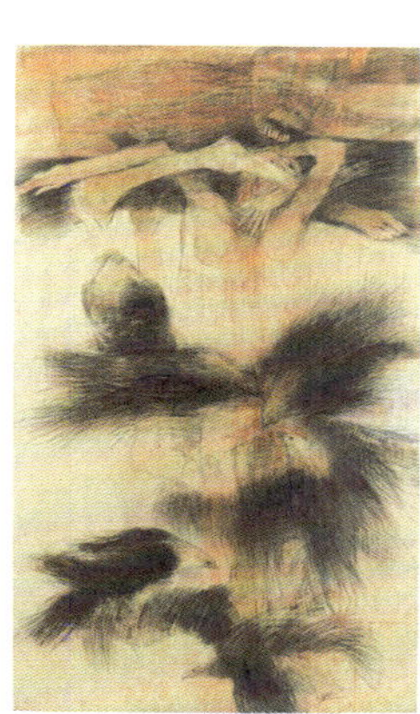

No. 20

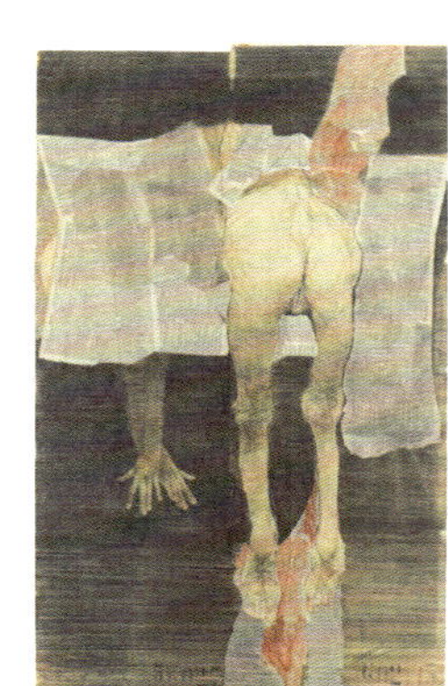

No. 21

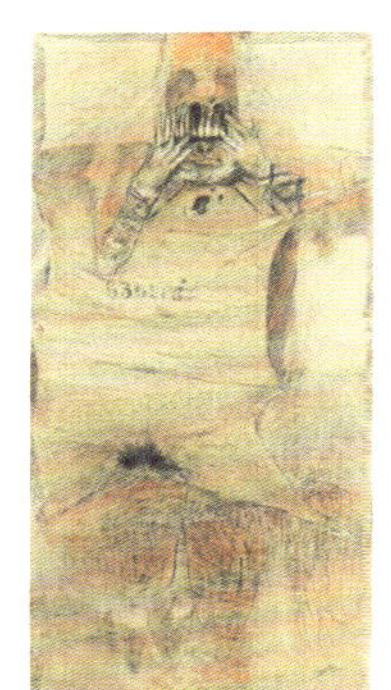

No. 22

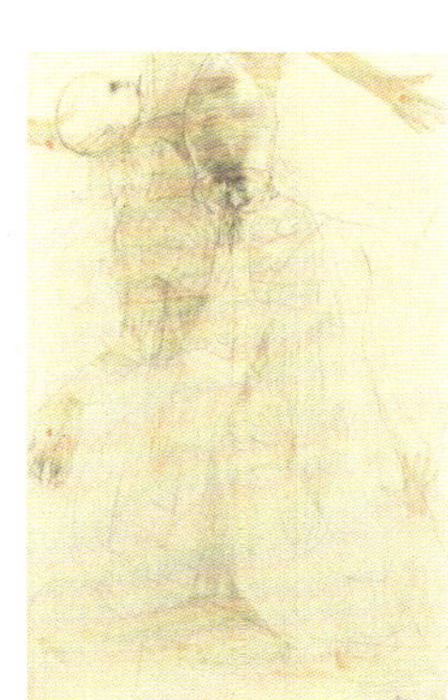

No. 23

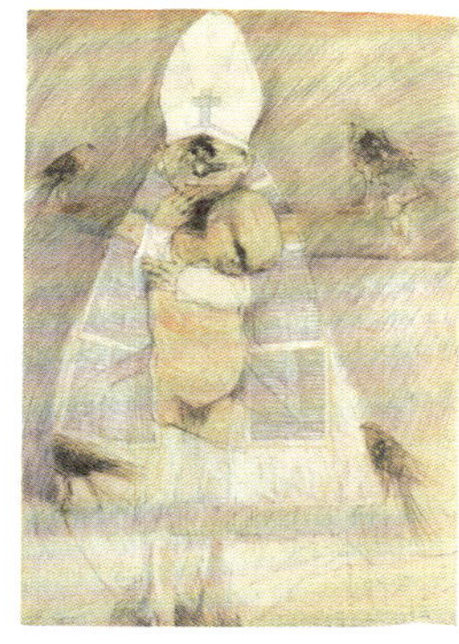

No. 24

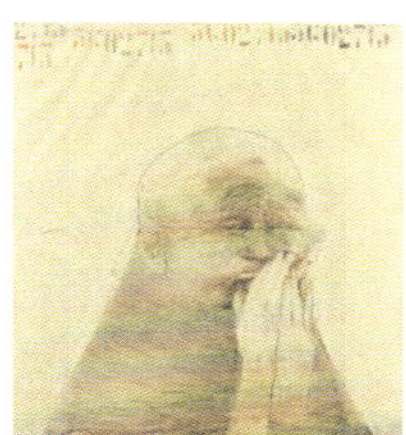

No. 25

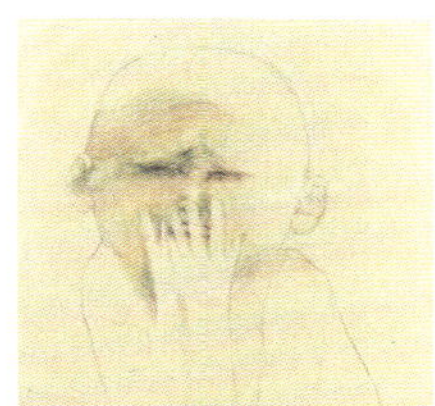

No. 26

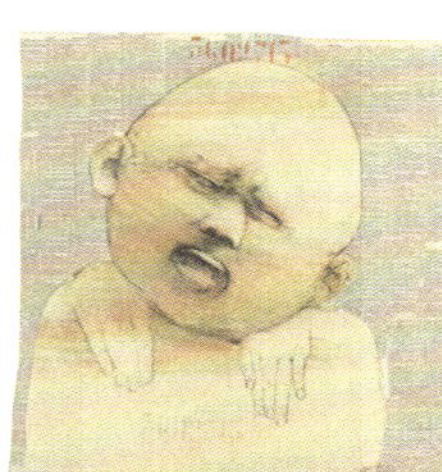

No. 27

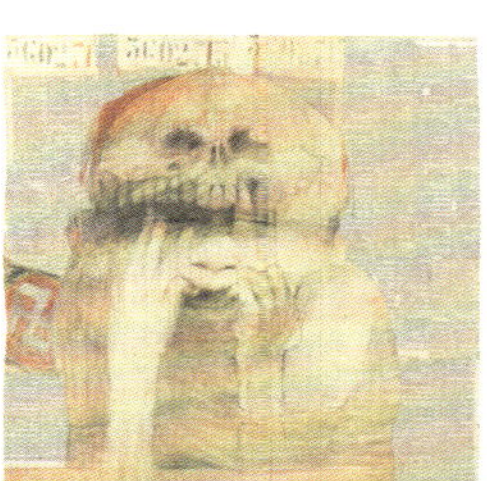

No. 28

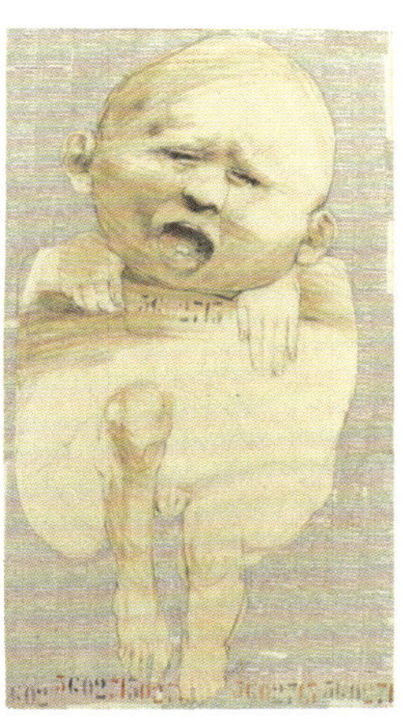

No. 29

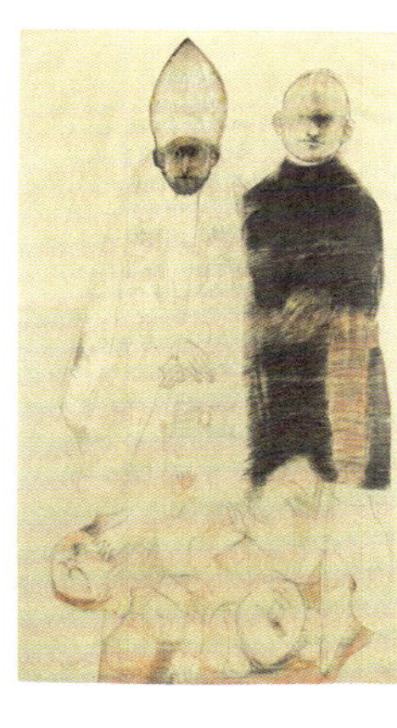

Triptych

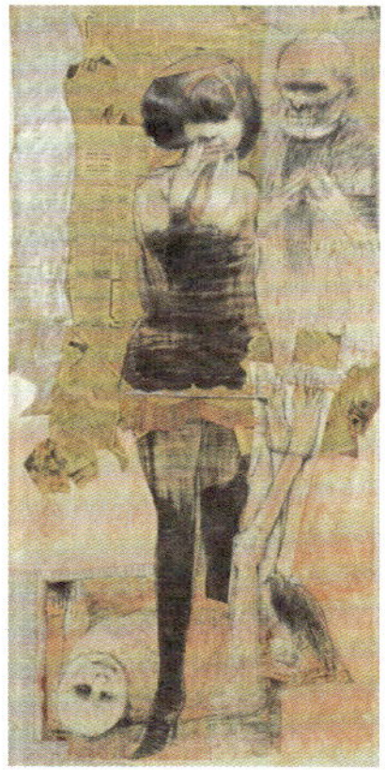

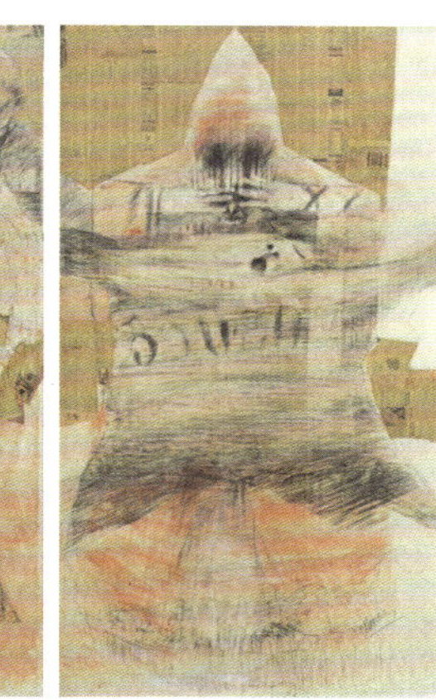

No. 30

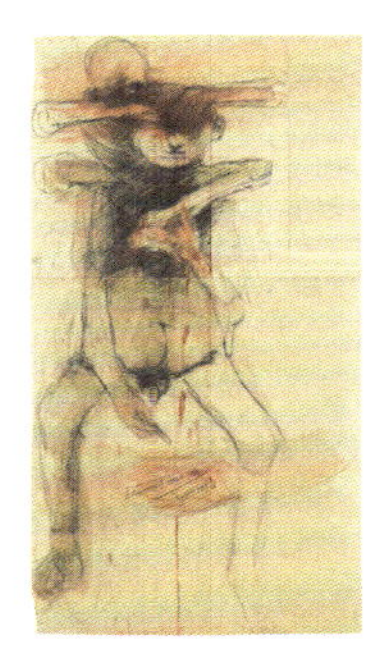

ENVISIONING EVIL: "THE NAZI DRAWINGS" BY MAURICIO LASANSKY

Rachel McGarry

When I made "The Nazi Drawings," I made them as an angry young man, I wanted to spit it out, my point of view, no rules, no nothing, an instinctive reaction. I was upset, I wanted people to know that the world was upset. I am the world, so are you! —Mauricio Lasansky, 1976[1]

Mauricio Lasansky embarked on "The Nazi Drawings" in 1961, and the series would occupy him for much of the next decade. *Nos. 1–30*—they had numbers, not titles—were completed between 1961 and 1966. *Triptych* was finished in 1971. The artist's anger is palpable in the drawings, which he executed with terse, jagged outlines and forceful, brash shading. He handled the paper roughly, tearing edges and corners, collaging ripped pieces of biblical scripture and newspaper. While working, he haphazardly tacked the drawings to plywood supports, which pocked the edges of the paper with pinholes. These were not to be refined works of art; Lasansky repeatedly stated that the brutal subject was beyond aesthetic expression.[2]

Graphic footage of the Nazi camps, with emaciated corpses inhumanely stacked one on top of another in fields and carts, and prisoners starved to the brink of death, compelled the artist to express his anger. "What woke me up were the millions and millions of people killed and screaming," Lasansky said.[3] Footage of the atrocities filmed by the U.S. and British armies was widely shown in the United States in newsreels in the spring of 1945,[4] after the camps were liberated, and in two early documentaries, *Hitler Lives* (Warner Bros., 1945) and *Nuremberg* (U.S. Department of the Army, 1946).[5] After that only a handful of films in the 1940s and 1950s incorporated footage, making it virtually inaccessible.[6] This changed in 1959 when CBS broadcast its fictional television play *Judgment at Nuremberg*. The production included actual camp footage, some of which had been screened as evidence at the Nazi war criminal trials in Nuremberg in 1945–46. (The footage came from a U.S. and British film compilation called *Nazi Concentration Camps*.[7]) One scene in the CBS broadcast showed bodies being bulldozed into mass graves at Bergen-Belsen following a deadly typhus outbreak. This grisly footage would be referenced in "The Nazi Drawings."

While Lasansky sought to express a universal message beyond the Nazis and the Holocaust, his life and background shaped his approach. News of Adolf Eichmann's capture in 1960 in Buenos Aires, Lasansky's hometown, clearly brought the Nazi crimes close to home. Lasansky's son Phillip (Luis Felipe) recalled watching news of the capture with his father and oldest brother, William (Guillermo). He remembered his father's emotional reaction, eyes fixed on newscaster Walter Cronkite, tuning out the boys' conversation so he could hear every word.[8] As details of Eichmann's crimes unfolded in 1960 and 1961, they exposed a gross travesty of justice: the war criminal had enjoyed a decade of freedom in Argentina with his family.

Lasansky's experience as a father—the youngest of his six children was just four years old when he began the drawings—may help explain his sensitivity to the torment and anguish of children. Sickened by the Nazis' massacre of children, he said he wanted the series to emphasize their suffering.[9] The deaths of two younger brothers in infancy, a loss Lasansky's mother mourned her entire life, undoubtedly influenced his deeply felt treatment of this theme as well.

While "The Nazi Drawings" has a number of specific references to the Holocaust, including its title, Lasansky did not intend it to be about Jewish victims alone. He was very selective in his use of overt symbols that would identify particular perpetrators or victims. Among the 33 drawings, there are just three with swastikas (*No. 5*; *No. 27*; *Triptych*, right panel) and one with the Star of David (*No. 23*). Lasansky himself was not religious.[10] He was an assimilated, nonobservant Jew married to a Roman Catholic. He and his wife, Emilia, raised their children in a secular household, and if religion was discussed, it was as an intellectual subject, not as a matter of faith.[11] Lasansky did not consider himself a Jewish artist in the sense that he did not focus on Judaism or Jewish subjects in his art or produce Jewish ritual objects. He was ecumenical in his choice of artistic influences, which included old master and modern prints, Spanish painting, medieval Christian devotional art, and pre-Columbian and African art, which he collected.[12] Nevertheless, as discussed in the essay "The Holocaust in Press, Culture, and Art," many American Jews found that their Jewish identity and heritage became more important to them as more details and shocking stories about the Holocaust came to light beginning in the 1960s,[13] and Lasansky was no different. "The Nazi Drawings" and "Kaddish" (1976–78), a print series that celebrates aspects of the Jewish faith and tradition, seem to demonstrate this.

Lasansky would again show a personal interest in his Jewish heritage when during his first visit to the United States Holocaust Memorial Museum (Washington, D.C.) he sought specific information about the Lithuanian

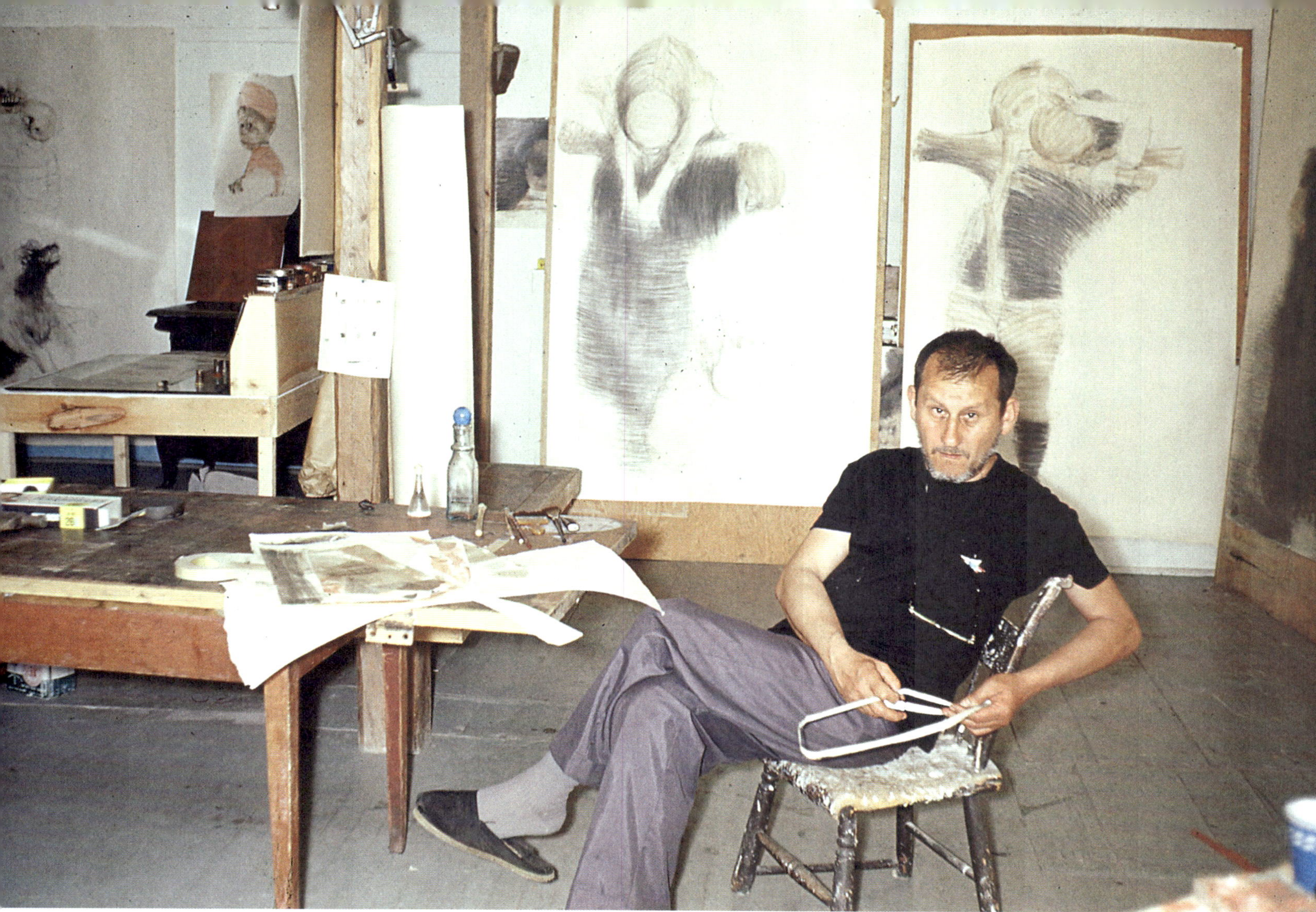

Fig. 4.1 Mauricio Lasansky working on "The Nazi Drawings" in his studio, 1962, Vinalhaven, Maine

towns where his family came from.[14] By 1944, the Nazis and their collaborators had annihilated 95 percent of Lithuania's Jews. In Vilna (Vilnius), Lasansky's father's hometown, an estimated 70,000 to 100,000 Jews were murdered, mostly in mass shootings by *Einsatzgruppen* in the Ponary forest outside the city.[15] In his mother's hometown of Kaunas, some 30,000 Jews were murdered. Yad Vashem's Central Database of Shoah Victims' Names lists likely family members among the dead, with the surnames Kahn and Kagan from Kaunas, and Lashansky, Milikovski, and Milejkowskis from Vilna.[16]

The early drawings of Nazi soldiers (*Nos. 1–5*) and parts of *Triptych* are probably the only works Lasansky created in his adopted hometown of Iowa City, Iowa. Most were executed during his summers in Maine while on break from teaching printmaking. Every May, he and Emilia would load the family into their Mercury Commuter wagon and make the trek to their cottage on the island of Vinalhaven. There, in his studio in an old barn, he had the solitude and space to undertake these solemn, large-scale works. Phillip, who was five when the series was initiated, remembered his father suffering emotional stress and terrible headaches while working on the drawings. He said the artist would lock himself in the studio for long stretches every day, beginning at 7 a.m. and returning home at 5 p.m. drained.[17] His son Leonardo recalled that his father would try to decompress on the 10-minute walk from the studio before entering the chaotic, joyful house full of children, but that emotions stirred up by the day's work often followed him.[18]

Five or six drawings could be in progress at any one time. *Nos. 1–5* were made first, but the rest were executed at various times, not in the order suggested by the final numbering. Some were numbered below the artist's signature and then renumbered after Lasansky executed more works and grouped the drawings by theme rather than chronology. Some are dated, and we know a *terminus post quem* date of a few others based on the news articles collaged onto them. He ultimately rejected as many as 10 drawings he made for the series. Some he tore up; two he reworked later. At least six of these are known from photographs, such as the drawing of two skeleton figures with a barking German shepherd hanging in his Maine studio (see fig. 4.1, far left).[19] Such dogs were fixtures of the concentration camps, especially at the women's camps, where there were fewer guards.[20]

Throughout the series, Lasansky incorporated powerful iconographic archetypes—the Dance of Death, the Crucifixion and Pietà, and other enduring imagery. Drawing from his deep reservoir of art historical knowledge—of Goya, Munch, the German artists George Grosz and Otto Dix, early Christian art, devotional painting, portraiture—he created in "The Nazi Drawings" something wholly original and commanding. Goya's prints had a particularly significant impact, especially "The Disasters of War" ("Los Desastres de la guerra," 1810–20) and its representation of innocent victims. This series presents an eyewitness account of the atrocities (murder, torture, mass execution, defilement of victims, starvation) committed during Spain's struggle for independence following the invasion of Napoleon's troops in 1808. Lasansky was deeply affected by Goya's stark, unheroic treatment of war, studying the prints at New York's Metropolitan Museum of Art in 1943–44 and later collecting them himself. Lasansky drew inspiration from an array of other sources as well—newspapers, popular culture, literature, film footage, *Life* magazine—which made "The Nazi Drawings" resonate with contemporary audiences. In the spring of 1967, when the series was shown at the newly built Whitney Museum of American Art on Madison Avenue in New York, crowds lined up around the block (p. 11, fig. A.3). The accompanying catalogue featured an essay by Edwin Honig, a poet and playwright who had translated such celebrated Spanish writers as Federico García Lorca and Miguel de Cervantes. Honig had also served in the U.S. Army in Europe during World War II. His astute literary description of the initial 30 "Nazi Drawings" introduces the series this way:

> Looking with shock-fascinated eyes at the drawings, it comes to us that we are the prurient observers, the guilty bystanders who survived these terrors of human history. We have survived, but at what price, with what knowledge and understanding of our own participation in events now rigidified in the nightmare of the past? Now that those events have become matters of innocent curiosity to human beings born since, we keep wondering how we could continue in silent anguish of that period all these years.[21]

It is our task now to historicize "The Nazi Drawings," to consider them in the context in which they were made. The imagery reflects specific issues debated at the time of their inception and how the Holocaust was then understood. As the historian Peter Novick observes, "Every generation frames the Holocaust, represents the Holocaust, in ways that suit the mood."[22] Lasansky, for instance, directly implicated the Roman Catholic Church in the Holocaust in three of the drawings, reflecting contemporary debates surrounding the Vatican's silence, inaction, and culpability and the role of Christian doctrine, as examined in Rabbi Barry Cytron's essay in this book. The prevalence of prostitutes in the series may surprise many 21st-century viewers, but concentration camp brothels were much discussed in Holocaust literature and films in the 1960s. Recent scholarship has uncovered more facts about this subject, and attitudes toward sex trafficking have changed, yet this group of drawings brings attention to sexual violence in war, a pervasive crime all too often overlooked. The goal of this essay is not to project 21st-century attitudes and judgments about the Holocaust, World War II, sex trafficking, religion, race, and gender onto "The Nazi Drawings," but to try to reconstruct and understand their historical and cultural context 50 to 60 years ago, when the series was created (1961–71) and first viewed (1967–70).

The Nazis: *Nos. 1–6*

I was merely a little cog in the machinery that carried out the directives and orders of the German Reich. I was neither a murderer nor a mass-murderer. I was a man of average character, with good qualities and many faults. . . . —Adolf Eichmann, 1957[23]

By the will of the Reichsführer SS [Heinrich Himmler], Auschwitz became the greatest human extermination center of all time. . . . It was certainly an extraordinary and monstrous order. Nonetheless the reasons behind the extermination program seemed to me right. I did not reflect on it at the time: I had been given an order, and I had to carry it out. Whether this mass extermination of the Jews was necessary or not was something on which I could not allow myself to form an opinion, for I lacked the necessary breadth of view. —Auschwitz Commandant Rudolf Höss, 1947[24]

One can hardly call upon the whole world and gather correspondents from the four corners of the earth in order to display Bluebeard in the dock. The trouble with Eichmann was precisely that so many were like him, and that the many were neither perverted nor sadistic, that they were, and still are, terribly and terrifyingly normal. From the viewpoint of our legal institutions, and of our moral standards of judgment, this normality was much more terrifying . . . that this new type of criminal, who is in actual fact the enemy of mankind, commits his crimes under circumstances that make it well-nigh impossible for him to know or to feel that he is doing wrong. —Hannah Arendt, *Eichmann in Jerusalem*, 1963[25]

Lasansky began "The Nazi Drawings" with six lone Nazi soldiers. The first five drawings show the figures as they are devoured by menacing skull-helmets and ultimately, in *No. 6*, by an entire skeleton. The faces in the first four portraits are enveloped by uniforms but are individuated by their distinct noses and ears. Their visors, made of skeletal teeth, shade or cover eyes blinded by rough black charcoal strokes. High-collared jackets brace these figures' chins and partly cover their lips, as if to muzzle them. In the end, the skull, a universal symbol of death, has subsumed them. The motif of skull as helmet may also allude to the SS *Totenkopf* (skull and crossbones) pin worn on SS officers' military caps. The range of uniforms brings to mind the docket of Nazi defendants at the first

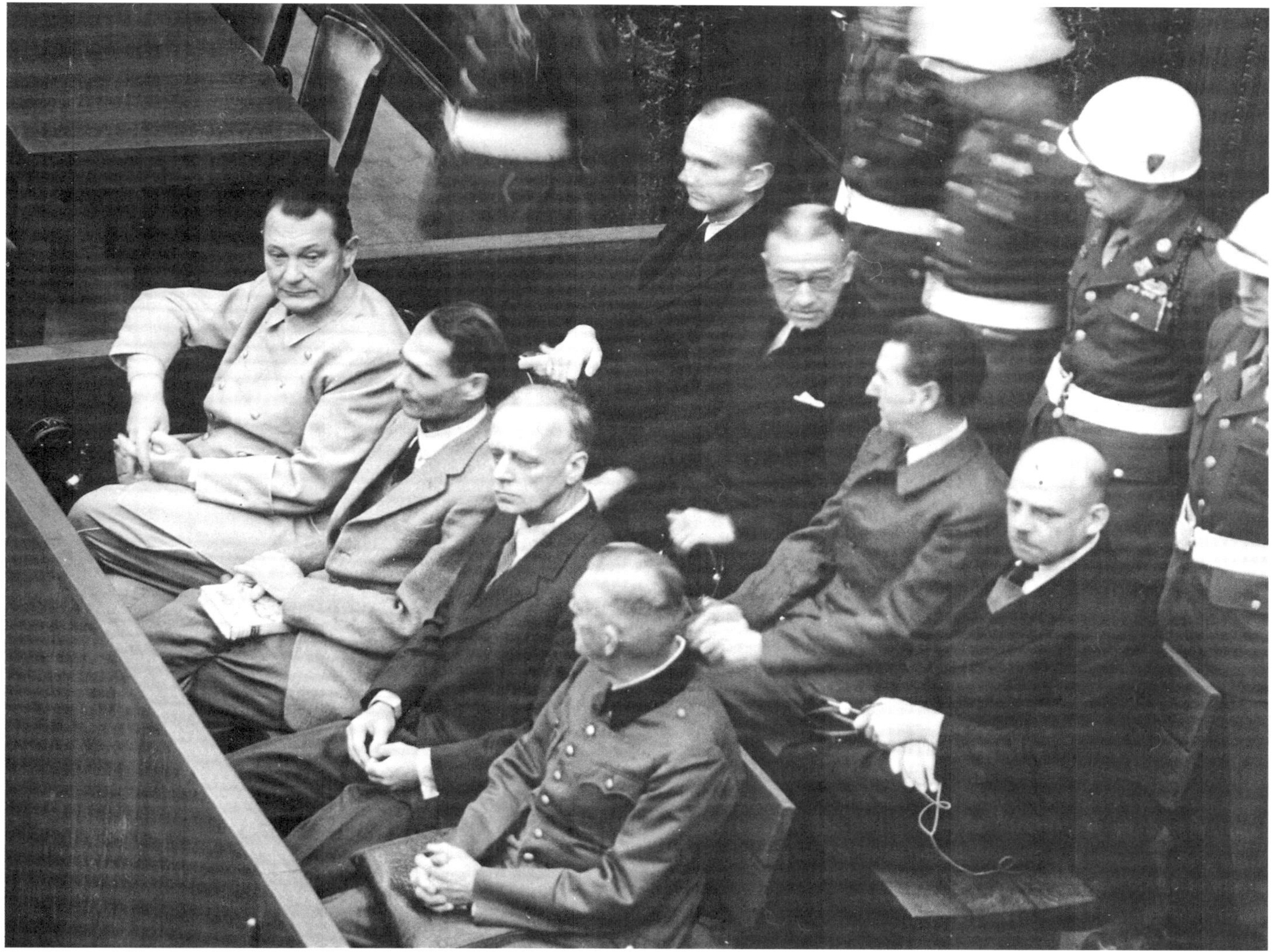

Fig. 4.2 Nazi defendants, Nuremberg trials, 1945–46. National Archives, Washington, D.C.
Twenty-two Nazi leaders were tried for war crimes by the International Military Tribunal in the first Nuremberg trial. The accused included Hermann Göring (front row at left), commander in chief of the *Luftwaffe* (German air force) and founder of the Nazi Gestapo (secret police). He led efforts to confiscate Jewish property in Germany and occupied countries and in 1941 ordered Reinhard Heydrich to implement the "Final Solution" to the Jewish question.

Nuremberg trial, notably Hermann Göring in his pale double-breasted jacket (fig. 4.2). *Judgment at Nuremberg* (1959), only recently televised, began with actual footage of the Nuremberg defendants as their guilty verdicts and death sentences were read. Most memorable was Göring's reaction. Reportedly cured of his drug addiction while in custody, Göring appeared addled and overly alert, furiously blinking and expressly dismissive of his conviction.[26]

The Nazi in *No. 4* marks the first of several references to the Christian faith. The figure's jacket suggests a priestly vestment, complete with a clerical collar and a cross or two. Lasansky abruptly cut the sheet in two, slicing the paper right through the Nazi's neck, then reattached the pieces.

After the first four, the drawings become larger. *No. 5* depicts a Nazi with his right arm raised in the *heil* salute and dripping with blood. Behind his back, we see the hand of his other arm forcefully, threateningly clenched. His sombrero-shaped helmet (trimmed with enormous teeth), white military jacket laden with medals, and little yellow shorts (revealing pale, thin legs) suggest that this Nazi lives in a warm climate—perhaps South America, a known haven for Nazi war criminals at the time.

By *No. 6*, the skull and captive have become more beastly; features are demonic, hands and feet resemble claws. It is not just death capturing people's minds and silencing their consciences, Lasansky seems to say, but evil. This Nazi has been entirely consumed by a monstrous, puppeteering skeleton hooked over his shoulders. The command of his hands has been assumed by the skeleton. His large body and familiar Nazi uniform (tall boots, jodhpurs, long, pocketed coat) are lightly sketched, as if his individual identity has faded away in the presence of this wicked master. Indeed, his face is barely recognizable as human.

Nos. 1–5 were probably completed in 1961. The world at this moment was fixated on SS *Obersturmbannführer* (Lt. Col.) Adolf Eichmann, head of Jewish affairs for the Gestapo, whose four-month trial began on April 11, 1961. He was accused of, among other things, implementing the Nazi plan to annihilate the Jews and transporting millions to extermination camps. In an article published the first week of the trial, *Life* magazine called him "a symbol of the hatreds and unspeakable hideousness of Hitler's Germany." The accompanying photos showed the Nazi doing everyday things like brushing his teeth, washing his clothes, and walking the prison yard (see p. 37, fig. 1.21).[27] Observers were shocked and distressed by the ordinariness of his looks and demeanor. Photos of him in his glass box at the trial showed a slight, 55-year-old man with glasses, ill-fitting dentures, and thinning hair (see p. 37, fig. 1.22). It was difficult to reconcile the mass murderer who transported millions to their deaths with this man who appeared so "terribly and terrifyingly normal," as the German American political thinker and journalist Hannah Arendt wrote.

Eichmann seemed at ease with his past and the crimes he had committed, essentially admitting his large role in the genocide, saying he regretted nothing, and then pleading not guilty "in the spirit of the indictment."[28] This provoked serious philosophical debates about the nature of evil (and its "banality," as Arendt controversially described it) and the political structures and circumstances that could breed it. The details of the crimes that emerged at the trial showed that the Holocaust went beyond Eichmann and a small group of powerful, wicked sadists who were tried for war crimes. Its massive scale involved innumerable hands—thousands of guards, executioners, administrators, and collaborators—complex, long-term planning, international cooperation, and willful indifference by an uncountable number of bystanders. The perpetrators were racist and cruel, to be sure, but other qualities were needed, such as a regard for hierarchy over human life, a blatant, dangerous abandonment of personal responsibility, blind thoughtlessness, and a lack of conscience. Lasansky's initial drawings examine this aspect of Nazi criminals.

Another important influence was undoubtedly the 1959 English publication of *Commandant of Auschwitz: The Autobiography of Rudolf Höss* (Warsaw 1951). Höss, Auschwitz's longest-serving commandant, was executed by the Polish government in 1947, but while in custody he wrote a memoir at the suggestion of a Polish prosecutor and psychologist. He confessed to ordering 2.5 million victims to death by gassing and burning, and was responsible for at least another half million at Auschwitz dying from starvation. The book's unflinching account of the gas chambers and firing squads, the horrific living conditions of the camps, and the suffering and abuse of the prisoners is only intermittently punctuated by expressions of sadness or pity (except for himself; his own "sufferings" are amply recounted). The victims are mostly faceless for Höss, embodiments of their prisoner group—racial or otherwise: Gypsies, Jews, homosexuals, prostitutes, criminals, politicals. He prided himself on his ruthless execution of every order, no matter how cruel. In one instance he recounted that he showed no emotion while they tried to squeeze more children into the gas chamber, so that he could serve as a model for other guards.[29] The memoir begins with recollections of a disconcertingly happy childhood; Höss writes of growing up in a "house full of love," with warm memories of his love of animals and stint as an altar boy.[30] He was a bully as a teenager, seriously injuring a boy he pushed down a stairwell. Later he served time for murder. Höss joined the SS in 1934 and began working at the camps immediately. Of his unthinking obedience under the Nazis, he wrote, "I gave it no thought. . . . The soldier's life held me in thrall." Ordered to prepare installations at Auschwitz for the murder of millions of human beings, here, too, he wrote, "I did not reflect on it at the time."[31] Thoughtless, obedient, and lacking remorse—Höss represented the dangerous kind of evil that the Nazis harnessed against humanity.

The Italian writer and Auschwitz survivor Primo Levi, in his final book, *The Drowned and the Saved* (1986), considered the rationalizations and the memories of Nazi perpetrators like Eichmann and Höss. Their repeated, universal defense was that they were following orders, were not responsible for decisions, and should not be punished. Such people, Levi observed, needed a drastic manipulation of memory in order to hold such beliefs. This was how they lived with their crimes, and the lies they told and retold must have slowly become true even to themselves.[32]

Nos. 1–6 represent the process of corrupting seemingly ordinary men like Eichmann and empowering criminals like Höss to become murderous Nazis—blinding and silencing them, indoctrinating them into absolute obedience, obliterating their thoughts and consciences. Ultimately the incurable contagion distorted their memories, too.

Sex and Sexual Violence in War: *Nos. 7–13, 16–17, 19*

Women are central in "The Nazi Drawings." Lasansky depicted them as protective mothers, tortured bodies, dead victims, rape victims, and temptresses. The sexualized depiction of women in the drawings may strike us today as disquieting or taboo. Lasansky borrowed deeply from art history to infuse them with symbolic meaning while also touching on such issues as prostitution, concentration camp brothels, sexual slavery, collaboration with the Nazis, rape, death, and desecration of the dead.

Like the soldiers, many of the women wear toothy skull headwear or are ensnared by skeleton beasts. The latter refers to the *danse macabre*, or Dance of Death. This motif, popular since the Middle Ages, depicts skeletons dancing with people from all walks of life, from princes and street peddlers to young brides and toddlers. These memento mori remind us that death arrives unexpectedly, and no one escapes its grasp.

Death and the Maiden is a well-established subcategory within this genre, one that artists have eroticized for centuries. Few relished the subject as much as the German Renaissance artist Sebald Beham, whose prints Lasansky knew well. His *Death Seizing a Woman* (fig. 4.3) is a reminder that life is transient, that beauty and youth are fleeting. Lasansky's *No. 10* and *No. 12*, each portraying a woman ravenously devoured by Death, go beyond the traditional iconography to show the figures engaged in a sexual encounter. Beasts attack passive, scantily clad women as if they were prey. Rather than show expressions of surprise, fear, or aversion, however, these women have upturned lips, signaling their consent and perhaps a certain masochistic pleasure.

Edvard Munch's *Death and the Maiden* (fig. 4.4), portraying a beautiful young woman dancing with Death, may have been Lasansky's reference point for *No. 9* and *No. 12*. Munch's maiden shows herself to be a willing, amorous consort, like the figure in *No. 9*. Lasansky closely imitated the woman's body and embracing gesture, although he put her paramour, who wears a military uniform, in a reclining position. In *No. 12*, Lasansky subtly mimicked Munch's dance by giving Death a lightly drawn second pair of legs, which are intertwined with his partner's in an arrangement similar to Munch's couple.

Lasansky portrayed many of the women in the series as prostitutes. In eight of the works (*Nos. 7–13* and *Triptych*, left panel) they are naked or skimpily dressed in black high heels, corsets, and stockings. The smiling woman in *No. 11* is handed cash as she pleasures a line of seated and standing customers. Like her, many of Lasansky's prostitutes seem to enjoy what they are doing, whether seducing men, embracing or being embraced, or engaging in sexual acts. The skull headwear in *Nos. 7–12* suggests that these women have been corrupted

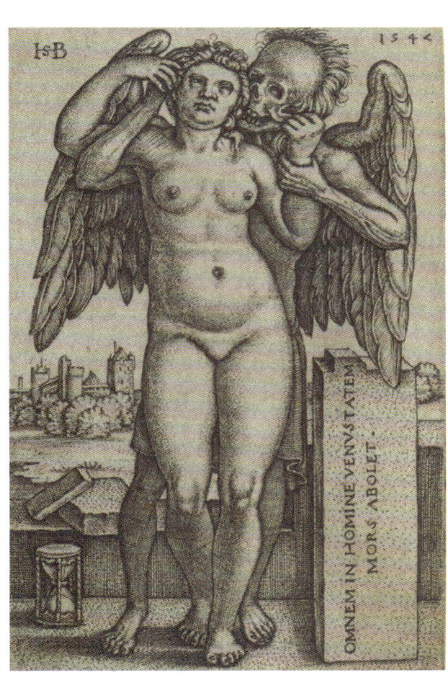

Fig. 4.3 Sebald Beham, *Death Seizing a Woman*, 1547, engraving, $2\frac{15}{16} \times 1\frac{15}{16}$ in. (7.5 x 4.9 cm), Minneapolis Institute of Art, gift of Tom Rassieur in memory of Tracey Albainy, 2010.71

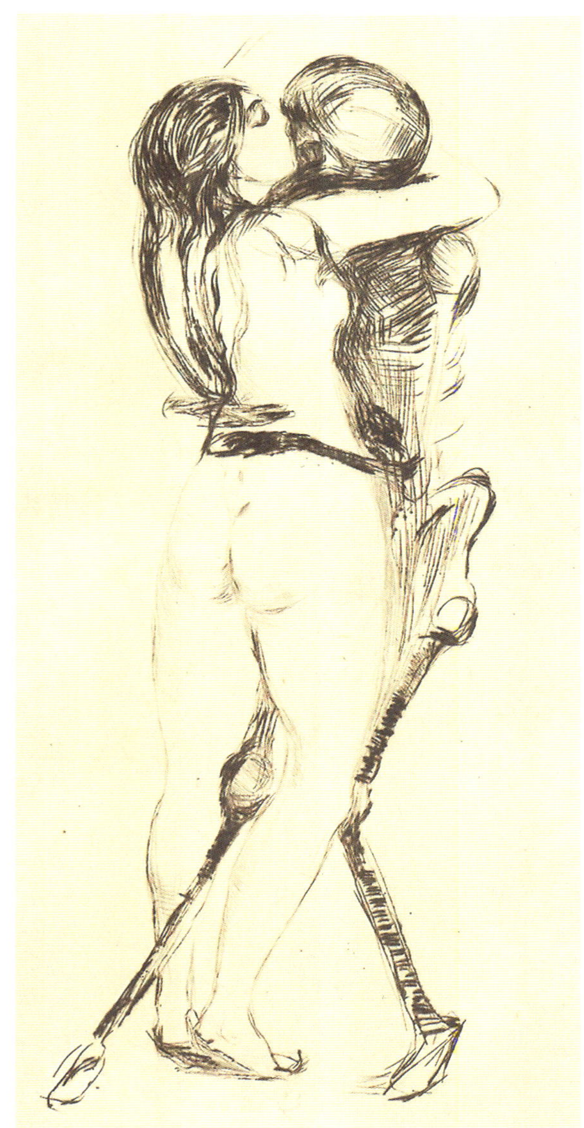

Fig. 4.4 Edvard Munch, *Death and the Maiden* (detail), 1894, drypoint, $12 \times 8\frac{1}{2}$ in. (30.4 x 21.7 cm) (plate), Art Institute of Chicago, Clarence Buckingham Collection, 1963.274

and blinded; they appear as coconspirators to their Nazi counterparts. In a finished drawing that Lasansky eliminated (fig. 4.5), a helmet-wearing prostitute, stripped below the waist and her legs splayed in a high kick, holds a Nazi flag as a swastika banner waves behind her. Lasansky may have felt that the graphic sexuality and the Nazi symbolism were too overt for the more universal message he wanted to achieve.

Lasansky's treatment of prostitution drew partly from the work of Dix, Grosz, and other German artists working in the interwar years. The theme figured prominently in their art in the 1920s as a symbol of the degeneration of modern society. Dix and Grosz used the subject not to moralize but rather to create shocking images that showed the bestial, barbarous nature of humanity. Dix's print series "The War" ("Der Krieg," 1924) is based on the horrors he witnessed firsthand as an infantryman in World War I. It includes a number of brothel scenes. One, *A Visit to Madame Germane in Méricourt* (fig. 4.6), in which prostitute and soldier leer and fondle, is farcical in the way her large body weighs on the shallow lap of the small, wounded, pockmarked client. Physically grotesque and crude, they appear sickly, perhaps syphilitic. Although the composition is reversed in *No. 11*, it seems to allude directly to Dix's famous print. In their respective series, Lasansky and Dix depicted the base instincts of human behavior—aggression, dominance, hunger, and a ruthless drive to procreate and survive. Both artists set out to expose human nature at its most reptilian and animalistic, particularly in war.

Lasansky displayed a rawer, more energetic drawing technique in this group compared to the earlier sheets. He drew the figures with more pentimenti, employed splatters of wash, and shaded large areas of the compositions with broad, black lines. The repeated charcoal strokes in the black clothing (see, for instance, the bustier in *No. 10*) are drawn with such force that the grain of Lasansky's plywood work surface is visible. His rough tears to the paper in *No. 7* and *No. 8* created jagged edges that cut right through the bust and gut of the women.

In his Artist Statement for "The Nazi Drawings" (see p. 102), Lasansky specifically excoriated the Nazis' negation of human dignity, which turned men into animals. Sex shown in its most depraved form—violent, lewd, bought and sold—in "The Nazi Drawings" is a powerful expression of Nazi transgression. Prostitution and sexual slavery were also conspicuous fixtures of Nazi Germany. Although Hitler decried prostitution as morally destructive behavior that polluted the Reich, it was not only legal during his rule but increased substantially.[33] Some 500 military brothels operated in German-occupied Europe in 1942, and at least 34,140 women are estimated to have been forced into sexual slavery.[34] The German government dictated prices, medical exams and blood tests for venereal diseases, and strict enforcement of the Nuremberg racial laws, which forbade sexual relations between "German or related blood" and Jews.

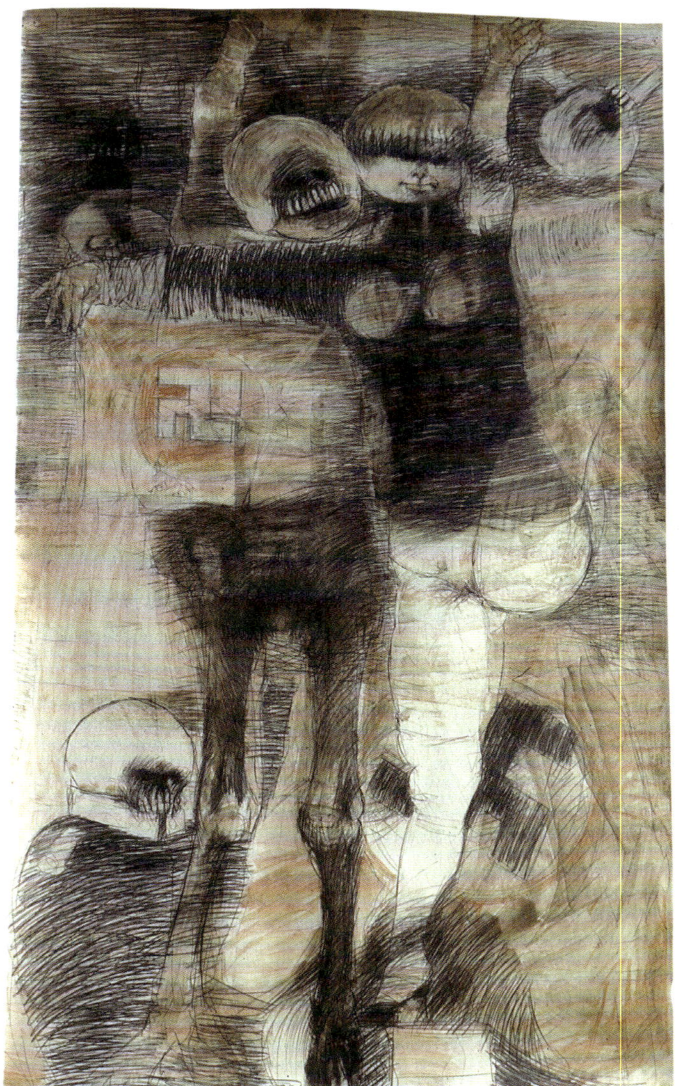

Fig. 4.5 Mauricio Lasansky, drawing eliminated from "The Nazi Drawings" (destroyed)

Concentration camp brothels were established in 1942 by Heinrich Himmler, who, as head of the SS (*Schutzstaffel*, or "protection squads"), oversaw the administration of the concentration and extermination camps. The brothels were part of an incentive system for prison laborers,[35] with the first one opening at Mauthausen and 11 camps with brothels in operation by 1944.[36] Only privileged prisoners were granted access: *Kapos* (supervising prisoners, usually common criminals), block chiefs, and other prisoners with authority.[37] Ukrainian SS men were not permitted entry in brothels with German prostitutes; Jewish prisoners and Russian POWs were forbidden altogether. Most of the brothel workers were forced into service or offered prostitution as an alternative to life-threatening work details. They received assurances of improved living conditions and food (thus survival); many were given false promises of early release.[38] The majority came from the large women's concentration camp at Ravensbrück, whose population included political prisoners and former prostitutes, some of whom had been rounded up as *Asoziale* (asocial elements)—only to be forced into prostitution again.[39] At Auschwitz, women were chosen by doctors and guards upon arrival at the camp. The women were ordered to have intercourse with 6, 8, even 12 men every evening. They were replaced by new recruits or rotated to different camp brothels every four to six months.[40] Pregnancy was dangerous; some women were sterilized, others underwent forced abortions, and some who became pregnant were executed.[41] While brothel workers were more likely to survive than other inmates,[42] few spoke of their experiences after the war because of the shame and trauma, and the disgrace it would bring them in their communities.[43]

News of Nazi brothels appeared occasionally during the war.[44] In 1942, a book detailing Nazi crimes in occupied Poland from the Polish government-in-exile included numerous reports of young Polish women and girls being rounded up and sent to brothels for Nazi

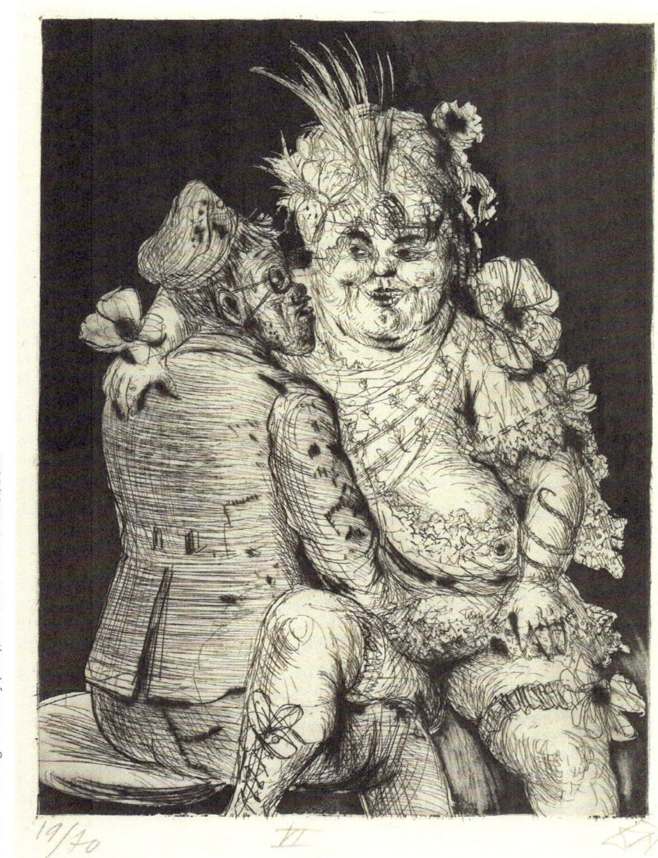

Fig. 4.6 Otto Dix, *A Visit to Madame Germane in Méricourt*, 1924, etching, aquatint, and drypoint, 10 1/16 × 7 1/2 in. (25.6 × 19.1 cm), plate 36 from "The War" ("Der Krieg") (Berlin, Karl Nierendorf, 1924), Minneapolis Institute of Art, the John R. Van Derlip Fund and gift of funds from Alfred and Ingrid Lenz Harrison and the Regis Foundation, 2005.16.1.32

soldiers.[45] The camp brothels were documented in the liberation footage of the camps, and they appeared again in Alain Resnais's influential documentary *Nuit et brouillard* (*Night and Fog*) of 1955.[46] Scholar Robert Sommer's extensive research of SS documents and testimonies shows that an estimated 210 women were enslaved in these camp brothels—this in addition to the tens of thousands forced to work in the German-run military brothels across Europe. Many millions more women were victims of sexual violence in Europe during and immediately after World War II.[47] In the 1960s, however, it was the concentration camp brothels that captured the public's attention. They had an outsize reputation in terms of the realities of camp life, which undoubtedly led to their prominence in Lasansky's "Nazi Drawings."

The novels of Yehiel Dinur, a Holocaust survivor who went by the pen name Ka-Tzetnik 135633 (Concentration Camp Inmate 135633),[48] contributed to their notoriety as well. *Beit habubot* (Tel Aviv, 1953; *House of Dolls*, New York, 1955) follows the author's purported sister, Daniella, from her life in the ghetto to her enslavement as a teen in a concentration camp brothel, where she commits suicide. The novel describes the abusive sex and torture she and other young Jewish women endured, including sterilization and having their chests branded with the words *Feld-Hure* (field whore). Ka-Tzetnik 135633's novel *Piepel*, published in 1961 in Hebrew and English, is the story of his purported younger brother, Moni, also sexually enslaved, this time by a Jewish *Kapo* at Auschwitz.[49] The book includes a grisly vision of an enslaved boy being roasted and fed to starving prisoners. Both novels were widely read in the 1960s and became required reading for high school students in Israel in the 1960s and again in the 1990s.[50]

By 1968, *House of Dolls* had sold more than 5 million copies. The 1960 paperback edition (fig. 4.7), with its cover image of an anguished woman displaying the degrading label on her chest,[51] may have influenced Lasanswky's conception of the woman in *No. 19*, shown with a large prison number tattooed on her chest and her head and neck similarly strained. (Lasansky's victim, however, is being strangled by a hooded Death figure and tormented by a flock of eagles.) Ka-Tzetnik 135633's books have been criticized as pornographic, kitschy, and deceptive,[52] yet also applauded for examining a subject that many survivors rarely discussed.[53] One inescapable fact is that the books created an inaccurate and somewhat sensationalized picture of Nazi camp brothels. Because the author was a survivor, many readers initially believed them to be factual, even though they were works of fiction.[54] *House of Dolls* also established the mistaken but widely held belief that many Jewish women were forced into sexual slavery in camp brothels.[55] While Jewish women suffered rape, assault, and sexual exploitation during and after the war, recent research has shown that they were spared work in the official camp brothels due to Nazi racial laws.[56] Similarly, branding women in brothels as "field whores" was not standard practice.[57]

The brothel theme appeared in films during the 1960s as well. Sidney Lumet's *The Pawnbroker* (1966) is told from the viewpoint of Holocaust survivor Sol Nazerman, played by Rod Steiger.[58] Living in the slums of New York

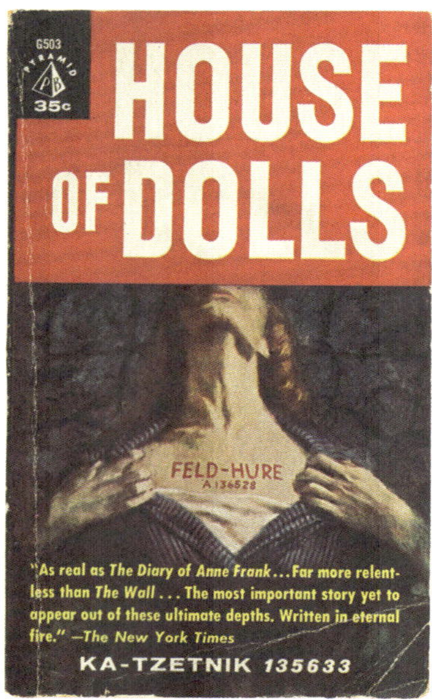

Fig. 4.7 Ka-Tzetnik 135633, *House of Dolls*, Pyramid Books, New York, 1960
The cover art for this English paperback edition is by Dick Shelton.

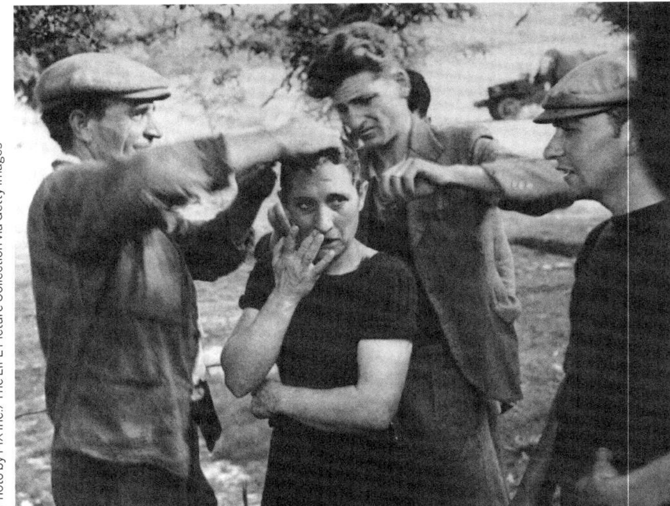

Photo by PIX Inc./The LIFE Picture Collection via Getty Images

Fig. 4.8 Photograph from *Life* magazine photo-essay, "Corsicans Punish Traitorous Women," July 17, 1944, photographer unknown
This story features three women accused of consorting with German troops following the liberation of Corsica in October 1943—an office worker (illustrated) who quit her job to live with a German officer, a "peasant girl," and a prostitute. The women's heads were publicly shorn, and they were stripped and made to walk home naked.

after the war, Nazerman continues to suffer trauma from life in the camps. He is haunted by memories of his wife's enslavement in a camp brothel and being forced to watch her perform. The Yugoslavian film *Witness Out of Hell* (1966), directed by Živorad Mitrović, also took on the theme.[59] A far more common form of sexual exploitation, both inside and outside the camps, was that of women forced to barter sex for their survival. This was the subject of Gillo Pontecorvo's 1959 Italian film *Kapò*, released in the United States in 1960 and nominated for an Academy Award for best foreign film. After witnessing her parents being sent to the gas chambers, the protagonist hides her Jewish identity and assumes that of a criminal. She is moved to a labor camp, where she uses her body to survive, trading her virginity for food. She finds protection among the Nazis and eventually becomes a *Kapo* at the camp.[60]

Memoirs of Auschwitz survivors, which were more widely read in the 1960s, also made note of the sexual exploitation and violence women confronted at the camps daily.[61] Primo Levi recorded a few incidents, including how an Italian woman who was a forced laborer at Auschwitz secretly slept with a "cooperative of German and Polish Kapos" for bread.[62] Female survivors often went into more detail, although they were more apt to discuss incidents that happened to other prisoners rather than to themselves.[63] Olga Lengyel wrote about how, soon after arriving at the camp, she was offered potatoes in exchange for sex (she refused). She discovered that many women, starved after months or years at the camp, were willing to do anything for food. She reported that a black market for sex flourished between male and female prisoners in the latrine during the rest hour.[64] Survivor Raya Kagan explained, "The root cause of it all was hunger, the cruel hunger that occurs with particular viciousness in winter, that drove women into the arms of the men."[65]

When Lengyel arrived at Auschwitz, a German doctor told her not to have her hair shorn along with the other female prisoners.[66] Although she does not write this, it may have meant she was being singled out for the brothels. (She lined up to have her hair shaved, an act for which she was whipped.) Brothel recruiters sought young women who still possessed their hair and were not too thin; thus, at Auschwitz, they were mostly new arrivals.[67] If women in the brothels did have shaved heads, they were permitted to grow their hair out.

Two prostitutes in "The Nazi Drawings," those in *Nos. 8* and 12, have shaved heads, which seems to locate them in the camps. The others retain their hair. With or without hair, all appear to have healthy weight and good color, indicating that they either partake of the special privileges granted to them in the camp brothels (hair, adequate food, civilian clothes), or that Lasansky was portraying prostitutes in a more general way. As noted above, they wear skull headwear and are represented as willing, happy Nazi companions. This depiction may also allude to the so-called horizontal collaborators, women across occupied Europe who consorted with the Nazis, whether they fell in love, bartered sex for food, or opportunistically collaborated with the enemy. Following the liberations of France, Belgium, the Netherlands, Italy, Norway, and Finland, such women were rounded up by mobs. As discussed in the essay "The Holocaust in Press, Culture, and Art," their heads were publicly shaved and they were paraded through streets, sometimes covered with pitch or swastikas or stripped down to their shoes. In 1944, *Life* magazine ran two stories featuring photographs of some of the 20,000 French *tondues* (shorn women) (figs. 4.8 and 1.14, p. 27).[68]

The blushing woman in *No. 8*, head shaved and naked except for shoes, resembles the images of *collaboratrices* that circulated in the press in the 1940s. (This would also explain the officer's coat and her flirtatious expression in the drawing.) The unusual pose of the woman in the left panel of Lasansky's *Triptych* coincidentally echoes one of the accused women pictured in *Life* in 1944. She was described as initially calm and resigned during her public shaving, but "toward the end began to show signs of guilt and grief."[69]

Rape: *Nos. 13, 16, 17*

"The Nazi Drawings" also treat the age-old war crime of rape, showing women and children raped and murdered or murdered and then raped, or both. Lasansky depicted these victims without the usual skull helmets: they are innocents preyed upon by Nazi beasts who savagely, brutally violate and desecrate their bodies. Throughout history, soldiers have raped, pillaged, and plundered their vanquished enemies, but World War II was exceptionally violent, with crimes committed by both Axis and Allied forces.[70] This dimension of the war has been largely marginalized in official accounts, as well as by historians, writers, artists, and the courts. (Rape was only explicitly defined and prosecuted as a war crime in international law beginning in the 1990s, with the Bosnian and Rwandan wars.[71]) There are no reliable records documenting the number of women raped by Nazi soldiers, as the crimes were not prosecuted after the war, and the Nazis tried very few of their soldiers who committed rape in occupied countries.[72] Nonetheless, the evidence of testimonies, spotty documents and police records, the spread of venereal disease, and the high incidence of pregnancies indicate that rape was endemic, with some scholars estimating a total in the millions.[73] Already by 1942, Nazi documents had recorded some 750,000 babies born to Russian mothers by German soldiers. Nazi soldiers did not discriminate by ethnicity; Polish, Jewish, Ukrainian, Russian, and Roma and Sinti women all were vulnerable to rape. Incidents were higher where women were more powerless, such as in the ghettos, prisons, and camps of Eastern Europe. There are even reports of Jewish women being raped in their last hours of life by guards at the extermination camps of Treblinka, Sobibor, and Bełżec.[74]

Soldiers in the Russian Red Army were particularly relentless and brutal, raping and pillaging the countries they "liberated"—Poland, the Baltic States, Hungary, Czechoslovakia, Yugoslavia, Austria, and, finally, Germany.[75] Clinics and doctors reported that in Vienna, 87,000 women were raped in three weeks. This statistic does not include those raped in surrounding towns and villages or the many women who did not report the crime. In Berlin, in the six days leading up to Germany's surrender, it is estimated (conservatively) that Russian soldiers raped between 110,000 and 130,000 women.[76] The victims' ages reportedly ranged between 12 and 80; many were gang-raped and raped multiple times, as many as 60 times.[77] Some 2 million German women are estimated to have been raped between March and November 1945.[78] Hundreds of thousands died as a result, with death rates higher for those in occupied Poland and the first German lands to be conquered by the Red Army, namely East Prussia, Pomerania, and Silesia.[79] The Soviets did not punish the serial-raping soldiers in their forces, even in the innumerable instances of mutilation and murder.[80] While artists often overlook this brutal subject in works about war, Lasansky treated it head on, just as Goya had.

Lasansky conveyed a sense of these horrors in *No. 13*, which shows a woman's corpse suspended from a kind of scaffolding, as a helmeted beast with a large carcass on its back stands to her right and skeletons congregate around

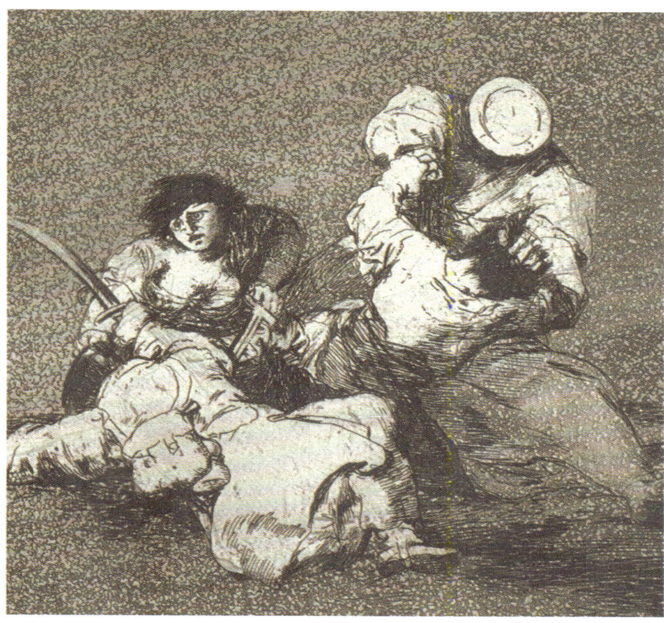

Fig. 4.9 Francisco de Goya y Lucientes, *The Women Give Courage* (*Las mugeres dan valor*) (detail), 1810–14 (published 1863), etching, burnished aquatint, drypoint, burin and burnisher, plate 4 from "The Disasters of War" ("Los Desastres de la guerra"), Minneapolis Institute of Art, the William Hood Dunwoody Fund, by exchange, P.71.20

her. Strung up by her own pink belt, her dress crumpled about her knees, the victim is almost naked except for her black boots. Her hands are clasped above her head as if in prayer. The menacing figures grab at her fallen dress and dangling legs and feet. A hand chillingly emerges from the ground to grip her left heel. There are motifs familiar from Goya's "Disasters of War" that depict defiled corpses left hanging from trees to frighten future victims, as in the etching *Not [in This Case] Either* (*Tampoco*, pl. 36). In *The Women Give Courage* (*Las mugeres dan valor*, pl. 4) (fig. 4.9), women are shown viciously tortured. Dix's and Grosz's *Lustmord*, or sexual murder, works from the 1920s, inspired by actual murders of prostitutes, also come to mind. Intended to be provocative expressions of humankind's perverse, savage nature, such works depict the violation and dismemberment of women's bodies in disturbing detail.[81] By showing the victim in *No. 13* from behind, Lasansky spares us graphic mutilation. Still, the figures lurking around her are at work. A bird of prey rendered in hard, gestural graphite lines perches on the helmet, waiting to feast on her corpse.

In *No. 16*, a dead girl is crudely assaulted by a beastly skeleton-soldier (note the military medals pinned jointly to the skeleton and army coat). One arm holds her lifeless body while the other grips her genitals.[82] The horrors are equally graphic in *No. 17*, which is set in a gas chamber. A soldier in a gas mask raises his bloody hand in the Nazi *heil* salute, while a skeleton on his shoulders directs the shower head toward the young victims. The Nazi bares his bushy groin with his other hand to rape the anguished young child before him. The child's eyes are squeezed tight in agony. At left, still-pink bodies form a pile of contorted limbs and jumbled heads. With just these few corpses, Lasansky conveyed the scale of the Holocaust and the depravity of the perpetrators. The piled heads and limbs are reminiscent of concentration camp films showing bodies bulldozed into mass pits at Bergen-Belsen, images that particularly upset Lasansky. Goya's "Disasters" series, too, has echoes of mistreated, abandoned bodies (*Even Worse [Tanto y mas]*, pl. 22, and *Harvest of the Dead [Muertos recogidos]*, pl. 63) and corpses hurriedly buried or robbed (*They Make Use of Them [Se aprovechan]*, pl. 16, and *Bury Them and Keep Quiet [Enterrar y callar]*, pl. 18). Goya's prints and the liberation films, distanced by more than 125 years, show how the horrors of history repeat themselves.

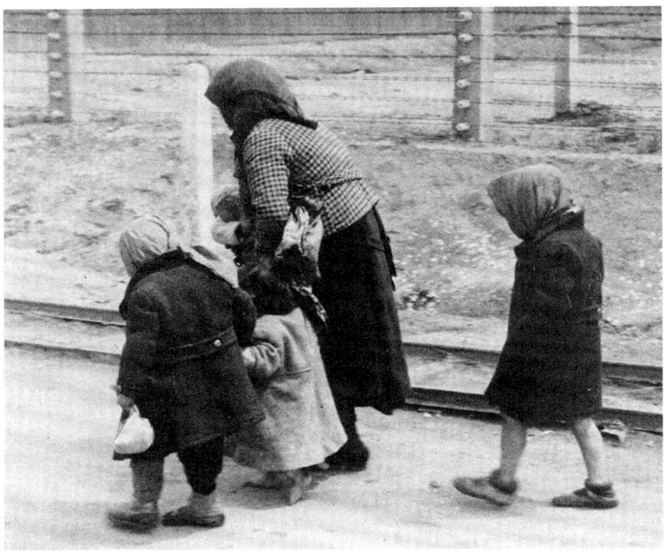

Fig. 4.10 A Jewish woman with three small children and a baby walking toward the gas chambers after selections at Auschwitz-Birkenau, May 1944. United States Holocaust Memorial Museum, courtesy of Yad Vashem, Jerusalem

The 6 Million: *Nos. 13–29*

Lasansky turned to the Nazis' murder victims, the 6 million, in this part of the series. In *No. 14*, for example, we see a small corpse, perhaps of a child, decomposing on the ground. Looking like the Grim Reaper, a Nazi—seemingly under the command of the skeleton on his back—grips the lifeless figure with his massive arms and hands, forcibly crushing its skull as he reaches inside the mouth, presumably searching for gold teeth. The job of looking for valuables usually went to *Sonderkommandos*, special units of forced prison laborers, but Lasansky has depicted a Nazi soldier doing it, identifiable by the long black coat of the Nazi uniform. Lasansky gave this drawing a date, 1963, and a number, 4, suggesting that he had initially intended to include *No. 14* within an early group of Nazi soldiers, *Nos. 1–6*, and it indeed fits logically within the progression.[83]

As he continued the series, Lasansky concentrated more squarely on the victims' suffering. This reflects a broader cultural shift in the 1960s, when survivors assumed a more central role in the events of the Holocaust. This change was largely prompted by the internationally televised Eichmann trial, where 90 survivors testified. The Nuremberg trials (1945–49) had focused on documenting the crimes of Nazi perpetrators. But as survivors told their harrowing stories at the Eichmann proceedings in Jerusalem, the world listened anew. For decades to come, the words and suffering of the survivors would form the memory of the Holocaust, and ultimately of much of World War II, as expressed in documentaries, books, art, memoirs, television, Holocaust memorials and museums, even podcasts.

In *No. 15*, Lasansky represented a mother seated with her children near a prison fence; a vertical scratched line running down the length of the sheet at left and marked with charcoal Xs and asterisks suggests barbed wire. A white beast descends upon them, placing its jaw of death over the mother's head and gripping her shoulder just where she holds her naked infant. Although the baby is still pink with life, she looks lifeless; her swollen belly suggests that she died of starvation. The little girl, wearing a light red cloak and bonnet, is nestled at her mother's side, resting her arms and tiny clasped hands on her mother's lap. Lasansky's pentimenti and erasures in the area of the child's feet and the erasures around the mother's coat imply movement, as Death's long, extended arm directs the group to the right. The scene recalls a 1944 photo from the "Auschwitz Album" (fig. 4.10) of a mother with three small children and a baby walking toward the gas chambers. Powerless and trapped between railroad tracks and barbed wire fences, they have nowhere else to go. The photo was reproduced in the 1959 edition of *Commandant of Auschwitz: The Autobiography of Rudolf Höss*.[84] Goya's *I Saw It Too (Yo lo vi*, pl. 44) shows a similar scene, a mother holding a lifeless infant and grabbing the hand of a small child while fleeing a terrible yet unseen threat.

Crucifixions, Pietàs, and the Martyred Jews: *Nos. 18–23*

In this group, Lasansky explored a range of martyred victims. He deployed the iconography of Christ's martyrdom to powerful ends, adopting the Crucifixion and Pietà as symbols of the suffering of the Jewish people in the Holocaust. Marc Chagall's famous *White Crucifixion* (1938, Art Institute of Chicago) is an early example of an artist using Christian symbols to represent the Nazi persecution of the Jews. Chagall's painting depicts the crucified Christ wearing a Jewish prayer shawl as a loincloth, and his traditional emblem on the cross, *INRI*, meaning "Jesus of Nazareth, King of the Jews," is shown with an Aramaic translation of these words. The Crucifixion is surrounded with scenes of Jewish men and women fleeing pogroms and violence. Scholar Ziva Amishai-Maisels traces the iconography of the "Crucified Jew" throughout Holocaust art, from Chagall to Lasansky, and observes that different artists use this deeply resonant imagery to "address and condemn the Christian world."[85] She notes that while Chagall's use of the Crucifixion "identifies Jesus as the archetypal Jewish martyr," many subsequent artists, including Lasansky, substituted the bodies of other Jewish martyrs from the Holocaust for Jesus on the cross.

In *No. 18*, a dead mother and infant are martyred on a monumental cross, crucified upside down like Saint Peter. The chubby baby lies on its mother's belly in the same position it would have been inside her womb. The mother's body is mutilated, broken and held by the ropes that bind her and her child to the cross. Her face is frozen in a silent scream; blood streams from her neck and mouth, and from her feet onto the baby. Lasansky employed two forceful conventions used by artists since the Renaissance to signify death here and elsewhere in the series. He showed the bottom of the victim's feet and palms of her hands—parts of the body not customarily represented on the living—and depicted the bodies in extreme foreshortening. We implicitly understand the meaning of this perspective: it indicates the loss of all bodily control and will, that is, death.

The cross is collaged newspaper, torn and pasted, with a second, smaller cross painted in red that appears to drip blood. The uppermost clipping comes from the *Daily Iowan*. Dated April 7, 1964, and titled "'Kill Him,' Germans Yell at SS Soldier," it reports on the Auschwitz trials in Frankfurt, West Germany (1963–65), which charged 22 defendants for their crimes at the Auschwitz-Birkenau death camp. Coming on the heels of the Eichmann trial, this trial again brought significant worldwide attention to the Holocaust, particularly in Germany. Fritz Bauer, a prosecutor who played a critical role in Eichmann's capture, called some 210 survivors to testify.[86] The headline refers to emotional outbursts in the courtroom following an upsetting day of testimony. A witness recounted how the SS guard Oswald Kaduk, one of the defendants, forced Jewish children into the gas chambers at gunpoint, with some as young as age four begging to work rather than die. Also collaged onto the cross are *New York Times* classified ads from Sunday, May 19, 1963, for chartered yachts and boats for sale. There are also ads for cars, especially used foreign cars, with prominence given to German automakers like Mercedes-Benz and Volkswagen. Ads for Alfa Romeos, Rolls-Royces, and Cadillacs are included as well.[87] Among the various pet listings, German breeds are highlighted—German shepherds, Doberman pinschers, Weimaraners, schnauzers. One clipping is a short notice about the upcoming 1964 Olympics in Tokyo and a joint North and South Korean team.[88] (North Korea would later withdraw its athletes.)

The besieged victim in *No. 19*, whose large chest tattoo was discussed earlier in connection with the supposed branding of brothel workers, also appears to be martyred on a cross. The composition is reminiscent of conventional Descent from the Cross treatments, in which Joseph of Arimathea and Nicodemus help Mary and Joseph retrieve Christ's dead body for burial. Often either Joseph or Nicodemus is shown bending over the crossbar or ascending a ladder to pull the nails from Christ's hands and lower the body gently to the ground. Lasansky placed a deathly beast on the crossbar above the victim's head, from where it squeezes the life out of the woman with its legs and hands.

The woman in *No. 20* is splayed over another cross, this one covered with scraps of biblical scripture. The sharp protrusion on her back indicates that she has been impaled. Her bony backside and genitals are cruelly exposed as massive amounts of blood drain from her body. Her feet remain clenched, showing the pain and agony of her last moments. Her body and the collaged texts stand in sharp relief against the background, made of long horizontal strokes of charcoal and graphite that Lasansky drew obsessively across the width of the paper. He drew so vigorously, the background is shiny from the graphite and textured from the imprint of his plywood support. The number 5,602,715 stenciled along the bottom is one contemporary estimate of the number of Jewish victims murdered by the Nazis.

Six of the drawings have Bible pages collaged onto them, all taken from the same source: a 19th-century American Bible Lasansky found in the attic of his house in Maine.[89] He selected mostly Hebrew scripture, but he cropped pages, eliminated headings and titles, cut through paragraphs, crossed out lines, and covered passages with pigment or pasted them upside down, so that many of the texts are not legible or easily identifiable. He did not intend for viewers to draw deep, complex meanings from the texts he selected.[90] Rather, he mined the Bible for passages or words that resonated with the subject matter of "The Nazi Drawings." His references are to war, starvation, the wrath of tyrants, people's evil deeds and sins, violence against women and children, concubines, wickedness, grief, and the suffering, enslavement, and forced migrations of the Jewish people. Glued to the woman's back in *No. 20* is a passage from Ecclesiastes (6:3), given emphasis by a folded corner, saying that a stillborn child is better off than a man denied burial, even if blessed with a long life and a hundred children.

Various passages collaged onto *No. 20* contain vivid figurative language that seems to have inspired imagery in Lasansky's other drawings, such as this verse from Proverbs pasted near the victim's suspended leg: "There is a generation whose teeth are as swords, and their jaw-teeth as knives, to devour the poor from off the earth, and the needy from among men" (Proverbs 30:14). In a passage about preying birds, he underlined the last phrase: "The eye that mocketh at his father and despiseth to obey his mother, the ravens of the valley shall pick it out and the young eagles shall eat it" (Proverbs 30:17). Isaiah's vision of peace, which Lasansky included to the right of the figure, proclaims that peace and law will flow to all nations from the top of Mount Zion in Jerusalem. It contains the famous words, "They shall beat their swords into plowshares, and their spears into pruning-hooks; nation shall not lift up sword against nation, neither shall they learn war any more" (Isaiah 2:4).[91]

No. 21 depicts a flayed woman, her skin pierced, strung up, and stretched. Here Lasansky seems to be alluding to reports and film footage from Buchenwald showing lampshades and art made from human skin.[92] The woman's silent scream is eternally fixed in this wicked human trophy. More skin pelts hang in the background. In the midst of these bodily remnants a figure struggles to lift a skull helmet off his eyes, revealing a brutish face, trapped and blinded in the grip of Death. On his left forearm is a phylactery, a box containing Hebrew scripture inscribed on parchment, which is attached to a leather strap and worn by observant Jewish men during morning prayers. The striped sleeve on his right arm suggests a concentration camp uniform. (The comparison is clearer when this figure reappears in *Triptych*.) Lasansky explained that this drawing examines the Jewish men in the *Sonderkommando* units, prisoners forced to work for the Nazis as slave laborers in the gas chambers, killing fields, and crematoria. Scholar Amishai-Maisels interviewed Lasansky about this drawing in 1982 and reports his sentiments this way: "In his view, even an unwilling acceptance of a role in the Nazis' deadly system is a surrender to Death."[93] The drawing is heavily worked and raw, with rough, expressive lines and brushwork and extensive splatters of wash and erasures, revealing the depth of the artist's emotion.

The figure portrayed in *No. 22* is a high-ranking member of the Catholic Church and thus—as was becoming clearer in the 1950s and 1960s—a silent, passive witness to Nazi crimes. Shown wearing a white bishop's miter and an elaborate, voluminous cope ornamented with images of martyrdoms and haloed saints, he represents both the pope and the institution of the Church. Related prints Lasansky made in these years, *Pope* (1965), *Pope and Cardinal* (1966), and *Pope and Crying Boy* (1967), depict the same figure wearing the same white miter.[94]

In *No. 22* the pope stands before the crucified Christ and a dead child suspended from a meat hook that skewers his chin. The child's lifeless head is gently supported by Christ's hand. His small chest is tattooed with a number, and his feet bear the stigmata like Christ's hands. Lasansky thus directly links the martyrdom of this Jewish child in the Holocaust with the martyrdom of Christ, a Jew sacrificed for humanity nearly 2,000 years earlier. Disembodied hands of supplicants plead to this pope for help. But he stands still, eyes frozen, hands raised to his lips in the semblance of prayer.

The pope in *No. 23* holds a dead, naked child in a pose reminiscent of a Pietà, Italian for "pity," a common Catholic devotional image representing the mourning of Christ's dead body. Most frequently the theme is associated with the Virgin Mary, who appears alone, holding her grown dead son on her lap. Variants show other figures (Saint John the Evangelist, Joseph of Arimathea, Nicodemus, Mary Magdalene, and God the Father) and portray Christ held upright, embraced around the chest as here. This pitiable child, rather than being surrounded by a choir of angels, has four birds waiting to feast on his dead body, which is still nailed to the cross he was martyred on. The two birds perched on his arms have already started pecking at him. The child's face is covered by a toothy skull-helmet, and on his stomach, above his tattooed prison number, are two lightly drawn Stars of David (see detail on p. 45), the only Stars of David Lasansky drew in the whole series. Here again Christian iconography has become, in the artist's rendering, a symbol of Jewish suffering. Amishai-Maisels writes of this group in "The Nazi Drawings," "Lasansky reverses the old blood libel: it is not the Jews who kill the Christian child, but the Church that helps to crucify the Jewish children, the kin of Christ."[95] As in *No. 20*, pages of Hebrew scripture contribute meaning. Texts from Genesis and Exodus, which make up the pope's cope, recount Joseph's and Moses' travels back and forth to Egypt and the plagues unleashed on Pharaoh's people for enslaving the Israelites. The pope's expression of pity seems genuine, but his hand covers his mouth, rendering him inaudible and submissive. The background is a chaotic pattern of diagonal, uneven lines with a red band along the top, suggestive of an apocalyptic landscape.

Massacre of the Innocents: *Nos. 24–28*

Approximately 1.5 million Jewish children were murdered in the Holocaust, and tens of thousands of Sinti and Roma and Polish children and adolescents were also targeted, as well as children who were disabled.[96] Jewish children, upon arrival at the death camps, were often separated from their parents and immediately sent to the gas chambers. Lasansky depicted their suffering in *Nos. 24–28*, creating haunting, colossal images of young, powerless infants and children, alone, vulnerable, and terrified.[97] Their tiny hands cover their screams, their eyes are squeezed closed to erase the horrors they have seen or the nightmares they are living. There is no one to protect them.[98] The number 5,602,715, an estimate of Holocaust victims when Lasansky was working, is stenciled repeatedly on this group of drawings.[99] These children represent five of the many millions.

The child in *No. 25* is lightly drawn in pencil, which, combined with the erasures throughout the sheet, give the impression that this child is weak or fading away. Lasansky wallpapered the backgrounds of *Nos. 26–28* with scripture from Deuteronomy, Joshua, Samuel, Judges, and Chronicles, recounting the perpetual wars that Jews had fought for millennia. The text describes the battles waged, the thousands upon thousands killed, the tests and punishments from God, the constant threats, the recurring disasters, and the evil committed by men. In *No. 27*, a red swastika is painted over some text describing rape and adultery, burning cities, and violent acts against men, women, and children. The anguished child in this drawing appears enmeshed in Lasansky's trademark skull and tooth helmet, here coated in blood.

Nos. 26 and *28* are portraits of crying infants who appear crippled, with short arms or thin, immobile legs. The Nazis murdered children who were disabled (and chronically or mentally ill), but Lasansky here was also referring to a wave of birth defects caused by the medication thalidomide. Prescribed to pregnant women for nausea from 1957 to 1962, it was found to cause malformed limbs in fetuses. Thousands of babies were affected. Lasansky's son Leonardo remembers his father cursing the Germans "again" after reading that the epidemic was traced to a German pharmaceutical company.[100] The story was widely reported in the spring and summer of 1962. That August, *Life* magazine featured an X-ray of a thalidomide victim whose legs and hips closely resemble those of the infant Lasansky drew in *No. 28*.[101] This drawing is also the largest in the entire series, indicating how strongly he wanted to emphasize the suffering and murder of children.

Indicting the Church: *No. 29*

Lasansky used *Nos. 22, 23,* and *29* to take aim at the indifference of Pope Pius XII (1939–58) and the Catholic Church toward the suffering of the Jews during the Holocaust. In *No. 29*, he laid the bodies (and the blame) at the feet of the Church hierarchy. Rabbi Cytron's essay in this book, "Art and Faith: Crafting a Renewed Relationship After Auschwitz," reflects on how the Roman Catholic Church's role in the Holocaust was examined in the 1950s and 1960s. The impact of its theology and teachings on antisemitism and the inaction of Pope Pius during wartime were the subjects of much debate at this time.[102] Just as Lasansky's pope and cardinal are oblivious to the young victims below them, Pius failed to lead the Church in any meaningful way, to speak out against the genocide, to assist Jews, or, at the very least, to lend support (financial and

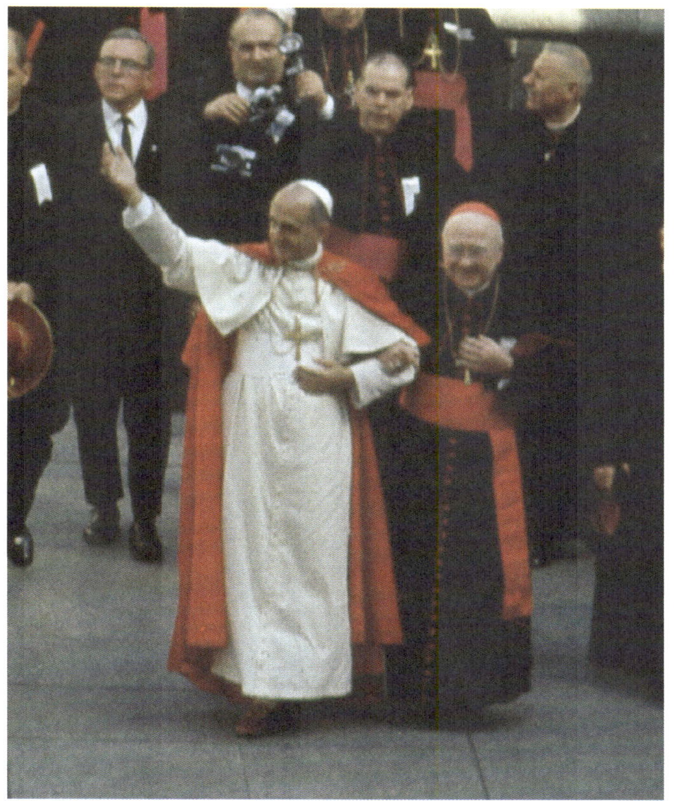

The LIFE Picture Collection via Getty Images

Fig. 4.11 Pope Paul VI's visit to St. Patrick's Cathedral, New York, escorted by Cardinal Spellman; photo by Francis Miller, featured in "Pope Paul VI in America," *Life* magazine, October 15, 1965

moral) to those who did help them.[103] Forced underground, Catholic rescue efforts were dispersed and localized, and Catholic Nazis and collaborators continued to deport and murder Jews without moral condemnation from their foremost (and doctrinally "infallible") religious leader.[104] After the war, some Vatican officials actively participated in the so-called ratlines, or Nazi escape routes from Europe, assisting Eichmann and other war criminals to secure passports and passage to a safe haven in South America. For Lasansky, who grew up in Argentina, where the Catholic Church and fascist dictators had strong ties, allied in their fear of the spread of communism, the issue of the Church's complicity was particularly sensitive. The dollar bill Lasansky drew on the pope's cope symbolizes how easily the Church could be bought. This echoes the cash being handed to the prostitute in *No. 11*, but in the pope's case, Lasansky seems to say, it comes at the expense of millions of innocent victims.[105]

Lasansky's composition recalls photos of the 1965 visit Pope Paul VI (1963–78) made to St. Patrick's Cathedral in New York with Cardinal Francis Spellman. The cardinal's religious dress in *No. 29* is identical to Spellman's in the photos, too (fig. 4.11).[106] Lasansky's pope, however, is portrayed as an older, hunched, weakened, cowardly cleric. His head, with its dark, wizened face, big ears, and large miter, appears in several of Lasansky's prints depicting popes (1965–67). For this work, he printed from that same intaglio plate, cutting out the head and hat and collaging the print onto the drawing.[107]

Triptych (1963–71)

"The Nazi Drawings" close with *Triptych*, a monumental altarpiece of sorts. In it, Lasansky synthesized many of the themes and motifs he explored in the series while offering other traumas to consider, such as America's racial injustice and war in Vietnam. News clippings collaged onto *Triptych* date from 1963, 1965, and 1967, indicating that Lasansky had been contemplating this work for many years, although it was not completed until 1971.[108]

The left panel represents a young woman dressed in the now-familiar prostitute uniform (black heels, stockings, and bustier). The number stenciled on her skirt marks her as a concentration camp prisoner, as does the number itself, 5,602,715. A dead inmate lies prostrate at her feet, and a threatening figure of Death, dressed as a cleric, lurks behind her. With a coquettish smile, she covers her mouth in a gesture feigning surprise or modesty. Here again is the Death and the Maiden motif, with a reference perhaps to Albrecht Dürer's *Coat of Arms with Skull* (1503), which represents a young bride in a wedding crown and fancy dress who lets a lustful wild man press himself on her and caress her hair.[109] The foreboding skull on the shield in front of her is positioned much like the head at the woman's feet in *Triptych*.

Lasansky located this scene in the here and now, giving the woman a stylish 1960s hairstyle, her long bangs nearly covering her eyes, and using recent newspaper clippings—crinkled, folded, torn, and cut—to form a complex collage around her. Paper, card, and slim extracts of Bible scripture are pasted to form the figures. The most prominent news story, to the left of the woman's skirt, is "Protestant Leaders in Germany Urge Support of Vatican Draft on Jews" (see p. 73, fig. 3.4), a 1965 *New York Times* article about a Protestant congress at which German church leaders asked all Christians to act in the spirit of the proposed Vatican II (1962–65) declaration on the Jews aimed at mitigating antisemitism—and urged Rome to approve it.[110] (The statement mentions a need for Protestant repentance as well; Martin Luther had tried to expel Jews from Saxony in 1537 and published *On the Jews and Their Lies* in 1543.) Just above the news clipping is a 1967 excerpt from the *Times*, cropped and turned on its side, about U.S. troops in Vietnam and the threat of Communist China's involvement there.[111] On the opposite side of the woman are clippings from the *Times* editorial pages from May 19, 1963, about racism and the civil rights movement in the South, as President John F. Kennedy had traveled to Alabama the day before to meet with segregationist governor George Wallace about the increasing violence in Birmingham. The collaged clippings are mostly obscured. One is a cartoon of the Alabama governor protesting federal intervention in racial integration, with the partly covered caption, "Ask the Un-American

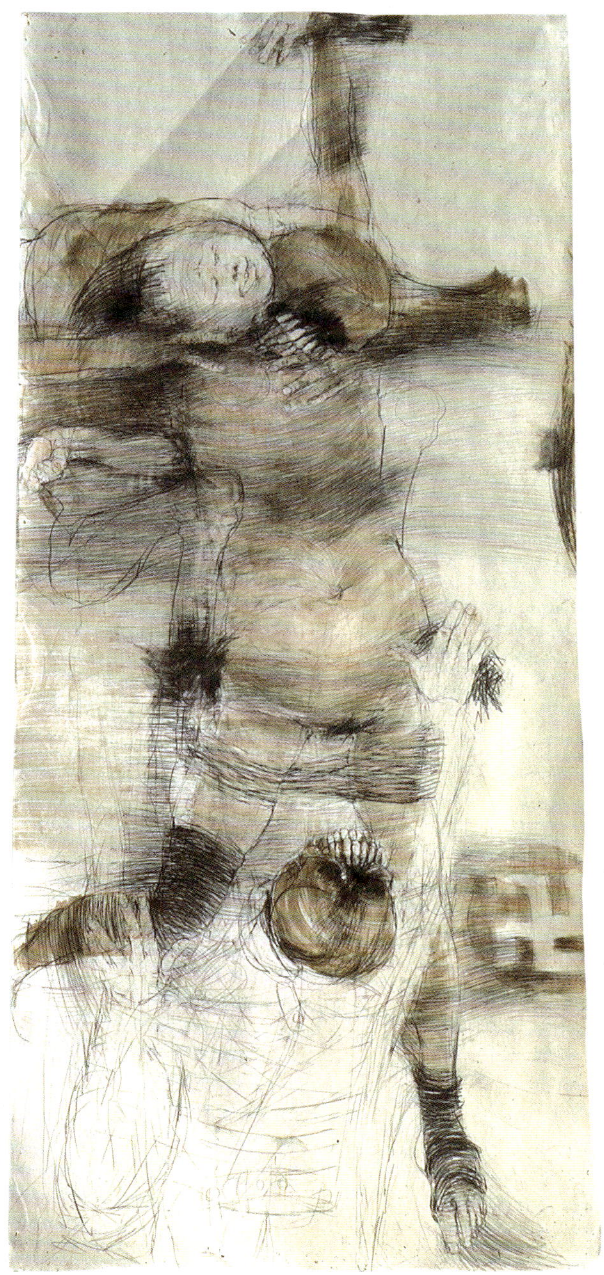

Fig. 4.12 Mauricio Lasansky, *Triptych*, right panel, unfinished state, 1960s
The artist would make significant changes to the composition.

Activities [Committee to investigate] what this strange flag is [doing down here]." Cut from the image is the governor pointing furiously at the American flag and a German sign in his office, "Alabama Uber Alles" (Alabama above All)—a direct reference to the opening line of Nazi Germany's national anthem, "Deutschland, Deutschland über alles" (Germany, Germany above all).[112] Lasansky also took a cartoon from a German newspaper about racism in America and cropped it to show only the dark silhouette of the Statue of Liberty's raised arm.[113] Another story discusses Kennedy's desire for peaceful integration in the South and his support of United Nations' efforts to secure independence and immediate self-government for the nations of Africa.[114] Collaged on and around the skirt of the Jacqueline Kennedy–styled woman are several more stories about the president—his efforts to curb pesticides and improve railroads, his presumed upcoming run

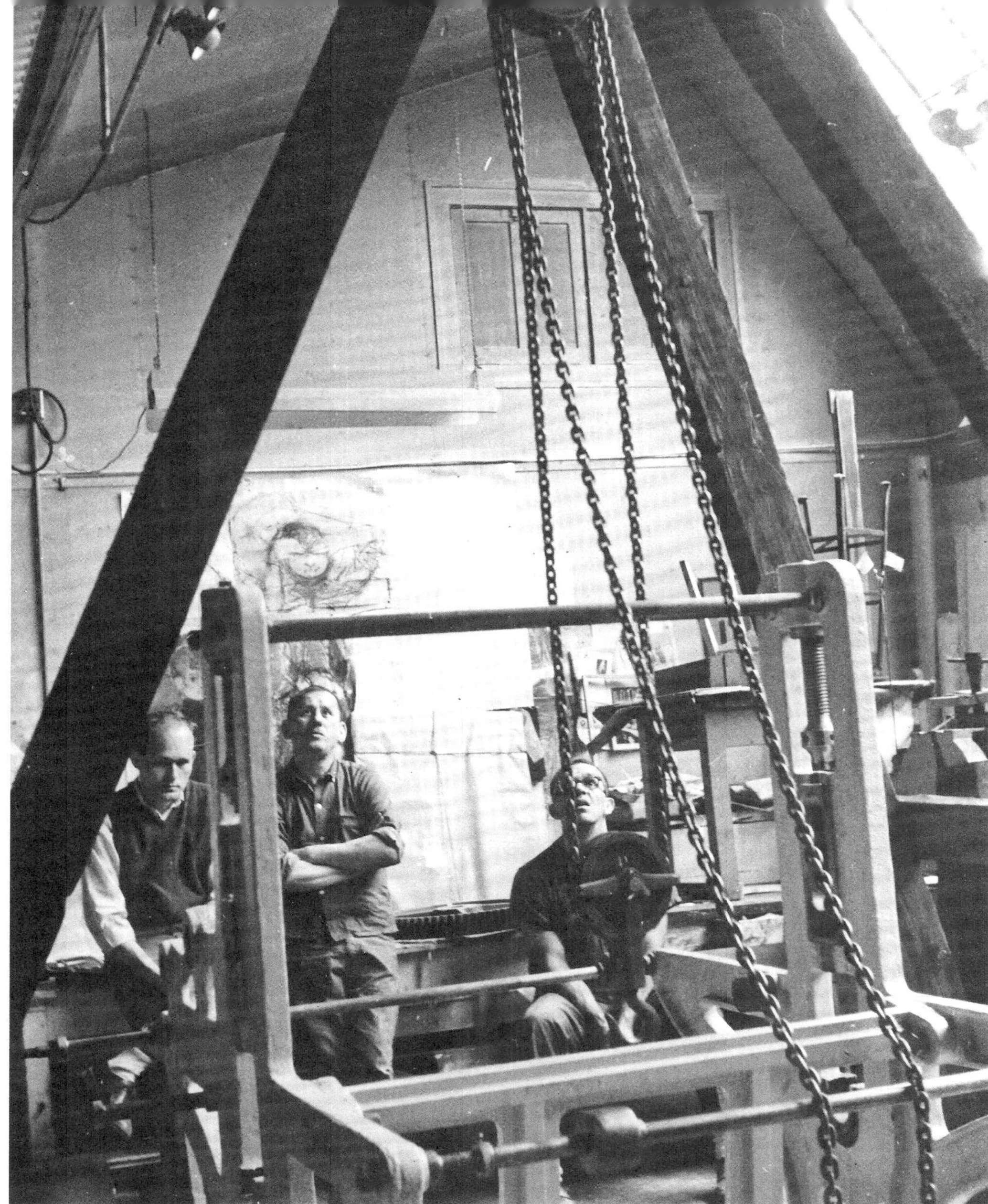

Fig. 4.13 Mauricio Lasansky (center) in his Iowa print studio with an early iteration of *No. 30* of "The Nazi Drawings" tacked to the wall. This photo was taken between 1958 and 1962.

against Governor Nelson Rockefeller, his support of the space program.[115] One story highlights the president's 1963 telephone call to the astronaut Gordon Cooper following his 22 orbits around the earth.[116]

Given all the Kennedy references, it seems possible that the pink wash over the woman's dress and diadem is an allusion to the suit Jacqueline Kennedy wore when Kennedy was assassinated. There are also splatters of blood on the priestly figure of Death. Near the woman's lips are biblical texts too fragmented to read, except for the words "cried also."[117] The biblical scripture that lines her dress and black heels is mostly covered with pigment and illegible except for the word "Ruth" at the bottom of her heel, who was also widowed. Also immortalized on the drawing is Iowan Florence McCall, whose May 1967 obituary is among the clippings Lasansky used to decorate the woman's dress.[118] The clippings papering the background include classified ads for jobs (teachers, librarians, coaches, engineers) and science and business articles, particularly regarding the fluctuating financial markets in August 1967.[119] Additional excerpts from the *Times* 1963 editorial pages deal with prefabricated outdoor fireplaces, the United Nations, and the opposition of university professors to Idaho's loyalty oath.[120] The square cutout in the groin area of Death is an ad for jobs at the Grumman Aerospace Corporation, the chief contractor for the Apollo space program, and, during World War II, supplier of fighter aircraft. These mostly unreadable clippings seem to surround the figures with so much dull chatter, reflecting a sense of business as usual, even as Death and evil continue to wreak suffering in the form of racism, the Vietnam War, and the assassination of President Kennedy.

The central panel of *Triptych* revisits the flayed victim and Jewish *Sonderkommando* (wearing a phylactery and a striped prison uniform) represented in *No. 21*. Blood gushes from the flayed body and covers the distraught figure undertaking his task. Here, however, the death helmet has become a *capirote*, a pointed hood similar to those worn by members of the Ku Klux Klan.[121] To the left of the figure, Lasansky included an article addressing the escalating civil rights struggle in Birmingham, Alabama.[122] In early May, peaceful demonstrations there against segregation had been broken up by police with fire hoses, tear gas, and police dogs, with hundreds of protesters arrested and beaten. On May 11, Klan members bombed the house of A. D. King, brother of Martin Luther King and a leader of the Birmingham integration campaign, and the Gaston Motel, a meeting place of civil rights activists. Massive protests and riots ensued, leading Kennedy to alert federal troops for deployment, against Governor Wallace's wishes. The article discusses the worsening violence in Alabama, as well as the systemic racism that endures in both the North and South—in employment, education, and housing—and calls on the federal government (and Birmingham's business community) to intervene. Lasansky thus appears to link Nazi racial crimes to contemporary racial violence and hatred perpetrated by white supremacists in the United States. This indictment of America is subtle,[123] easily overlooked in the sea of other clippings, mostly taken from the *Times* business section (August 13, 1967)—trading on the American and New York stock exchanges, market charts and reports, and classified ads for jobs, as well as a few sports stories on horse racing, auto racing, and fencing.[124] Evil, Lasansky seems to suggest here, hides and persists in plain sight.

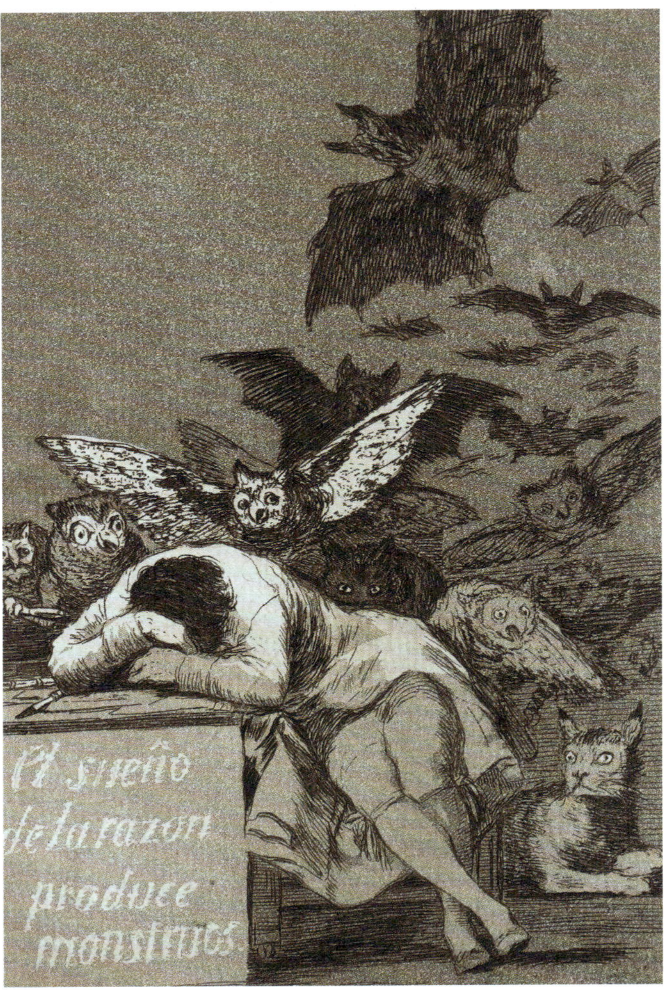

4.14 Francisco de Goya y Lucientes, *The Sleep of Reason Produces Monsters* (*El sueño de la razón produce monstruos*), 1799, etching and aquatint, plate 43 from "The Caprices" ("Los Caprichos"), Minneapolis Institute of Art, the William Hood Dunwoody Fund by exchange, and gift of funds from Mr. and Mrs. John T. Adams, Dr. and Mrs. David Bradford, Mr. and Mrs. Benton J. Case, Mr. and Mrs. W. John Driscoll, Mr. and Mrs. Reuel Harmon, P.83.57.43

On the right panel, the horse racing story from the central panel continues, trailing into the left side of the drawing.[125] Here a dead woman wearing a skeletal helmet hangs by her arms as skeletal beasts attack her. The figures' bony limbs form a kind of ladder that extends the length of the drawing, from the victim's feet to her clasped hands; one of the "crossbars" is the victim's fallen underwear. A photograph of this drawing in an unfinished state (fig. 4.12) reveals that Lasansky originally conceived of a young woman being raped by two skeletons, one attacking her over the shoulders, the other from between her knees. Lasansky apparently decided to erase the victim's head and long hair and soften her nude body so that it recedes into the composition, although traces of her chest and head can still be seen. The ladder and martyred body again allude to Descent from the Cross imagery, only these attendants are not here to bury the body, but to fight over it and desecrate it. An arm extends from below the ladder and grips the bent leg of the victim.

The Evil within Us: *No. 30*

Even though *Triptych* was finished last, Lasansky wanted the series to end with *No. 30*, a self-portrait. The drawing shows the artist's mind, body, and soul being mutilated by a skeleton. The artist holds the drawing utensil he has just used to sign and title the series in a pool of his own blood—blood that drips from his obliterated eyes and damaged heart. A large preliminary sketch for this work is visible in a photo of Lasansky in his Iowa print studio, taken sometime between 1958 and 1962 (fig. 4.13). It depicts the primary figure covering his own eyes, with a barely sketched second figure looming above his shoulders. Clearly the subject festered in Lasansky for years.

The final drawing seems to be a reconsideration of Goya's famous print *The Sleep of Reason Produces Monsters* (*El sueño de la razón produce monstruos*, pl. 43) from "The Caprices" ("Los Caprichos," 1797–99) (fig. 4.14). Goya depicted an artist (himself) who has set down his drawing tool and fallen asleep, which unleashes a flock of devilish owls and bats to descend upon him. The image carries many layers of meaning (including the role of the artist to combine reason and fantasy), but it has come to represent first and foremost the nightmare world that would exist without reason, and the kind of world we would have if artists failed to expose the monsters. Lasansky chose to show the artist (himself) literally torn apart and tormented by the act of making "The Nazi Drawings," with their monsters, corpses, and crimes. Just as the death skeleton ensnared so many figures over the course of this series, it now, too, ensnares the artist. Lasansky, in this final image, warned that evil may lurk within us all.

Mauricio Lasansky, *No. 30* (detail), "The Nazi Drawings"

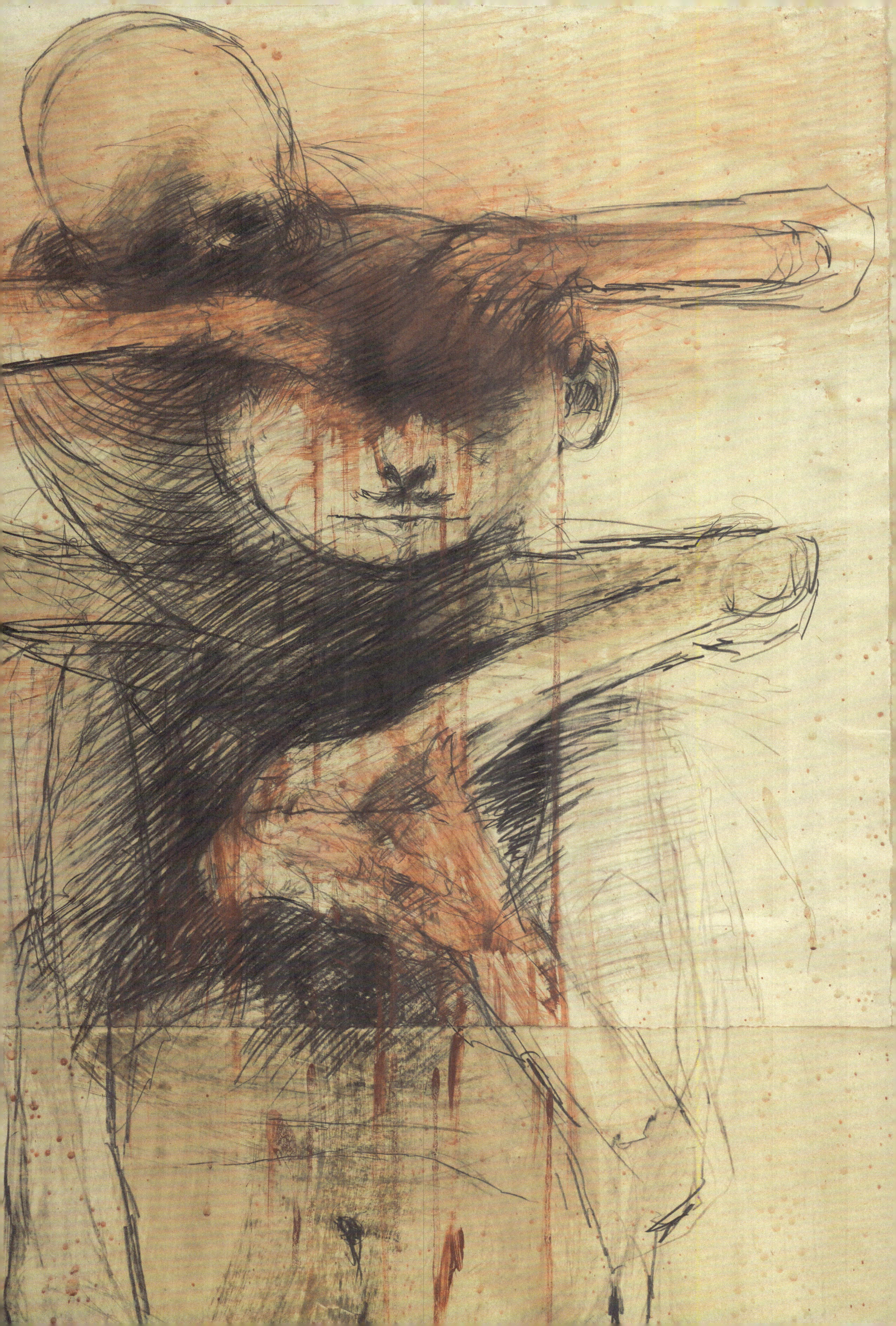

NOTES

1. Interview with the artist by Jan K. Muhlert, in Joann Moser et al., *Mauricio Lasansky: A Retrospective Exhibition of His Prints and Drawings* (exh. cat.), University of Iowa Museum of Art and other venues (Iowa City, 1976), with essays by Joann Moser and I. Michael Danoff, p. 22.

2. See Lasansky's comments noted in Hoke Norris, "A Cold Look at Horror," *Chicago Daily News*, April 29, 1970, p. 4, and Charlotte Willard, "Drawings from Hell," *Look*, February 21, 1967, p. 80.

3. Lane Wyrick and Mauricio Lasansky, "Interview with Lasansky," *The Nazi Drawings by Artist Mauricio Lasansky*, directed by Lane Wyrick (1999; Iowa City, Iowa: Xap Interactive Inc., 2004), DVD.

4. The U.S. and British army film footage of the camps was featured in newsreels from all five major American newsreel companies in late April and May of 1945. Billy Wilder's *Death Mills* (*Die Todesmühlen*), 22 minutes, was made for German audiences and shown throughout West Germany in January 1946, and also shown in limited release in the U.S.; *Nazi Concentration Camps* (1945), an hour-long compilation of footage, was aired at the Nuremberg trials but not in the U.S. until 1959.

5. Larry D. Wilcox, "'Shadows of a Distant Nightmare': Visualizing the Unimaginable Holocaust in Early Documentary Films," in *Remembering for the Future: The Holocaust in the Age of Genocide* (New York, 2001), eds. John Roth and Elisabeth Maxwell, vol. 3, pp. 478–500. The film *Hitler Lives* incorporates the U.S. War Department's short occupational film *Your Job in Germany*, directed by Frank Capra and written by Theodor Geisel (Dr. Seuss). Warner Bros. won the 1945 Academy Award for best short documentary for *Hitler Lives*, although they gave no credit to *Your Job in Germany*. *Nuremberg*, a 76-minute film, was "made available for television" in 1946 by the U.S. Army Department, but few Americans had televisions at the time. Wilcox has researched the distribution of the film and suggests that it was probably seen by most audiences in movie theaters, but lack of early film reviews suggests limited distribution. Lasansky may also have seen some of the footage reported to have circulated among American college campuses in 1946 and 1947 for faculty viewings. Access to camp footage after that was very limited in the U.S.

6. As discussed in "The Holocaust in Press, Culture, and Art," the trauma and rebuilding efforts of the early postwar period pushed many of the tragedies of the war out of mind. Governments discouraged showing the atrocity footage as the Cold War realigned European political alliances, and Hollywood frequently censored it, partly in response to audience appetites. Nancy Copeland Halbgewachs recently studied how Hollywood's Production Code Administration censored atrocity footage from films, particularly graphic footage, before 1980. She traces the role played by the Hollywood studio system and demonstrates that very few films about the Holocaust were produced in Hollywood before the studio system collapse (Nancy Copeland Halbgewachs, "Censorship and Holocaust Film in the Hollywood Studio System" [PhD diss., University of New Mexico, 2012]). A few Hollywood films in the 1940s nonetheless incorporated actual footage, such as Orson Welles's *The Stranger* (1946) and Lewis Allen's *Sealed Verdict* (1948). In Britain, *German Concentration Camps Factual Survey*, an official British documentary produced by Sidney Bernstein, with the assistance of Alfred Hitchcock, was abandoned in 1945, although footage was screened at the Nuremberg trials. Alain Resnais's *Nuit et brouillard* (*Night and Fog*, 1955) also incorporates footage, but it was distributed in the U.S. only in 1962 and in very limited markets. The flashbacks in Sidney Lumet's *The Pawnbroker* (1964) depict fictive camps created on the movie set.

7. Jeffrey Shandler, *While America Watches: Televising the Holocaust* (New York, 1999), pp. 18–22. The camp footage shown in *Judgment at Nuremberg*, both on television (CBS, 1959) and Hollywood film (1961), was taken from *Nazi Concentration Camps* (1945); see note 4 for more on the compilation.

8. Phillip Lasansky, in conversation with the author, August 8, 2017. William explained to young Phillip why Israel had gone undercover to arrest Eichmann. William, who was born in Argentina and was six years old when the family moved to the U.S., believed that Argentina never would have given up Eichmann to Israel. While Israel announced Eichmann's arrest on May 23, 1960, the story of his secret kidnapping in Argentina by Mossad agents was told two weeks later in *Time* magazine (June 10, 1960), so the family must have learned this news at their summer place in Maine, because they left Iowa for Maine every May. Phillip said they almost never watched television in Maine, as they did not have a set there and had to go to a neighbor's house, as they did for the moon landing in July 1969.

9. Wyrick and Lasansky 2004.

10. See Catherine Quehl-Engel, "Christian Theology after the Jewish Use of Christological Imagery in Holocaust Art," in *The Holocaust: Lessons for the Third Generation*, eds. Dominick A. Iorio, Richard Libowitz, and Marcia Sachs Littell (Lanham, Md., 1997), pp. 86, 90n13, citing interview with the artist in 1993. This was also noted by his sons Phillip (2017) and Leonardo Lasansky (2017–20) in conversation with me.

11. Phillip Lasansky, conversation, 2017.

12. Nina Barragan, "When Fiction Becomes Memory," *North American Review*, open-space, September 17, 2019. She discusses the Lasanskys' art collection, and, in particular, the medieval wooden Corpus Christi sculpture they acquired in Spain. The Lasanskys formed a major collection of African and pre-Columbian art; "African, Oceanic and Pre-Columbian Art Including Property from the Krugier and Lasansky Collections," Sotheby's, New York, May 16, 2014. In his early years in Argentina, Lasansky even dabbled in Christian imagery; see, e.g., *The Annunciation*, 1938, drypoint on zinc (plate destroyed), in John Thein and Phillip Lasansky, *Lasansky, Printmaker* (Iowa City, Iowa, 1975), no. 41.

13. Ziva Amishai-Maisels, "The Crucified Jew," in *Depiction and Interpretation: The Influence of the Holocaust on the Visual Arts* (Oxford, 1993), pp. 86–87, 123, 318, discusses the impact of the Eichmann trial on R. B. Kitaj, among others; see also Peter Novick, *The Holocaust in American Life* (New York, 1999), pp. 2–7, 198–200.

14. Phillip Lasansky, conversation, 2017.

15. Arūnas Bubnys, "Holocaust in Lithuania: An Outline of the Major Stages and Their Results," in *The Vanished World of Lithuanian Jews*, eds. Alvydas Nikžentaitis, Stefan Schreiner, and Darius Staliūnas (Amsterdam and New York, 2004), pp. 218–19; "Vilnius," YIVO Encyclopedia of Jews in Eastern Europe, YIVO Institute for Jewish Research, accessed May 5, 2020, https://yivoencyclopedia.org/article.aspx/Vilnius.

16. As well as alternative spellings: Kahan, Kann, Leszańskis, Milakowsky, Milikowska, Milikovski, Milejkowski, Mileykovski, Melakovski. Lasansky's mother, Ana Kahn [Kagan] (1888–1971), was from Kovno (Kaunas). His father, Abrahm Isaac Lasansky [Laschansky] (1883–1938), lived in Vilna (Vilnius). Milikovski was the name of Lasansky's paternal grandmother's family. I would like to thank Yehudit Shendar for her assistance in researching Yad Vashem's documents and database for Lasansky's relatives, and Nina Barragan, pen name of Rocio Lasansky Weinstein, Mauricio Lasansky's eldest daughter, for sharing her research into her family's heritage with me.

17. Phillip Lasansky, conversation, 2017.

18. Leonardo Lasansky, in conversation with the author, February 6, 2020.

19. This drawing was later reworked by Lasansky, and extended on the right to make room for the six figures and three dogs. He also added color and collage elements. The drawing is in the possession of the Lasansky Corporation, along with another reworked drawing in color.

20. Rudolf Höss, *Commandant of Auschwitz: The Autobiography of Rudolf Höss* (New York and Cleveland, 1959), p. 155.

21. Edwin Honig, "The Nazi Drawings of Mauricio Lasansky," in Mauricio Lasansky, *The Nazi Drawings* (exh. cat.), Philadelphia Museum of Art and eight other venues (Philadelphia, 1966), nine-page essay, unnumbered.

22. Novick 1999, p. 120.

23. "Confessions of Adolf Eichmann," *Life*, November 28, 1960, p. 21. In 1957, Eichmann participated in extensive recorded interviews in Argentina with the Dutch Nazi collaborator and former SS journalist Willem Sassen. Sassen sold the abridged "memoirs" by Eichmann, drawn from these interviews, to *Der Stern* and *Life* magazines after Eichmann's arrest.

24. Höss 1959, p. 160. Höss's memoir was first published in Warsaw in 1951, and in English in 1959.

25. Hannah Arendt, *Eichmann in Jerusalem: A Report on the Banality of Evil*, 2006 ed. (New York, 1963), p. 276.

26. Among other things, Göring, commander in chief of the Luftwaffe (German air force) and founder of the Nazi Gestapo (secret police), established the first concentration camps. He led efforts to confiscate Jewish property in Germany and occupied countries, and in 1941 ordered Reinhard Heydrich to implement the Nazis' so-called Final Solution to the Jewish question. He committed suicide in prison after the trial by taking a capsule of poison, but the other 11 Nazis sentenced to death were executed. The 1959 television play shows the actual hanging of Julius Streicher—his walk up the plank, his head covered with a hood, a priest reciting a Latin prayer, his hanging, his body afterward, and the simple coffin marked with a cross in which he would be buried. Streicher was instrumental in inciting his compatriots to persecute the Jews as the publisher of *Der Stürmer* (*The Stormtrooper*), a malicious antisemitic newspaper.

27. "Eichmann Is at Bay on Eve of Trial: An Intimate Study," *Life*, April 14, 1961, p. 22, with photos by Gjon Mili.

28. Eichmann pleaded "not guilty in the spirit [or sense] of the indictment" to each charge of the 15-count indictment, that is, not guilty as charged. Eichmann famously declared, "To sum it all up, I must say that I regret nothing," in his abridged memoir published in *Life* magazine, "Eichmann's Own Story Part II," *Life*, December 5, 1960, p. 161.

29. Höss 1959, see, e.g., pp. 170–75.

30. Höss 1959, pp. 29–35. As Höss continues his story, bullying and injuring a schoolmate, and later murdering a fellow mercenary soldier, it becomes clear that his violent and sociopathic qualities preceded his decision to join the SS in 1934.

31. Höss 1959, pp. 69, 160.

32. Primo Levi, *I sommersi e i salvati* (*The Drowned and the Saved*, Turin, 1986), in *The Complete Works of Primo Levi*, ed. Ann Goldstein (New York, 2015), vol. 3, pp. 2420–27.

33. Julia Roos, "Backlash against Prostitutes' Rights: Origins and Dynamics of Nazi Prostitution Policies," *Journal of the History of Sexuality*, vol. 11 (2002), pp. 67–94.

34. Christa Paul, *Zwangsprostitution: staatlich errichtete Bordelle im Nationalsozialismus* (Berlin, 1994), p. 102. Paul notes that brothels would move as the war front changed, so the number was in flux.

35. Robert Sommer, "Sexual Exploitation of Women in Nazi Concentration Camp Brothels," in *Sexual Violence against Jewish Women during the Holocaust*, eds. Sonja M. Hedgepeth and Rochelle G. Saidel (Hanover, N.H., 2010). Bonus vouchers were given to privileged prisoners and could be used for cigarettes, food, or a brothel visit.

36. Hester Baer and Elizabeth R. Baer, introduction to *The Blessed Abyss: Inmate #6582 in Ravensbrück Concentration Camp for Women*, by Nanda Herbermann, eds. Hester Baer and Elizabeth R. Baer, trans. Hester Baer (Detroit, 2000), pp. 32–34.

37. Levi, *Se questo è un uomo* (*If This Is a Man*, Turin, 1947), in Levi 2015, vol. 1, pp. 28, 76. Primo Levi describes one of the brothels at Auschwitz: "Block 29, which always has its windows closed, because it is the Frauenblock, the camp brothel, serviced by Polish *Hafltling* [prisoner] girls and reserved for the Reichsdeutsche [Germans of the Reich]," which he earlier explains meant it was for "the criminals and politicals; not for the Jews." In most literature, Block 24, not Block 29, is identified as the main brothel at Auschwitz.

38. Sommer 2010, p. 48.

39. Sommer 2010, pp. 52–53, 57n20. Over the course of the war (1939–45), Ravensbrück imprisoned an estimated 130,000 women, with about 40,000 women thought to have survived the war. About 80 percent of the women forced into sex slavery at the official camp brothels outside Auschwitz can be documented. Well over half were German, many of whom were registered as "asocial." Sommer estimates that about a quarter of the women were Polish, a proportion likely higher at Auschwitz. Separate brothels were built for Ukrainian SS guards, since they were not permitted to have intercourse with German women, and Nazis sought Polish women for them; Jessica R. Anderson Hughes, in her 2011 PhD dissertation for Rutgers University, titled "Forced Prostitution: The Competing and Contested Uses of the Concentration Camp Brothel" (pp. 120, 136), notes that among the women classified as asocials were prostitutes, alcoholics, or "work-shy," and at risk of sterilization. While prostitution was legal in Nazi Germany, it was still cause for arrest. There were political prisoners, criminals, and lesbians at Ravensbrück as well, and she notes that many political prisoners were also forced into the brothels.

40. Anderson Hughes (2011, p. 151) notes that length of time in the brothel varied by camp. Nanda Herbermann, a Catholic activist and political prisoner at Ravensbrück from 1941 to 1943, who was conscripted to work as a block supervisor there, published a memoir of the camp in 1946 (Herbermann 2000 ed., pp. 42–44, 103–4). It includes a brief, important account of how the camp brothels operated, which was little discussed by the actual women forced to work in them. Herbermann learned from the women coming and going from Ravensbrück to the Mauthausen camp brothel and others and writes of women being rotated at the brothel every three months. Herbermann did not have any knowledge of the Auschwitz brothels, as Ravensbrück prisoners were not sent there, but Primo Levi describes there "the changing of the guard at the Frauenblock [women's block], with the arrival of a fresh contingent of robust Polish girls" (Levi 1947, in Levi 2015, vol. 1, p. 76).

41. Anderson Hughes 2011, pp. 164–66. Her research shows that there was no standard policy across the camp brothels in dealing with pregnancy, but that survivor testimonies describe women being shot for becoming pregnant. In her 1946 memoir, survivor Nanda Herbermann reported of some brothel prisoners never returning to Ravensbrück, and she assumed they were killed (Herbermann 2000 ed., pp. 43–44). While camp brothel records are far from complete, particularly for the three at Auschwitz and its satellite, Sommer states there is no record of a woman in a brothel camp being executed (Sommer 2010, p. 54).

42. Sommer 2010, p. 54.

43. On female survivors' tendency to remain silent after the war about sexual abuse they suffered, see S. Lillian Kremer, "Sexual Abuse in Holocaust Literature: Memoir and Fiction," in Hedgepeth and Saidel 2010, pp. 177–99, and Nomi Levenkron, "Death and the Maidens: 'Prostitution,' Rape, and Sexual Slavery during World War II," in Hedgepeth and Saidel 2010, pp. 13–28. Levenkron discusses the hostility victims of sexual assault met within their own communities after the war. Christa Paul, in her pioneering study on the camp brothels, brought new attention and clarity to the subject (Paul 1994). In her research, she tracked down and interviewed some of the female victims, as well as male prisoners who visited the brothels. Sommer notes that the stigma surrounding these victims was lifelong, and the women who were arrested as asocials were denied restitution following the war in West Germany until the 1980s, and in East Germany unless they integrated themselves into the socialist fabric of Soviet occupation (Sommer 2010, p. 55).

44. See, e.g., C. L. Sulzberger, "Anti-Axis Revolt Rife in Slovenia," *New York Times*, January 23, 1943; Harold Denny, "Despair Blankets Buchenwald Camp," *New York Times*, April 20, 1945. Also widely reported was a fake suicide note purported to have been written by a student of the Bais Yaakov school of girls in the Kraków ghetto, who martyred herself in a mass suicide by poison, one of 93 Jewish young women (pupils and students), to escape the forced prostitution of the Nazis ("93 Choose Suicide Before Nazi Shame," *New York Times*, January 8, 1943, p. 8). There is vast literature on this letter, see, e.g., Judith Tydor Baumel and Jacob J. Schacter, "The Ninety-Three Bais Yaakov Girls of Cracow: History or Typology?" in *Reverence, Righteousness and Rahamanut: Essays in Memory of Rabbi Dr. Leo Jung*, ed. Jacob J. Schacter (Northvale, N.J., 1992), pp. 93–130, and Zev Garber, "The 93 Beit Ya-akov Martyrs: Toward the Making of a Historiography," in *Shoah: The Paradigmatic Genocide: Essays in Exegesis and Eisegesis* (New York, 1994), pp. 97–118.

45. The Polish Ministry of Information, *The Black Book of Poland* (New York and London, 1942), pp. 98, 104–13.

46. The British *German Concentration Camps Factual Survey* (1945), discussed above, which was screened at the Nuremberg trials, discusses and films the brothel at Dachau.

47. Sommer 2010, pp. 52, 55. Sommer observes that while camp brothels "had little relevance for most camp prisoners," they represented a cynical and extreme dimension of Nazi terror, in which victims at camps become perpetrators. The broader statistics concerning sexual violence during the war are discussed below.

48. Dina Porat, "An Author as His Own Biographer—Ka-Tzetnik: A Man and A Tattooed Number," in *Holocaust History and the Readings of Ka-Tzetnik*, ed. Annette F. Timm (New York, 2018), pp. 13–36. Yehiel Dinur (1909–2001) was born Yehiel Feiner in Poland. After the war, he took the name "Dinur," meaning "of the fire" in Aramaic, and used his Auschwitz prison number, Ka-Tzetnik 135633, as his pen name, publishing a number of novels about his and his family's persecution in Nazi-occupied Poland, in the ghetto, labor camps, and at Auschwitz.

49. Ka-Tzetnik 135633's *Kar'u lo pipl (They Called Him Piepel*, Tel Aviv, 1961) was published in English first as *Piepel* (London, 1961), and then as *Moni: A Novel of Auschwitz* (New York, 1963) and *Atrocity* (New York, 1963).

50. David Mikics, "Holocaust Pulp Fiction," *Tablet*, April 19, 2012, Arts and Letters section, accessed December 10, 2019, https://www.tabletmag.com/jewish-arts-and-culture/books/97160/ka-tzetnik. In 1994 Israel's Ministry of Education reissued the books as part of the country's high school curriculum; Miryam Sivan, "'Stoning the Messenger': Yehiel Dinur's *House of Dolls* and *Piepel*," in Hedgepeth and Saidel 2010, pp. 200–216.

51. The cover art of the 1960 paperback of Ka-Tzetnik's *House of Dolls* (New York, Pyramid Books, 1960), by Dick Shelton, was used for a series of printings. The 1968 cover published by Panther Books, on the other hand, incorporated a photograph, rather than a drawing, of a woman similarly branded and posed, although decidedly more eroticized, with her cleavage exposed and her expression sexually suggestive. The photograph was used again for the 1977 edition published by Mayflower and again in 1989 (Grafton).

52. See, e.g., Omer Bartov, "Kitsch and Sadism in Ka-Tzetnik's Other Planet: Israeli Youth Imagine the Holocaust," *Jewish Social Studies*, vol. 3 (1997), pp. 42–76; Kremer 2010, pp. 177–99. Kremer observes that men writing fictionalized accounts of the camp brothels tend to eroticize them and describe the activities in the brothel more explicitly than female memoirists and survivor testimonials. She cites as examples Tadeusz Borowski, *This Way for the Gas, Ladies and Gentlemen* (New York, 1967, first published in Polish in 1948), Arnošt Lustig, *Lovely Green Eyes* (New York, 2001, first published in Czech, 2000), and Arthur Miller's *Playing for Time* (CBS, 1980). Kremer argues that such graphic titillation by these male writers, both survivors and men who have no personal experience of the Holocaust, can give "rise to charges of Holocaust exploitation" (p. 193). This tendency seems applicable to a number of artists and filmmakers treating the subject as well.

53. See, e.g., Sivan 2010, pp. 208–9.

54. Timm 2018, passim. Pascale Bos observes ("Sexual Violence in Ka-Tzetnik's *House of Dolls*," in Timm 2018, p. 119) that Dinur's literary conceit of coming into possession of his "sister's" diary lent authenticity to his imagined account of life inside the brothels.

55. Na'ama Shik, "Sexual Abuse of Jewish Women in Auschwitz-Birkenau," in *Brutality and Desire: War and Sexuality in Europe's Twentieth Century*, ed. Dagmar Herzog (New York, 2009). Shik's essay grew out of a doctoral dissertation that concluded that *House of Dolls* is a fiction. Nazi race laws pervaded both camp brothels and civilian life, and Jewish prostitutes were illegal after 1939. Porat (2018, p. 32) points out that as a consequence of the rumor that Jewish women were forced into sexual slavery in the camps, survivors were barraged frequently with questions about camp brothels in these years. Bos writes of *House of Dolls*, "As such imagined stories of prostitution took hold, it unfortunately sensationalized and scandalized the subject. The sexual violence is not analyzed as a phenomenon in its own right, but as part of the overall barbarity, brutality, and depravity of the enemy soldier force. It is scandalized for the sake of publicity and to generate moral outrage and activism but it comes to overshadow the actual events of sexual violence during the Holocaust." Bos 2018, p. 125.

56. Sommer notes that there were many reports of rape and sexual exploitation of Jewish women outside the official camp system, but he could trace only one Jewish woman in the brothel records, which document the identity of 80 percent of those forced into the official brothels. He suggests that this Jewish woman may have worked in an administrative and organizational capacity in the brothel rather than as a sex worker. Records are not complete, but Sommer argues that chances are slim that there were other Jewish women forced into official brothel service there (Sommer 2010, pp. 45, 52–55). The records at Auschwitz appear to be less complete, and the brothels at this camp were run outside the rest of the system. Anderson Hughes (2011, p. 179) also traces a few instances when Jewish women were accidentally selected for the brothels at Auschwitz-Birkenau, but finds only those in which "the error" was corrected.

57. For fictitious details in the novel, including the "field whore" tattoo, see Bos 2018, pp. 119–20, 137n75. A photograph by the Israeli photographer Paul Goldman of an unidentified female survivor (her face cropped from the picture) shows a woman with her chest branded with a prison number and label "Feld-Hure," which appears to be a unique record of this practice. The photo, usually dated to 1945, was taken in Israel so is presumed to record a Jewish woman who survived Auschwitz, but no details are known of the subject or circumstances of the photo. Holocaust survivor Arnošt Lustig incorporated this detail into his novel *Lovely Green Eyes* (2000).

58. *The Pawnbroker* was adapted from a 1961 novel by Edward Lewis Wallant. Rod Steiger's performance earned him an Academy Award nomination.

59. Inspired by the Frankfurt Auschwitz trials (1963–65), the film is about the prosecution of Nazi criminals. It follows a potential witness at the trial who refuses to testify, a Jewish survivor, Lea Weiss, who had been forced to work in a camp brothel and also endure medical experiments. The terrifying prospect of reliving her trauma and facing the doctor who tortured her drives the victim to suicide. The film was released in Germany in 1967.

60. Edith falls in love with a Russian POW, which saves her spirit, but she dies leading an unsuccessful prison escape. *Kapò* was heavily criticized by French director and critic Jacques Rivette for a tracking shot that depicts the electrocution of a prisoner. Rivette describes the approach of the Italian Jewish filmmaker, Gillo Pontecorvo, as the aestheticizing of atrocity. A debate over Holocaust cinema ensued that continues to this day.

61. Olga Lengyel's *Souvenirs de l'au-delà (Memoirs from the Beyond*, Paris, 1946) was published in English as *Five Chimneys: The Story of Auschwitz* (Chicago, 1947). Lengyel's memoir of the camps represents one of the earlier published accounts written from a female perspective. She describes incidents of sexual exploitation and risk with more detail and feeling than most survivor memoirs. Primo Levi's sensitive accounts of the Holocaust in *If This Is a Man* (1947) and *La tregua (The Truce*, Turin, 1963) note episodes of sexual violence against women as a matter of course, indicating it was commonplace.

62. Levi 1947 and 1963, in Levi 2015, vol. 1, pp. 341–42, 354–57, 361–62. In *The Truce* (1963), Levi describes Flora, an Italian woman sent to Germany as a forced laborer, who swept floors at a work camp of Auschwitz, where she had "meetings" in a secret "closet under the stairs with a cooperative of German and Polish Kapos" for food. He sees the same woman after the war, on their long journey back to Italy, living with an Italian, "not as a spouse, but as a slave" who "beat her savagely." He also mentions offhandedly two German women caught in Russia following the war, living in the woods, who worked as prostitutes for food and "protection." Rape by the Red Army after the war is also discussed.

63. For discussion of gender and Holocaust testimonies, and tendency toward silence about personal abuses suffered and fear of disgrace, see Levenkron, Kremer, and Sivan in Hedgepeth and Saidel 2010. Herbermann in her 1946 memoir (2000 ed., pp. 53–150) discusses the prisoners selected from her block at Ravensbrück for brothels. She initially judged the imprisoned prostitutes and those who "volunteered" for the camp brothels uncharitably and to be immoral, but she became more empathetic to their situation over her years at the camp, and afterward. See also Baer and Baer 2000, pp. 30–40.

64. Olga Lengyel, *Five Chimneys: The Story of Auschwitz* (1947), 2nd ed. (Chicago, 1995), pp. 59–63.

65. Raya Kagan, *Nashim be-lishkat ha-gehinom (Women in the Office of Hell*, Merḥavyah, Israel, 1947), p. 136, as cited by Levenkron 2010, p. 21.

66. Lengyel 1947, 1995 ed., pp. 28–29.

67. Anderson Hughes (2011, pp. 124–27, 179) notes various Nazi camp documents discussing how women working in the brothel should appear (see also pp. 124n97, 126n101). Lengyel was Jewish, so it is not clear if she was being selected for the official brothels or some other kind of exploitation. Anderson Hughes traces a few instances when Jewish women were mistakenly selected for brothels and later dismissed. For women retaining hair in brothels, see also *German Concentration Camps Factual Survey* (1945), the unfinished British documentary discussed above,

which shows footage of the Dachau brothel, where the women not only have their hair, but appear well fed and dressed in civilian clothes; Monika J. Flaschka, "'Only Pretty Women Were Raped': The Effect of Sexual Violence on Gender Identities in the Concentration Camps," in Hedgepeth and Saidel 2010, pp. 79–85. Flaschka discusses the subject of women's hair and the trauma of losing it at the camps, as well as the widely held perception by prisoners that women who retained their hair risked rape.

68. "Corsicans Punish Traitorous Women," *Life*, July 17, 1944, and "Woman Collaborationist," *Life*, August 18, 1944. The Corsican photos, taken by an unknown photographer, were initially censored and only published nine months after the public shaving.

69. *Life*, July 17, 1944, p. 33.

70. Sexual violence—rape, sexual enslavement, harassment, assault—committed by Japanese troops was rampant. During the Nanking massacre in 1937, for instance, Japanese forces were estimated to have killed over 300,000 soldiers and civilians in six weeks and raped between 20,000 and 80,000 women (including the elderly) and children (Iris Chang, *The Rape of Nanking: The Forgotten Holocaust of World War II* [New York, 1997]). In the European theater of World War II, the rape committed by Nazi and Russian troops far outweighed that by other forces. For U.S. forces in Europe, one scholar has documented some 14,000 women raped by American soldiers, mostly in Germany (11,000), a number some question as too low (J. Robert Lilly, *Taken by Force: Rape and American GIs in Europe during World War II* (New York, 2007).

71. The U.N.'s International Criminal Tribunals first specifically addressed rape, forced prostitution, and sexual slavery as war crimes (rather than private crime) systematically and widely employed against civilians in conflicts with their courts in the former Yugoslavia (1993) and Rwanda (1994). The United Nations addressed the abuse with a human rights law in 2000, with the U.N. Security Council since continuing to update and improve the resolutions with stronger protections for the victims.

72. Fabrice Virgili, "Les Viols commis par l'armée allemande en France (1940–1944)," *Vingtième Siècle. Revue D'Histoire*, vol. 130, no. 2 (2016), pp. 103–20; Wendy Jo Gertjejanssen, "Victims, Heroes, Survivors: Sexual Violence on the Eastern Front during World War II" (PhD diss., University of Minnesota, 2004), pp. 121–53, 253–353; Birgit Beck, "Rape: The Military Trials of Sexual Crimes Committed by Soldiers in the Wehrmacht, 1939–1944," in *Home/Front: The Military, War and Gender in Twentieth-Century Germany*, eds. Karen Hagemann and Stefanie Schüler-Springorum (Oxford, 2002), pp. 255–74. Beck's study shows most crimes of sexual violence by Nazi soldiers went unpunished in occupied Poland and countries on the eastern front, even for rape-murders, and it was only when the crimes attracted widespread scandal with the local population that anything was done.

73. Maren Röger, "The Sexual Policies and Sexual Realities of the German Occupiers in Poland in the Second World War," *Contemporary European History*, vol. 23 (2014), pp. 1–21; Pascale R. Bos, "Feminists Interpreting the Politics of Wartime Rape: Berlin, 1945; Yugoslavia, 1992–1993," *Signs*, vol. 31 (2006), pp. 995–1025; Virgili 2016, pp. 103–20; Gertjejanssen (2004, p. 30) writes, "Sexual violence during World War II was a reality for hundreds of thousands, if not millions of people, primarily women and girls, on the eastern front. These crimes were in the form of sexual harassment and abuse, forced abduction into military and concentration camp brothels, rape, and mutilation."

74. Sommer 2010, p. 53; Levenkron (2010, pp. 18–19) discusses assaults at Auschwitz, citing testimony of survivor Raya Kagan.

75. Tony Judt, *Postwar: A History of Europe since 1945* (New York, 2005), p. 20; Levi 1963, in Levi 2015, vol. 1, pp. 361–62. Primo Levi also notes having to hide and protect women months after the war when they were in DP camps in Russia. Red Army soldiers invaded the women's quarters, climbing across roofs and gutters, so they had to set up night patrols, and the women ultimately were forced to leave their dormitory to stay with the men in less private but securer quarters.

76. Antony Beevor, *Berlin: The Downfall 1945* (2002), 2nd ed. (New York, 2020), pp. 410–12; Barbara Johr, "Die Ereignisse in Zahlen," in *Befreier und Befreite: Krieg, Vergewaltigungen, Kinder*, eds. Helke Sander and Barbara Johr (Munich, 1992), p. 11; Atina Grossmann, "The 'Big Rape': Sex and Sexual Violence, War, and Occupation in Post-World War II Memory and Imagination," in *Sexual Violence in Conflict Zones, from the Ancient World to the Era of Human Rights*, ed. Elizabeth D. Heineman (Philadelphia, 2011), pp. 137–51; Atina Grossmann, "A Question of Silence: The Rape of German Women by Occupation Soldiers," *October*, vol. 72 (1995), *Berlin 1945: War and Rape "Liberators Take Liberties,"* pp. 42–63. Beevor notes that some 10,000 of the Berlin victims died, many from suicide (p. 10).

77. William Hitchcock, *The Struggle for Europe: The Turbulent History of a Divided Continent, 1945 to the Present* (New York, 2004), p. 14; Beevor 2020, pp. 28–30, 410. Beevor's extensive discussion of the mass rapes by the Red Army led to his book being banned in Russia in 2015; Natalya Gesse, a Russian correspondent reporting from the front, wrote, "The Russian soldiers were raping every German female from eight to 80." Richard Lourie, *Russia Speaks: An Oral History from the Revolution to the Present* (New York, 1991), pp. 253–54.

78. Johr 1992, p. 591. Some 150,000–200,000 "Russian babies" were born in the Soviet-occupied zone of Germany in 1945–46 (Judt 2005, pp. 20–21). In Berlin, only 995 women were granted abortions due to Red Army rapes in 1945 (Grossmann 1995, p. 42).

79. Beevor 2020, pp. 32, 326, 410–12. Beevor estimates that the Red Army raped some 1.4 million women in East Prussia, Pomerania, and Silesia alone, with higher death rates than their subsequent rampages in Germany. Red Army soldiers also raped Russian, Belarusian, and Ukrainian women they "liberated" from German slave labor, and Jewish women recently freed from Nazi camps and prisons (pp. 30–31, 65, 67, 345–46).

80. Judt 2005, pp. 20–21; Beevor 2020, pp. 28–29. Beevor cites as sources contemporary reports on the rapes by the Soviet secret police (NKVD) military units at the front as well as the unpublished notes of the Red Army war correspondent Vasily Grossman. Judt notes that Stalin's no-leave policy for the soldiers during the six-year duration of the war contributed to the problem. He remarks that Stalin gave tacit approval to the sexual violence committed by his troops and quotes Stalin's response to a Yugoslavian official's objection to the Russians' mass rape: "Can't he understand the soldier who has been through blood and fire and death, if he has fun with a woman or takes a trifle?"

81. Dix and Grosz focused on the violence and mutilation rather than the suffering of the prostitute victim.

82. Lasansky experimented with this composition in a related drawing that he eliminated from the series, which was photographed before it was destroyed. It shows the same female victim and skeleton in the same poses, but the skeleton sits atop a horse's back rather than a soldier's. He wears a doctor's head mirror and fiddles in the mouth of a dead victim, presumably searching for gold teeth.

83. *No. 10*, which depicts a prostitute devoured by a skeleton on her back, positioned similarly to the skeleton in *No. 14*, was originally numbered "5" by Lasansky, so would have followed *No. 14*, originally numbered "4," in his earlier conception of the series.

84. Höss 1959, fig. 7. I do not know if Lasansky owned a copy of this book, but the University of Iowa library possesses a copy of this edition. The photo from the "Auschwitz Album," taken by SS Officer Bernhardt Walter, head of the Auschwitz photographic laboratory, or his assistant Ernst Hofmann, is cropped in the 1959 book at the top, just above the mother's head and white fence post, so that Lasansky's composition resonates even more closely with the book image.

85. Amishai-Maisels 1993, pp. 179–97.

86. Fritz Bauer, a German Jew, had been imprisoned in a Nazi concentration camp in 1933 before escaping into exile during the war. When his efforts to prosecute Nazi criminals in West Germany were stymied in the 1950s by government officials, with many former Nazis still holding high-ranking positions there, he passed along tips about Eichmann's whereabouts to Israel and confirmed Eichmann's location there. It took several years for Mossad to arrest Eichmann. Following the Eichmann trial, there was a new resolve in prosecuting Nazi war crimes, particularly in Germany, where the statute of limitations for murder was extended (1963, 1969) and then eliminated (1979) so that World War II–related crimes could continue to be prosecuted. In the 1965 Auschwitz Frankfurt trial judgment, 18 of the accused were sentenced to prison, eight with life sentences, including SS guard Oswald Kaduk, discussed below.

87. There is also a *Times* ad calling for the listing of household items for sale, and some excerpts from the sports section. Lasansky collaged clippings from this same *New York Times* issue (May 19, 1963) on *Triptych*. Though not used in the

drawing, a review of Hannah Arendt's *Eichmann in Jerusalem* was also featured in this same issue of the *Times*. The review, by Justice Michael Musmanno of the Pennsylvania Supreme Court, who served as a judge of the Nuremberg trial of the *Einsatzgruppen* and was a witness at the Eichmann trial, featured a large photo of Eichmann in prison in Israel.

88. This article from Reuters, dated May 18, 1963, may have run in the Iowa or Maine edition of the *New York Times*, May 19, 1963, sports section, but it did not run in the New York edition until May 22, 1963 (p.46), where it ran with the headline, "Berlin a Candidate to Stage 1968 Olympics."

89. *The Holy Bible, containing the Old and New Testaments; translated out of the original tongues; and with the former translations diligently compared and revised, with Canne's marginal references* . . . was issued by the American Bible Society and printed numerous times throughout the 19th century, beginning in 1817. The later editions reprinted the text with the same pagination and font, so it is not possible to date the exact edition Lasansky used. This Bible, which includes annotations by the 17th-century Baptist minister John Canne, seeks to make parallels between the Old and New Testament in search of prophesies of Christ. Thus Christ appears in some of the margin notes in the Hebrew scripture.

90. See Amishai-Maisels 1993, p. 423n149, citing an interview with Lasansky in 1982.

91. This oft-cited quotation from Isaiah is inscribed on the "Isaiah Wall," erected in 1948 in the municipal park near the United Nations headquarters in New York.

92. Amishai-Maisels 1993, pp. 214, 449n151.

93. Amishai-Maisels 1993, p. 214.

94. Thein and Lasansky 1975, nos. 112, 119, 123, the latter of which also incorporates the crying baby of *No.* 25 from "The Nazi Drawings."

95. Amishai-Maisels 1993, p. 197.

96. "Children's Memorial," Yad Vashem, accessed March 2, 2020, https://www.yadvashem.org/remembrance/commemorative-sites/children-memorial.html; "Children during the Holocaust," United States Holocaust Memorial Museum, accessed March 2, 2020, https://encyclopedia.ushmm.org/content/en/article/children-during-the-holocaust; see also "Non-Jewish Victims of Persecution in Germany," Yad Vashem, accessed March 2, 2020, https://www.yadvashem.org/holocaust/about/nazi-germany-1933-39/non-jewish-victims.html.

97. Two related drawings Lasansky ultimately did not include in the series and likely destroyed but are known from photographs of his Maine studio represent portrait heads of two camp prisoners, one the head and bust of a solemn (not crying) baby, which is more realistically drawn than the suffering children in the series, and the other a dead or near-dead older male figure with his eyes closed.

98. Goya's *Unhappy Mother!* (*Madre infeliz!* pl. 50, "Disasters of War") presents a helpless child orphaned by war; the little girl, heartbroken, cries in the darkness as her mother's lifeless body is carried away.

99. In *No.* 26, three of the stenciled numbers, drawn in green chalk, have faded, and two are no longer visible. The statistic originally appeared on this drawing five times, yet now only two are clear, with traces of a third visible on the child's chest.

100. Leonardo Lasansky, conversation, 2017. The drug was launched by Chemie Grünenthal in 1957 and marketed in 46 countries, but an official at the FDA held up its approval, mitigating the drug's effect in the U.S.

101. "The Full Story of the Drug Thalidomide: The 5,000 Deformed Babies," *Life*, August 10, 1962, pp. 24–36.

102. This debate was partly stirred up by the controversial German play *The Deputy*, which directly implicates Pius XII in the Holocaust. The play was written by Rolf Hochhuth, a German Protestant, and first performed in West Berlin, on February 20, 1963, with title *Der Stellvertreter: Ein christliches Trauerspiel* (*The Deputy: A Christian Tragedy*). Subsequent performances in the U.K., Sweden, Germany, Switzerland, Denmark, and France had various titles: *The Deputy: A Christian Tragedy, The Representative*, and *The Vicar of Christ*. A condensed version by Jerome Rothenberg opened on Broadway in 1964. It provoked strong reactions wherever it was performed—weeping (Berlin), fist fights (Basel, Switzerland), actors being assaulted (Paris), canceled second acts (Rome), and protests in every city. All of this was widely covered by the press.

103. Michael Phayer, *The Catholic Church and the Holocaust, 1930–65* (Bloomington, Ind., 2000). Phayer presents a balanced, critical examination of Pius XII's record and the Catholic Church during the Holocaust, and addresses the controversial assessment of John Cornwell in *Hitler's Pope: The Secret History of Pius XII* (London, 1999).

104. Phayer 2000, pp. 24–132. Phayer examines the actions of European bishops and Catholic rescuers, as well as Catholic killers. He looks at Pius XII's diplomatic career in Germany, and considers the pope's concerns that a public condemnation from the Church of the Nazi persecution and murder of Jews would further endanger Jews in occupied countries (as was the case in the Netherlands, when Dutch Catholic officials spoke out against deportations), as well as retribution against Catholics. For new research into Pius XII's role in the Holocaust and the opening of the Vatican Secret Archive, see Rabbi Cytron's essay in this book.

105. While the issue sparked fierce debate in the 1960s, Cytron's essay shows that this period also fostered a productive dialogue among faiths and bridge building, particularly with Vatican II (1962–65).

106. See especially, "Pope Paul VI in America," *Life*, October 15, 1965, p. 42, photos by Francis Miller, and, for the pope's dress, see photo by Bill Eppridge of Paul VI's visit to Yankee Stadium, front matter, unnumbered, preceding B1.

107. Lasansky's intaglio plate *Pope* (1965), representing the head and bust of the pope, was also incorporated into his larger prints *Pope and Cardinal* (1966) and *Pope and Crying Boy* (1967); see Thein and Lasansky 1975, nos. 112, 119, 123. The intaglio print is executed with a variety of techniques: engraving, etching, drypoint, aquatint, grease ground, electric stippling, scraping, and burnishing.

108. I would like to thank Leonardo Lasansky for researching the family archives to determine the year *Triptych* was completed.

109. Dürer's engraving relates to the medieval folklore tradition of men dressing up at wedding feasts as wild men and playfully lusting after women.

110. John Cogley, *New York Times*, August 8, 1965, p. 54.

111. "Far East, Again a Question of China," *New York Times*, August 27, 1967, Week in Review section, p. 1. Further sections of this editorial are pasted to the upper edge of the drawing: "In Vietnam, More Pressure on Hanoi" and "In Hong Kong, More Pressure on Britain."

112. Cartoon by Herblock, *New York Times*, May 19, 1963, Week in Review section, p. 9.

113. Cartoon by Hartung, for *Die Welt*, Hamburg (Germany), reprinted in *New York Times*, May 19, 1963, Week in Review section, p. 2.

114. "Race Turmoil" and "G.O.P. and Kennedy," *New York Times*, May 19, 1963, Week in Review section, pp. 1–2, 8.

115. "Pesticide Problem," "Rails and Jobs," "Wagner's Future," *New York Times*, May 19, 1963, Week in Review section, p. 2. There is also a Kennedy story from the *Cedar Rapids Gazette*, May 29, 1967, p. 11, "O'Brien Urges Real JFK Personality Not Be Lost," relating to a commemorative stamp issued in honor of President Kennedy on what would have been his 50th birthday. The article addresses how the hero worship of Kennedy might obscure the president's achievements in the "cynical age" of the 1960s, "marked by lack of values and a dull sense of drift, anchorless on a dark and angry sea."

116. "Space Triumph," *New York Times*, May 19, 1963, Week in Review section, p. 1.

117. Ezekiel 9:1–2, "He cried also in mine ears with a loud voice, saying, Cause them that have charge over the city to draw near, even every man with his destroying weapon in his hand. And, behold, six men came from the way of the higher gate . . . every man a slaughter weapon in his hand." The lengthier excerpted scripture in the lower left corner, from Ezekiel 32 and 38, recounts various destructions and plagues to be unleashed by God on those who come against Israel.

118. "Obituaries," *Cedar Rapids Gazette*, May 29, 1967, p. 8. This same issue had a story about Lasansky: "Lasansky Named Hancher Professor, Iowa City—Mauricio Lasansky, world-famous printmaker and teacher, Monday was designated Virgil M. Hancher Professor of Art at the University of Iowa, where he has taught since 1945" (p. 5). Other stories from this paper are collaged onto the work, including "Farmer Burned When Nitrogen Hose Breaks," "$48 Take In Three Breakins," "Open House Is Wednesday for Coe Computer," and an excerpt from a ruling related to an Iowa murder trial (p. 8).

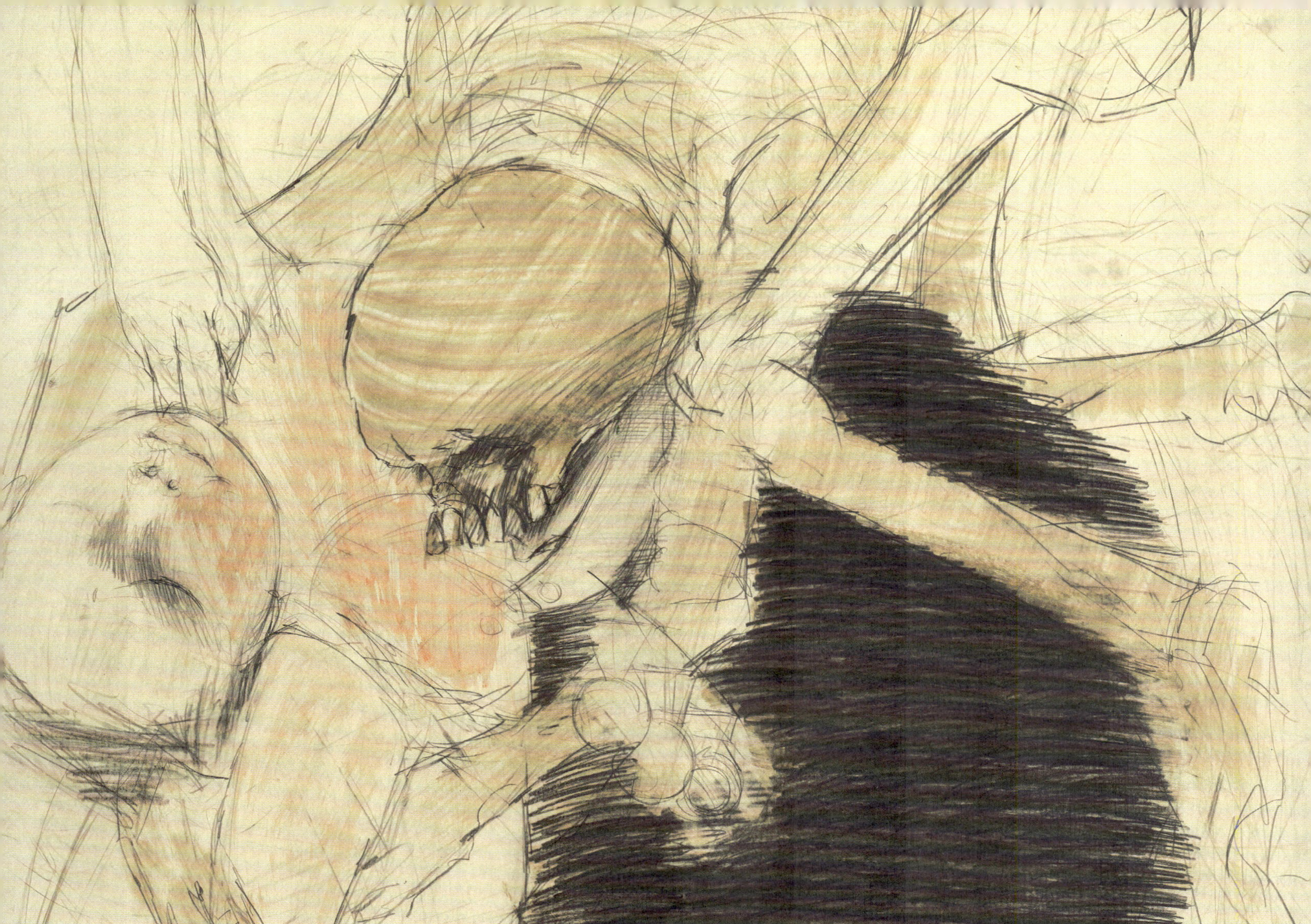

Mauricio Lasansky, *No. 16* (detail), "The Nazi Drawings"

119. Most of the classifieds and articles here were taken from the *New York Times*, May 19, 1963, particularly the Week in Review section, including pp. 1, 9, and the business section, p. 16. Another, "Volume is Slow for Preferreds," *New York Times*, August 13, 1967, is from the business section, p. 5.

120. *New York Times*, May 19, 1963, Week in Review section, including p. 8, "The U.N.'s Budget Problems," "Idaho's Campus Loyalty," and "Prefab Fireplace: Bought for Men, Turn Back Time, Heave and Light, The Dying Glow." This page also includes a short essay about the scarlet tanager, and Sarah Singer's poem "Mirror, Mirror."

121. The American press covered many stories about the Klan in the 1960s, particularly following the Klan's bombings in Birmingham in 1963 of the Gaston Hotel, A. D. King's house, and the 16th Street Baptist Church, the latter of which killed four young girls and sparked a national outcry, galvanizing the civil rights movement. Near the 1965 *Times* article about German Protestant reforms that Lasansky prominently collaged onto the left panel of *Triptych* was an entire page of stories about desegregation efforts in the South, suspension of poll taxes, lawsuits against literacy tests, and a large photo of a Klan march in North Carolina. In the picture, a white-robed member rides a horse beside a young Black child standing next to his bicycle and staring up at him ("Klan Parades in North Carolina," *New York Times*, August 8, 1965, p. 58). The page also features an Associated Press story, "Negro Boy Stabbed in Jackson Protest."

122. Anthony Lewis's article, "Negroes Press Harder for Basic Rights: Birmingham Reflects Their Growing Restiveness and The Many Hurdles in the Path Toward Equality," from the *Times* Week in Review section (May 19, 1963 p. 10), is featured without the headline or author's name (a Pulitzer Prize–winning journalist) and is pasted sideways.

123. Lasansky's chilling allusion to the Ku Klux Klan stands in contrast to Philip Guston's more direct, cartoonish, and frequent depictions of Klansmen in the late 1960s and 1970s. Guston described the hooded figures in his works as self-portraits. "I almost tried to imagine that I was living with the Klan," he said. "What would it be like to be evil? To plan and to plot." In *The Studio* (1969, private collection), for instance, Guston represented a red-handed Klansman smoking a cigarette and painting a self-portrait. His Jewish-émigré parents had fled pogroms and antisemitism in Ukraine in 1904/5, only to encounter pervasive racism and violence in Los Angeles, where Guston's family settled in the 1920s; Harry Cooper, *Philip Guston Now* (exh. cat.), National Gallery of Art and other venues (Washington, D.C., 2020), pp. 5–14, 83–92, 94–106, 108–16, 118–21, pl. 116; Glenn Ligon, "In the Hood," p. 117. Guston depicted murderous Klansmen in a few works in the 1930s before embracing abstraction in the 1940s and 1950s. He then returned to figuration later in his career to make work about the pressing issues of his times, following a similar trajectory as Lasansky. Despite their distinct artistic approaches to the subject of Klansmen, both Guston and Lasansky offer biting critiques of racism and white complicity in America.

124. *New York Times*, August 13, 1967, business section, pp. 2, 4, 11, 15, 36. Among the articles included are "Jobless Get Word of Jobs on TV; Other Cities to See Chicago Show," "Labor Costs in Manufacturing," "Industrial Zone Helping Taiwan," "Honolulu Dole Company Is Processing Record Pineapple Crop" and "U.S. Industry Set To Feed the Poor," and, prominently, the American Stock Exchange and New York Stock Exchange listings. "Retail Sales" and classified ads for jobs ("MONEY!"), manufacturing facilities, and printing machinery are also shown. *New York Times*, May 19, 1963, sports section, pp. 1, 4, including clippings from these articles: "Davis's Death Shocks Family; 'Perfect Athlete' Is Mourned," "Spicy Living, 15–1, Wins at Aqueduct," "Britain Wins Top Prize in Rome Horse Show," "Qualifying Mark Broken by Jones," and "U.S. Fencers Capture World Military Titles."

125. Excerpts from *New York Times*, May 19, 1963, sports section, "Spicy Living, 15–1, Wins at Aqueduct," about the Acorn race of fillies at Belmont, and two ads—one for a Yankees-Angels baseball series, another for jobs for electronic technicians—are also featured in the clipping.

“THE NAZI DRAWINGS”

Mauricio Lasansky
***Nos.* 1–30 and *Triptych*, 1961–71**
Lent by the Levitt Foundation

ARTIST STATEMENT

Dignity is not a symbol bestowed on man, nor does the word itself possess force. Man’s dignity is a force and the only modus vivendi by which man and his history survive. When mid-twentieth century Germany did not let man live and die with this right, man became an animal. No matter how technologically advanced or sophisticated, when man negates this divine right, he not only becomes self-destructive, but castrates his history and poisons our future. This is what “The Nazi Drawings” are about.

—Mauricio Lasansky, 1966

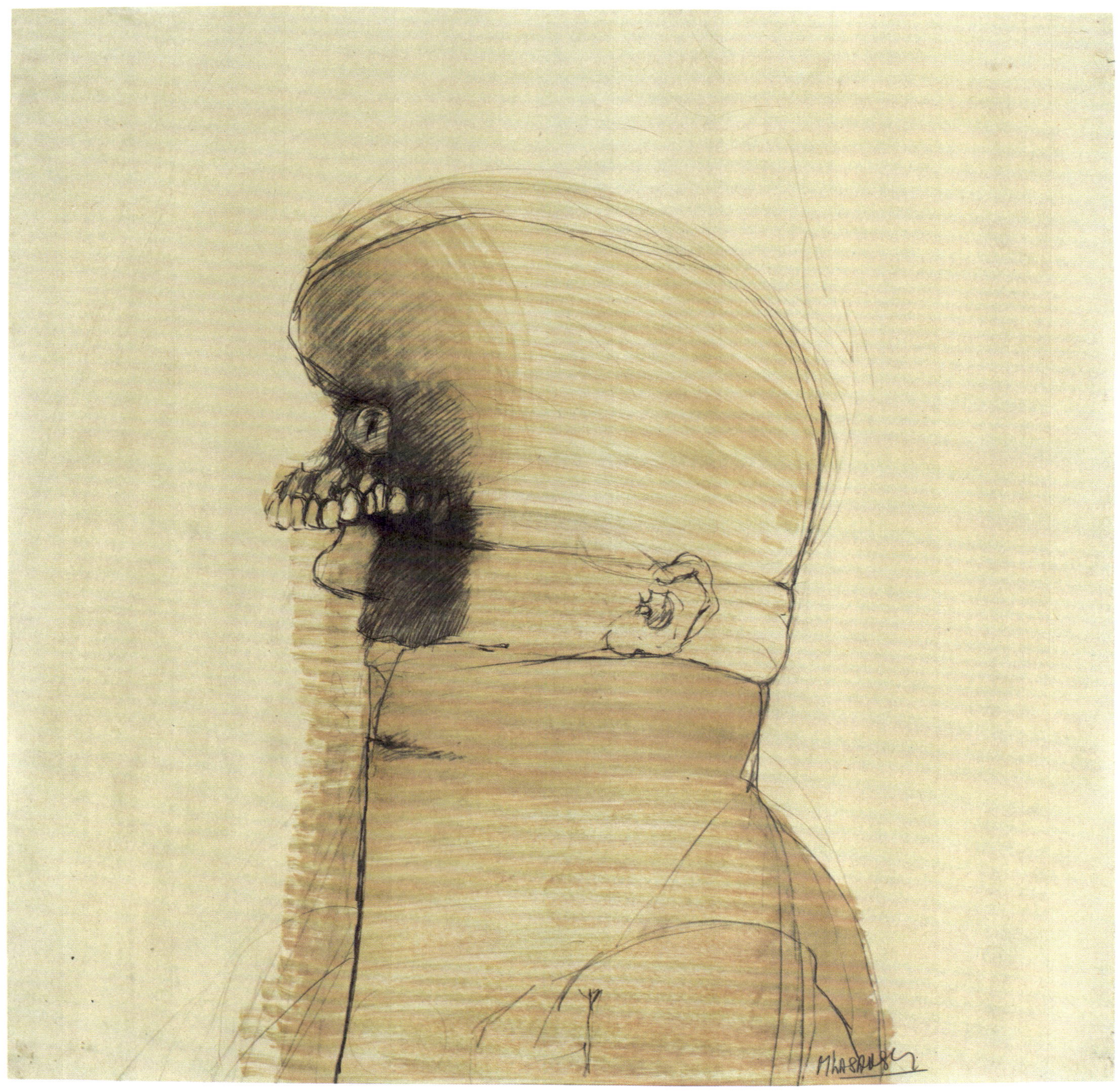

No. 1 1961

Graphite, charcoal, brush and asphaltum turpentine wash, on card paper

23½ × 23¼ in. (59.7 × 59.1 cm) (sheet)

Signed at lower right in charcoal: M LASANSKY

Levitt Foundation

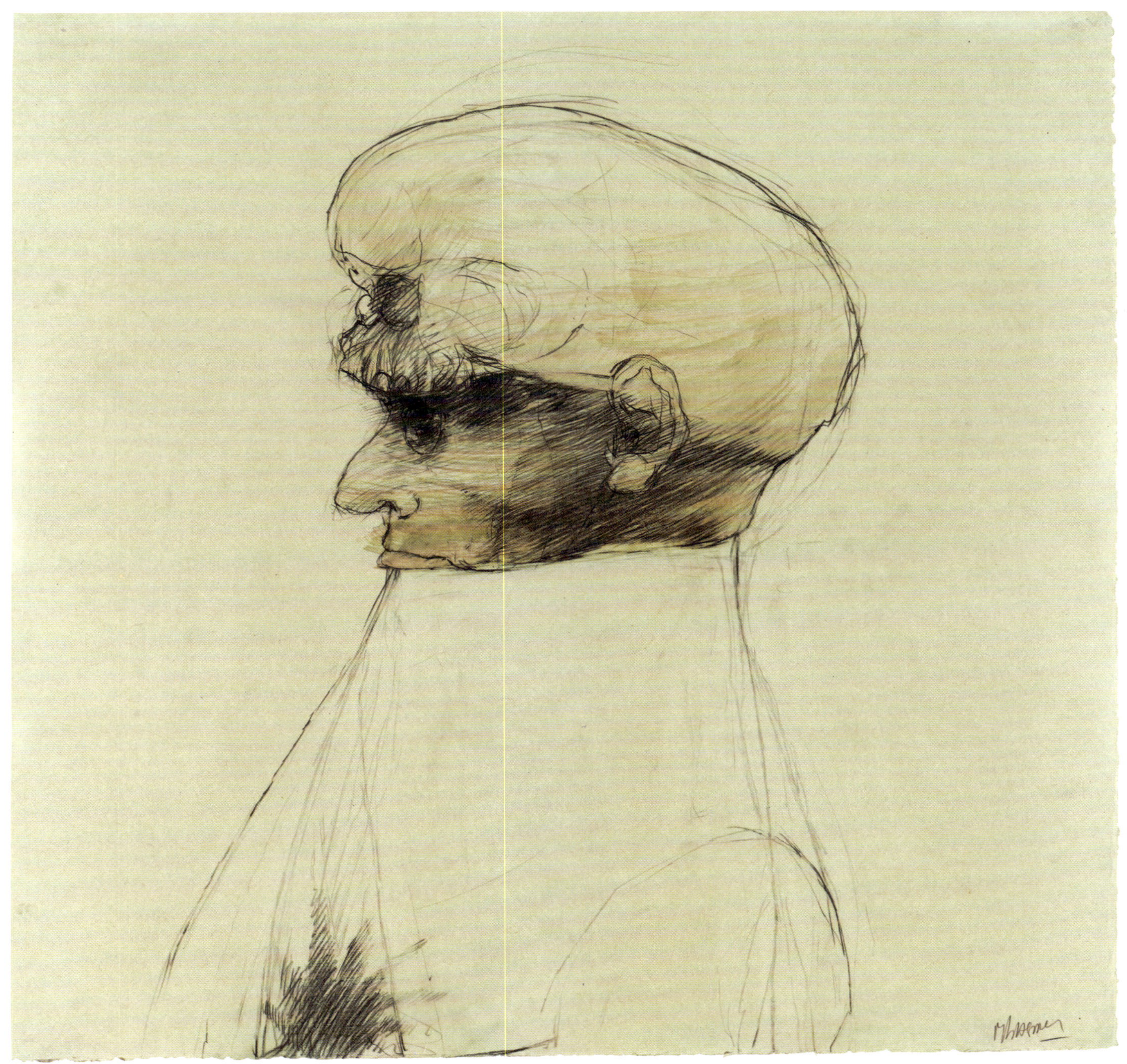

No. 2 1961

Graphite and charcoal, with erasures, brush and asphaltum turpentine wash, on card paper, with torn edges

23 × 23½ in. (58.4 × 59.7 cm) (sheet)

Signed at lower right corner in charcoal: M LASANSKY

Levitt Foundation

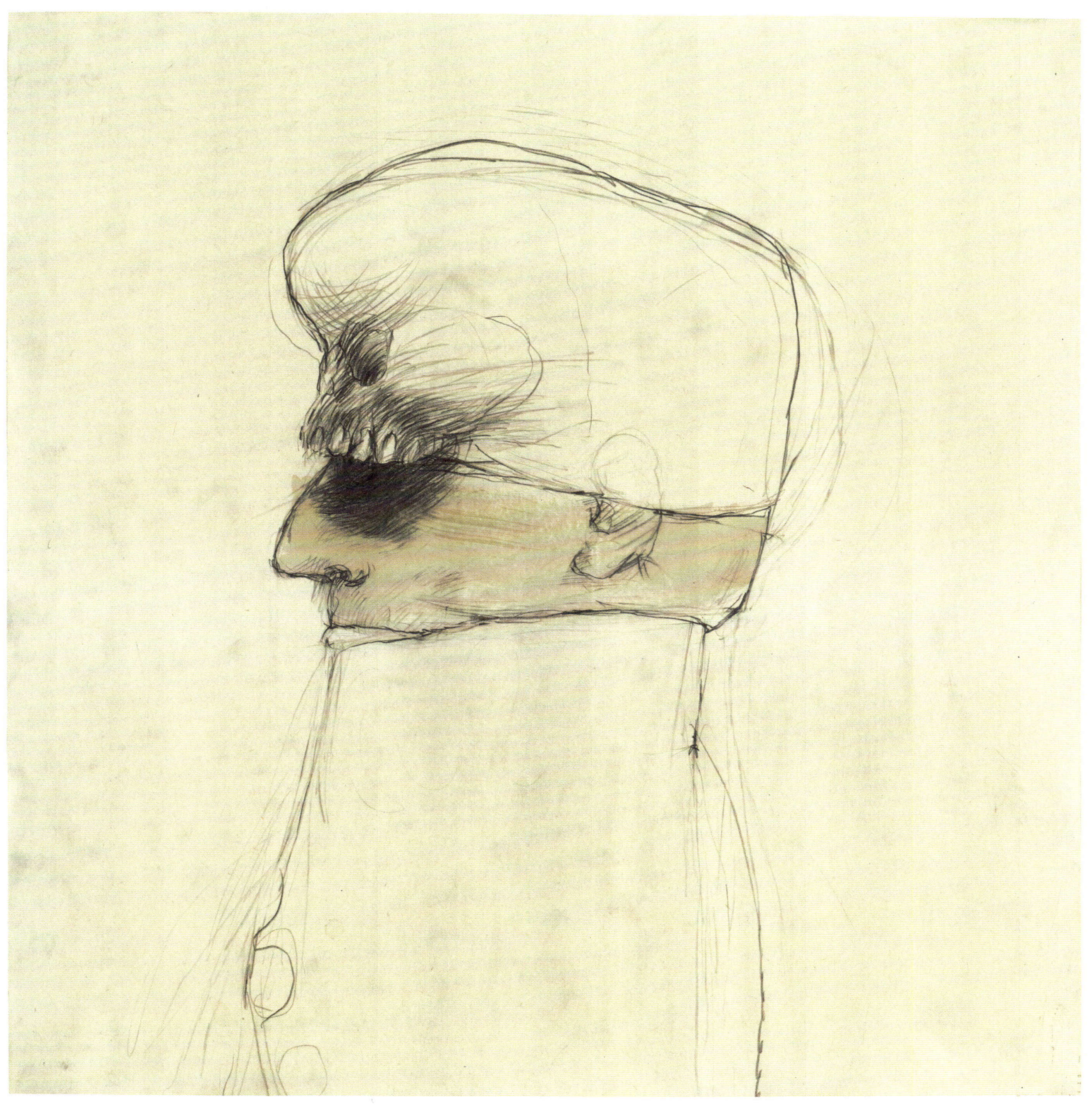

No. 3 1961

Graphite, charcoal, brush and asphaltum turpentine wash, on card paper

23⅜ × 22½ in. (59.4 × 57.2 cm) (sheet)

[Unsigned]

Levitt Foundation

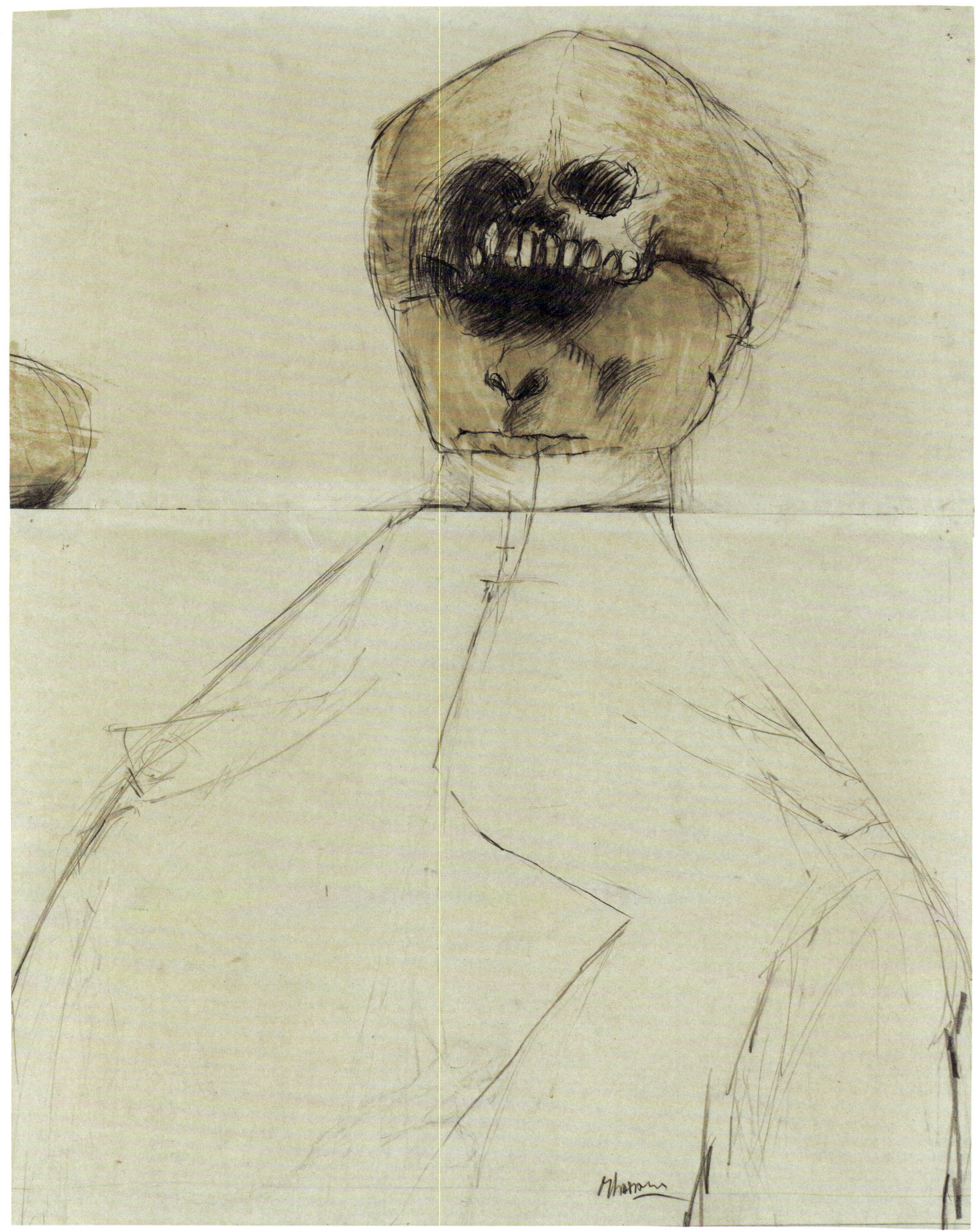

No. 4 1961

Graphite, charcoal, brush and asphaltum turpentine wash, on card paper, two sheets

25¾ × 19¾ in. (65.4 × 50.2 cm) (overall)

Signed at lower center in charcoal: M LASANSKY

Levitt Foundation

Right: detail, actual size

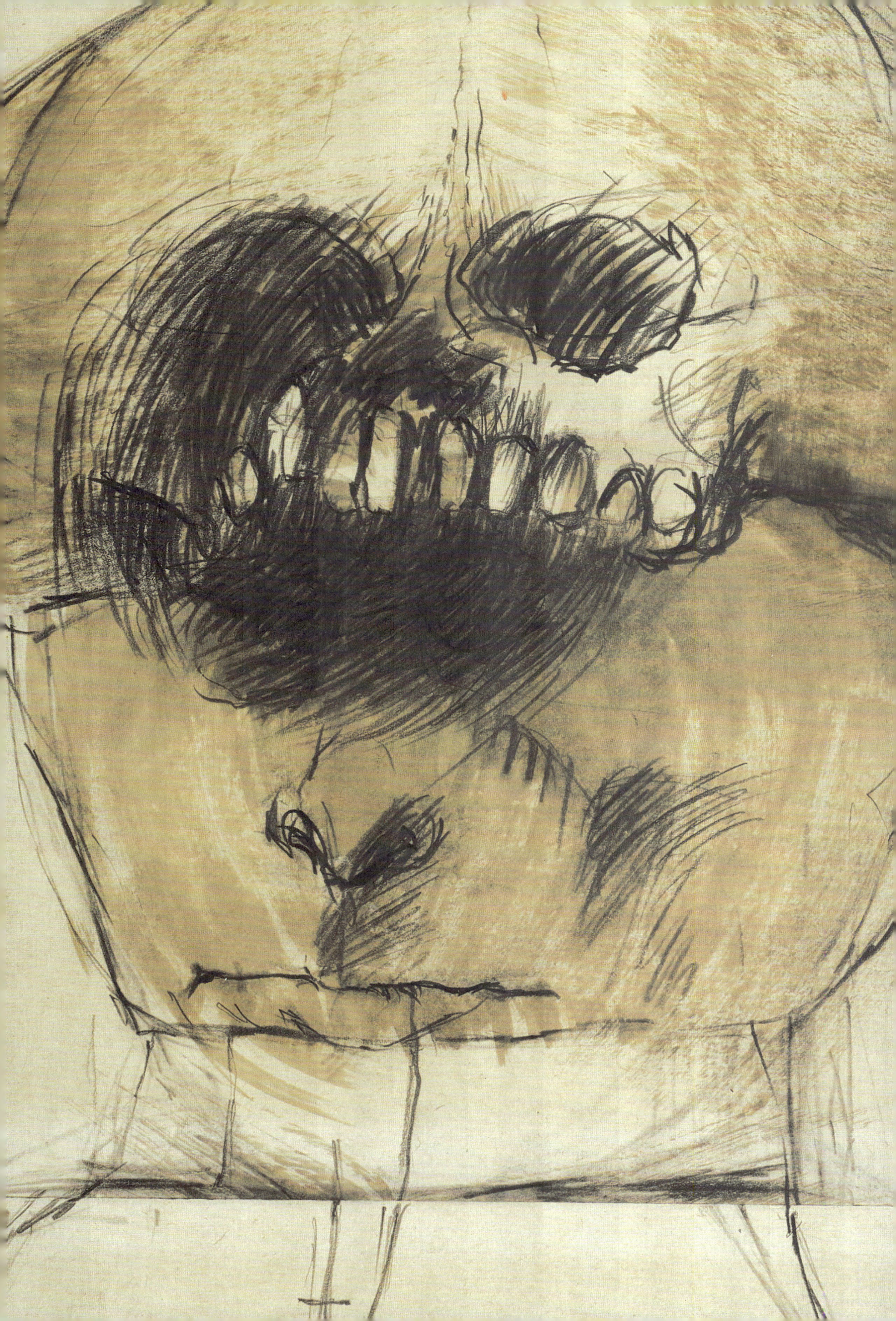

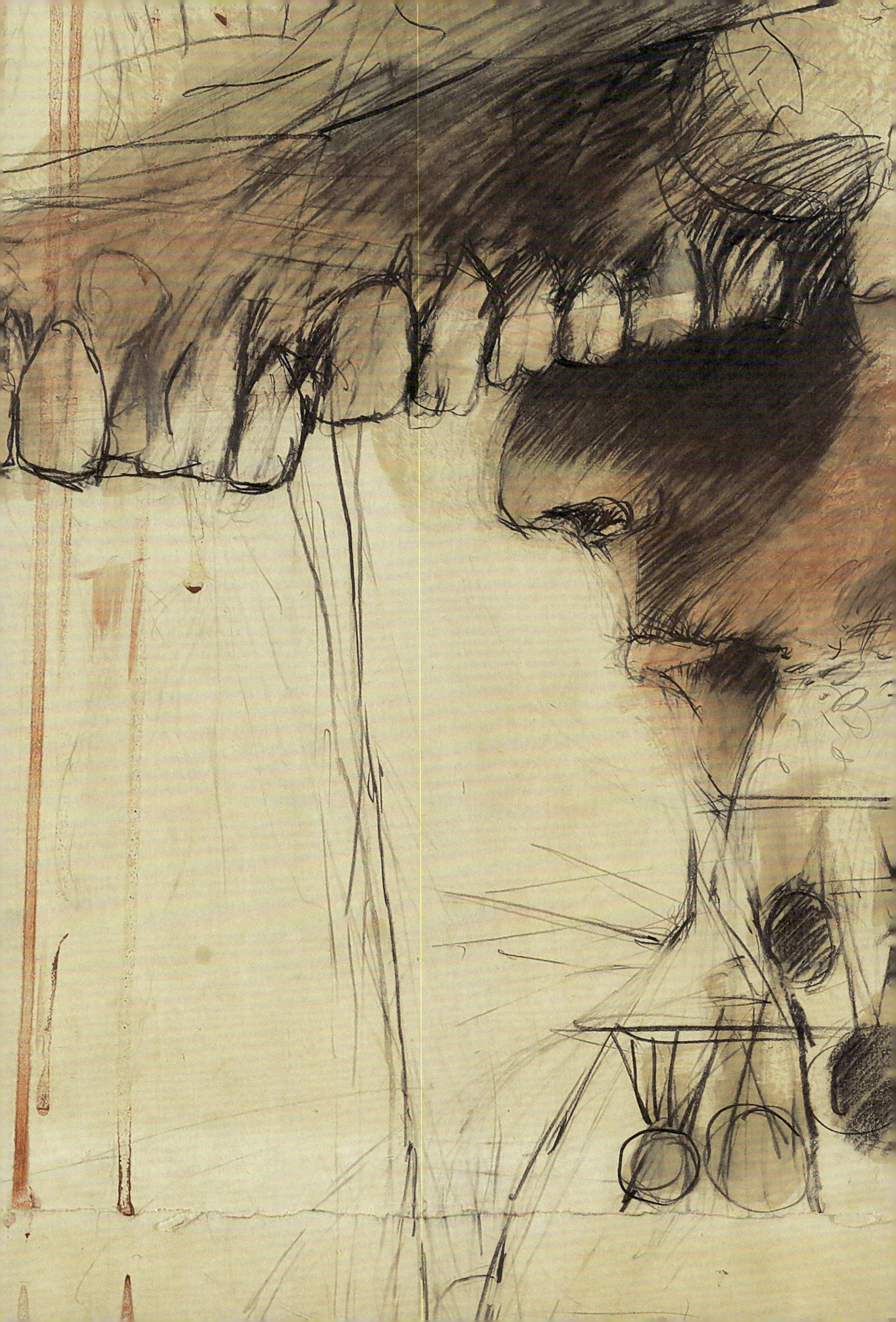

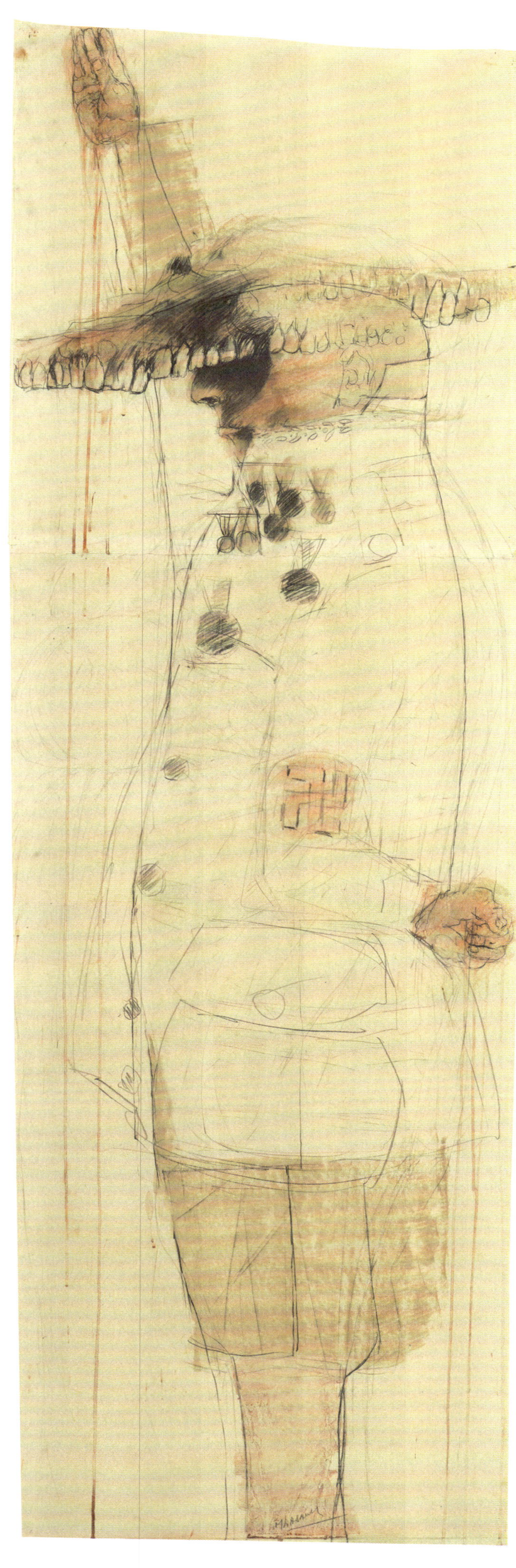

No. 5 1961

Graphite, charcoal, brush and asphaltum turpentine and red wash, on card paper, two sheets, with some torn edges

68½ × 22¼ in. (174 × 56.5 cm) (overall, irregular)

Signed at lower center in charcoal: M LASANSKY

Levitt Foundation

Left: detail, actual size

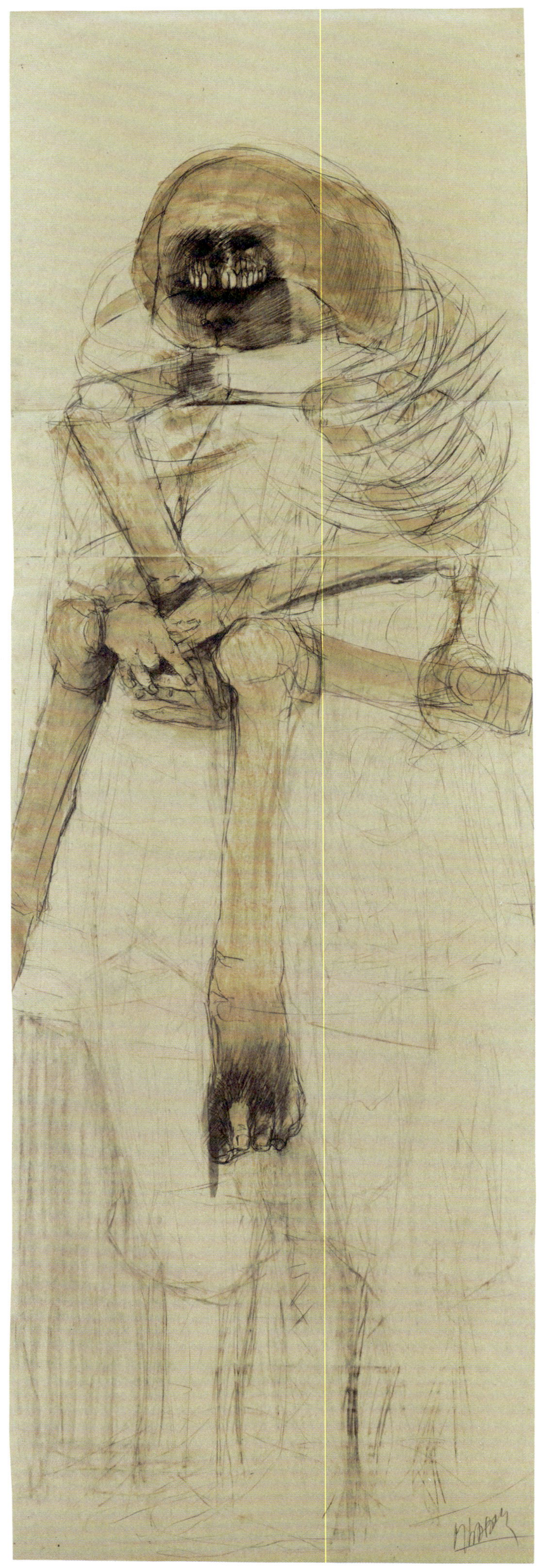

No. 6 1961–66

Graphite, charcoal, brush and asphaltum turpentine wash, on card paper, three sheets, with some torn edges

70⅝ × 22⅞ in. (179.4 × 58.1 cm) (overall)

Signed at lower right corner in charcoal: M LASANSKY

Levitt Foundation

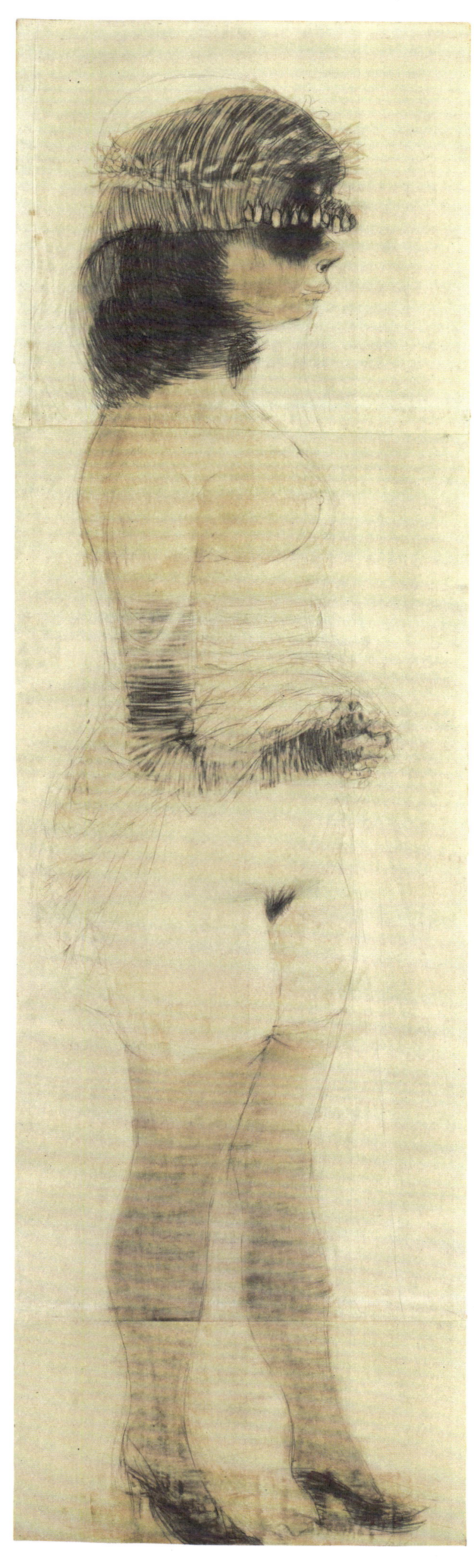

No. 7 1961–66

Graphite, charcoal, brush and asphaltum turpentine wash, on card paper, three sheets

76½ × 22⅛ in. (194.3 × 56.2 cm) (overall)

[Unsigned]

Levitt Foundation

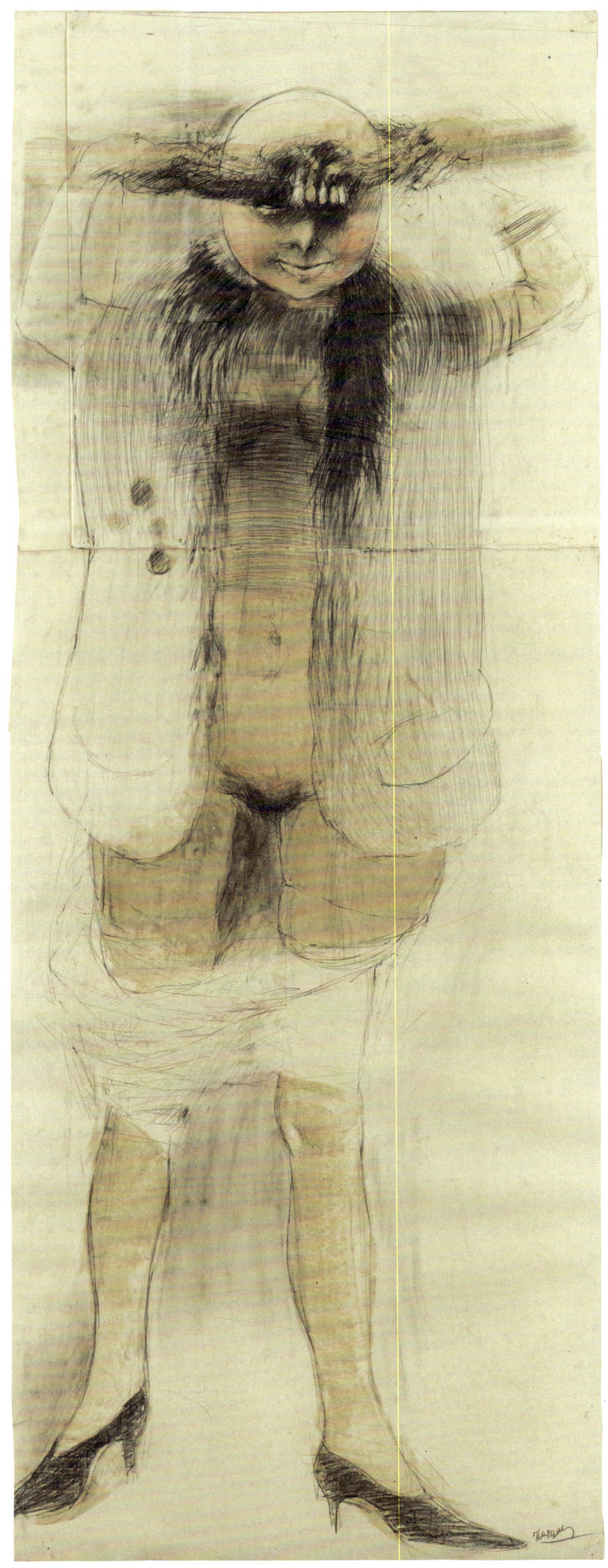

No. 8 1961–66

Graphite, charcoal, brush and asphaltum turpentine and red wash, on card paper, three sheets, with some torn edges

69 × 25½ in. (175.3 × 64.8 cm) (overall)

Signed at lower right corner in charcoal: M LASANSKY

Levitt Foundation

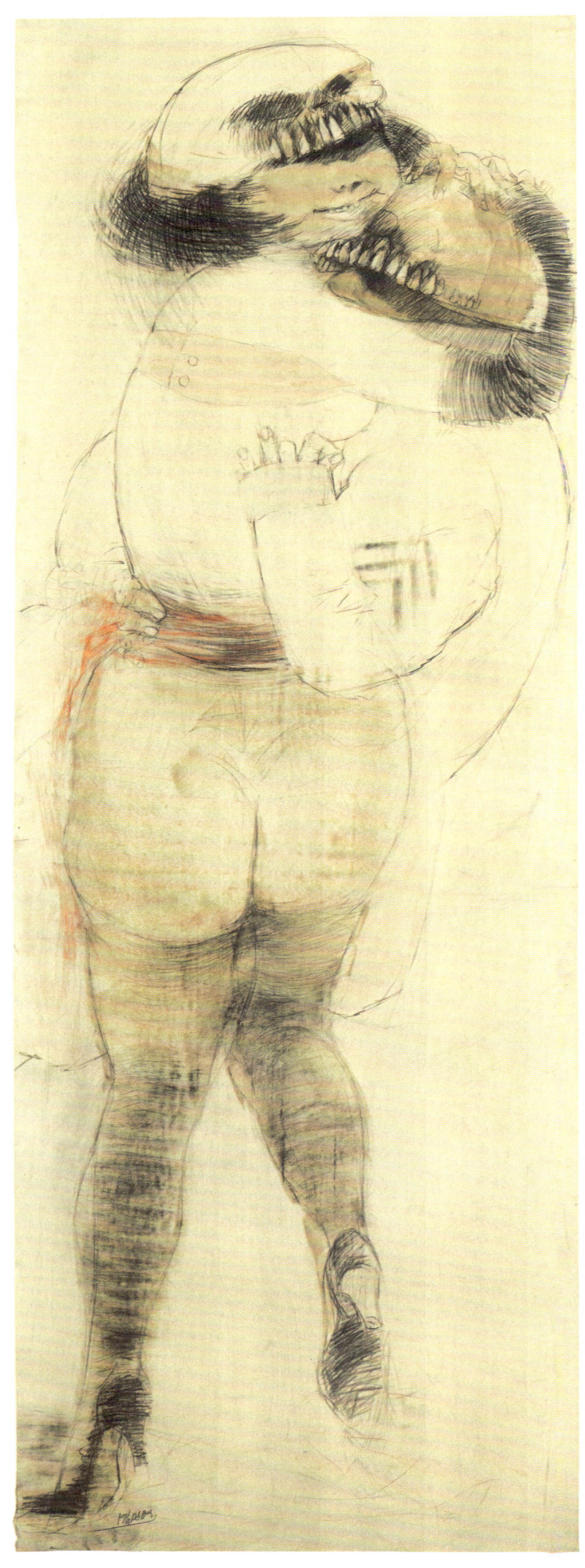

No. 9 1961–66

Graphite, charcoal, brush and asphaltum turpentine and red wash, with touches of red chalk, on card paper

68 × 24 in. (172.7 × 61 cm) (sheet, irregular)

Signed at lower left corner in charcoal: M LASANSKY

Levitt Foundation

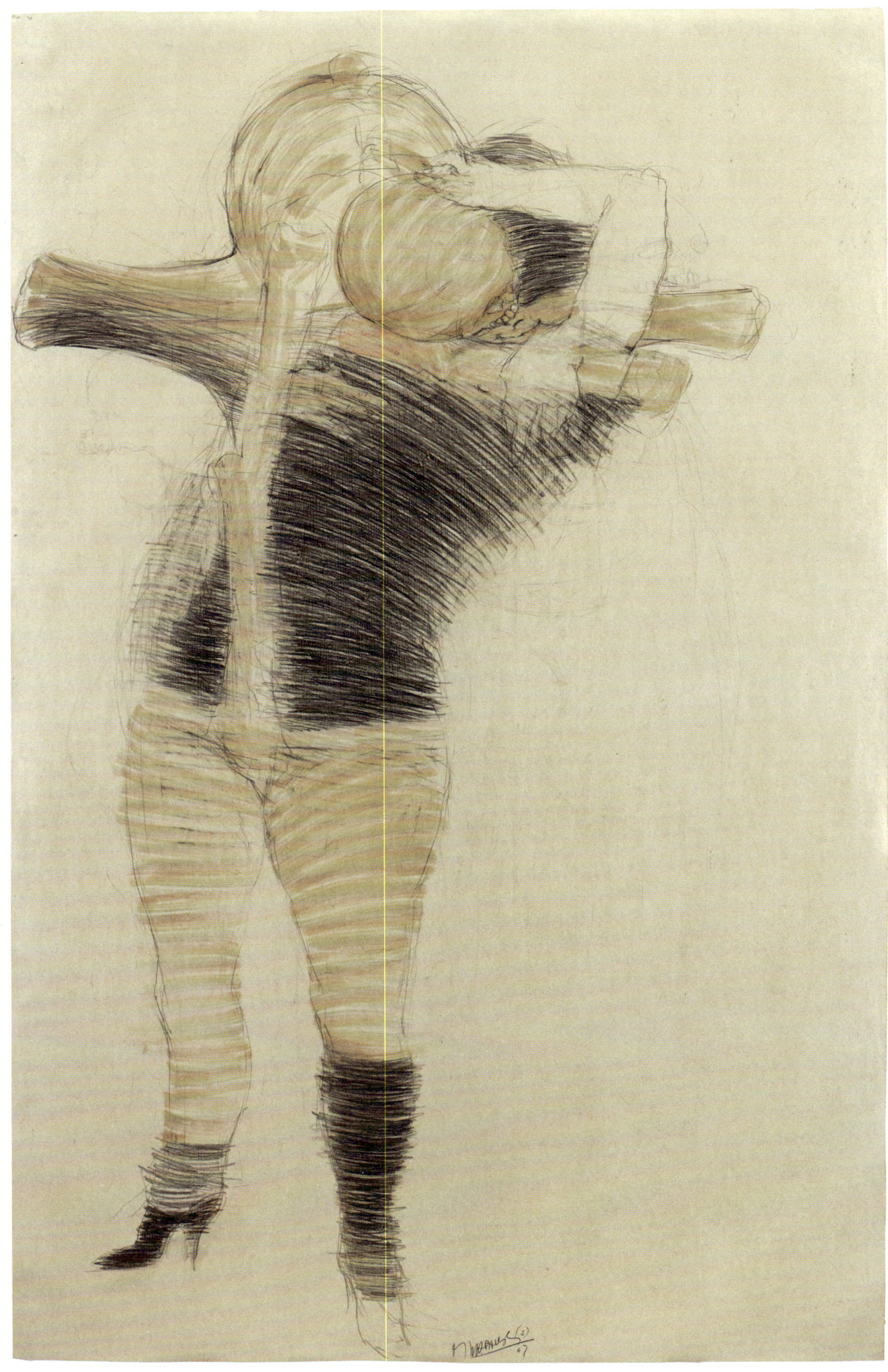

No. 10 1962–63

Graphite and charcoal, with erasures, brush and asphaltum turpentine wash, with touches of red wash, on card paper

73 × 44½ in. (185.4 × 113 cm) (sheet)

Signed, numbered, and dated at lower center in charcoal: M LASANSKY (5) / 63

Levitt Foundation

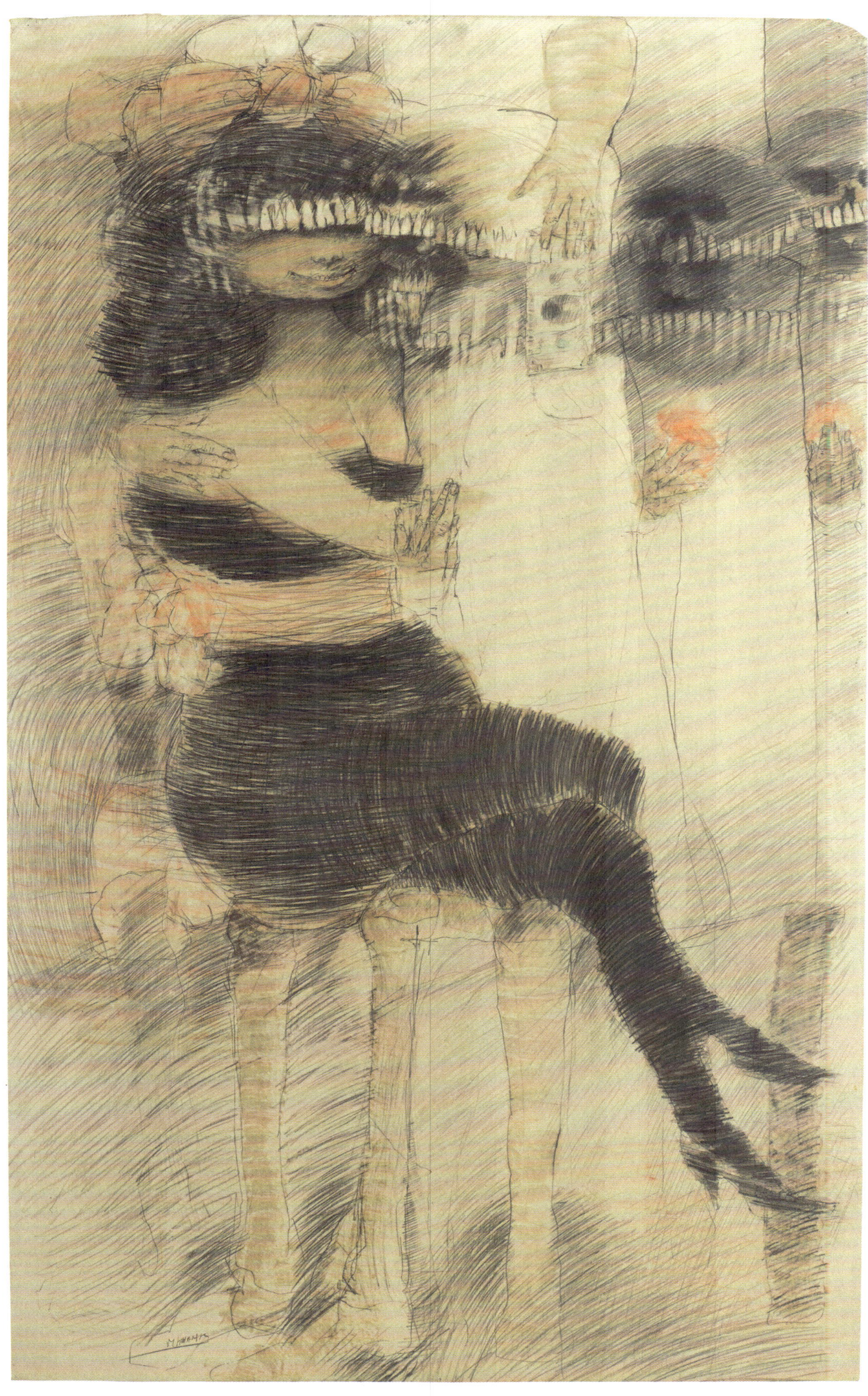

No. 11 1961–66

Graphite and charcoal, with erasures, brush and asphaltum turpentine and red wash, with touches of red chalk and green pastel, on card paper, with some torn edges

73⅞ × 44¾ in. (187.6 × 113.7 cm) (sheet, irregular)

Signed at lower left in charcoal: M LASANSKY

Levitt Foundation

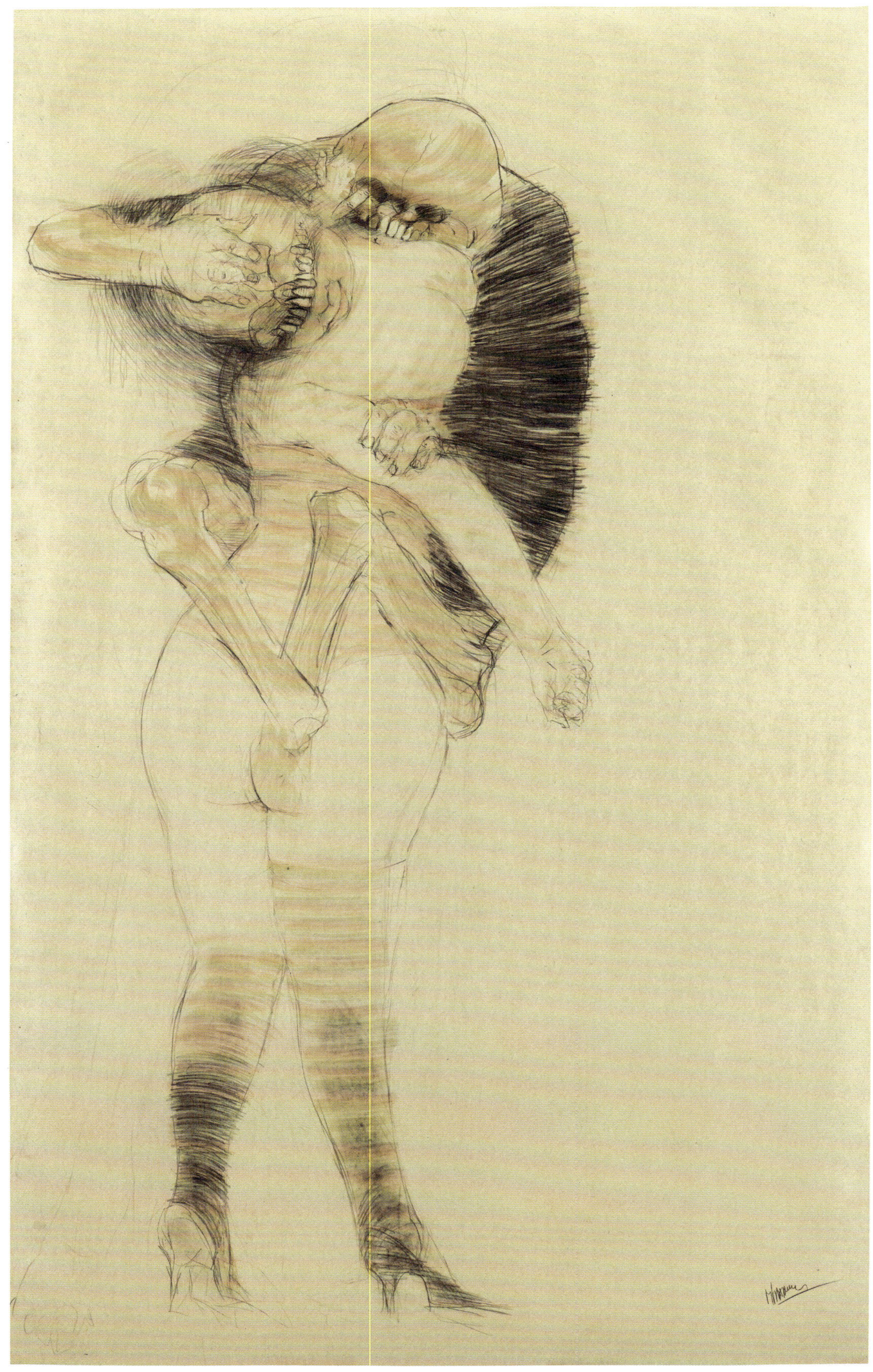

No. 12 1961–66

Graphite, charcoal, brush and asphaltum turpentine and red wash, on card paper

71¼ × 44¾ in. (181 × 113.7 cm) (sheet)

Signed at lower right corner in charcoal: M LASANSKY

Levitt Foundation

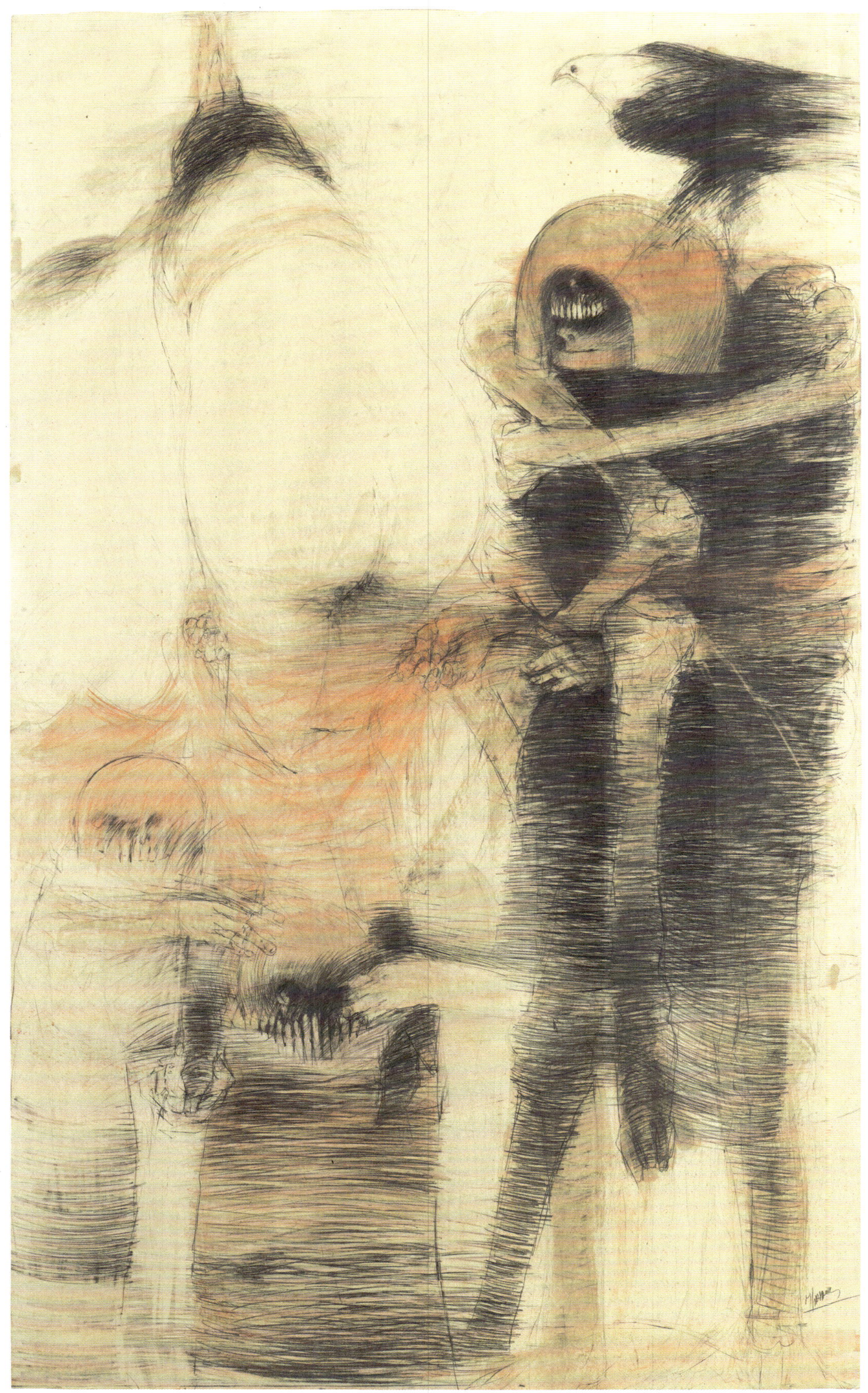

No. 13 1961–66

Graphite and charcoal, with erasures, brush and asphaltum turpentine and red wash, with touches of red chalk, on card paper, with some torn edges

75 5/16 × 45 in. (191.3 × 114.3 cm) (sheet, irregular)

Signed at lower right corner in charcoal: M LASANSKY

Levitt Foundation

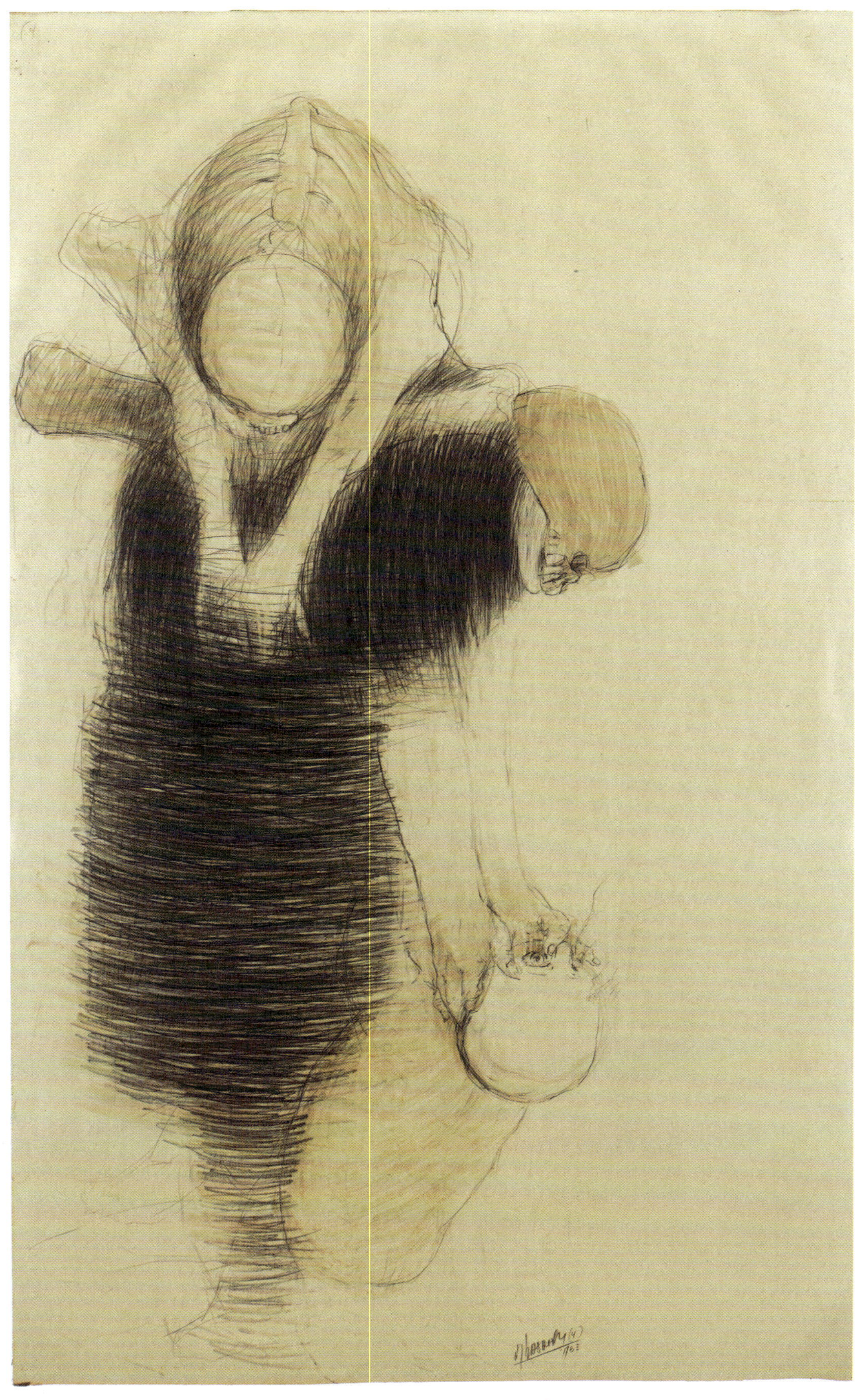

No. 14 1962–63

Graphite and charcoal, with erasures, brush and asphaltum turpentine, on card paper, with some torn edges

73 × 43¼ in. (185.4 × 109.9 cm) (sheet, irregular)

Signed, numbered, and dated at lower center in charcoal: M LASANSKY (4) / 63

Levitt Foundation

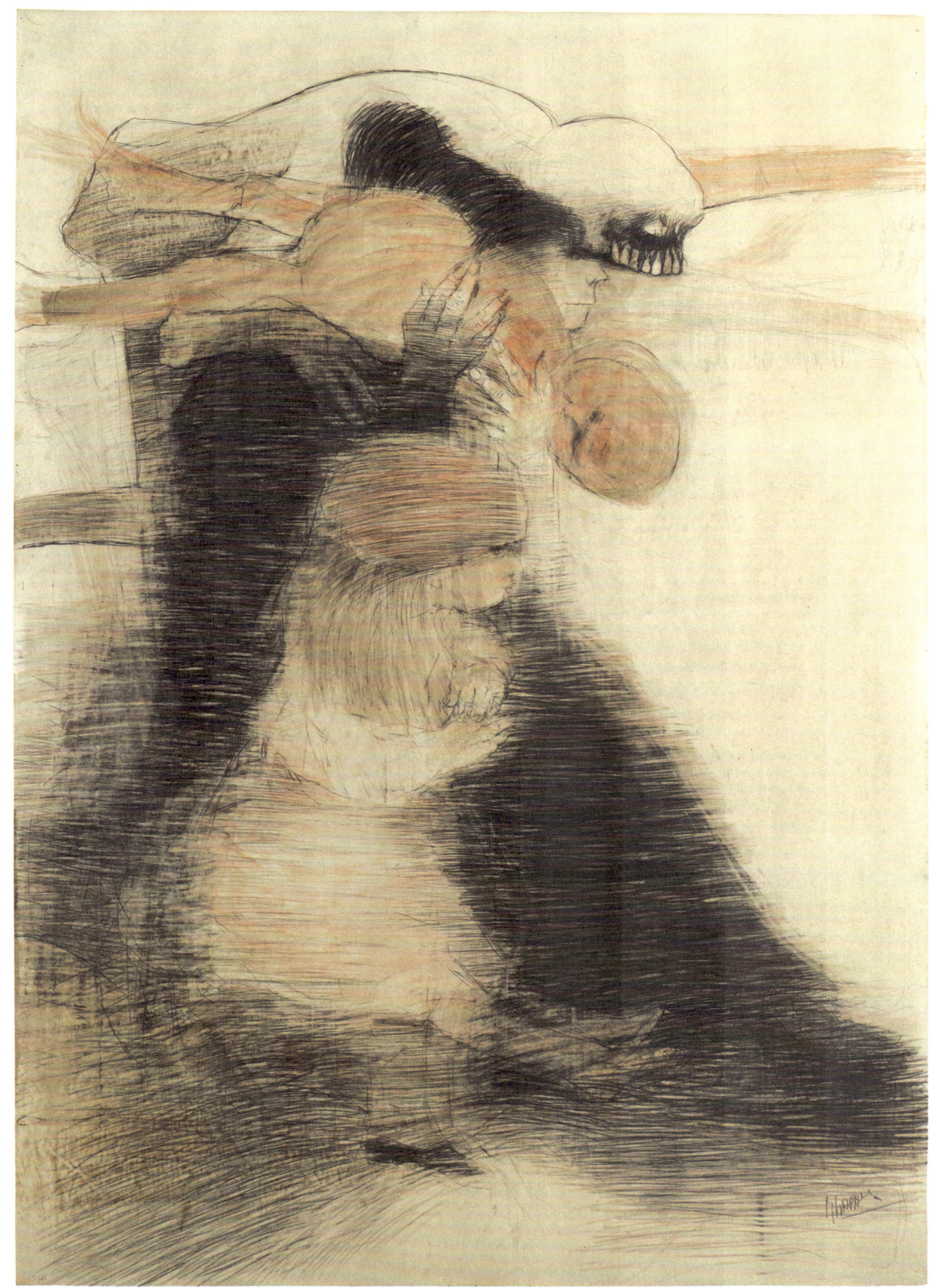

No. 15 1961–66

Graphite and charcoal, with erasures, brush and asphaltum turpentine and red wash, on card paper

65 × 45 in. (165.1 × 114.3 cm) (sheet, irregular)

Signed at lower right corner in charcoal: M LASANSKY

Levitt Foundation

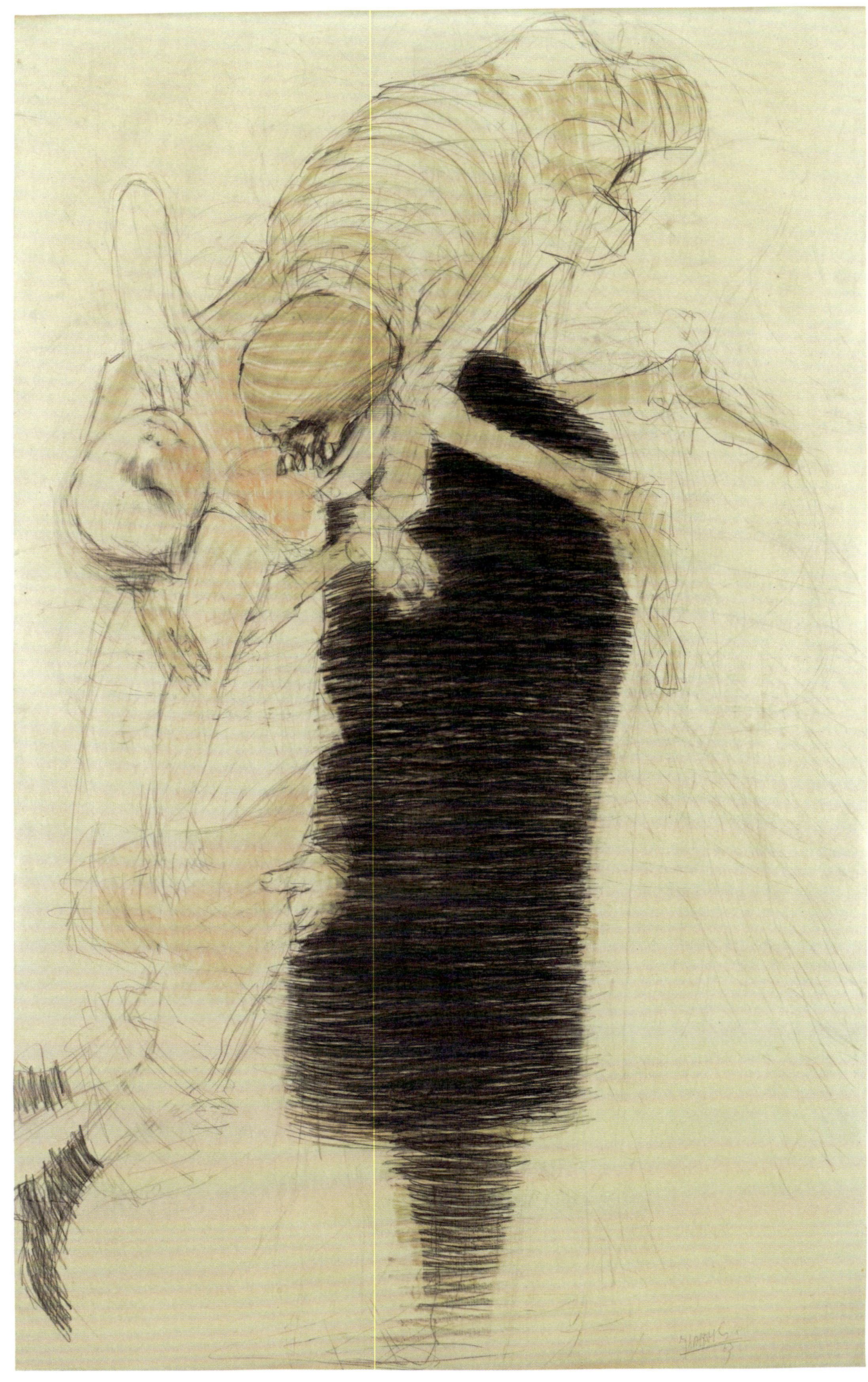

No. 16 1963

Graphite and charcoal, with erasures, brush and asphaltum turpentine and red wash, on card paper

71⅛ × 43⅛ in. (180.7 × 109.5 cm) (sheet)

Signed at lower right in pencil: M LASANSKY / 8 / 63

Levitt Foundation

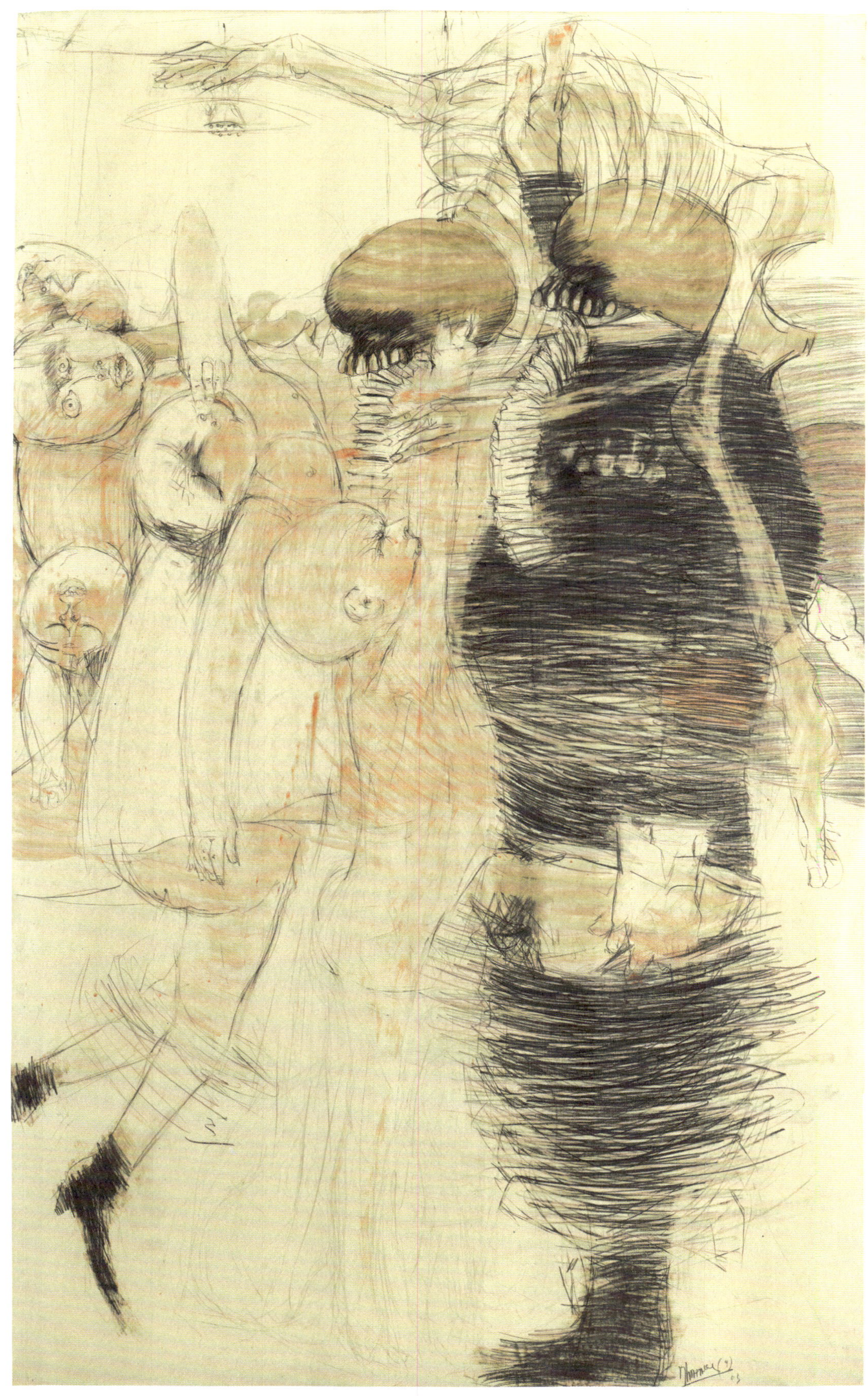

No. 17 1963

Graphite and charcoal, with erasures, brush and asphaltum turpentine and red wash, with splatters of red wash, on card paper, with torn edges

74⅞ × 44⅞ in. (190.2 × 114 cm) (sheet, irregular)

Signed, numbered, and dated at lower right corner in charcoal: M LASANSKY (9) / 63

Levitt Foundation

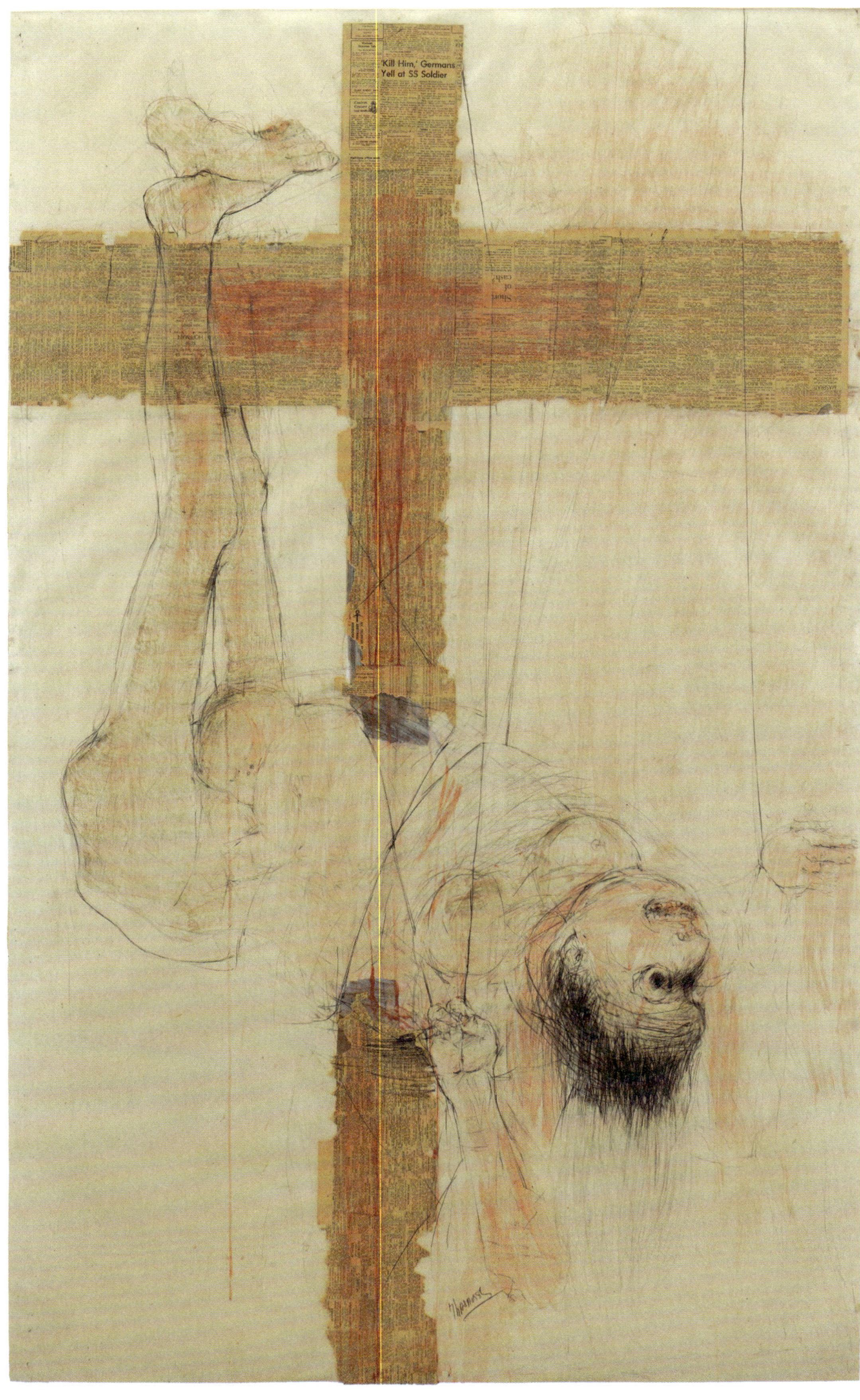

No. 18 1963–66

Graphite and charcoal, with erasures, brush and asphaltum turpentine, red, and white wash, torn and pasted newspaper, on card paper

75 5/16 × 45¼ in. (191.3 × 114.9 cm) (sheet, irregular)

Signed at lower center in charcoal: M LASANSKY

Levitt Foundation

Collaged excerpts from *Daily Iowan*, April 7, 1964, and *New York Times*, May 19, 1963, classified advertisements and articles from sports section

Right: detail

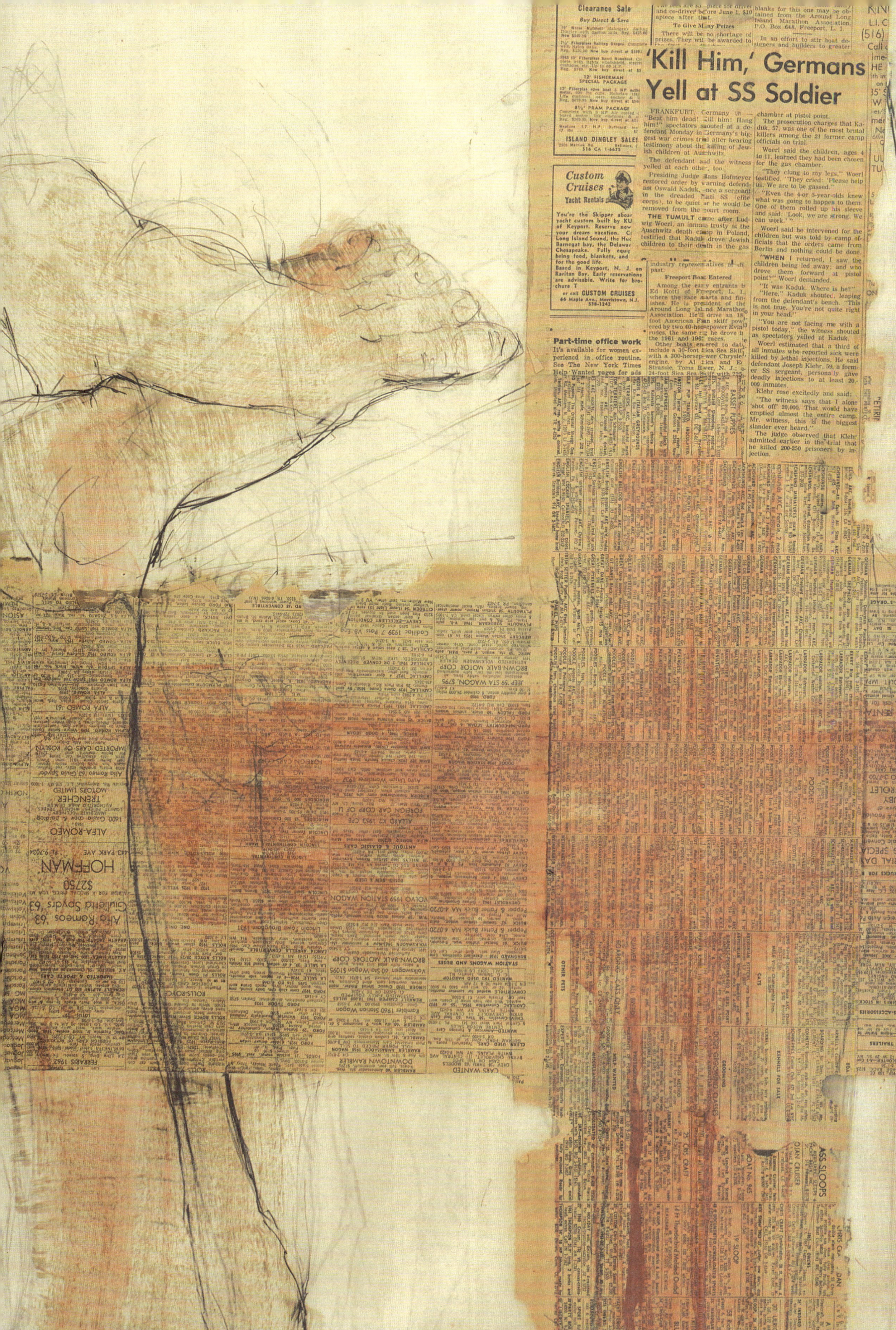
'Kill Him,' Germans Yell at SS Soldier
FRANKFURT, Germany — "Beat him dead! Kill him! Hang him!" spectators shouted at a defendant Monday in Germany's biggest war crimes trial after hearing testimony about the killing of Jewish children at Auschwitz.
The defendant and the witness yelled at each other, too.
Presiding Judge Hans Hofmeyer restored order by warning defendant Oswald Kaduk, once a sergeant in the dreaded Nazi SS (elite corps), to be quiet or he would be removed from the court room.
THE TUMULT came after Ludwig Woerl, an inmate trusty at the Auschwitz death camp in Poland, testified that Kaduk drove Jewish children to their death in the gas chamber at pistol point.
The prosecution charges that Kaduk, 57, was one of the most brutal killers among the 21 former camp officials on trial.
Woerl said the children, ages 4 to 11, learned they had been chosen for the gas chamber.
"They clung to my legs," Woerl testified. "They cried: 'Please help us. We are to be gassed.'"
"Even the 4-or 5-year-olds knew what was going to happen to them. One of them rolled up his sleeve and said: 'Look, we are strong. We can work.'"
Woerl said he intervened for the children but was told by camp officials that the orders came from Berlin and nothing could be done.
"WHEN I returned, I saw the children being led away; and who drove them forward at pistol point?" Woerl demanded.
"It was Kaduk. Where is he?"
"Here," Kaduk shouted, leaping from the defendant's bench. "This is not true. You're not quite right in your head."
"You are not facing me with a pistol today," the witness shouted as spectators yelled at Kaduk.
Woerl estimated that a third of all inmates who reported sick were killed by lethal injections. He said defendant Joseph Klehr, 59, a former SS sergeant, personally gave deadly injections to at least 20,000 inmates.
Klehr rose excitedly and said:
"The witness says that I alone 'shot off' 20,000. That would have emptied almost the entire camp. Mr. witness, this is the biggest slander ever heard."
The judge observed that Klehr admitted earlier in the trial that he killed 200-250 prisoners by injection.
To Give Many Prizes
Freeport Boat Entered
Clearance Sale
Custom Cruises
Yacht Rentals
Part-time office work
BASSET PUPPIES
STATION WAGON
BROWN-BALK MOTOR CORP
HOFFMAN
ALFA-ROMEO

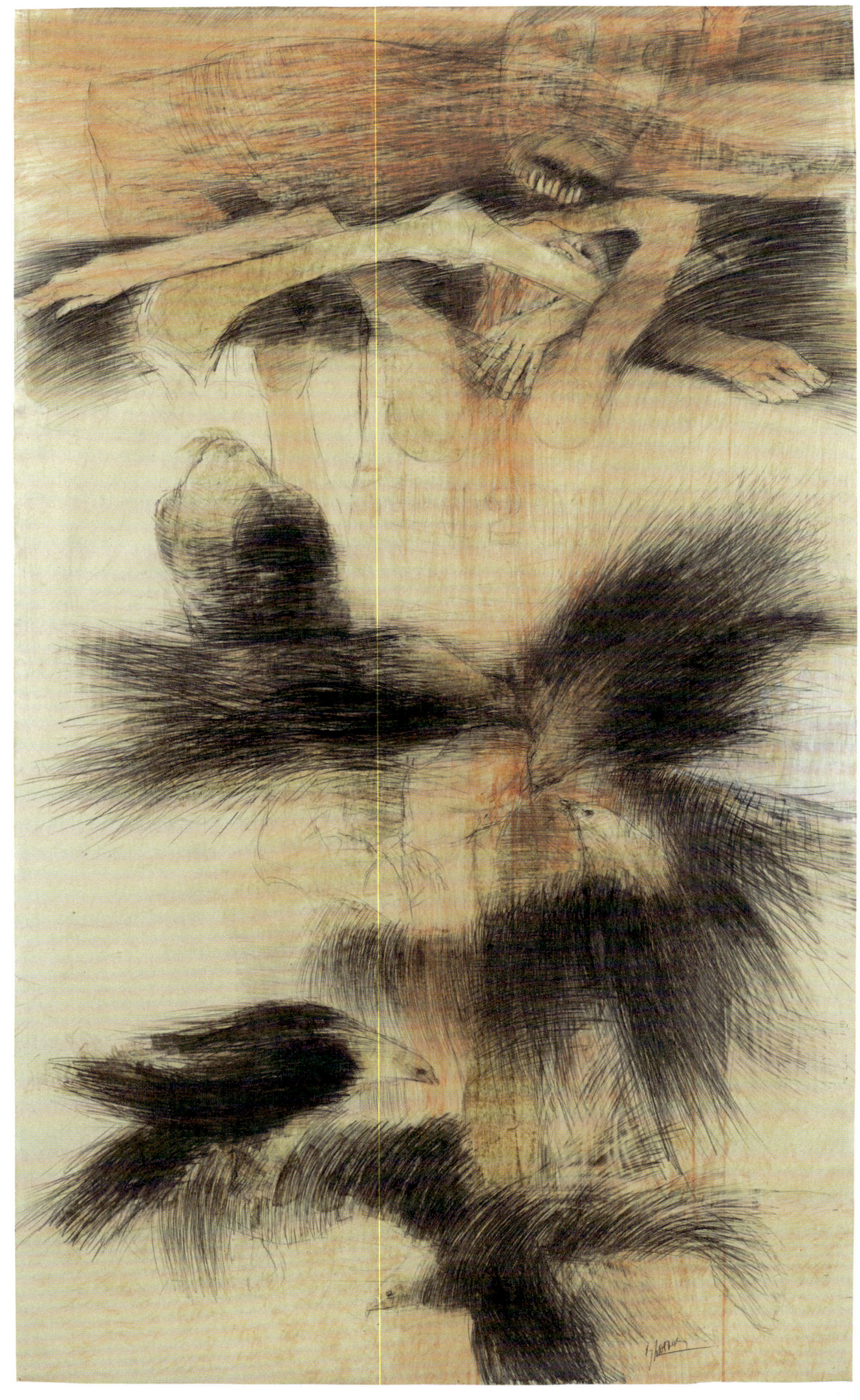

No. 19 1961–66

Graphite and charcoal, with erasures, brush and asphaltum turpentine, red, and white wash, on card paper

76 × 44⅞ in. (193 × 114 cm) (sheet, irregular)

Signed at lower right in charcoal: M LASANSKY

Levitt Foundation

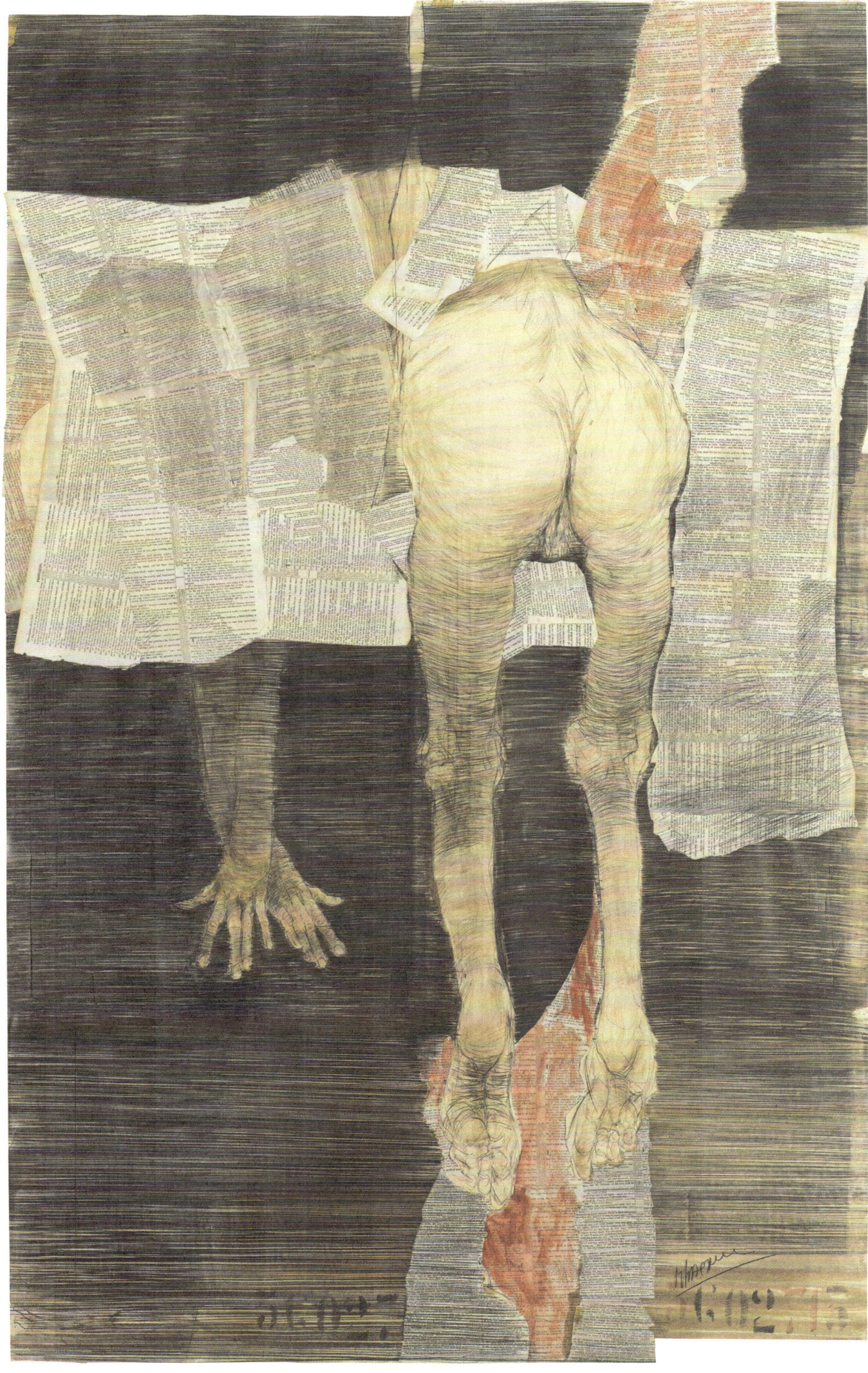

No. 20 1961–66

Graphite, charcoal, brush and asphaltum turpentine and red wash, tape, stencil, and cut, torn, folded, and pasted biblical scripture and paper, on card paper

74⅞ × 46⅜ in. (190.2 × 117.8 cm) (sheet, irregular)

Signed at lower right in charcoal: M LASANSKY

Levitt Foundation

Collaged excerpts from Judges 15; 1 Kings 4–6, 11–12, 14–15, 16–18; 2 Kings 2–3; Psalms 25–27, 30–32, 139–40, 143; Proverbs 25–26; Ecclesiastes 6–8; Isaiah 1–5, 8–9, 12, 16–19, 29; Baruch 4, 6; Acts of the Apostles 17–18

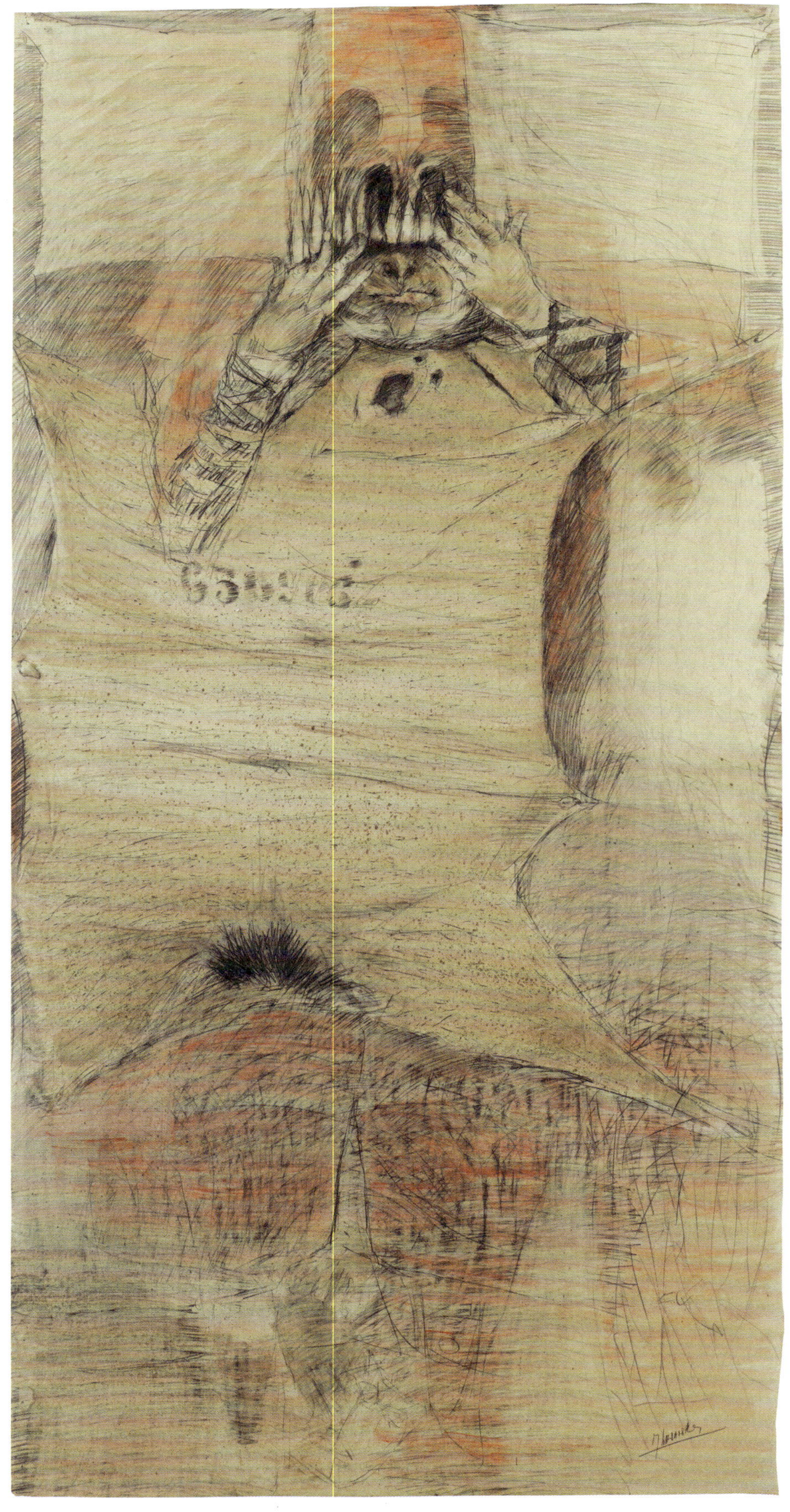

No. 21 1961–66

Graphite and charcoal, with erasures, brush and asphaltum turpentine and red wash, with splatters of red wash and touches of red chalk, on card paper, with torn corners

70 × 35 in. (177.8 × 88.9 cm) (sheet, irregular)

Signed at lower right corner in charcoal: M LASANSKY

Levitt Foundation

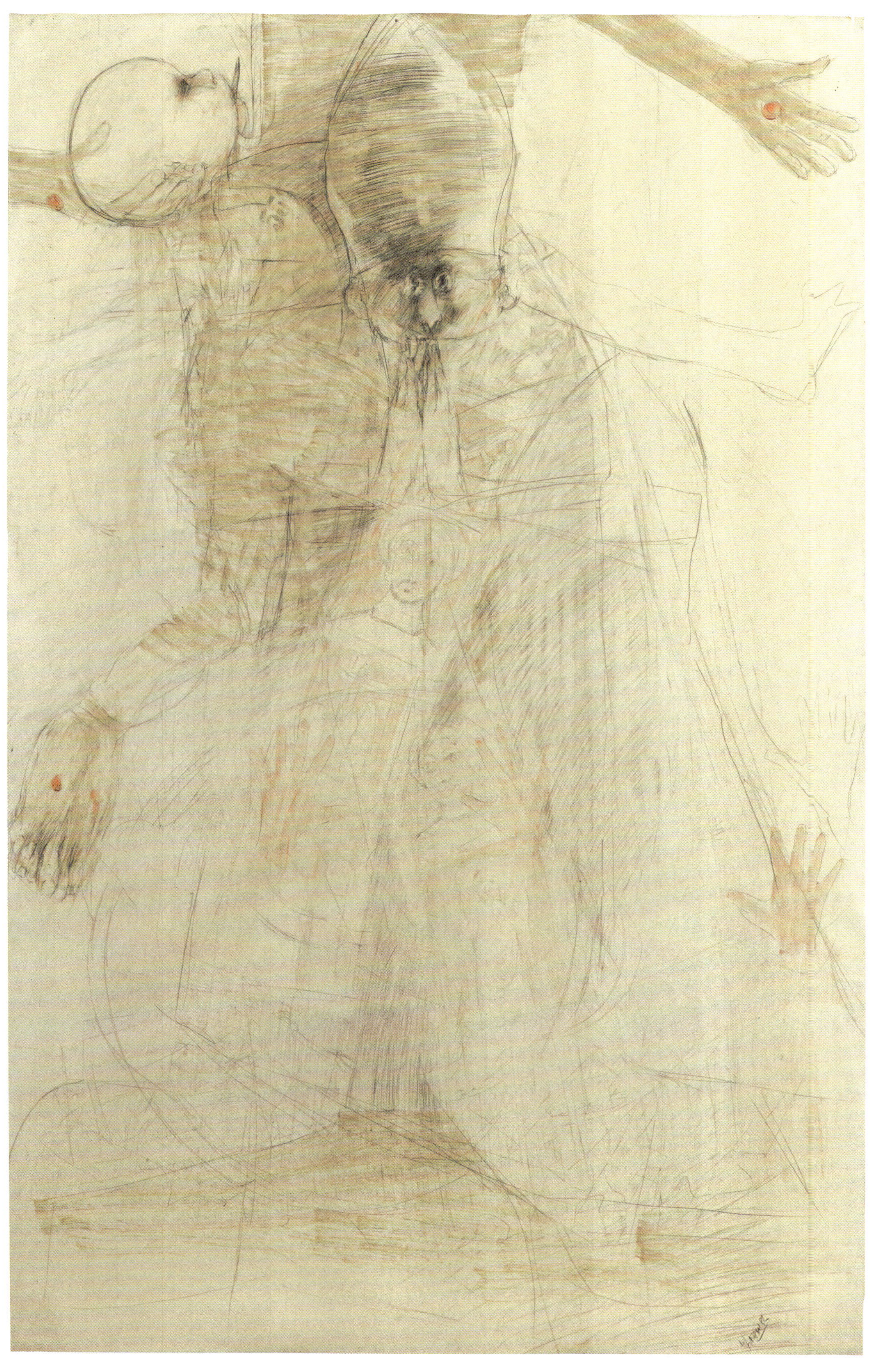

No. 22 c. 1964–66

Graphite and charcoal, with erasures, brush and asphaltum turpentine and red wash, with touches of red chalk, on card paper

72⅞ × 45⅛ in. (185.1 × 114.6 cm) (sheet, irregular)

Signed at lower right corner in charcoal: M LASANSKY

Levitt Foundation

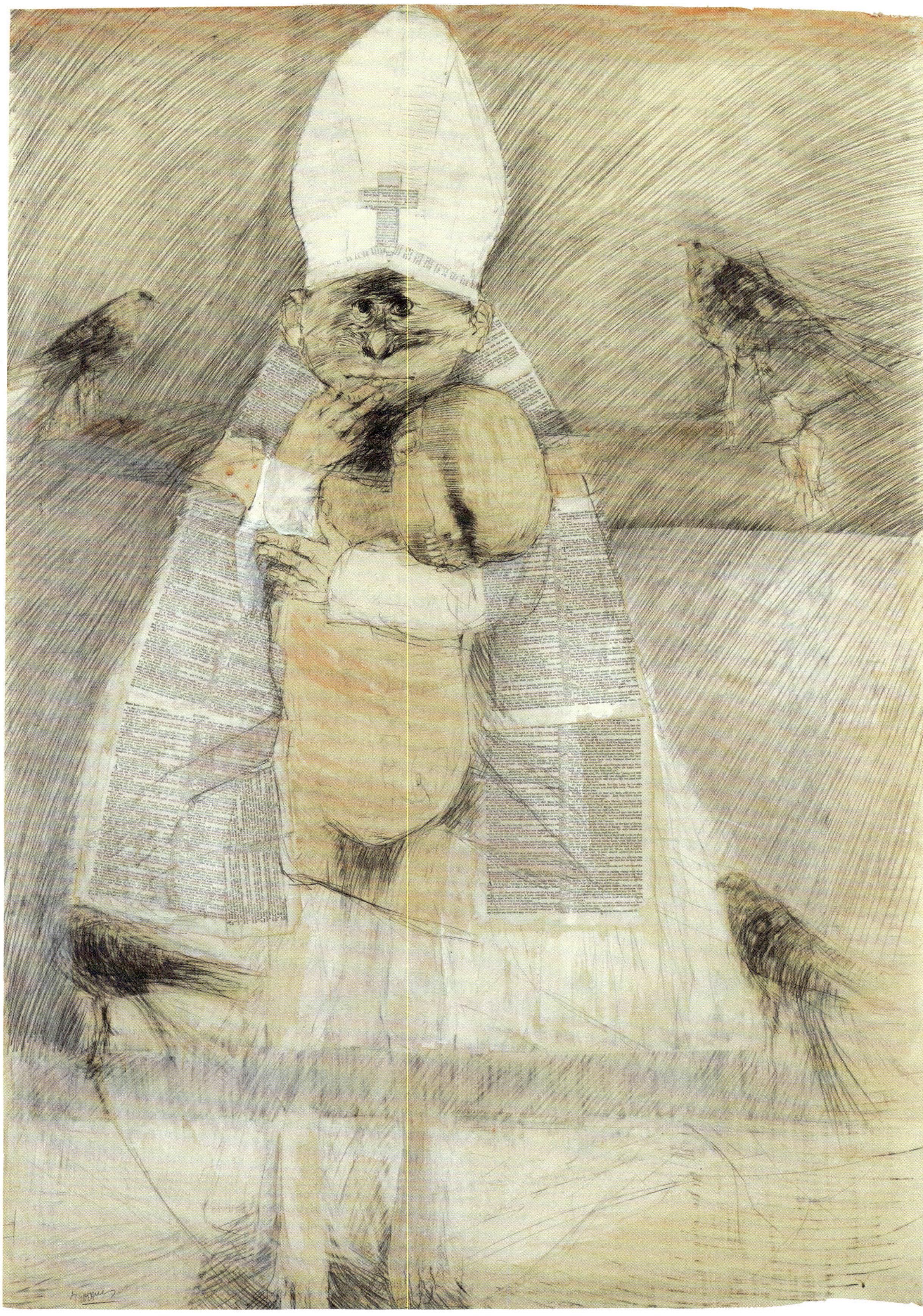

No. 23 c. 1964–66

Graphite and charcoal, with erasures, brush and asphaltum turpentine, red, and white wash, with touches of red chalk, cut and pasted biblical scripture and paper, on card paper, torn at right corners

66⅞ × 45¹¹⁄₁₆ in. (169.9 × 116 cm) (sheet, irregular)

Signed at lower left corner in charcoal: M LASANSKY

Levitt Foundation

Collaged excerpts from Genesis 44–48; Exodus 1–4, 8–10

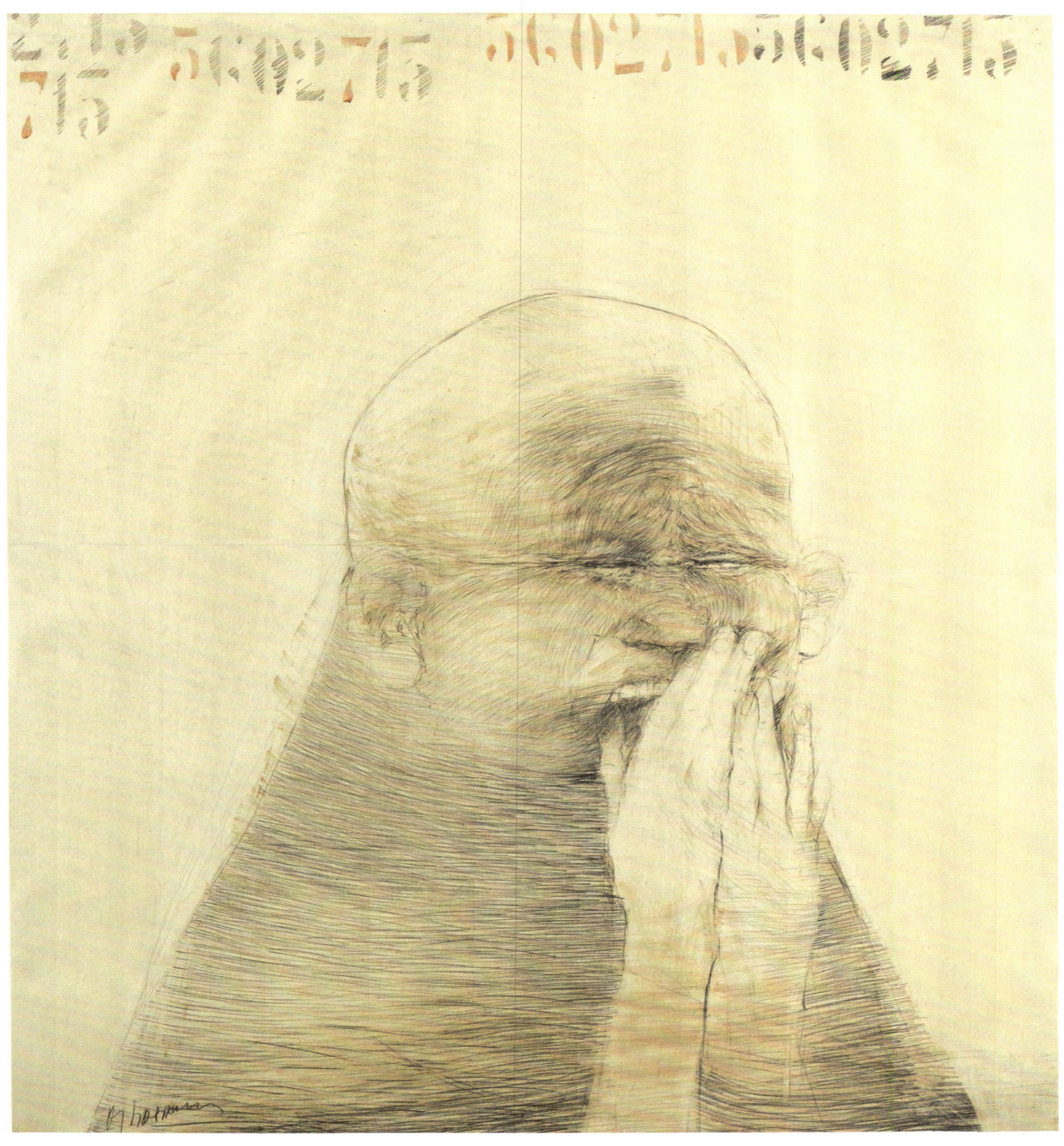

No. 24 1961–66

Graphite with erasures, brush and asphaltum turpentine and red wash, with touches of charcoal, stencil, on card paper

$43\frac{3}{8} \times 39\frac{1}{4}$ in. (110.2 × 99.7 cm) (sheet)

Signed at lower left in charcoal: M LASANSKY

Levitt Foundation

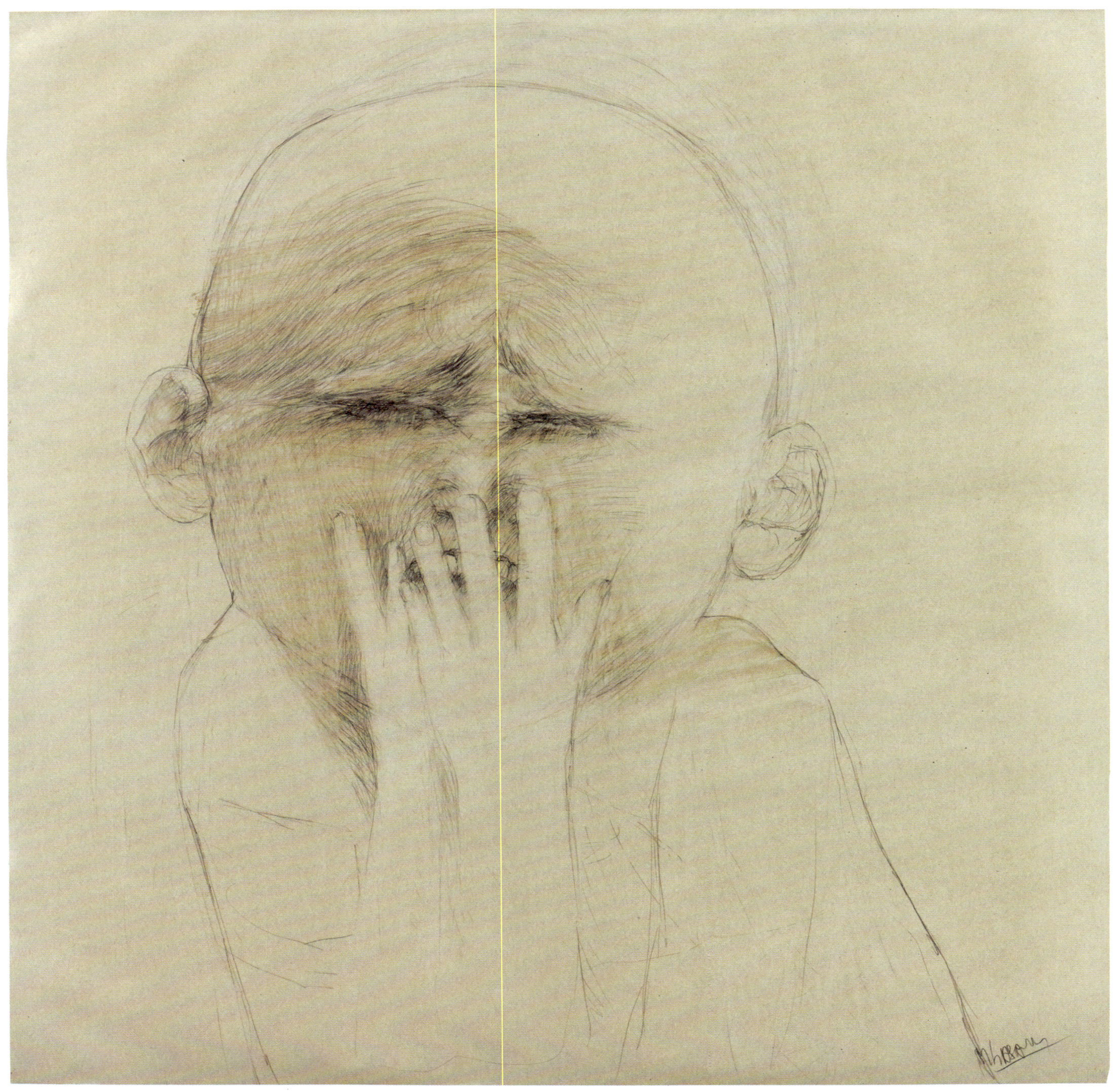

No. 25 1961–66

Graphite with erasures, brush and asphaltum turpentine wash, with touches of charcoal, on card paper

43 × 42$\frac{9}{16}$ in. (109.2 × 108.1 cm) (sheet)

Signed at lower right corner in charcoal: M LASANSKY

Levitt Foundation

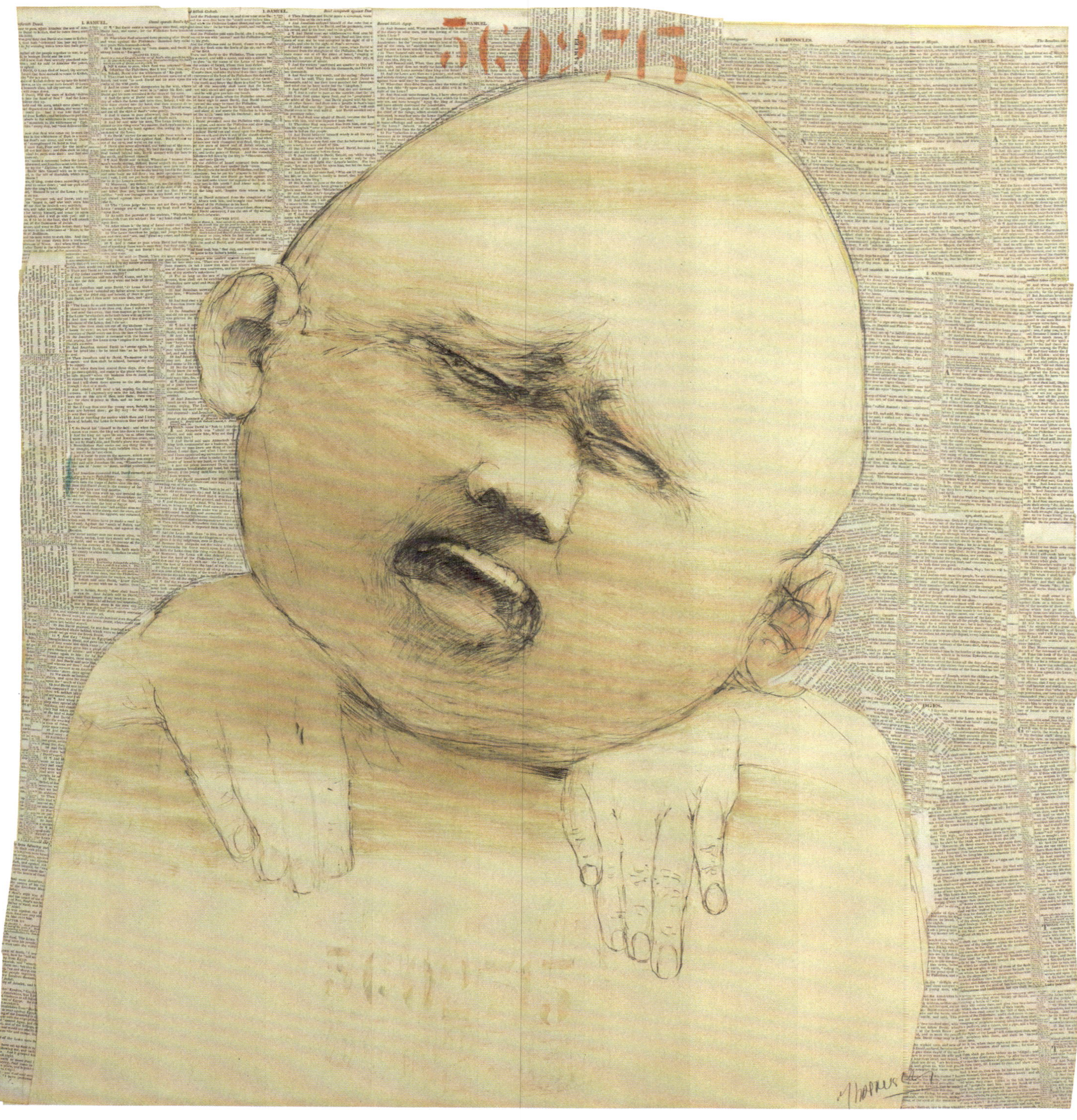

No. 26 1961–66

Graphite, charcoal, brush and asphaltum turpentine and red wash, with touches of green pastel (where three stenciled "5,602,715" in green have faded), stencil, and cut, torn, and pasted biblical scripture, on card paper, with some torn edges

45¼ × 43⅜ in. (114.9 × 110.2 cm) (sheet, irregular)

Signed at lower right in charcoal: M LASANSKY

Levitt Foundation

Collaged excerpts from Deuteronomy 28–32; Joshua 25; Judges 1; 1 Samuel 2–4, 6–9, 14–18, 20–21, 23–24, 27–28, 30–31; 2 Samuel 2, 9; 1 Chronicles 16–17

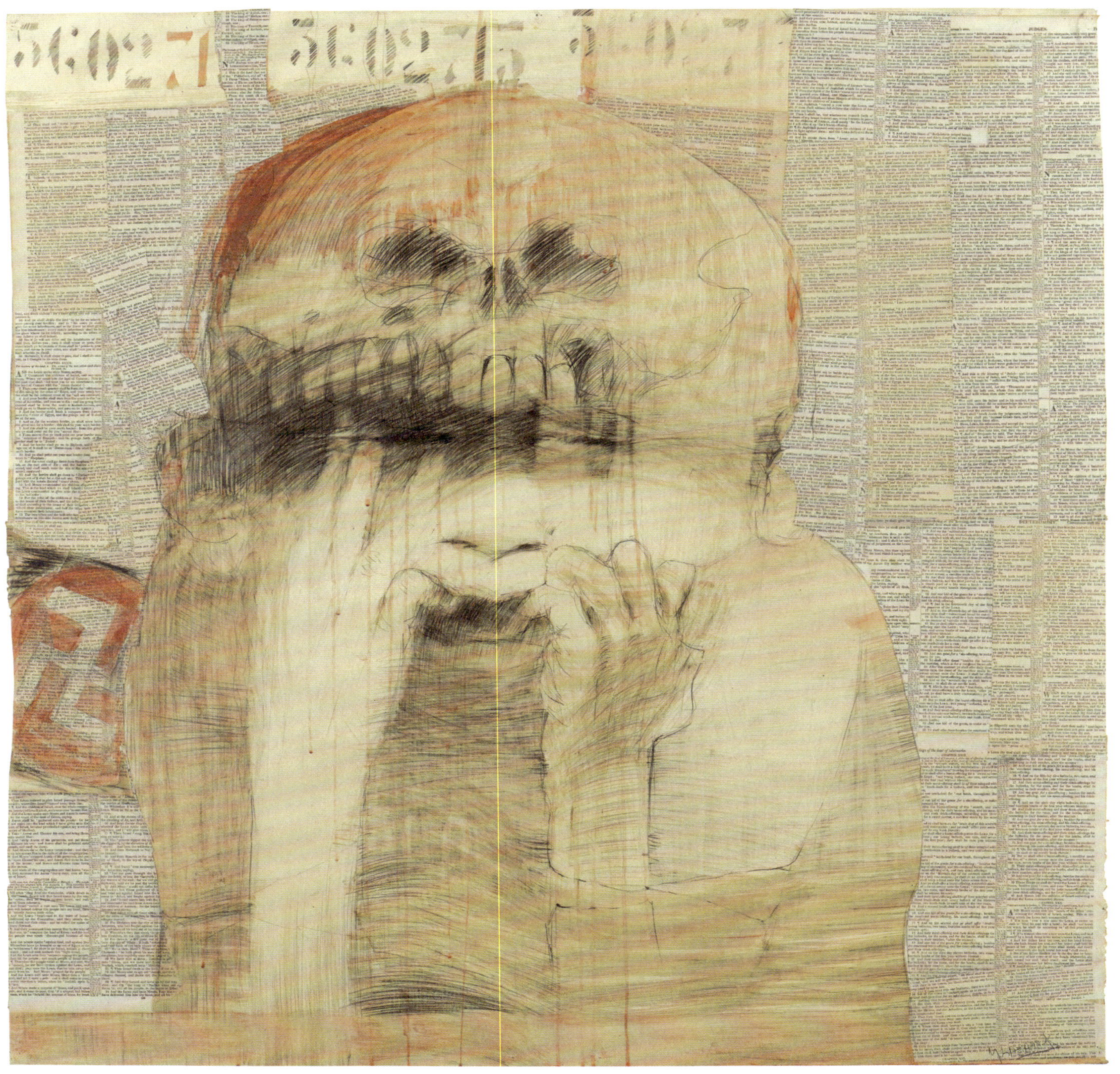

No. 27 1961–66

Graphite and charcoal, with erasures, brush and asphaltum turpentine and red wash, stencil, and cut, torn, and pasted biblical scripture and paper, on card paper

45⅞ × 46 in. (116.5 × 116.8 cm) (sheet, irregular)

Signed at lower right corner in charcoal: M LASANSKY

Levitt Foundation

Collaged excerpts from Numbers 20–21, 29–30, 33–34; Deuteronomy 2, 5–7, 12–17, 19, 20–22, 33–34; Joshua 2–3, 8–10, 12–14; Judges 1–12, 20

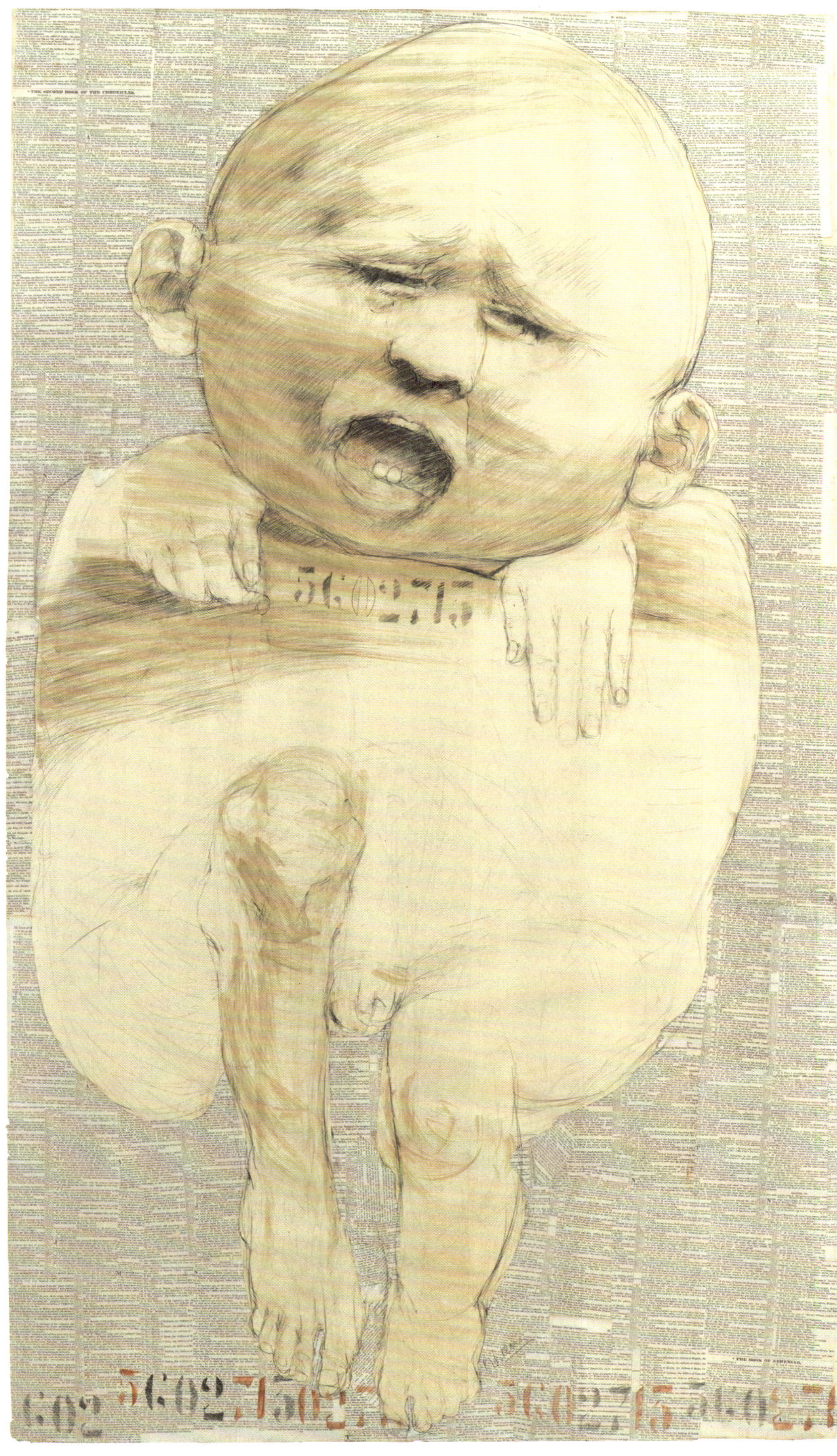

No. 28 1961–66

Graphite and charcoal, brush and asphaltum turpentine and red wash, stencil, and cut, torn, and pasted biblical scripture and paper, on card paper, with torn edges

82 × 45¾ in. (208.3 × 116.2 cm) (sheet, irregular)

Signed at lower center in charcoal: M LASANSKY

Levitt Foundation

Collaged excerpts from 1 Kings 2–4, 10; 2 Kings 8–10, 12–13, 15, 17–18, 19–25; 1 Chronicles 2, 5, 13–14, 19–21, 26–29; 2 Chronicles 1–2, 9–11, 18, 23–26, 32–34; Ezra 2, 5–8; Nehemiah 1, 7, 15; Esther 1–2, 5

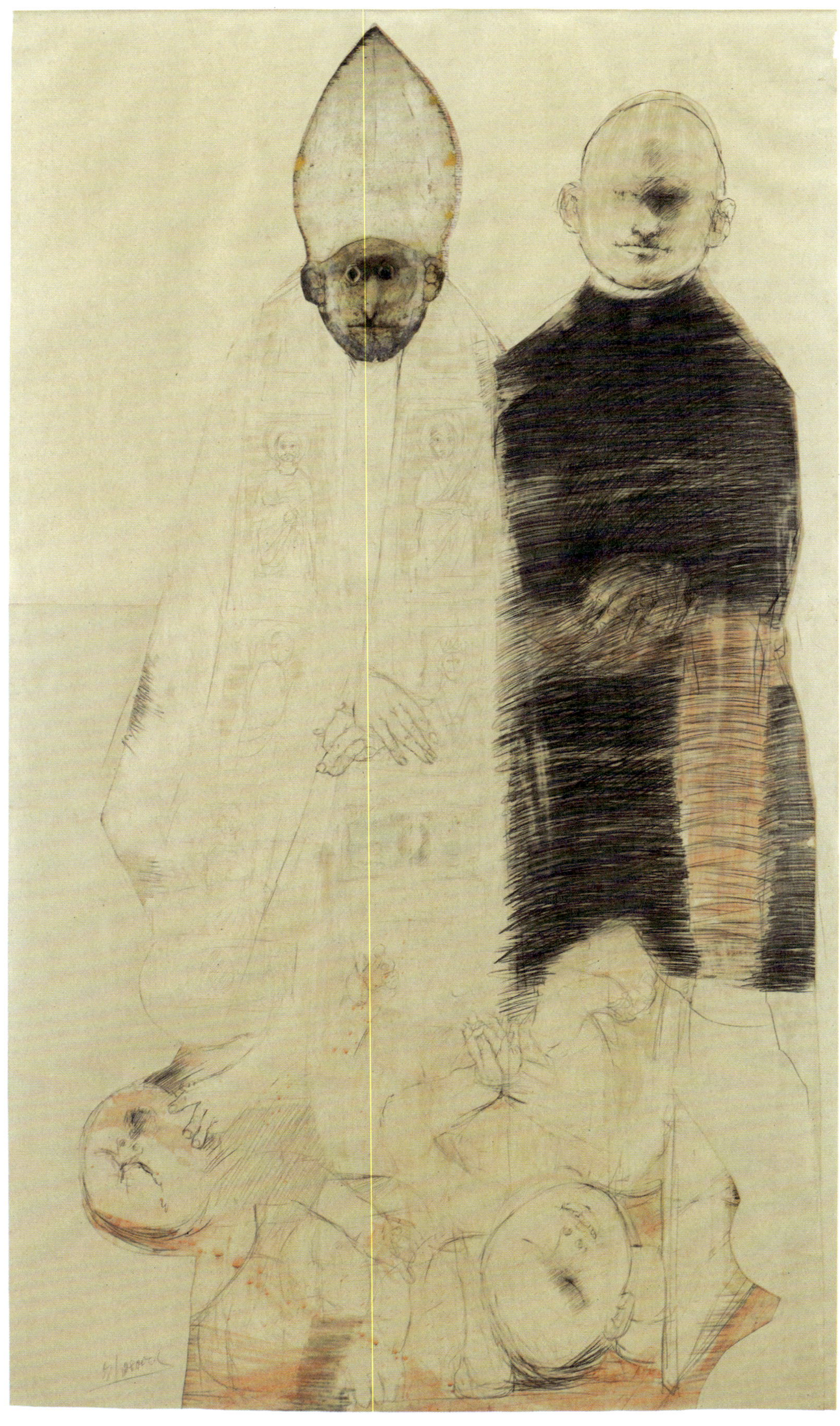

No. 29 c. 1965–66

Graphite and charcoal, with erasures, brush and asphaltum turpentine and red wash, with splatters of red wash and touches of green pastel, cut and pasted intaglio print (pope's head and miter hat), tape, biblical scripture and paper, on card paper, two sheets, with torn upper corners

77 × 44⅛ in. (195.6 × 112.1 cm) (overall, irregular)

Signed at lower left in graphite: M LASANSKY

Levitt Foundation

Right: detail

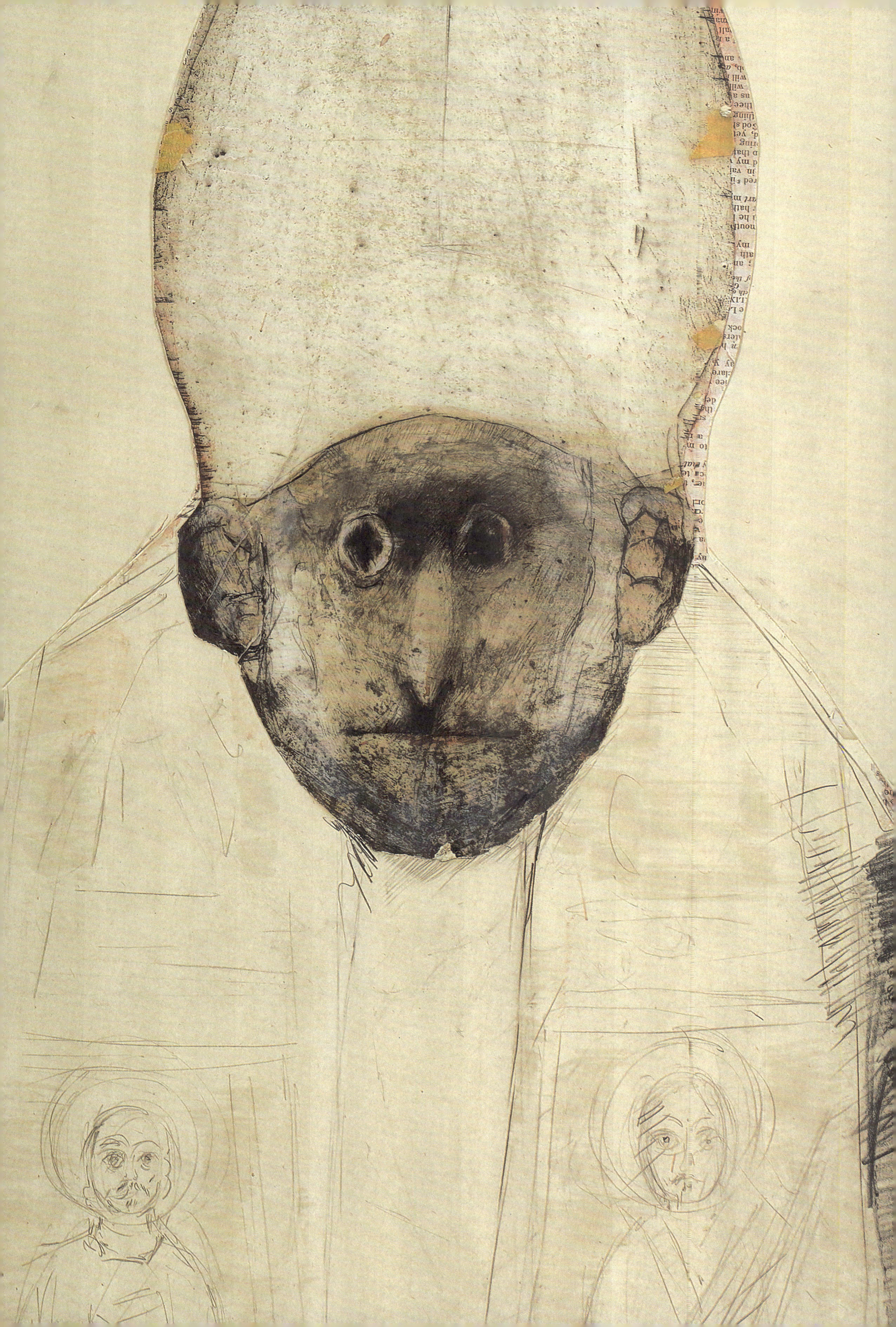

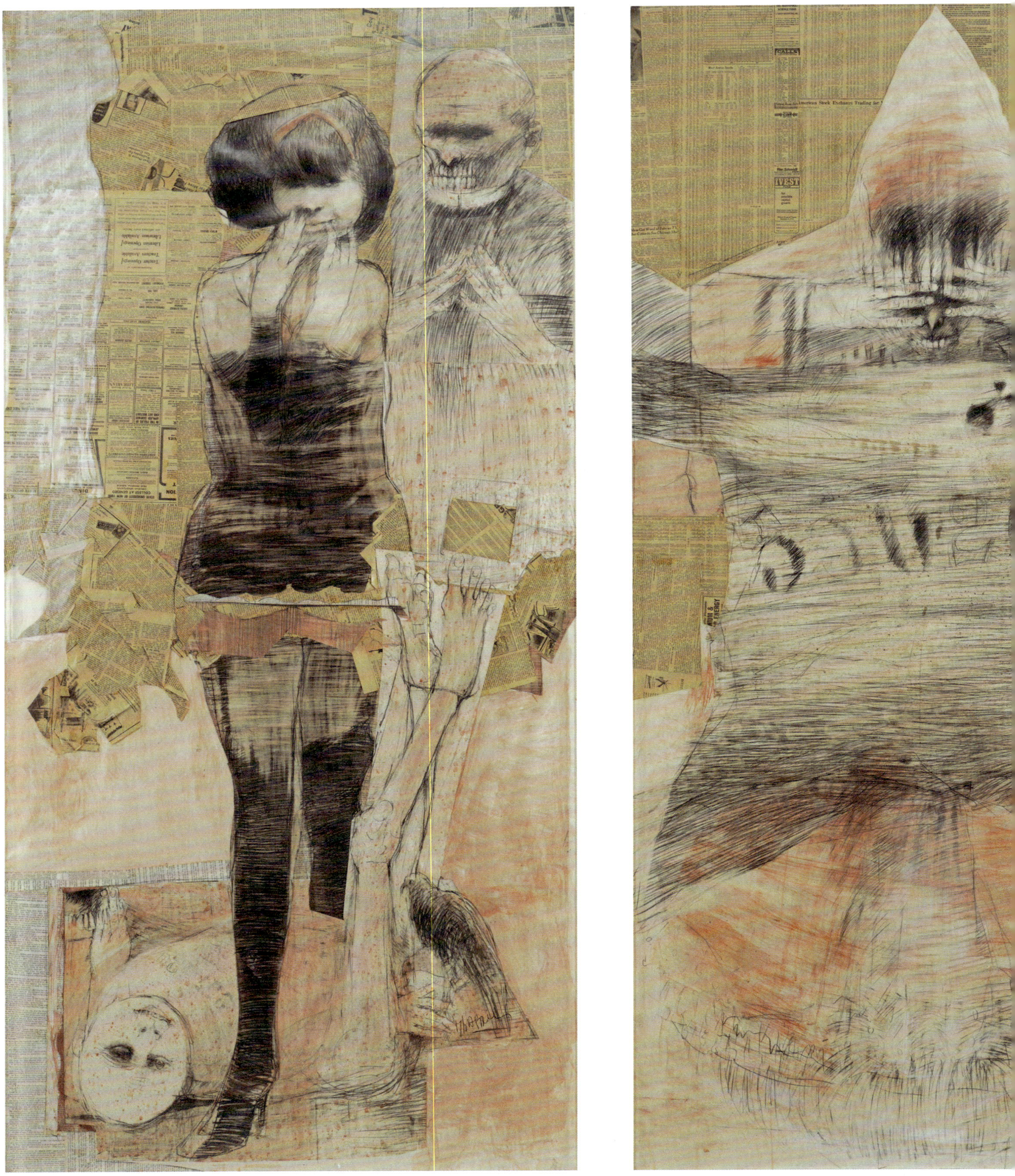

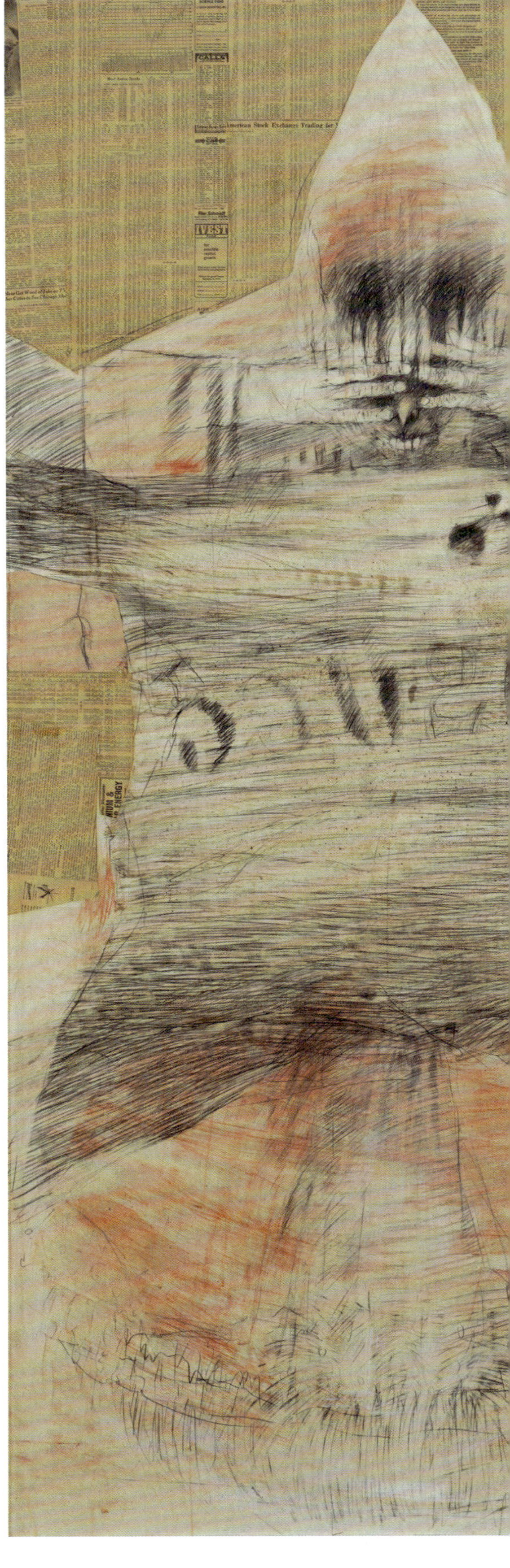

Triptych 1963–71

Graphite and charcoal, with erasures, brush and asphaltum turpentine, red, and white wash, with splatters of red wash, cut, torn, folded, and pasted newspaper, biblical scripture, and paper, on card paper, with some torn edges

Left and right panels: 79⅝ × 37⅝ in. (202.2 × 95.6 cm) (sheets, irregular); center panel: 79⅝ × 44½ in. (202.2 × 113 cm) (sheet); overall: 79⅝ × 119¾ in. (202.2 × 304.2 cm) (irregular)

Signed on each panel at lower right in charcoal: M LASANSKY

Levitt Foundation

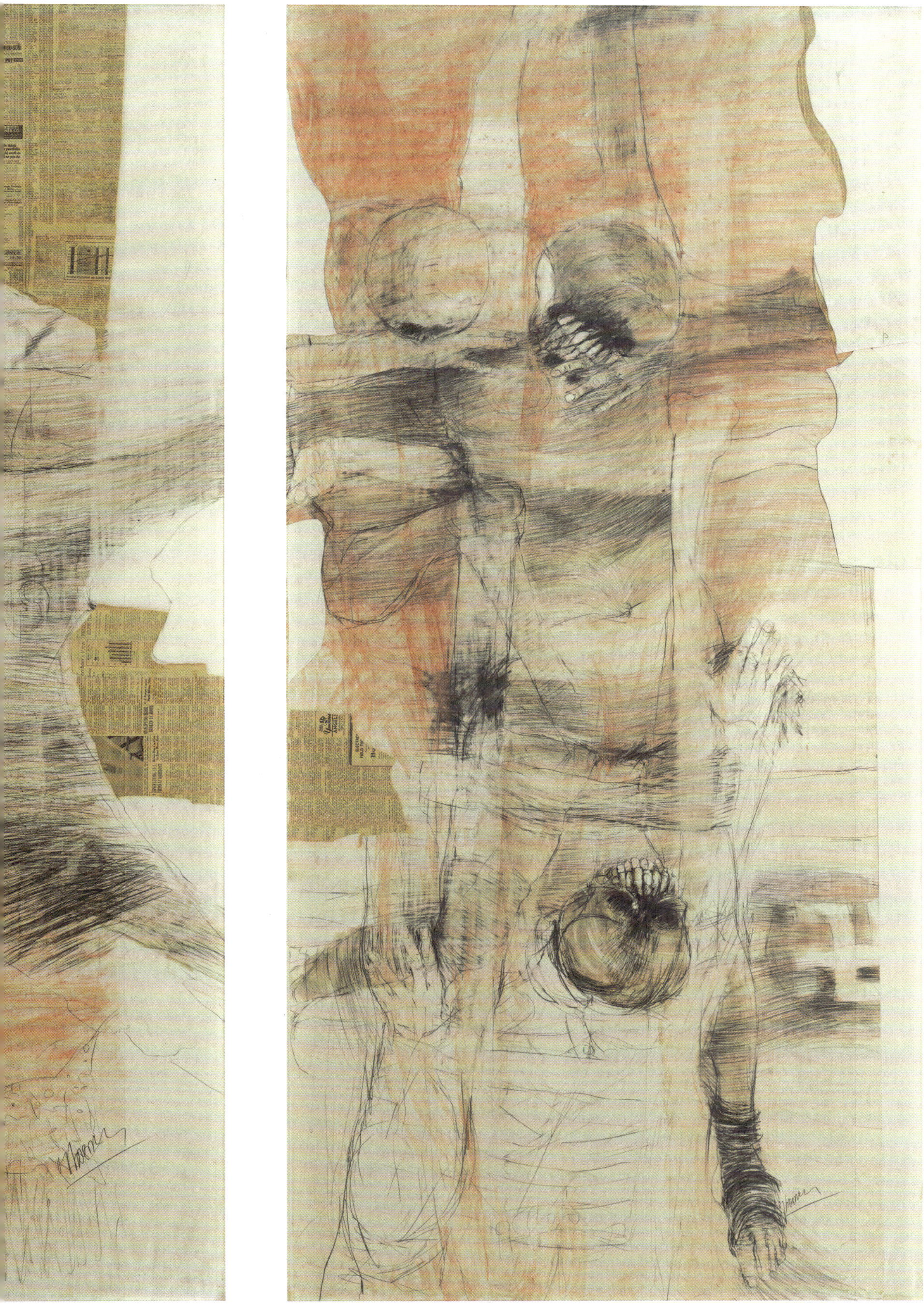

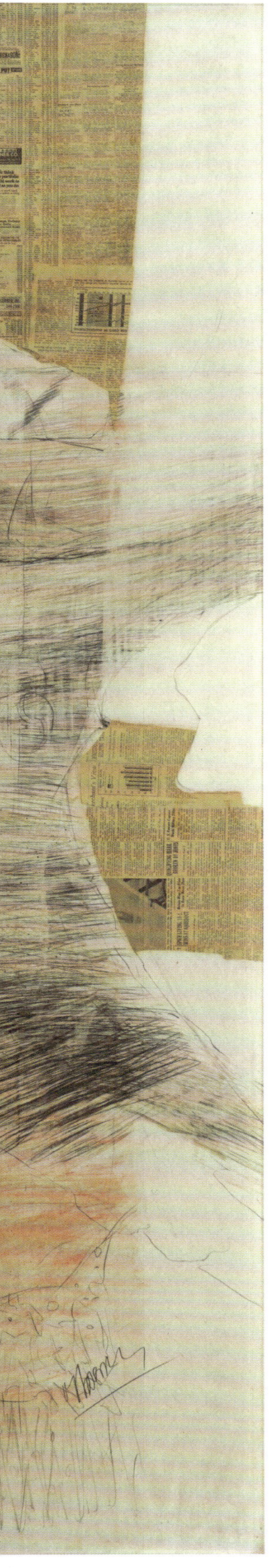

Collaged excerpts from, left panel: *New York Times*, May 19, 1963 (articles from Week in Review and business sections, and classified ads); *New York Times*, August 8, 1965; *Cedar Rapids Gazette*, May 29, 1967; *New York Times*, August 13, 1967 (articles from business section); *New York Times*, August 27, 1967 (articles from Week in Review); and Ezekiel 9, 32, 38; Jeremiah 6; center panel: *New York Times*, May 19, 1963 (business and sports sections); *New York Times*, August 13, 1967 (articles from business section, stock exchange trading); right panel: *New York Times*, May 19, 1963 (articles from sports section)

Next three pages: details, left, center, and right panels

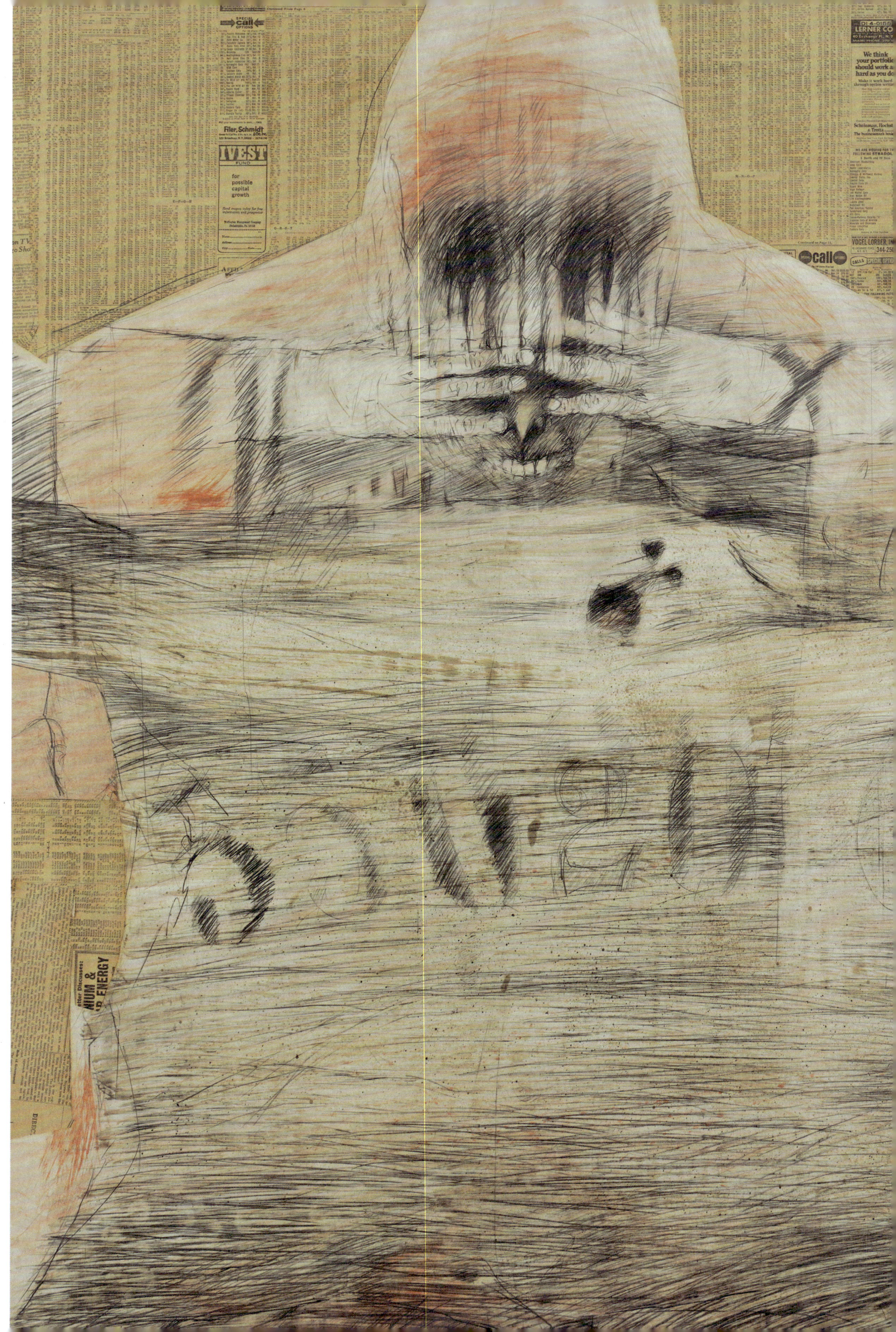
call
Filer, Schmidt
IVEST
FUND
for
possible
capital
growth
LERNER CO
We think
your portfolio
should work a
hard as you do
VOGEL-LORBER, INC
call
NIUM &
ENERGY

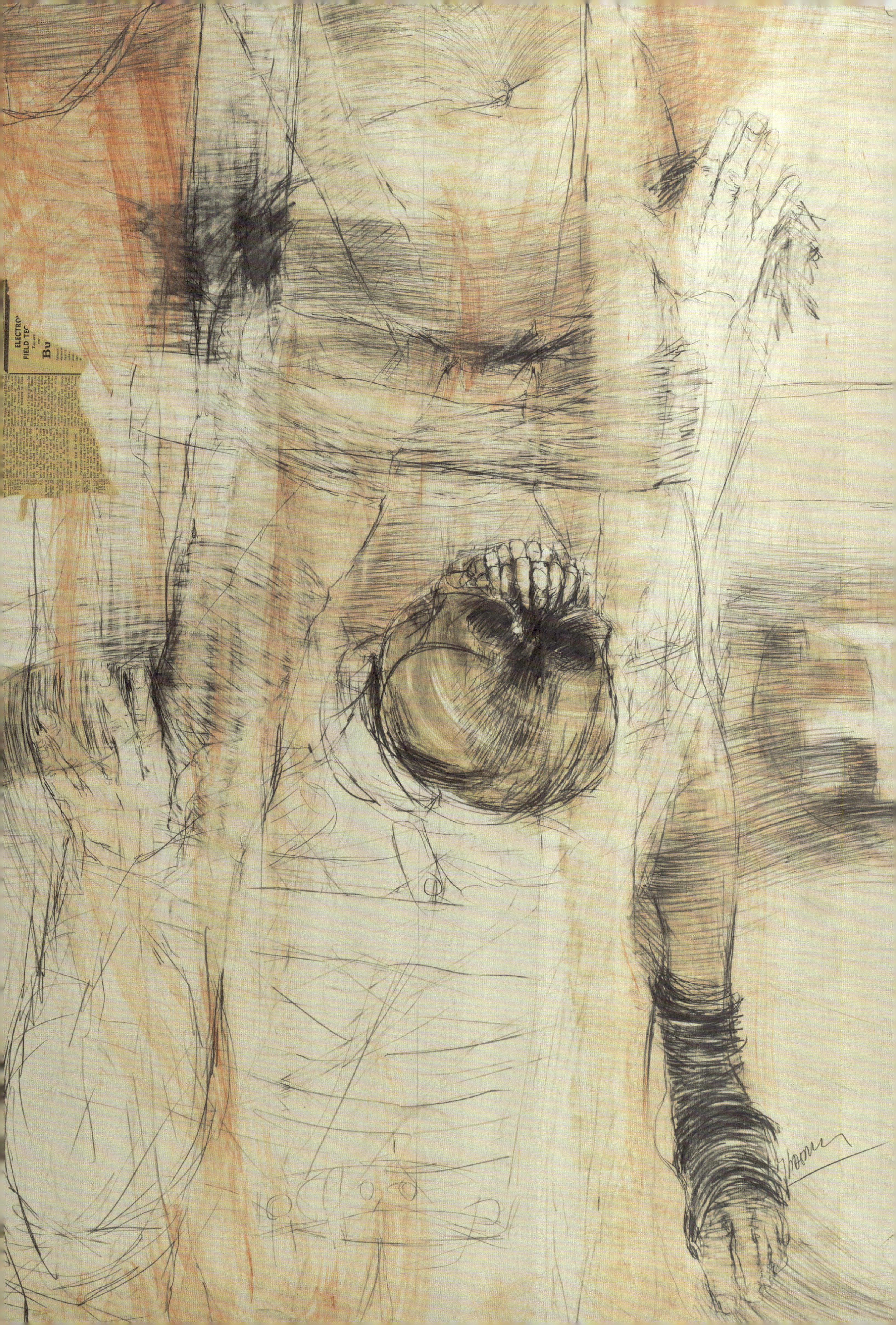

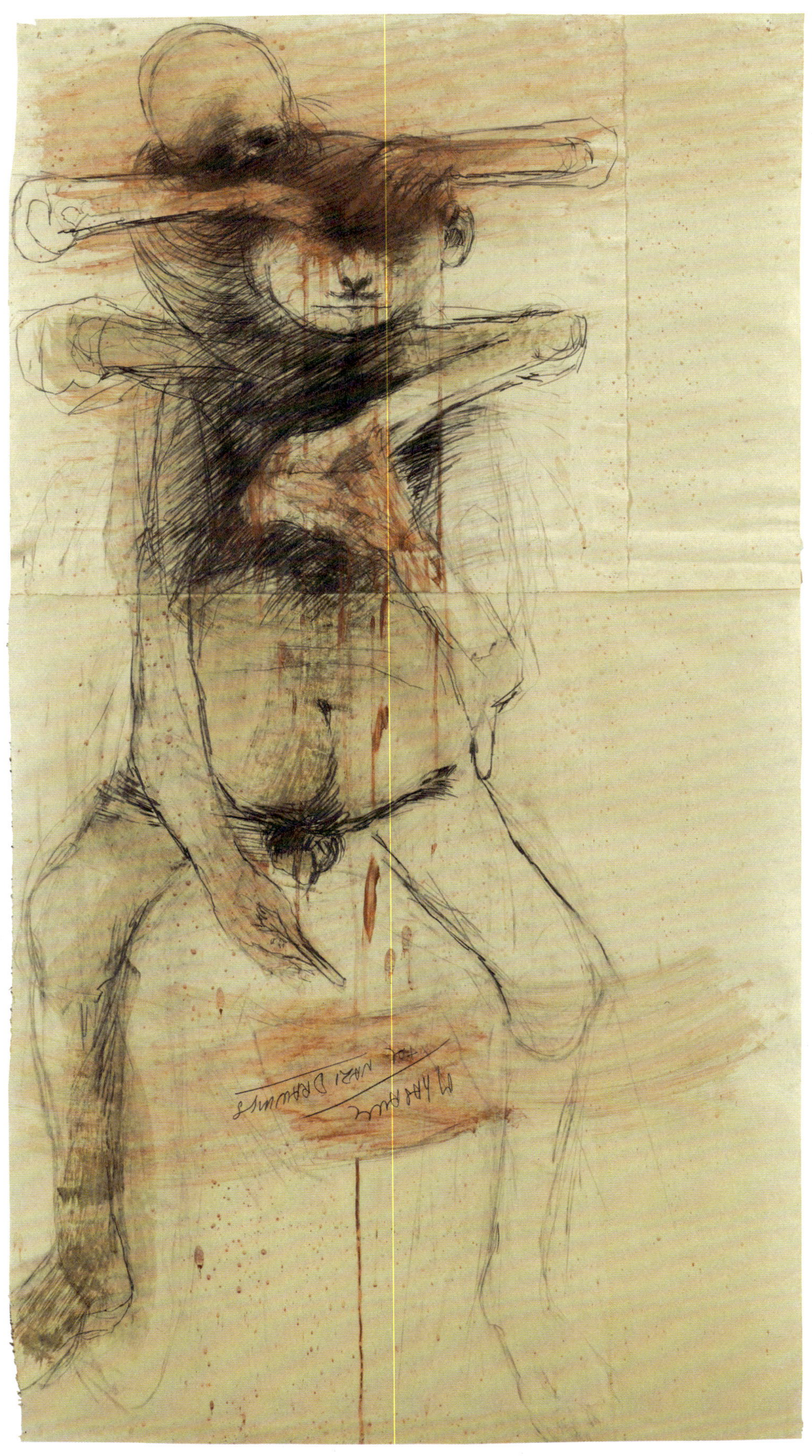

No. 30 c. 1961–66

Graphite and charcoal, brush and asphaltum turpentine and red wash, with splatters of red wash and fingerprints, on card paper, three sheets, with some torn edges

55⅞ × 29⅞ in. (141.9 × 75.9 cm) (overall, irregular)

Signed and titled at lower center in charcoal: M LASANSKY / THE NAZI DRAWINGS

Levitt Foundation

TIMELINE: THE HOLOCAUST IN LITERATURE, ART, AND POPULAR CULTURE, 1945–70

Rachel McGarry

On January 27, 1945, the Auschwitz-Birkenau camps in Poland were liberated by the Soviet Red Army. Press coverage was initially limited. The Nazis had attempted to destroy the gas chambers and crematoria to hide their crimes and evacuated all able-bodied prisoners on death marches west to Germany. In April and May, the Allied forces liberated the remaining concentration and death camps, beginning with the U.S. forces at Buchenwald (April 11) and British at Bergen-Belsen (April 15). The world was shocked by the horrors of the reports, photos, and footage of what were already being called "Nazi death factories." Hitler committed suicide on April 30 in an underground bunker in Berlin as the Red Army laid siege to the city. Germany surrendered on May 7. On August 6 the United States dropped an atomic bomb on the Japanese city of Hiroshima and a second atomic bomb on Nagasaki three days later. Emperor Hirohito announced the surrender of Japan on August 15.

Lasansky was living in New York when news broke of the Nazi atrocities. He learned of its horrors as others in the U.S. did, through newspapers, newsreels, magazines, radio, and subsequently films, books—histories, survivor memoirs, Nazi war criminals' accounts, novels—and television. Although this timeline is not comprehensive, the works noted here often resulted, at least temporarily, in heightened awareness of the Holocaust and its aftermath.

1945

NEWSREELS

Nazi Murder Mills, April 26, Universal, narrated by Ed Herlihy; *Nazi Horrors Shock the World*, May 2, Paramount. In May, America's five major newsreel companies devote their reports to Nazi atrocities, and RKO-Pathé film footage is shown to U.S. Congress on April 30 and May 1. The newsreels covering the Nazi camp liberations fail to mention the high number of Jewish victims.

MAGAZINE

"Atrocities," *Life*, May 7, 1945, features photographs of concentration camps by George Rodger, Margaret Bourke-White, and others. Six-page story makes no mention of Jewish victims in the Nazi camps.

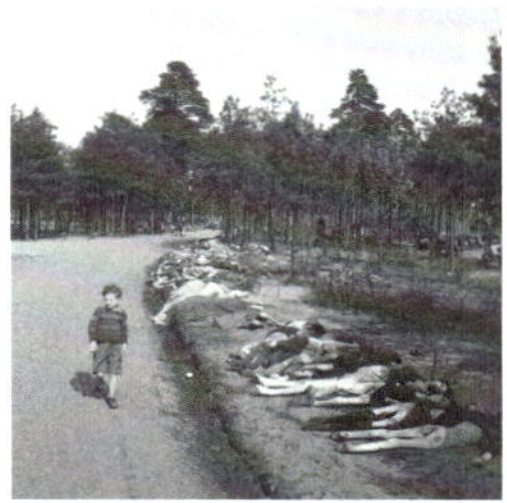

LITERATURE

Yitzhak Katzenelson, *Dos lid fun oysgehargetn yidishn folk* (*The Song of the Murdered Jewish People*, Paris). Before his deportation, Polish Jewish writer Katzenelson (killed at Auschwitz in 1944) buries one copy of his epic Yiddish poem in a bottle at Vittel detention camp in France; he smuggles another to relatives in Palestine. Translations published in Hebrew, German, Italian, French, English, and Polish (1948–82).

BOOKS

Lest We Forget (*Daily Mail*, London). Eighty-page book features "the horrors of Nazi concentration camps revealed for all time in the most terrible photographs ever published."

Léon Delarbre, *Dora, Auschwitz, Buchenwald, Bergen-Belsen, croquis clandestins* (*Dora, Auschwitz, Buchenwald, Bergen-Belsen, Clandestine Sketches*, Paris). Book reproduces 44 drawings of the concentration camps at which the artist, a member of the French Resistance, was imprisoned.

Henri Pieck, *Buchenwald: Reproducties naar zijn teekeningen uit het concentratiekamp* (*Buchenwald: Reproductions of His Drawings from the Concentration Camp*, The Hague); *Seven origineele kleurenlitho's van beelden uit het concentratiekamp Buchenwald* (*Seven Original Color Lithographs of Images from Buchenwald Concentration Camp*, The Hague). Pieck, a member of the Communist party in the Netherlands, was arrested in 1941 for resistance activities. Two books reproduce drawings he made at Buchenwald.

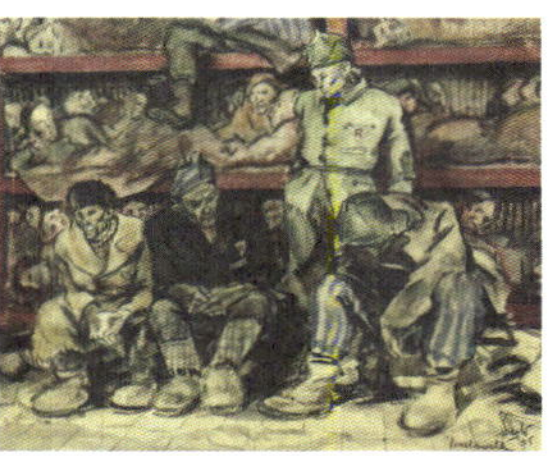

FILMS

Death Mills (*Die Todesmühlen*), directed by Billy Wilder and Hans Herbert Burger. This U.S. government film explains Nazi crimes to German audiences. It is shown in West Germany in January 1946.

Hitler Lives, Warner Bros., wins the 1945 Academy Award for best short documentary. It incorporates the U.S. War Department film *Your Job in Germany*, directed by Frank Capra and written by Theodor Geisel (Dr. Seuss).

EXHIBITION

Lest We Forget, organized by Joseph Pulitzer in collaboration with the U.S. government. Show features 25 photo murals of Nazi camps by U.S. Army Signal Corps, Associated Press, and British Army. The film *Your Job in Germany* and U.S. forces footage are also shown. Exhibition opens in St. Louis, June 1945, and travels to Washington, D.C., Boston, Cleveland, and New York, among other cities. It is seen by hundreds of thousands of Americans.

NUREMBERG TRIALS, 1945–49

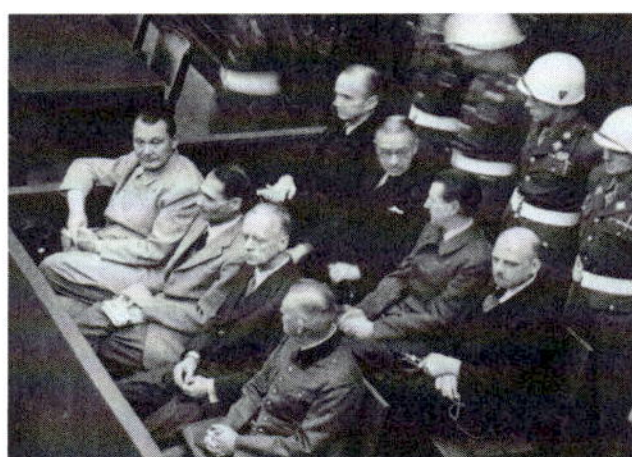

Immediately after the war, trials of war criminals and collaborators get under way across Europe, prosecuted in various courts, by governments of former occupied countries, military tribunals, and the International Military Tribunal (IMT), formed by Great Britain, France, the Soviet Union, and the United States. The IMT prosecutes 22 high-ranking Nazi officials in Nuremberg (November 20, 1945–October 1, 1946) for conspiracy, crimes against peace, war crimes, and crimes against humanity, sentencing 12 to death. The U.S. military court holds 12 additional trials at Nuremberg (1946–49), trying 166 defendants—SS officers, generals, doctors, judges, business executives from IG Farben and Krupp and so on—and further trials at Dachau and Wiesbaden. The British military court prosecutes war crimes at Belsen and Ravensbrück concentration camps. The Polish government prosecutes war criminals at Chełmno and Auschwitz, among other places. Norway tries 3 percent of its population for Nazi collaboration, nearly 100,000 people; the Netherlands, twice as many. The ongoing coverage of these trials is not cited in this Timeline. The Nuremberg trials receive the most coverage in the American press and newsreels, particularly the first trial.

NUREMBERG NEWSREELS

These are among many newsreels covering the first Nuremberg trial:

The Hitler Gang Goes on Trial, November 21, 1945, RKO-Pathé

Nuremberg War Crime Trial Opens, November 29, 1945, Universal

Nazis Face War Crime Evidence, December 6, 1945, Universal

End of Nuremberg Trial, September 30, 1946, Universal

21 Nazi Chiefs Guilty, October 8, 1946, Universal

NUREMBERG FILMS

These are among the films shown at the Nuremberg trials:

Nazi Concentration Camps, a compilation of U.S. and British army footage of the liberations of Nazi camps at Leipzig, Penig, Ohrdruf, Meppene, Mauthausen, Buchenwald, Dachau, and Bergen-Belsen. Film describes inmates as "political prisoners" and representing "every European nationality . . . they came from Germany, Poland, Czech, Russia, France, and Holland." The 58-minute film includes footage of corpses bulldozed into mass graves at Belsen (following a deadly typhus outbreak); it is screened on November 29, 1945.

German Concentration Camps Factual Survey, a British documentary produced by Sidney Bernstein, with the assistance of Alfred Hitchcock, is abandoned in 1945. Footage is screened at the trial on November 29, 1945. The incomplete surviving reels of the film are released in 1984 with the title *Memory of the Camps* (televised release, PBS, 1985). *Night Will Fall* (2014), a documentary directed by Andre Singer, examines the film's production history.

The Nazi Plan, directed by George Stevens, is screened on December 11, 1945.

Nuremberg: Its Lesson for Today (*Nürnberg und seine Lehre*), a U.S. Army documentary produced by Pare Lorentz and directed by Stuart Schulberg, incorporates footage of Hitler's rise to power and the Nazi atrocities. Completed in 1947, the film is widely screened in Germany in 1948–49 as part of American denazification, reeducation efforts, but sees only limited release in the States. American and German officials worry it will stir up anti-German sentiments amid shifting U.S. alliances in Europe with the escalation of the Cold War.

1946

LITERATURE

Jean Cayrol, *Poèmes de la nuit et du brouillard* (*Poems of the Night and of the Fog*, Paris). A member of the French Resistance, the Catholic poet Cayrol had been interned at the Mauthausen concentration camp. He later publishes *Lazare parmi nous* (*Lazarus among Us*, Paris, 1950).

David Rousset, *L'Univers concentrationnaire* (*The Concentrationary Universe*, Paris). Rousset, a Communist and member of the French Resistance, had been captured by the Gestapo in 1943, sent to salt mines, then Buchenwald. His book wins the Renaudot Prize. It is published in English as *The Other Kingdom* (New York, 1947) and *A World Apart* (London, 1951).

Olga Lengyel, *Souvenirs de l'au-delà* (*Memoirs from the Beyond*, Paris). Lengyel, a Hungarian Jewish survivor of Auschwitz, had lost her children and parents to the gas chamber; her husband was shot by a camp guard. Her memoir is published in English as *Five Chimneys: The Story of Auschwitz* (Chicago, 1947) and in paperback as *I Survived Hitler's Ovens* (New York, 1947).

Viktor Frankl, *. . . trotzdem Ja zum Leben sagen: Ein Psychologe erlebt das Konzentrationslager* (*. . . Nevertheless Say "Yes" to Life: A Psychologist Experiences the Concentration Camp*, Vienna). It is better known by its later English title, *Man's Search for Meaning* (New York, 1963).

Ka-Tzetnik 135633, *Salamandra* (Tel Aviv). Polish Holocaust survivor Yehiel Dinur writes under his pen name, meaning "Concentration Camp Inmate 135633." Born Yehiel Feiner, he takes the name Dinur ("of the fire" in Aramaic) after the war. He publishes a number of novels about the Holocaust. His true identity is made public when he testifies at the Eichmann trial (1961) and collapses on the stand. The English version is published as *Sunrise over Hell* (London, 1977).

Tadeusz Borowski, Janusz Nel Siedlecki, and Krystyn Olszewski, *Byliśmy w Oświęcimiu* (*We Were in Auschwitz*, Munich). Literary account of Auschwitz by three Polish political prisoners.

Nanda Herbermann, *Der gesegnete Abgrund: Schutzhäftling Nr. 6582 im Frauenkonzentrationslager Ravensbrück* (*The Blessed Abyss: Protective Custody Inmate #6582 in Ravensbrück Concentration Camp for Women*, Nuremberg). The Roman Catholic critic of the Nazi regime was imprisoned at Ravensbrück (English translation, Detroit, 2000).

Rudolf Reder, *Bełżec* (Kraków, Poland). Reder recounts his deportation from the Lemberg ghetto (Lviv, Poland), and his survival and escape from the Bełżec extermination camp (English translation, Kraków, Poland, 1999).

Leon Weliczker Wells, *Brygada śmierci (Sonderkommando 1005): pamiętnik* (*Death Brigade [Sonderkommando 1005]: Diary*, Łódź). An account of a Polish Jewish survivor who was enslaved as a laborer in a *Sonderkommando* unit. After the author testifies at the Eichmann trial (1961), it is published in English as *The Janowska Road* (New York, 1963) and *The Death Brigade* (New York, 1978).

Ota Kraus and Erich Kulka, *Továrna na smrt* (*The Death Factory*, Prague). Historical account of Auschwitz based on the authors' experiences as Czech Jewish prisoners, as well as interviews with other survivors. Published in English as *The Death Factory: Document on Auschwitz* (Oxford, 1966).

Eugen Kogon, *Der SS-Staat: Das System der deutschen Konzentrationslager* (*The SS-State: The System of the German Concentration Camps*, Frankfurt). Kogon, a German political prisoner, had spent six years at Buchenwald. Published in English as *The Theory and Practice of Hell: The German Concentration Camps and the System behind Them* (New York, 1950).

Ernst Wiechert, *Der Totenwald: ein Bericht* (*The Forest of the Dead: A Report*, Zurich). The celebrated German author had been arrested as a political prisoner in 1938 and kept in "protective custody" for five months. This account of his internment at Buchenwald is published in English in 1947 as *The Forest of the Dead* (New York).

Béla Zsolt, *Kilenc koffer* (*Nine Suitcases*) appears first in installments in the Hungarian periodical *Haladás* (Budapest, 1946–47). The Hungarian Jewish writer describes his survival of the Holocaust as "miraculous" (English translation, London, 2004).

BOOKS

Margaret Bourke-White, *Dear Fatherland, Rest Quietly: A Report on the Collapse of Hitler's "Thousand Years"* (New York). Book features 128 wartime photos.

Boris Taslitzky, *111 dessins faits à Buchenwald 1944–1945* (*111 Drawings Made at Buchenwald, 1944–45*, Paris), preface by Julien Cain. French Jewish artist Taslitzky was deported to Buchenwald for his activities in the French Resistance and made numerous drawings at the camp.

FILMS

The Stranger, directed by Orson Welles. Nazi fugitive (Welles) hides in small-town America; includes documentary footage of concentration camps.

Die Mörder sind unter uns (*Murderers among Us*), directed by Wolfgang Staudte, is the first German postwar film. It examines Nazi crimes and postwar trauma amid the ruins of World War II and introduces the "rubble film" genre. Staudte had acted in the notorious antisemitic Nazi propaganda film *Jud Süss* (*Süss the Jew*, 1941).

EXHIBITIONS

Art et résistance (*Art and Resistance*), Musée des Arts Modernes, Paris, February 15–March 15. Organized by friends of a French Communist resistance group, the show features hundreds of works by French Resistance members and paintings by Matisse, Bonnard, and Picasso (*The Charnel House*, 1944–45).

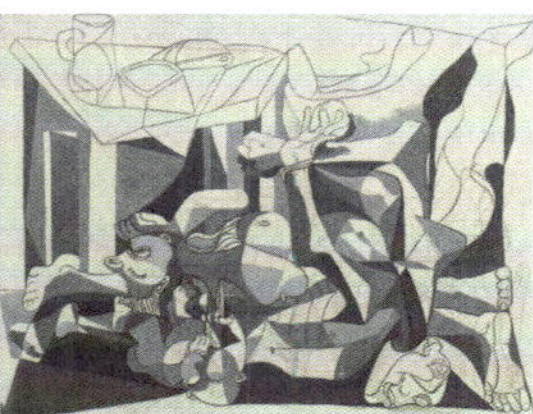

Boris Taslitzky, *Témoignage* (*Testimony*), Galerie La Gentilhommière, Paris, June. Paintings inspired by the drawings the artist made during his imprisonment at Buchenwald.

Ben-Zion, *De Profundis Gouaches*, Bertha Schaefer Gallery, New York, December. Ben-Zion's artist statement for the show states that his works are a tribute to the "six million Jewish people" murdered, an explicit reference and memorial to the Holocaust rare in the immediate aftermath of the war.

1947

LITERATURE

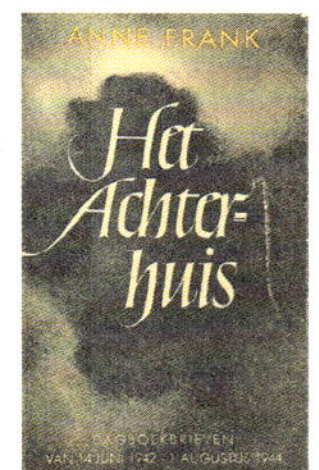

Anne Frank, *Het achterhuis, dagboekbrieven 14 Juni 1942–1 Augustus 1944* (*The Secret Annex: Diary Notes 14 June 1942–1 August 1944*, Amsterdam). Three thousand copies are printed in the first edition. Frank had spent much of World War II in hiding in Amsterdam. She and her family were discovered in 1944 and deported to Auschwitz. She died at Bergen-Belsen concentration camp in 1945, at age 15.

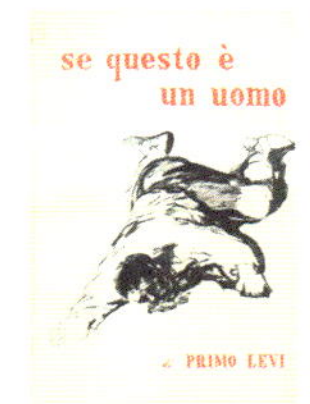

Primo Levi, *Se questo è un uomo* (*If This Is a Man*, Turin). Memoir of Auschwitz survivor is rejected by major publishers until De Silva takes a chance and publishes 2,500 copies (just 1,400 sold). Reissue by Einaudi (Turin, 1958) begins belated success of acclaimed book. Levi writes several more books and essays on the Holocaust. He commits suicide in 1987.

Raya Kagan, *Nashim be-lishkat ha-gehinom* (*Women in the Office of Hell*, Merḥavyah, Israel). Kagan's Holocaust memoir recounts her work in the prisoner registration department at Auschwitz. She will be a critical witness at the Eichmann trial (1961) and Frankfurt Auschwitz trials (1964), providing detailed accounts of operations of the camp.

Eugene Weinstock, *Beyond the Last Path* (New York). Account by Hungarian Jewish author who survived Buchenwald.

BOOK

Leo Haas, *12 puvodnich litografii z nemeckych koncentracnich taboru* (*12 Original Lithographs of German Concentration Camps*, Prague). Czech Jewish artist Haas publishes artwork documenting his imprisonment at Terezín and Auschwitz.

MEMORIALS AND MUSEUMS

Auschwitz concentration camp is declared a museum by the Polish parliament; the first exhibition opens in the barracks.

Memorial of National Suffering opens at Terezín (Theresienstadt), the ghetto–concentration camp near Prague. Jewish persecution begins to be addressed specifically when the Ghetto Museum opens there in 1991.

TRIAL

Auschwitz trials, Kraków, Poland, November 24–December 22. Polish government prosecutes 41 former Auschwitz camp guards and doctors for crimes against humanity. Twenty-one defendants are executed, including Rudolf Höss, the camp's longest-serving commandant, who confesses to overseeing the executions of 2.5 million victims by gassing and burning, and estimates at least another half million died of starvation. Around 8,000 personnel worked at Auschwitz and its satellite camps (Birkenau, Buna, Monowitz), but only a tiny fraction are brought to trial.

1948

LITERATURE

Tadeusz Borowski, *Pożegnanie z Marią* (*Farewell to Maria*) and *Kamienny świat* (*The World of Stone*) (Warsaw). Polish political prisoner publishes selection of short stories about his experience at Auschwitz. He commits suicide in 1951. Twelve stories appear posthumously in English as *This Way for the Gas, Ladies and Gentlemen* (New York and London, 1967).

Paul Celan, *Der Sand aus den Urnen: Gedichte* (*The Sands from the Urns*, Vienna). Celan is the pseudonym of the Romanian Jewish poet Paul Antschel. The poem "Todesfuge" ("Death Fugue," 1944–45) is about the Nazi camps. He later writes, "There is nothing in the world for which a poet will give up writing, not even when he is a Jew and the language of his poems is German." Celan lives in France after the war and commits suicide in 1970.

PERIODICAL

Hannah Arendt, "The Concentration Camps," *Partisan Review*. The political philosopher and writer examines Nazi and Soviet concentration camps and death camps and sees them as the most extreme manifestation of totalitarian governments.

FILMS

Germania anno zero (*Germany Year Zero*), directed by Roberto Rossellini. Filmed in the ruins of Berlin.

Lang ist der Weg (*Long Is the Road*), directed by Herbert B. Fredersdorf and Marek Goldstein. Portrays Holocaust from the viewpoint of a Polish Jewish family. Released in Germany and the U.S.

Morituri, directed by Eugen York and produced by Artur Brauner. German film about the escape of concentration camp prisoners who hide in a forest near the end of the war. The title comes from the Latin phrase meaning "those who are about to die."

The Search, directed by Fred Zinnemann and starring Montgomery Clift. Film treats the plight of displaced persons, especially children, in centering on the story of a young Czech (non-Jewish) Auschwitz survivor searching for his mother after the war. It is nominated for seven Academy Awards.

Sealed Verdict, directed by Lewis Allen. Explores Nazi war crimes trials, death camps, and acknowledges the Nazis' attempt to eradicate the Jews from Europe.

MEMORIAL

Nathan Rapoport, *Monument to the Ghetto Heroes*, bronze and stone sculpture. The work is erected on the site of the former Warsaw ghetto leveled by the Nazis and unveiled on April 19, the fifth anniversary of the Jewish uprising.

1949

FILMS

Ostatni etap (*The Last Stage*, 1948), directed and cowritten by the Polish Auschwitz survivor Wanda Jakubowska, is released in the U.S. It is one of the earliest films to dramatize life in Nazi extermination camps.

Daleká cesta (*Distant Journey*), directed by Alfréd Radok. Czech film examines the plight of Jews in Prague during the Holocaust and their deportations to Nazi camps and ghettos. It follows the story of a Jewish woman married to a gentile. Film incorporates explicit archival footage of Nazi atrocities.

MUSEUM AND MEMORIAL

Ghetto Fighters' House (Yitzhak Katzenelson Holocaust and Jewish Resistance Heritage Museum) is founded by Holocaust survivors on a kibbutz in Israel on April 19, the sixth anniversary of the Warsaw ghetto revolt.

1950

LITERATURE

John Hersey, *The Wall* (New York). Novel about an escape from the Warsaw ghetto.

Paul Rassinier, *Le Mensonge d'Ulysse, regard sur la littérature concentrationnaire* (*The Lie of Ulysses, a Study of Concentration Camp Literature*, Paris). Rassinier, known as the "Father of Holocaust Denial," attempts to debunk the Nazis' intention to annihilate the Jews and their use of gas chambers. Published in English as *The Holocaust Story and the Lies of Ulysses: A Study of the German Concentration Camps and the Alleged Extermination of European Jewry* (Newport Beach, Calif., 1978).

1951

LITERATURE

Theodor Adorno, "Kulturkritik und Gesellschaft" ("Cultural Criticism and Society"), 1949 essay published in Festschrift *Soziologische Forschung in unserer Zeit. Leopold von Wiese zum 75. Geburtstag* (Cologne). He famously pronounces, "To write poetry after Auschwitz is barbaric."

Rudolf Höss, "Autobiografia Rudolfa Hoessa," with introduction by Stanisław Batawia, *Biuletyn Głównej Komisji Badania Zbrod ni Hitlerowskich w Polsce* (*Bulletin of the Main Commission for the Investigation of German Crimes in Poland*), vol. 7 (Warsaw). Nazi war criminal, executed in 1947, had written his memoir while awaiting trial. It is published posthumously in Polish (*Wspomnienia Rudolfa Hoessa komendanta obozu oświęcimskiego* (*Memoirs of Rudolf Höss, the Commandant of Auschwitz Camp*, Warsaw, 1956), German (1958), English (1959), and Hebrew (1964).

TRIAL

IG Farben lawsuit, November 3, 1951–June 10, 1953, Frankfurt. Twenty-four directors of the German corporation had been prosecuted in Nuremberg (1947–48), but only 13 received prison sentences (six months to eight years). Survivor Norbert Wollheim, a forced laborer at Buna/Monowitz concentration camp, sues company for enslavement; court finds in his favor (and on appeal in 1957). IG Farben is ordered to pay Wollheim and a claims group of former forced laborers at Buna/Monowitz camps and subcamps 30 million Deutschmarks.

1952

LITERATURE

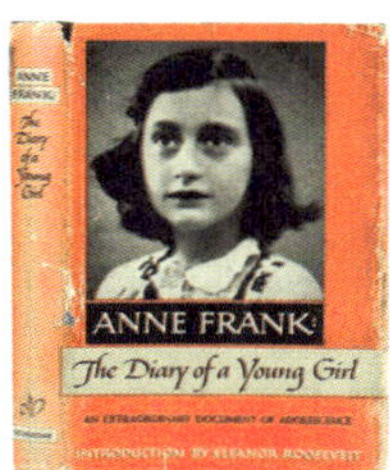

Anne Frank: The Diary of a Young Girl is published in English (New York and London) after being rejected by 16 English-language publishers. Published first in Amsterdam (1947), it is released in Germany and France in 1950. German paperback edition (1955) becomes the best-selling paperback in Germany to date, selling over 700,000 copies by 1960. More than 30 million copies of Frank's diary will sell worldwide.

Peter Bamm, *Die unsichtbare Flagge* (*The Invisible Flag*, Munich). Apologist memoir of German army doctor on the Russian front who seeks to distinguish ordinary German soldiers from Nazi SS. His book argues that soldiers' protests of the mass murder of Jews would have been futile, only leading to their executions.

TELEVISION

"Anne Frank: Diary of a Young Girl," half-hour television drama, written by Morton Wishengrad, airs on CBS Sunday evening series *Frontiers of Faith*.

REPARATIONS

West Germany signs reparations agreement with Israel to pay for Jewish economic losses, the resettlement of 500,000 survivors in Israel, and to compensate individual survivors in installments of cash and goods over 14 years. The agreement is extended numerous times, and payments continue today to cover lifetime of survivors and their spouses. By 2002, Germany has sent an estimated $500 million to Israel. Survivors outside Israel and those sent to ghettos or imprisoned as forced laborers are also compensated. By 2012, Germany has paid an estimated $89 million to victims of Nazi crimes. In 2013, Germany commits an additional $1 billion to home care of survivors and their spouses worldwide.

1953

LITERATURE

Gerald Reitlinger, *The Final Solution: The Attempt to Exterminate the Jews of Europe, 1939–1945* (London, New York, and Berlin).

MEMORIALS AND MUSEUMS

The Memorial of the Unknown Jewish Martyr is founded in Paris by Isaac Schneersohn and France's Contemporary Jewish Documentation Center, a massive archive secretly established by Schneersohn in 1943 to document the Holocaust in France. The cornerstone is laid on May 17 on a lot donated by the city, and the memorial is inaugurated in 1956. It would later become the Mémorial de la Shoah (2005).

Yad Vashem, World Holocaust Remembrance Center, is founded by Israel's Knesset on August 19. Cornerstone is laid in Jerusalem in 1954, and the memorial and museum open in 1957. The State of Israel wished to serve as the repository of Holocaust history and memory, and following the founding of the Paris memorial, the two organizations came to an agreement, with Yad Vashem managing the documented list of Holocaust victims.

FILMS

The Juggler, directed by Edward Dmytryk. Stars Kirk Douglas as a traumatized Jewish survivor of Auschwitz and refugee in Palestine.

The Glass Wall, directed by Maxwell Shane. A Jewish Hungarian survivor and displaced person seeks refuge in the U.S. Film highlights the plight of refugees in support of more liberal immigration policies.

TELEVISION

This Is Your Life (NBC) features Auschwitz survivor Hanna Bloch Kohner. The *New York Times* writes that the episode could be "television's first feature on a Holocaust survivor."

1954

LITERATURE

Lord Russell of Liverpool, *The Scourge of the Swastika: A Short History of Nazi War Crimes* (London). A chief British legal adviser at Nuremberg trials, Russell is forced to resign his post after refusing government calls to suppress his book and avoid stirring up anti-German sentiment. It becomes a best seller.

Henri Michel and Olga Wormser, *Tragédie de la déportation 1940–1945: Témoignages de survivants des camps de concentration allemands* (*Tragedy of the Deportation 1940–1945: Testimonies of Survivors of the German Concentration Camps*, Paris).

Léon Poliakov, *Harvest of Hate: The Nazi Program for the Destruction of Jews in Europe* (New York). Originally published in French as *Bréviaire de la haine: Le IIIe Reich et les Juifs* (Paris, 1951).

Philip Friedman, ed., *Martyrs and Fighters: The Epic of the Warsaw Ghetto* (New York). Friedman lived through the German occupation of Poland.

EXHIBITION

Résistance, liberation, deportation, Musée Pédagogique, Paris, 1954–55. Exhibition celebrating the decade anniversary of France's liberation from the Nazis, organized by Olga Wormser and Henri Michel.

1955

LITERATURE

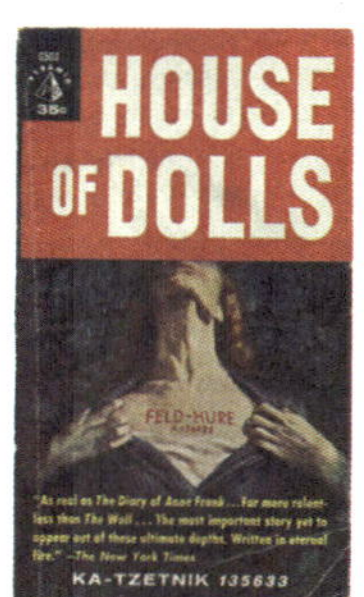

Ka-Tzetnik 135633, *House of Dolls* (New York). Pen name of Holocaust survivor Yehiel Dinur. Published in Hebrew as *Bet habubot* (Tel Aviv, 1953). Fictional account of the sex slavery of Jewish women in concentration camp brothels. It is translated into 16 languages (1960 U.S. paperback, ill.); it sells more than 5 million copies by 1968.

H. G. Adler, *Theresienstadt 1941–1945. Das Antlitz einer Zwangsgemeinschaft* (*Theresienstadt 1941–1945. The Face of an Enforced Community*). Academic study (900 pages) of Terezín, the Nazi concentration camp and ghetto in Czechoslovakia. Published in Germany; not yet translated into English.

FILM

Nuit et brouillard (*Night and Fog*), directed by Alain Resnais, narration written by Jean Cayrol, a political prisoner of Mauthausen concentration camp, and contributions by Olga Wormser and Henri Michel. The critically acclaimed French documentary is an account of the Nazi camps but gives little attention to Jewish victims. It is withdrawn from the 1956 Cannes Film Festival following objections by the German foreign ministry that it "would disturb the international harmony of the festival."

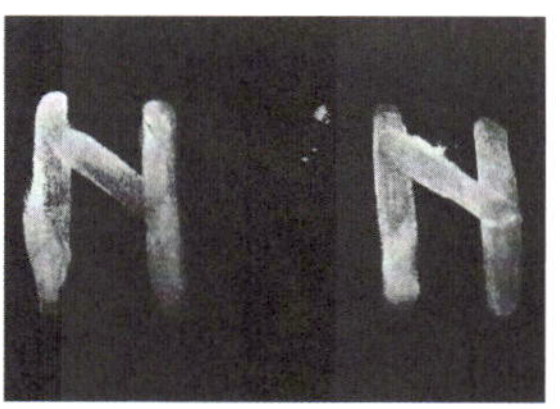

THEATER

The Diary of Anne Frank, directed by Garson Kanin and written by Albert Hackett and Frances Goodrich, debuts on Broadway. The hit play wins a Pulitzer Prize for drama and a Tony Award for best play. Over the next three years, it is performed in 30 countries in 21 languages.

1956

LITERATURE

Elie Wiesel, *Un di velt hot geshvign (And the World Remained Silent*, Buenos Aires). The 900-page memoir, written in Yiddish, is published in abridged form in French as *Nuit* (1958) and in English as *Night* (1960).

1957

BOOK

Maria and Kazimierz Piechotka, *Bóżice drewniane (Wooden Synagogues*, Warsaw). Polish architects document the synagogues of Poland, many of which were destroyed by the Nazis, with nearly 300 images. Published in English in 1959 (Warsaw).

1958

LITERATURE

Edith Bruck, *Chi ti ama cosi (Who Loves You like This*, Milan). An Auschwitz survivor's memoir of the Nazi persecution of Jews in Hungary and her experience at Auschwitz. It is published in English in 2001.

BOOK

1939–1945: Cierpienie i walka narodu polskiego, zdjęci-dokumenty (1939–1945: Suffering and Struggle of the Polish Nation: Photos-Documents), Stanisław Wrzos-Glinka, Tadeusz Mazur, Jerzy Tomaszewski, eds. (Warsaw). Book on Nazi atrocities in Poland includes the "*Sonderkommando* Photographs," four blurry pictures secretly taken by *Sonderkommandos* at Auschwitz, which show prisoners being stripped naked and sent to the gas chambers and corpses being cremated. They are the only known photos documenting the extermination process there. Published in translation in 1959 with the title *We Have Not Forgotten : Nous n'avons pas oublié : Wir haben es nicht vergessen* (Warsaw).

FILM

The Young Lions, directed by Edward Dmytryk and starring Marlon Brando, Montgomery Clift, and Dean Martin, based on Irwin Shaw's 1948 novel. Examines Nazi camps and the mass murder of Jews through the eyes of an American GI who is Jewish.

MEMORIAL

Buchenwald Memorial opens in East Germany on September 14. The monumental complex focuses on the imprisonment of German Communists and Resistance members. Only after the fall of the German Democratic Republic in 1990/91 are other victims—including Jews, Roma and Sinti, and Jehovah's Witnesses—formally addressed.

TRIAL

The Ulm *Einsatzgruppen* trial, Ulm, Germany, July 28–August 29. Ten Gestapo officers stand trial for the murder of 5,000 Jewish men, women, and children in Lithuania in 1941. In the first major Nazi crimes trial prosecuted by the West German government (as opposed to Allied tribunals after the war), gruesome crimes come to light and show that many ex-Nazi murderers resumed normal lives after the war. They are tried as accessories to murder for following orders and given light sentences of three to 15 years.

1959

LITERATURE

Primo Levi's 1947 memoir *If This Is a Man* is published in English (New York). A paperback edition is released in the U.S. in 1961 as *Survival in Auschwitz: The Nazi Assault on Humanity* (New York). Other translations quickly follow, including German, French, Finnish, and Dutch. Radio Canada and the Radiotelevisione Italiana produce radio adaptations. It is adapted for the stage in Turin in 1966.

Viktor Frankl's 1946 memoir is published in English as *From Death-Camp to Existentialism: A Psychiatrist's Path to a New Therapy* (Boston), then in paperback as *Man's Search for Meaning* (New York, 1963). Translated into 24 languages and reprinted 73 times, it will sell more than 10 million copies and be named in a Library of Congress survey as one of the 10 most influential books in America.

Nazi war criminal Rudolf Höss's 1947 memoir, *Commandant of Auschwitz: The Autobiography of Rudolf Höss*, is published in English (Cleveland and New York) and in 1992 with the title *Death Dealer: The Memoirs of the SS Kommandant at Auschwitz*.

FILM

The Diary of Anne Frank, directed by George Stevens and written by Albert Hackett and Frances Goodrich, is released. The film is nominated for eight Academy Awards (and wins three).

Rosen für den Staatsanwalt (Roses for the Prosecutor), directed by Wolfgang Staudte, examines Nazi war crimes, postwar memory, and Nazis hiding in plain sight.

TELEVISION

Judgment at Nuremberg, television drama written by Abby Mann and directed by George Roy Hill, airs on CBS. It includes archival footage of Nazi camps rarely shown in American films and television the decade prior.

The Final Ingredient, a half-hour television drama about Bergen-Belsen, airs on ABC.

French television broadcasts Alain Resnais's *Nuit et brouillard (Night and Fog)*. It is screened the following year in New York, along with Leni Riefenstahl's 1935 Nazi propaganda film *Triumph of the Will*.

MEMORIAL

Burdened Woman by sculptor Will Lammert (d. 1957), bronze, is unveiled posthumously at Ravensbrück concentration camp. In 1985, 13 unfinished figures designed by Lammert for the monument's base and cast by family members are installed by Mark Lammert, the artist's grandson, at the site of a transit camp for Jewish deportations in Berlin.

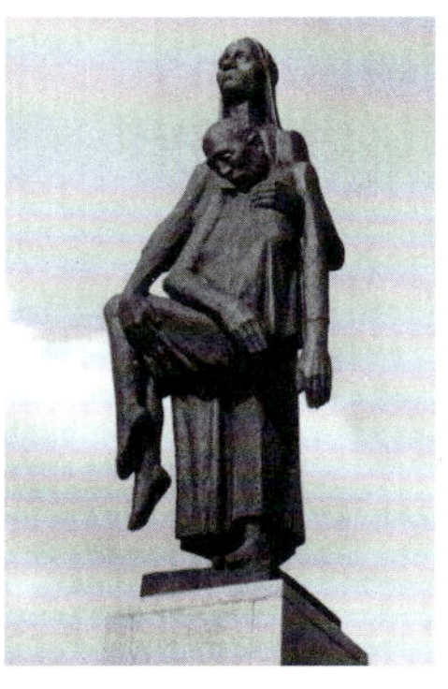

1960

HISTORIC EVENT

The notorious Nazi war criminal Adolf Eichmann, director of Jewish affairs and a key architect of the Holocaust, is captured in Argentina on May 11 by Israel's intelligence service to stand trial in Jerusalem. The story dominates the news cycle across the globe for months.

LITERATURE

Elie Wiesel's memoir, *Night* (New York), with a foreword by François Mauriac, is published in English. Wiesel will be awarded the Nobel Peace Prize in 1986.

André Schwarz-Bart, *The Last of the Just* (New York). The author's family was killed by Nazis. His novel, first published as *Le Dernier des justes* (Paris, 1959), wins the Goncourt Prize.

Miklos Nyiszli, *Auschwitz: A Doctor's Eyewitness Account* (Greenwich, Conn.). The 1947 memoir is posthumously translated into English from Hungarian and immediately published in paperback.

William L. Shirer, *The Rise and Fall of the Third Reich: A History of Nazi Germany* (New York). A Book-of-the-Month Club selection; 2 million copies are printed. It wins a National Book Award in 1961 and is serialized in *Reader's Digest*. One scholar estimates that 2 to 3 percent of the book is devoted to the Holocaust.

Several books are released in the wake of Eichmann's capture, including Quentin Reynolds, Ephraim Katz, and Zwy Aldouby, *Minister of Death: The Adolf Eichmann Story* (New York); Comer Clarke, *Eichmann: The Man and His Crimes* (New York); and Henry Zieger, *The Case against Adolf Eichmann* (New York).

MAGAZINES

Life (November 28 and December 5) publishes the two-part "Confessions of Adolf Eichmann." The account is drawn from interviews between Eichmann and Dutch Nazi collaborator and journalist Willem Sassen in Buenos Aires in 1957.

Life (December 26) publishes Margaret Bourke-White's photograph *The Living Dead at Buchenwald* in its anniversary issue, "Twenty-Five Years of Life."

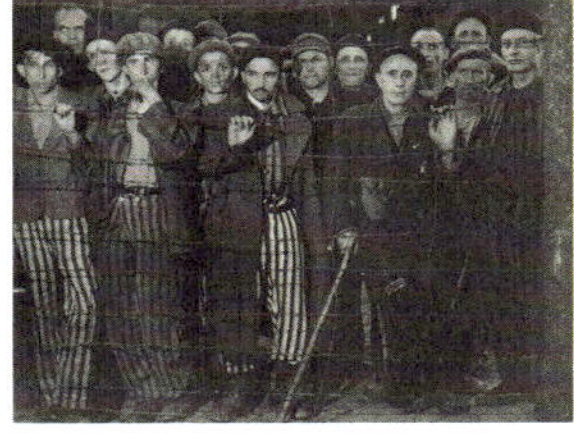

FILMS

Kapò, directed by Gillo Pontecorvo. The Italian film (1959), about the plight of a young Jewish teen in a concentration camp, is released in the U.S. and nominated for an Academy Award for best foreign film. Criticized by director and critic Jacques Rivette for aestheticizing atrocity and deserving "profound contempt," the film becomes a touchstone in the debate on Holocaust cinema.

Exodus, directed by Otto Preminger and starring Paul Newman, is based on Leon Uris's popular 1958 novel about the founding of modern Israel. It focuses on the plight of Holocaust survivors in 1947, homeless and nationless after the war, residing in displaced persons camps in Europe.

THEATER

John Hersey's novel *The Wall* (1950), about the Warsaw ghetto, is adapted for the New York stage and stars George C. Scott.

MEMORIALS AND MUSEUMS

The Anne Frank House museum opens in Amsterdam in the building where she and her family hid.

Pinkas Synagogue memorial in Prague opens. It displays the names of 78,000 Czech and Moravian victims of the Holocaust. (Closes 1968–89 during Soviet occupation; reopens in 1995 following major renovation.)

1961

TRIAL

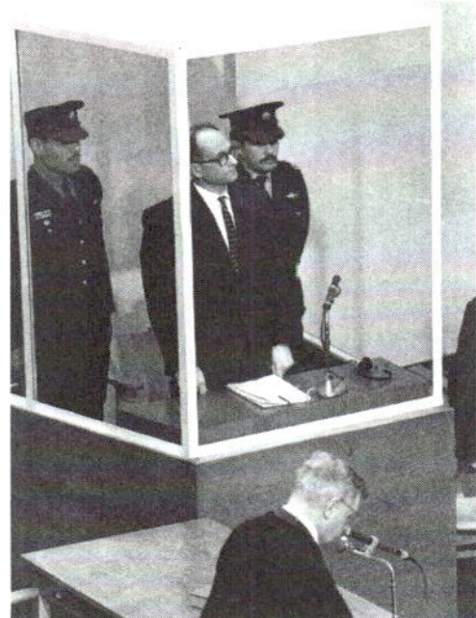

Eichmann trial, Jerusalem, April 10–December 11. Israel tries war criminal Adolf Eichmann. The first televised trial to be broadcast across the world, the case brings international attention to the Holocaust. The testimonies of 90 Holocaust survivors generate new interest in their stories. Eichmann is found guilty and executed by hanging on June 1, 1962.

TELEVISION

The Eichmann trial's televised coverage is produced by Milton Fruchtman of Capital Cities Broadcasting Corporation and directed by Leo Hurwitz. Distributed by subscription, it is broadcast in 38 countries over the course of the trial. America's major television networks and PBS air highlights daily, both on the nightly news and daytime news programs, as well as in-depth reports. Fruchtman and Capital win a Peabody Award for their televised production and for the half-hour special, "Verdict for Tomorrow," summarizing the proceedings (ABC, December 11).

LITERATURE

Raul Hilberg, *The Destruction of the European Jews* (Chicago and London).

Simon Wiesenthal, *Ich jagte Eichmann* (*I Hunted Eichmann*, Gütersloh, Germany). Book makes a celebrity of Wiesenthal, a Holocaust survivor and Nazi hunter. Critics claim he exaggerates his part in Eichmann's capture, but he plays an important role in the trials of other Nazis. In November he opens the Jewish Documentation Center in Vienna, dedicated to finding and legally prosecuting Nazi war criminals.

Michael A. Musmanno, *The Eichmann Kommandos* (Philadelphia). An account of the 1947 *Einsatzgruppen* (SS death squads) trials at Nuremberg, written by the presiding American judge. The trials were held to prosecute the commanding officers of the *Einsatzgruppen* in Eastern Europe.

Benjamin Murmelstein, *Terezin, il Ghetto Modello di Eichmann* (*Terezín, the Model Ghetto of Eichmann*, Bologna). Memoir of a Viennese rabbi who served on the Judenräten (Jewish Councils) in Vienna and Terezín (Theresienstadt) ghetto–concentration camp, implementing Nazi policies and organizing deportations of Jews to extermination camps. Murmelstein was the only Jewish council elder to survive the war and was briefly detained by the Czechoslovakian government as a Nazi collaborator. Claude Lanzmann's 2013 documentary, *The Last of the Unjust*, features interviews with Murmelstein in Rome in 1975.

Ka-Tzetnik 135633, *Kar'u lo pipl* (*They Called Him Piepel*, Tel Aviv). The novel depicts sexual abuse of boys at Auschwitz. Simultaneously published in English as *Piepel* (London), and later as *Moni: A Novel of Auschwitz* (New York, 1963) and *Atrocity* (New York, 1963).

Yevgeny Yevtushenko, "Babiyy Yar" ("Babi Yar"). Poem, published in a Russian literary magazine, breaks the silence in the Soviet Union about the Jewish victims of the Holocaust. The Soviets had memorialized victims of the "Great Patriotic War" in terms of their nationality without acknowledging the antisemitism and genocide of World War II. The poem would subsequently be set to music and published in English (*The Poetry of Yevgeny Yevtushenko*, New York, 1965).

FILM

Judgment at Nuremberg, directed by Stanley Kramer, based on the CBS television film by Abby Mann. Featuring an exceptional Hollywood cast—Spencer Tracy, Burt Lancaster, Judy Garland, Marlene Dietrich, Montgomery Clift—it is nominated for 11 Academy Awards and wins two, for best actor (Maximilian Schell) and screenplay (Mann).

MEMORIAL

Los Angeles Museum of the Holocaust opens; first of its kind in the U.S.

EXHIBITIONS

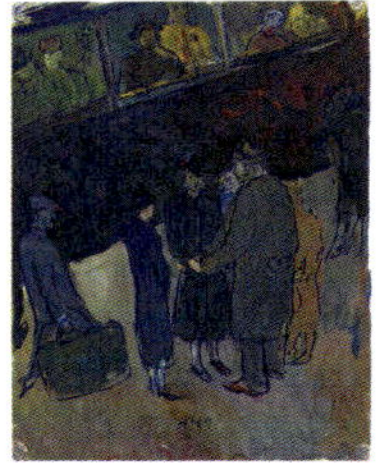

Charlotte Salomon, Museum Fodor, Amsterdam, February–March 5, featuring never-before-exhibited art by Salomon, a young Jewish artist who lived as a refugee in southern France before being murdered at Auschwitz in 1943. The exhibition travels to Tel Aviv (1962). In 1963 Paul Tillich and Emil Straus publish *Charlotte: A Diary in Pictures* (New York), the first of many books to be written about the artist.

Rico Lebrun: Paintings and Drawings, University of California, Los Angeles. Exhibition and catalogue feature the Italian American artist's series of works depicting Buchenwald and Dachau (1955–58).

1962

LITERATURE

Eberhard Kolb, *Bergen Belsen: Geschichte des "Aufenthaltslager," 1943–1945* (*Bergen-Belsen: History of a "Residence" Camp, 1943–1945*, Hannover, West Germany). Published in English as *Bergen-Belsen: From "Detention Camp" to Concentration Camp, 1943–1945* (Göttingen, West Germany, 1986).

Aharon Appelfeld, *Ashan* (*Smoke*, Jerusalem). Short stories about postwar persecution, trauma, and displacement by Romanian Holocaust survivor who emigrated to Israel in 1946. The English publication of his work, *In the Wilderness* (Jerusalem, 1965), includes these stories and those in *Ba-gai ha-poreh* (*In the Fertile Valley*, Jerusalem, 1963).

Edith Bruck, *Andremo in città* (*We'll Go to the City*, Milan). Holocaust survivor writes about the persecution of Jews during the war and the isolation they endure afterward. It is later adapted for film by her husband, Italian director Nelo Risi (1966).

1963

LITERATURE

Hannah Arendt, *Eichmann in Jerusalem: A Report on the Banality of Evil* (New York). Based on Arendt's reporting on the Eichmann trial for the *New Yorker*, which publishes the text in a five-part series, February 8–March 16. Arendt's controversial characterization of Eichmann and criticism of the cooperation of the Judenräten (Jewish Councils) spark an international furor that makes her a pariah for many years.

Moshe Pearlman, *The Capture and Trial of Adolf Eichmann* (New York).

Primo Levi, *La tregua* (*The Truce*, Turin). Documents Levi's nine-month journey home to Italy in 1945 from liberated Auschwitz. His memoir wins the Campiello literary prize and places third for Strega literary prize. Published in English in 1965 as *The Reawakening* (Boston) and as *The Truce* (London).

Jozef Lánik, *Čo Dante nevidel* (*What Dante Didn't See*, Bratislava, Czechoslovakia). Lánik is the pseudonym for Slovak writer Alfréd Wetzler, who escaped from Auschwitz with Rudolf Vrba (see below) by hiding in a woodpile. Their 1944 report, shared with diplomats, was the first reliable eyewitness account of Auschwitz. Wetzler's 1963 memoir is first published in 1964 and appears in English as *Escape from Hell: The True Story of the Auschwitz Protocol* (New York, 2007).

Rudolf Vrba with Alan Bestic, *I Cannot Forgive* (London). Vrba, a Slovak Jew, escaped from Auschwitz with Alfréd Wetzler. It is published in 1964 in German (*Ich kann nicht vergeben*, Munich) and in paperback as *Factory of Death* (London), and later in the U.S. as *Escape from Auschwitz* (New York, 2004).

FILM

Pasażerka (*Passenger*), directed by Andrzej Munk, who took part in the Warsaw ghetto uprising (1943). Munk died during production, but the film was completed by others. It is based on a play (1959), reworked into a novel (1962), and was partly filmed at Auschwitz.

TELEVISION

Storia del III Reich (*History of the Third Reich*), a documentary directed by Liliana Cavani, airs as a four-part television series in Italy.

THEATER

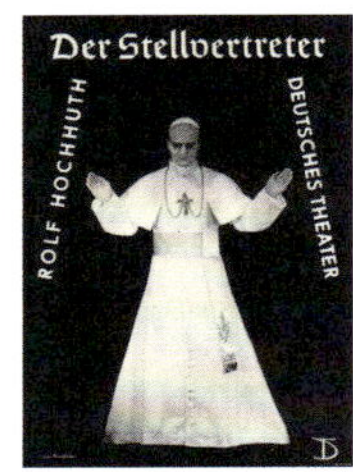

Der Stellvertreter: Ein christliches Trauerspiel (*The Deputy: A Christian Tragedy*), a drama by Rolf Hochhuth, a German Protestant, deals with Pope Pius XII's inaction during the Holocaust, and implicates him and the Catholic Church as culpable. First performed in West Berlin amid great controversy, with additional performances in the U.K., Sweden, Switzerland, Denmark, France, and elsewhere in Germany. In New York a condensed version, adapted by Jerome Rothenberg, debuts on Broadway in 1964 and runs for 316 performances.

TRIALS

Bełżec trial, August 18, 1963–January 21, 1965, Munich. Eight SS officers are charged with war crimes for mass murder; almost all are acquitted as having been following orders. Only SS officer Josef Oberhauser is found guilty of "accessory to murder" of 300,000 people, among other charges, and given four and a half years in prison (he serves half the sentence).

Auschwitz trials, Frankfurt, West Germany, December 20, 1963–August 19, 1965. Prosecution of 22 SS guards for crimes committed at the Auschwitz-Birkenau death camp. The case brings significant attention to the Holocaust in Germany. Fritz Bauer, a prosecutor who played a critical role in Eichmann's capture, calls some 210 survivors to testify. Eighteen defendants are sentenced to prison, eight with life sentences.

Sobibor trials, Kyiv, Ukraine, April. Prosecution of 11 Ukrainian guards for war crimes at Nazi extermination camp of Sobibor; 10 are found guilty and executed, one is sentenced to prison. At another trial in Kyiv in June 1965, three more former guards are found guilty and executed.

LAW

West Germany extends its 20-year statute of limitations for murder so that Nazi crimes can continue to be prosecuted. The statute is extended again in 1969 and abolished altogether in 1979.

1964

FILMS

The Pawnbroker, directed by Sidney Lumet and based on Edward Lewis Wallant's novel (1961), takes the viewpoint of a Holocaust survivor living in New York. Includes flashbacks of concentration camps. Rod Steiger is nominated for an Academy Award for best actor.

Herrenpartie (*Destination Death*), directed by Wolfgang Staudte. A group of German tourists confronts vengeful, traumatized women in a village where Nazis committed atrocities during the war.

THEATER

Fiddler on the Roof, directed by Jerome Robbins, opens on Broadway and wins nine Tony Awards (1965). The musical is inspired by Sholem Aleichem's Yiddish stories. Frances Butwin's *Tevya's Daughters* (New York, 1949), a translation of the stories, had been optioned by Rodgers and Hammerstein in 1949, then rejected. The 1971 film adapted from the play, directed by Norman Jewison, is nominated for eight Academy Awards (wins three).

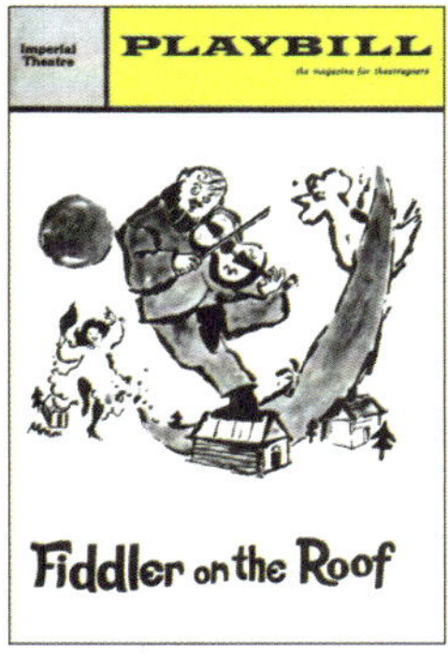

Arthur Miller, *Incident at Vichy*. One-act play premieres on Broadway. Ten detainees, mostly Jewish, are rounded up in Vichy, France, where they unknowingly await deportation. Miller adapts it for television in 1973.

MEMORIAL

Treblinka memorial, by sculptor Franciszek Duszenko and architect Adam Haupt, is unveiled at the Polish extermination camp, with 17,000 large inscribed stones set like tombstones around a central obelisk. It is one of many memorials erected at former Nazi camps and extermination sites in the 1960s. Monuments are commissioned at Sachsenhausen, Dachau, Auschwitz, Babi Yar, and Majdanek, among other places.

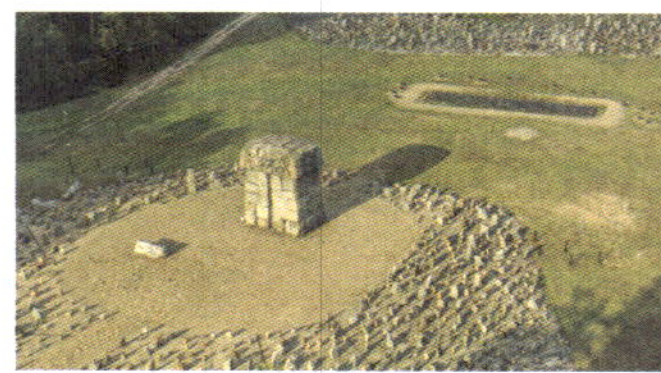

TRIAL

First Treblinka trial, Düsseldorf, West Germany, October 12, 1964–September 3, 1965. Eleven SS guards stand trial for war crimes at Treblinka extermination camp. Nine are sentenced to prison, four for life.

LAW

France enacts a crime against humanity law, with no statute of limitations, to prosecute Nazi war crimes.

1965

LITERATURE

Pery Broad, *KZ Auschwitz: Reminiscences of Pery Broad, SS-Man in the Auschwitz Concentration Camp* (Oświęcim, Poland). Auschwitz guard, clerk, and translator Broad was captured by the British after the war and released in 1947. He is tried in Frankfurt Auschwitz trials (1963–65) and sentenced to four years in prison.

FILM

Philippe Pétain: Processo a Vichy (*Philippe Pétain: Trial at Vichy*), a documentary directed by Liliana Cavani, examines France's wartime collaboration with the Nazis. It wins the Golden Lion at the Venice Film Festival.

MEMORIAL

Dachau Concentration Camp Memorial Site opens to the public. Between the late 1960s and 1970s, school group visits to Dachau increase more than tenfold.

TRIAL

Sobibor trial, Hagen, West Germany, September 6, 1965–December 20, 1966. Twelve SS guards stand trial for war crimes at Sobibor extermination camp. Five defendants are found guilty, six acquitted, and one commits suicide.

HISTORIC EVENT

Second Vatican Council, *Nostra aetate* (*In Our Time*), the Declaration on the Relation of the Church with Non-Christian Religions, addresses the Catholic Church's relationship with the Jewish people. The Church traces its theological beginnings to the Jewish faith as well as Christ's to the Jewish people. It acknowledges a special relationship between the Jewish people and God and a commitment to dialogue with the Jewish people. It rejects blaming Christ's Crucifixion on a Jewish conspiracy or the "Jews of today." It repudiates presenting the Jews as "rejected or accursed by God." It further states that the Church "deplores hatred, persecution, and displays of antisemitism directed against the Jews at any time or from any source."

1966

LITERATURE

Jean-François Steiner, *Treblinka: La Révolte d'un camp d'extermination* (*Treblinka: The Revolt of an Extermination Camp*, Paris), preface by Simone de Beauvoir. Best-selling, controversial book by young French Jewish journalist whose father was murdered in Nazi camps. Based on interviews with survivors and categorized by the author as nonfiction, it is told in the first person and adopts the form of a novel. Criticized for its portrayal of Jewish passivity and for seeming to blame members of Jewish *Sonderkommandos*. German and Swedish editions published in 1966; English, Danish, Dutch, Finnish, and Japanese editions in 1967.

Jean Améry (born Hans Maier), *Jenseits von Schuld und Sühne* (*Beyond Guilt and Atonement*, Munich). Political prisoner's account of the Nazi camps and the tortures he endured. Published in English as *At the Mind's Limits: Contemplations by a Survivor on Auschwitz and Its Realities* (Bloomington, Ind., 1980).

1967

LITERATURE

Chaim Potok, *The Chosen* (New York). Best-selling novel about two Jewish families in Brooklyn after the war, it is the first book to depict Hasidic Judaism for a larger American audience. A film, directed by Jeremy Kagan, is released in 1981. It incorporates graphic footage of the Nazi camps and emphasizes Jewish identity of victims.

Simon Wiesenthal, *The Murderers among Us: The Simon Wiesenthal Memoirs* (New York).

FILM

The Producers, written and directed by Mel Brooks, premieres in Pittsburgh following Embassy Pictures' refusal to distribute it. It features a satirical play within the film, *Springtime for Hitler*. In 1968 the movie finds wider release and critical acclaim, winning an Academy Award for best original screenplay, and a nomination for Gene Wilder as best supporting actor.

MEMORIAL

International Monument to the Victims of Fascism is unveiled at Auschwitz-Birkenau Memorial and Museum, with 200,000 people in attendance. This is the first large memorial inaugurated there, and it combines different proposals submitted to an unsuccessful competition organized by the sculptor Henry Moore in 1957–58. Those proposals were rejected due to plans to alter the camp, which is illegal.

EXHIBITION

Mauricio Lasansky, *The Nazi Drawings*, opens at the Philadelphia Museum of Art in January. Between 1967 and 1970, the show travels to eight other cities: New York (Whitney Museum of American Art); Des Moines (Iowa), Tacoma (Wash.), Indianapolis, Huntington (W. Va.), Chicago, Mexico City, and Iowa City.

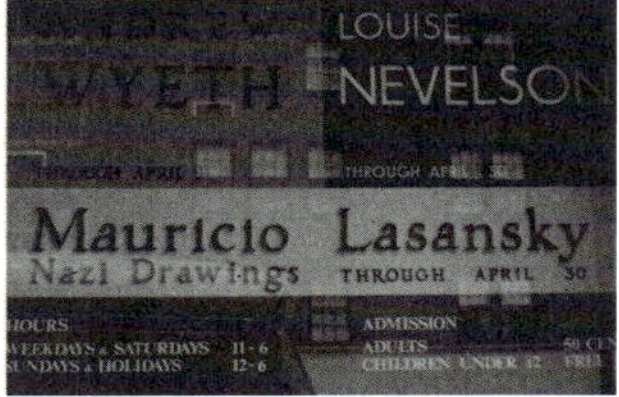

1969

FILM

Le Chagrin et la pitié (*The Sorrow and the Pity*), directed by Marcel Ophuls. The 250-minute documentary examines French collaboration and antisemitism during the Nazi occupation. Made for television, it is banned by French television until 1981. It premieres in West Germany in 1969. It receives an Academy Award in 1971 after its wider release in the U.K., U.S., Italy, and France, where, in Paris, it is shown in a small theater for 87 straight weeks.

LITERATURE

Albert Speer, *Erinnerungen* (*Inside the Third Reich*, Frankfurt, 1969; New York, 1970). Written while the Nazi war criminal was jailed and published after his release in 1966. Speer presents himself as a good, apolitical Nazi bureaucrat and claims (falsely) to have had no knowledge of the "Final Solution." The book is a best seller and makes Speer famous.

Myth of the Six Million, written by Holocaust denier David Hoggan (Los Angeles). Published anonymously (without author's permission) by antisemitic publisher Noontide Press, it is one of the first Holocaust denial books to be published in English.

MEMORIAL

Memorial of Struggle and Martyrdom by sculptor and Auschwitz survivor Wiktor Tolkin, a Polish political prisoner, and engineer Janusz Dembek, Majdanek camp, Poland. It features a towering monument gate and a mausoleum to hold victims' ashes.

1970

LITERATURE

Anatoly Kuznetsov (pen name A. Anatoli), *Babi Yar: A Document in the Form of a Novel* (New York). A censored version was printed in Russia in 1966.

MEMORIAL

Pillar of Heroism (1967–70) by Buki Schwartz, is the first of four monuments built at Yad Vashem. The impetus for this one is the Six Day Arab-Israeli War (1967). The 21-meter (69 feet) tower includes the inscription, "Now and forever in memory of those who rebelled in the camps and ghettos, fought in the woods, in the underground and with the Allied forces; braved their way to Eretz Israel; and those who died sanctifying the name of God."

TRIAL

Second Treblinka trial, Düsseldorf, West Germany, May 13–December 22. Franz Stangl stands trial following his extradition from Brazil (1967), where he lived under his own name and worked at a Volkswagen car factory. He is sentenced to life in prison for his role in the murder of 900,000 people as commandant of Treblinka death camp (1942–43) and Sobibor death camp (1942). Austria's prosecution of Stangl for his role in a euthanasia program, killing incurable and mentally disabled prisoners at Hartheim concentration camp (1940–41), ends in 1971 when the defendant dies of heart failure.

HISTORIC EVENT

Chancellor Willy Brandt of West Germany visits the Warsaw ghetto memorial and drops to his knees. His symbolic act is widely covered in the international press.

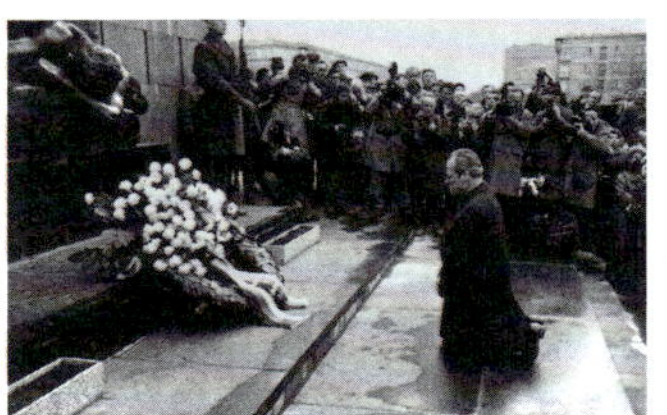

BEYOND THE POSTWAR ERA

1978

TELEVISION

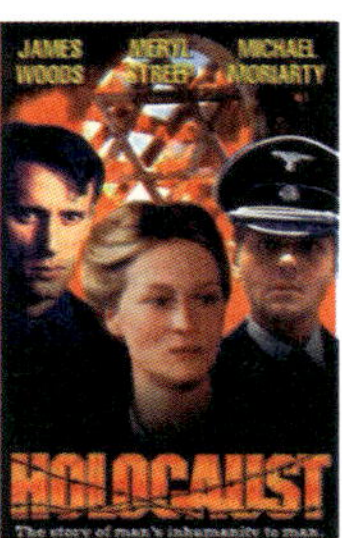

An estimated 100 million Americans watch *Holocaust: The Story of the Family Weiss*, a miniseries on NBC that airs in April. The four-part program runs nine and a half hours. It is widely criticized for being offensive, commercialized, and oversimplified, and the quip "There's no business like Shoah business" is frequently applied to the show. Yet it has an extraordinary reach. The 1979 broadcast in West Germany is seen by an estimated 20 million viewers, over half the adult population. It is credited with advancing Germany's confrontation with the Holocaust and decision to abolish the statute of limitations for murder in 1979. Rebroadcast in the U.S. in 1979.

1985

FILM

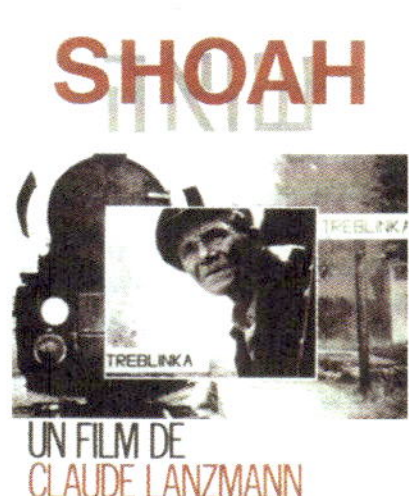

Shoah, directed by Claude Lanzmann, is released in Paris. The nine-hour film has taken 11 years to make and features interviews with survivors, witnesses, bystanders, and perpetrators. It features no liberation footage. Its focus is the "living words" of those who could bear witness and the extermination sites in Poland. (The film predates France's reckoning with its own collaboration in the deportation of Jews, administered by French police and militia.) First televised in 1987 during French trial of SS Gestapo officer Klaus Barbie, the so-called Butcher of Lyon, it draws some 4 million viewers over four nights in France, Great Britain, and the U.S.

1987

TRIAL

John Ivan Demjanjuk, a Ukrainian-born Russian POW, is tried for war crimes in Jerusalem and convicted as Ivan the Terrible, a notorious guard at the Treblinka extermination camp. His conviction and death sentence are overturned in 1993 when new evidence reveals Demjanjuk, following his capture by German troops, had served as a guard at Sobibor, not Treblinka. Following the war Demjanjuk had emigrated to the U.S., but his U.S. citizenship was stripped from him in 1981 following investigations into his wartime activities. It is restored in 1998 and lost again permanently in 2002. The U.S. seeks to deport him to Ukraine in 2004, and, following various court proceedings, deports him in 2009 to Germany, where he is charged on 28,060 counts of accessory to murder. He is convicted and sentenced to five years in prison but dies in a nursing home awaiting appeal.

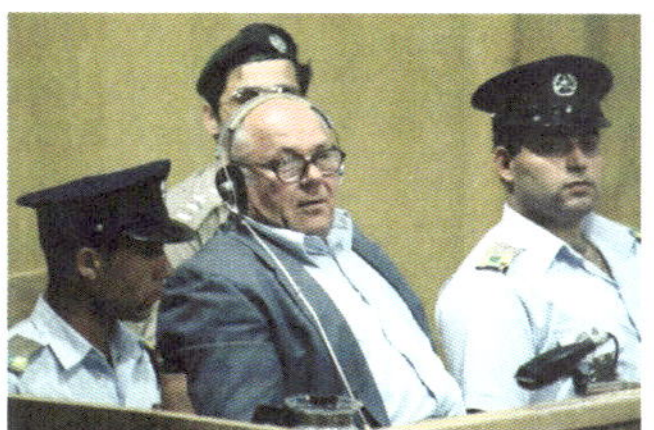

1993

FILM

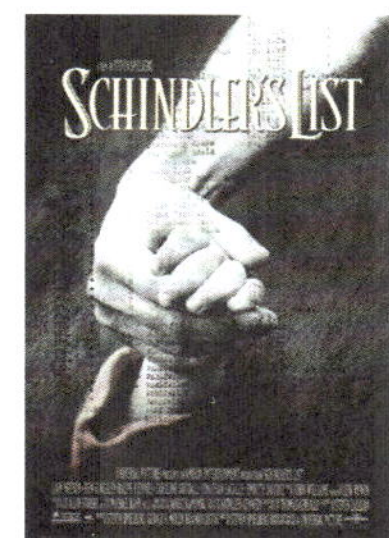

Schindler's List, directed by Steven Spielberg, grosses $322 million worldwide and wins seven Academy Awards (1994).

MEMORIAL AND MUSEUM

The United States Holocaust Memorial Museum opens on the National Mall in Washington, D.C.

Mauricio Lasansky, *No. 15* (detail), "The Nazi Drawings"

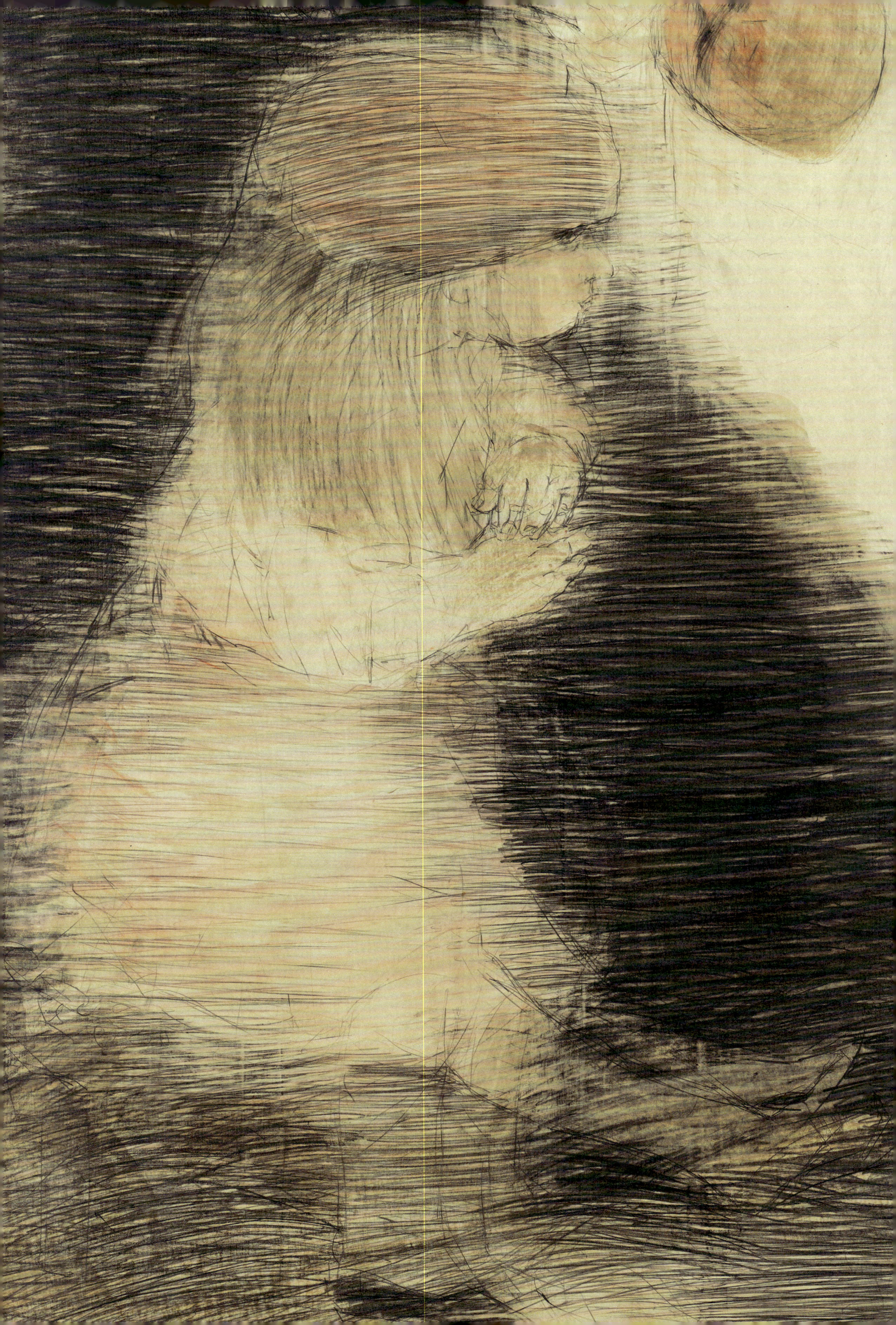

INDEX

Note: Page numbers in italic type indicate illustrations.

PHOTO REPRODUCTION CREDITS

Unless otherwise noted, all works in Mia's collection: Photo by Minneapolis Institute of Art

Front and inside covers: Levitt Foundation; © Lasansky Corporation

Front flap: photo courtesy the Lasansky Corporation

Frontispiece: Levitt Foundation; © Lasansky Corporation

Page 6: Levitt Foundation; © Lasansky Corporation

Page 10: fig. A.1, photo courtesy the Lasansky Corporation

Page 11: fig. A.2, photo courtesy the Lasansky Corporation

Page 11: fig. A.3, photo courtesy the Lasansky Corporation

Page 12: Levitt Foundation; © Lasansky Corporation

Page 14: fig. 1.1, National Archives, photo no. 238-NT-282, shared to Wikimedia Commons

Page 15: fig. 1.2, United States Holocaust Memorial Museum, courtesy of the National Archives

Page 16: fig. 1.3, United States Holocaust Memorial Museum, courtesy of Yad Vashem (public domain)

Page 17: fig. 1.4, photo by George Rodger / The LIFE Picture Collection via Getty Images

Page 18: fig. 1.5, National Archives, photo no. 208-AA-206K(31), shared to Wikimedia Commons

Page 19: fig. 1.6, Centro Primo Levi, New York

Page 21: fig. 1.7, © Thomas Fritta-Haas, long-term loan to the Jewish Museum Berlin

Page 22: fig. 1.8, Collection Jewish Historical Museum, Amsterdam © Charlotte Salomon Foundation

Page 22: fig. 1.9, Overloon War Museum, Netherlands

Page 23: fig. 1.10, Auschwitz-Birkenau State Museum, Oświęcim, Poland

Page 24: fig. 1.11, National Archives, photo no. 239-RC-24(28), shared to Wikimedia Commons

Page 25: fig. 1.12, National Archives, photo no. 286-ME-6(5), shared to Wikimedia Commons

Page 26: fig. 1.13, National Archives, photo no. 111-SC-196741, shared to Wikimedia Commons

Page 27: fig. 1.14, photo by Robert Capa © International Center of Photography / Magnum Photos

Page 28: fig. 1.15, Smithsonian American Art Museum, gift of Cissy and John Anderson, 1999.47; © The Estate of Leonard Baskin, photo: Smithsonian Museum of American Art

Page 29: fig. 1.16, The Museum of Modern Art, Mrs. Sam A. Lewisohn Bequest (by exchange), and Mrs. Marya Bernard Fund in memory of her husband Dr. Bernard Bernard, and anonymous funds 93.1971; © 2021 Estate of Pablo Picasso / Artists Rights Society (ARS), New York, Digital Image © The Museum of Modern Art / Licensed by SCALA I Art Resource, NY

Page 31: fig. 1.17, © 1956 Argos Films – Cocinor

Page 33: fig. 1.18, Collection Anne Frank House, Amsterdam, shared via Wikimedia Commons

Page 34: fig. 1.19, *The Diary of Anne Frank* © 1959 Twentieth Century-Fox. All rights reserved.

Page 36: fig. 1.20, Government Press Office of Israel, National Photo Collection

Page 37: fig. 1.21, photo by John Milli, Government Press Office of Israel, National Photo Collection

Page 37: fig. 1.22, Government Press Office of Israel, National Photo Collection

Page 38: fig. 1.23, Government Press Office of Israel, National Photo Collection

Page 38: fig. 1.24, Government Press Office of Israel, National Photo Collection

Page 38: fig. 1.25, Government Press Office of Israel, National Photo Collection

Page 39: fig. 1.26, Government Press Office of Israel, National Photo Collection

Page 41: fig. 1.27, Google Ngram (public domain)

Page 42: fig. 1.28, © 2021 Estate of Margaret Bourke-White / Licensed by VAGA at Artists Rights Society (ARS), NY

Page 43: fig. 1.29, © Alexandr Medvedkov / Dreamstime.com

Page 44: fig. 1.30, © Faces of Auschwitz / Marina Amaral / Auschwitz Memorial Museum, Oświęcim, Poland

Page 44: fig. 1.31, Auschwitz Memorial Museum, Oświęcim, Poland

Page 45: Levitt Foundation; © Lasansky Corporation

Page 56: fig. 2.1, © Lasansky Corporation

Page 57: fig. 2.2, photo courtesy the Lasansky Corporation

Page 58: fig. 2.3, © Lasansky Corporation; photo: Annex Galleries

Page 58: fig. 2.4, AméricaLee – Publicaciones latinoamericanas del siglo XX

Page 59: fig. 2.5, © Lasansky Corporation; Digital Image © The Museum of Modern Art / Licensed by SCALA / Art Resource, NY

Page 59: fig. 2.6, photo courtesy the Lasansky Corporation

Page 60: fig. 2.7, photo by Myron Davis / The LIFE Premium Collection via Getty Images

Page 60: fig. 2.8, photo by Hart Preston / The LIFE Picture Collection via Getty Images

Page 61: fig. 2.9, digital image © The Museum of Modern Art / Licensed by SCALA / Art Resource, NY

Page 62: fig. 2.10, © Lasansky Corporation

Page 63: fig. 2.11, © Lasansky Corporation

Page 63: fig. 2.12, © Lasansky Corporation

Page 64: fig. 2.13, photo courtesy the Lasansky Corporation

Page 65: fig. 2.14, © Lasansky Corporation

Page 65: fig. 2.15, Myron Kunin Collection of American Art, Minneapolis, MN; © Lasansky Corporation

Page 70: fig. 3.1, Government Press Office of Israel, National Photo Collection

Page 71: fig. 3.2, Levitt Foundation; © Lasansky Corporation

Page 72: fig. 3.3, Musées de Strasbourg, M. Bertola

Page 73: fig. 3.4, Levitt Foundation; © Lasansky Corporation

Pages 76–77: Levitt Foundation; © Lasansky Corporation

Page 79: fig. 4.1, photo courtesy the Lasansky Corporation

Page 81: fig. 4.2, National Archives, photo no. 238-NT-612, shared via Wikimedia Commons

Page 83: fig. 4.4, Art Institute of Chicago

Page 84: fig. 4.5, © Lasansky Corporation; photo courtesy the Lasansky Corporation

Page 85: fig. 4.6, © 2021 Artists Rights Society (ARS), New York / VG Bild-Kunst, Bonn

Page 85: fig. 4.7, Penguin Random House

Page 86: fig. 4.8, photo by PIX Inc. / The LIFE Picture Collection via Getty Images

Page 88: fig. 4.10, United States Holocaust Memorial Museum, courtesy of Yad Vashem (public domain)

Page 91: fig. 4.11, photo by Francis Miller / The LIFE Picture Collection via Getty Images

Page 92: fig. 4.12, © Lasansky Corporation; photo courtesy the Lasansky Corporation

Page 93: fig. 4.13, photo courtesy the Lasansky Corporation

Page 95: Levitt Foundation; © Lasansky Corporation

Page 101: Levitt Foundation; © Lasansky Corporation

Pages 103–41: Levitt Foundation; © Lasansky Corporation

Page 153: Levitt Foundation; © Lasansky Corporation

Back flap: © Lasansky Corporation

Back cover: photo courtesy the Lasansky Corporation

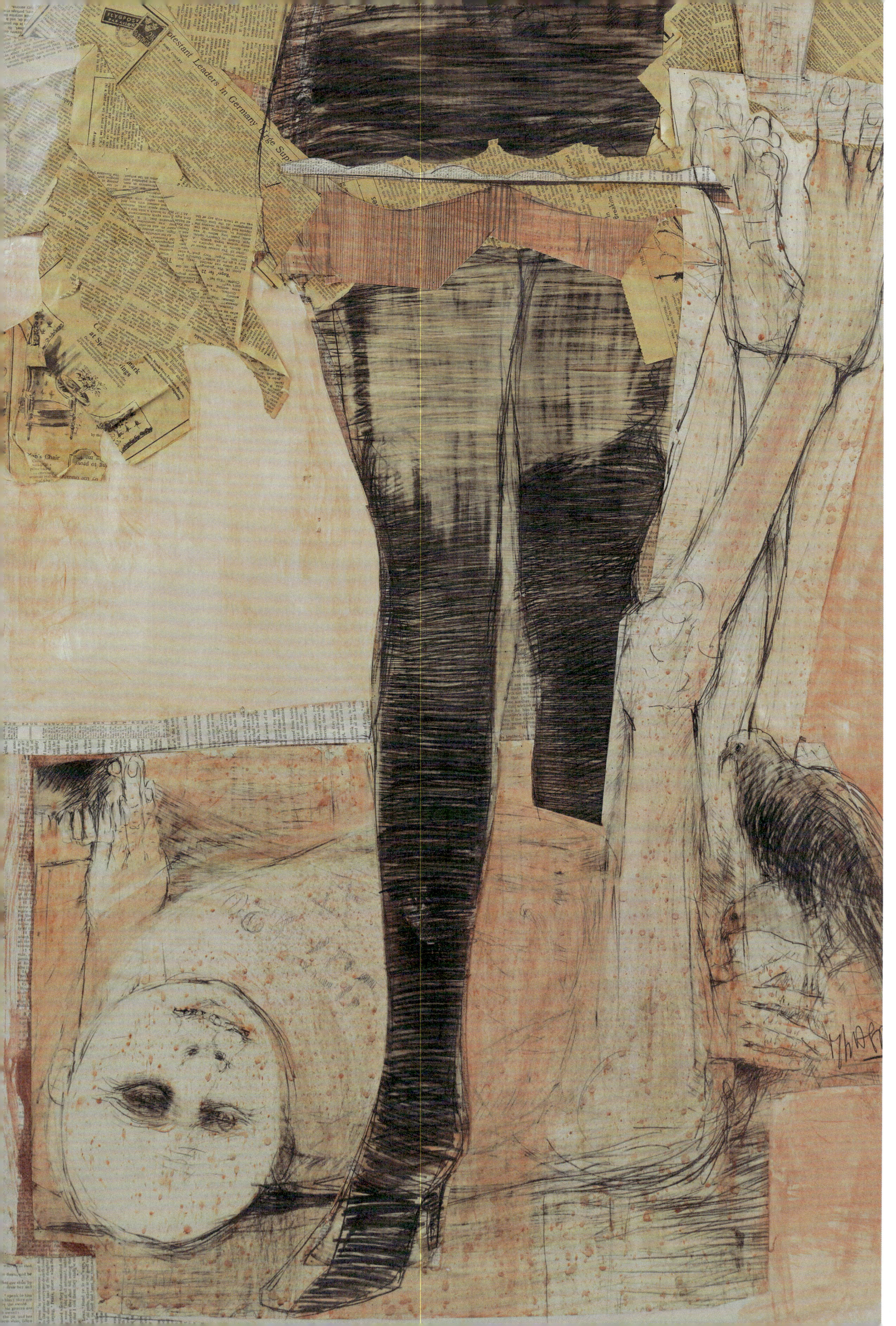